A JESUIT IN THE
FORBIDDEN CITY

A JESUIT IN THE
FORBIDDEN CITY:
MATTEO RICCI
1552–1610

R. PO-CHIA HSIA

OXFORD
UNIVERSITY PRESS

UNIVERSITY PRESS

Great Clarendon Street, Oxford OX2 6DP

Oxford University Press is a department of the University of Oxford.
It furthers the University's objective of excellence in research, scholarship,
and education by publishing worldwide in

Oxford New York

Auckland Cape Town Dar es Salaam Hong Kong Karachi
Kuala Lumpur Madrid Melbourne Mexico City Nairobi
New Delhi Shanghai Taipei Toronto

With offices in

Argentina Austria Brazil Chile Czech Republic France Greece
Guatemala Hungary Italy Japan Poland Portugal Singapore
South Korea Switzerland Thailand Turkey Ukraine Vietnam

Oxford is a registered trade mark of Oxford University Press
in the UK and in certain other countries

Published in the United States
by Oxford University Press Inc., New York

© R. Po-chia Hsia 2010

The moral rights of the author have been asserted
Database right Oxford University Press (maker)

First published 2010

British Library Cataloguing in Publication Data

Data available

Library of Congress Cataloging in Publication Data
Library of Congress Control Number: 2010930311

Typeset by SPI Publisher Services, Pondicherry, India
Printed in Great Britain
on acid-free paper by
MPG Books Group, Bodmin and King's Lynn

ISBN 978–0–19–959225–8

3 5 7 9 10 8 6 4 2

Acknowledgements

A sabbatical leave from the Pennsylvania State University allowed me to write the bulk of this book. I am grateful to the College of Liberal Arts and the Department of History for this lease of time. For their help in the completion of this work, I would like to express my appreciation to my colleague and friend On-cho Ng for his photographic eye during our trip to Ricci sites in Guangdong, to John Morrow for preparing the maps, to Ms Ellen Peachey of the American Philatelic Society for help in identifying Ricci commemorative stamps, and to Xiang Hongyan for help in preparing the manuscript for publication. A birthday gift in the form of a set of the *Fonti Ricciane* many years ago stoked my enthusiasm for the project: to Sophie de Schaepdrijver, historian, colleague, and inspiration, I owe the pleasure of many conversations over the years, when I defended and explained my interest in things Jesuitical. This book is dedicated to Mathilde Ming-wei and Eduard Ming-tse, in the hope that in the near future, they will have the same pleasure of discovering China as they have in discovering Europe.

A grant from the EDS-Stewart Endowment for Chinese-Western Cultural History at the Ricci Institute for Chinese-Western Cultural History, University of San Francisco Center for the Pacific Rim has made possible the reproductions of the color plates.

Contents

List of Figures

List of Plates

List of Maps

Abbreviations

ARSI Jap-Sin	Archivum Romanum Societatis Iesu, Japonica-Sinica
DI	*Documenta Indica, 1540–1597*, ed. Joseph Wicki, 18 vols. Rome: MHSI, 1948–88
FR	*Fonti Ricciane. Matteo Ricci: Storia dell'introduzione del Cristianesimo in Cina*, ed. Pasquale D'Elia, 3 vols. Rome: La Libreria dello Stato, 1942–9
HCC	*Handbook of Christianity in China*, i: *635–1800*, ed. Nicolas Standaert. Leiden: Brill, 2001
Lettere	*Matteo Ricci lettere (1580–1609)*, ed. Francesco D'Arelli. Macerata: Quodlibet, 2001
MHSI	Monumenta Historica Societatis Iesu
Ming Shi	*Ming shi*, 28 vols. Beijing: Zhonghua shuju, 1997
OS	*Opere storiche del P. Matteo Ricci S.I.*, ed. Pietro Tacchi-Venturi, 2 vols. Macerata: F. Giorgetti, 1913

Prologue

Even in death, Matteo Ricci triumphed over his enemies. On 1 November 1611, the Italian missionary was buried by his fellow Jesuits outside the walled city of Beijing, the capital of the Ming dynasty, the Empire of Great Brightness. The funeral mass took place in a newly constructed chapel, situated in the grounds of a confiscated villa that had belonged to a prominent and now disgraced palace eunuch, recently converted into a Buddhist temple, now bestowed by the emperor as a burial site for Ricci, once again converted into a Catholic church, freshly renovated and consecrated for the Christian burial. Hundreds of converts attended the funeral, among them the mandarins Xu Guangqi and Li Zhizao, good friends of the deceased, who were disconsolate. Still other mandarins, unbelievers, some belonging to the highest ranks, sent wreaths and condolences. For they all acknowledged Ricci to be a virtuous, upright, learned, and remarkable man, in whose honor the Emperor Wanli had granted the petition for imperial sponsorship of the burial. Between May and October 1610, with Ricci lying in a sealed casket, as was the custom of the long Chinese wake, streams of visitors paid their last respects at the Jesuit residence within Beijing, laying wreaths and bowing before a portrait of the westerner and his bodily remains, prior to its transfer to the last resting place in the fields outside the west gate of Beijing.

The idea to ask the emperor for a piece of burial ground came from Sun Yuanhua, a student of Xu Guangqi. The elegant prose of the petition came from Li Zhizao, the political backing from Ye Xianggao, a grand secretary, and other grand mandarins, all friends of the remarkable westerner. Once the site was chosen, the Jesuits had to fight off repeated attempts by the disgraced eunuch to reclaim his villa. Once their claim was assured, they took great pleasure in ordering the smashing of Buddhist statues and decorations, in pulverizing and mixing these dusts of 'idolatry' with the cement that would constitute the foundations of the Catholic church. Even in death, Ricci triumphed over his enemies in life, the eunuchs and

Buddhist monks, the source of many afflictions during his long years in China. Eighteen months elapsed between the submission of the petition and the burial; twenty-eight years had passed before Ricci gained the distinction of being the first foreigner in China, neither king nor envoy, to be honored by an imperial burial.

Ricci had come a long way. Born into a world torn asunder by the Protestant Reformation, he departed a Catholic Europe renewed in strength, restored in confidence, and restless in combat, against heretics and infidels, enemies of the Roman Church. Catholic orthodoxy aside, Ricci still imbibed the sweet nectar of the Renaissance, the humanistic studies of Greek and Latin, and the philosophy of nature. In the conviction that true knowledge and true doctrine were but two sides of the coin of salvation, Ricci, and the hundreds of Christian missionaries before him and the thousands after, strove to peddle their spiritual merchandise to the non-Christian world. These merchants of souls traveled the sea lanes opened up by the merchants of spices, the Portuguese, who had built a maritime network of trading posts and strongholds from the Madeira Islands to Bahia, Mozambique to Goa, and Malacca to Macao. At the last place, at the doorstep of China, Ricci crossed the threshold into the Realm of the Great Ming.

The mansion of the Ming Empire was anything but simple. To the casual visitor, impressed by its high walls, its large front courtyard, and its sumptuous reception hall, the best parts of the mansion remained hidden. Only intimates, family and close friends, gained access to the privileged spaces behind the screens that marked off the public and the private: the winding and covered corridors leading to the inner chambers, the eastern ones for men, the western for women, rooms opening out to gardens and ponds, with stone paths, twisting rocks, and gentle pavilions set in the midst of lotus and peonies, the calmness of the study and the library, the prayer chants from room altars, and beyond, the sounds and smells of the servants, cooking, cleaning, and bustling about. In the 1580s, when the Jesuits entered China, this mansion was anything but tranquil. Behind its prosperous and stately exterior, amidst the animated domestic scenes, the mansion was on fire. It was ablaze the way that life is consumed, by passions and desires, a metaphor used in the *Lotus Sutra*, the well-known Buddhist text, which compares the miseries of existence to a house ablaze, the residents carrying on unawares, until the whole structure collapses down on their heads. As the signs of crisis multiplied, mandarins, scholars, and the ordinary people looked for answers and solutions: to injustice, inequality, and the anxieties generated by the feeling of a rapidly changing world and an order that had failed to keep up with it.

Into this mansion ventured Matteo Ricci. By his intelligence, charm, and endurance, the Italian missionary gained access into the inner realm of Chinese civilization, denied to almost all visitors. To use a metaphor of the Jesuits, he had hoped to enter the house and compel its residents to exit with him in allegiance to the Catholic faith. How well Ricci succeeded in exploring the inner corridors and private chambers of the Chinese mansion was far beyond his first expectations. But it was a visit that allowed for no return. This is the story of Matteo Ricci and his world.

Types chinois. Modeste, et plutôt enfoui, étouffé, dirait-on, des yeux de detective, et aux pieds, des pantoufles de feutre, comme il se doit, et les usant du bout, les mains dans les manches, jésuite, avec une innocence cousue de fil blanc, mais prêt à tout.

(Henri Michaux, *Un barbare en Asie* (Paris: Gallimard, 1967; first pub. 1933), 148)

I

Macerata and Rome

M atteo Ricci was born on 6 October 1552 in Macerata to Giovanni Battista and Giovanna Angiolelli. With a population of 12,000 in the late sixteenth century, Macerata was the administrative capital of the Marches, the region of the Papal States richest in agricultural produce. Except for river valleys and a thin coastal plain, the Marches formed a landscape dotted by hill towns and villages, whose elevated locations provided protection against brigands and disease. Rugged terrain hindered north–south communication; and to travel east–west, one would ascend and descend the Apennines, the central spine of Italy. Built on a hill between two rivers, Macerata loomed over rolling fields of vineyards, olive groves, and wheat fields (see Figure 1). The town lies south of two important communes in the Marches. The Adriatic port of Ancona, gateway to the Levant, with bustling communities of Jewish, Greek, and Turkish merchants, had lost its autonomy to the Papal States in 1532; under Pope Paul IV, the Inquisition burned Portuguese *conversos* in the 1550s on the charge of secret adherence to Judaism, thus provoking a boycott of its commerce organized by the Jews in the Ottoman Empire. In contrast, Loreto thrived on pilgrims, not merchants. Reputed to be the second holiest city in Italy, Loreto attracted pilgrims who visited the Nazareth cottage where the Annunciation took place and where the Holy Family lived, which angels had borne away from the Holy Land in the thirteenth century, so the legend goes. While the Adriatic Sea lies only 15 miles to the east, Macerata is oriented to Rome by strong political and economic ties. In the sixteenth century, a steady traffic linked Rome and Macerata: pilgrims heading for Loreto; regular postal couriers traveling from Rome to Ancona, Rimini, and Venice; papal officials and soldiers escorting revenues from the Marches to the Apostolic Chamber (the tax office of the

Figure 1. Macerata, painting by Francesco Mingucci, 1626

Papal States); and wagons of grain from the wheat fields of the Marches to feed the growing population of Rome. All this flow moved on the ancient Roman road from Macerata to Tolentino, Camerino, Foligno, crossing the Apennines, before turning south to Spoleto, reaching Borghetto, where the bulk goods could be transferred to barges on the Tiber, and other travelers continued on the Via Flaminia to enter Rome from the north through the gate of the same name.

Descendant of a medieval patrician family in this provincial capital, Giovanni Battista Ricci cherished ambitions for his children. His pharmacy only a short walk from the Palazzo del Governo in the principal square of the city, Giovanni and his large family lived in a narrow side street just a few feet away from the Loggia dei Mercanti, close to the house where Matteo was born (see Figure 2). His proximity to the heart of Macerata reflected Giovanni's status. A prosperous shopkeeper, Giovanni had been elected to serve on the town council as well. The Ricci family was old and respectable; and perhaps in a future generation it could rise from the urban middle class to the nobility. Education was the key. Giovanni sent Matteo, who was

Figure 2. House where Ricci was born, Macerata. Photo by author

barely a toddler, to study Latin with the priest and schoolmaster Niccolò Bencivegni. When Bencivegni left to join the new religious order of the Society of Jesus in 1559, the 7-year-old Matteo continued his tutoring at home. We know less about his home life. Matteo lived in an ever growing family: Giovanna gave birth to nine boys and four girls, of whom Matteo was probably the eldest. Managing the large household left Giovanna little time, and his grandmother Laria 'raised him for some time as a second mother', as Matteo would recall years later, when he learned of her death. He seemed close to his brother Antonio Maria, and probably knew little of his youngest siblings, some of whom might not have been born before he left home.

In 1561, the city fathers invited the Jesuits to establish a college. Promising free tuition, excellence in the humanities, and strict discipline, Jesuit colleges were very much magnet schools for the urban elites. Giovanni Battista wasted no time to enroll young Matteo. The Jesuit College enrolled some 140 boys, many boarders, almost all from the leading families of the region. During his seven years with the fathers, young Matteo acquired a formative experience that would mark his intellectual and emotional personality for life.

The teachers at the Jesuit College, so the later *Ratio Studiorum*, or General Plan of Jesuit Education, specifies, 'should train the youths who are entrusted to the Society's education in such a way that, along with letters, they also and above all interiorize the moral behavior worthy of a Christian. However, his special attention, both in the lessons whenever the occasion arises and apart from them, should be directed at preparing their impressionable young minds for the devoted service and love of God and the virtues by which we ought to please him.'[1]

The first goal, acquiring knowledge of Latin and Greek, was achieved in a graduated program of Lower Studies beginning with the lowest grammar class and rising through the grades of middle and upper grammar, humanities to rhetoric. In Matteo's seven years at the Macerata Jesuit College, he spent the first years mastering Latin grammar and acquiring the rudiments of Greek syntax. As he graduated into the class of humanities, Matteo had spent two to three years reciting the letters of Cicero and some Roman poets, while learning Greek grammar. Then, a large dose of Latin—Cicero, Caesar, Sallust, Livy, Curtius for prosody, Virgil and Horace for poetry (with indecent verses expurgated of course), and more difficult Greek prose—prepared the student for the class of rhetoric. The intense exercise of memory, through oral declamations and written compositions, translations and reviews, was upheld by the rule of Latin conversation among the pupils, except during breaks from the full academic routine, which saw classes in the mornings and afternoons, six days a week, except on feast days. For students in the class of rhetoric, memory became more important than ever, as they were expected to recite long passages of Cicero, as well as perfecting their knowledge of Greek by reading Demosthenes, Plato, Thucydides, Homer, Hesiod, and Pindar, in addition to the Church Fathers Gregory Nazianzen, Basil, and Chrysostom. But the heart of Greek learning was Aristotle, just as Cicero's work dominated the Latin curriculum: Aristotle's *Rhetoric* and *Poetics* constituted the main texts for this grade, a foretaste of a full-blasted Aristotelian program in the next stage of Jesuit education. The Jesuits kept up the élan of their pupils by weekly and monthly exercises, competitions and prizes, and public disputations that presented the pomp of academic exercises to the civic community. The fathers rewarded excellence, noted the mediocre, punished the lax, and dismissed the undisciplined.

The second goal, to inculcate the moral virtues of a Christian, was achieved by routine and example. All classes at the Jesuit College began with prayers; all pupils attended daily mass; all were enjoined to confess monthly. The more fervent joined the Marian sodalities established at the colleges; some enjoyed pious private conversations with the fathers. The most fervent and the brightest pupils served as officers at the sodality and academies for their grades, thus learning the joining of virtue and intelligence so prized by the Society.

Among the pupils and Matteo's friends, two would later join the Society of Jesus. The first was Girolamo Costa, from a Macerata noble family, just about Matteo's age and a close companion throughout the college years. He became a Jesuit in Rome in 1574, and rose to important administrative ranks within the Society. The two friends would keep up a lifelong correspondence. The other was Giulio Alaleoni, who became a Jesuit novice in Rome in 1577; ten years later, his younger brother Girolamo, whom Matteo knew, also joined the Society.

Although Macerata claimed a university, founded on a late thirteenth-century Law Faculty, the town was too small for a talented boy like Matteo and for his ambitious father. This commune of lovely red-tiled roofs, graced by its medieval cathedral tower, perched on a hill above green gentle valleys, was tucked far away in the Marches of the Papal States. But there, beyond the Apennines, was Rome, capital of the Papal States, of Italy, of the Catholic world, *caput mundi*, the most magnificent city of the world to many who lauded its glory.

In 1568, Giovanni Battista sent his son to Rome. Matteo left the steep steps of his native town for the Roman plains (see Figure 3). He traveled along the well-trodden route that took him across the Apennines to the banks of the Tiber. Matteo enrolled at the university, *La Sapienza*, and studied law. Jurisprudence was a nobler profession than pharmacy. Not all sons had to stay at home, and the brightest should go the furthest. In his father's eyes, Matteo would rise in the world as a lawyer, ascending the ladder of success in the administration of the Papal States, earning a decent living for himself for certain, and a noble title perhaps in the next generation. We know next to nothing about Matteo at the university. Suffice to say mastering the texts of the Civil and Canon Codes required good memory, technical expertise, and perhaps patience for dullness. Close association with the Jesuits provided the young student with a sense of continuity with his hometown: Matteo confessed with the fathers and joined the Sodality of the Annunciation at the Roman College of the Jesuits. On 15 August, 1571, just short of his nineteenth birthday, Matteo

Figure 3. The steep steps of Macerata. Photo by author

went to the Jesuit Novitiate on the Quirinale Hill and asked to be admitted to the Society.

The church of the Jesuit Novitiate visible today was designed by Bernini in the seventeenth century. Sant'Andrea del Quirinale stands on the site of the first structure, Sant'Andrea in Monte Cavallo, a parish church donated to the Jesuits by Andrea Croce, Bishop of Tivoli, a few years before Ricci joined the Society. The modest building belied the many novices who had entered its doors who would become illustrious in the annals of church history.

When Giovanni Battista heard the news, the upset father left for Rome to dissuade his son. The elder Ricci wanted a brilliant career in the world for his son, whose talent must not be thrown away on a clerical vocation. Hardly a few hours en route, Giovanni Battista was seized by a fit of high fever in the town of Tolentino, barely 12 miles away, forcing him to return to Macerata. The pharmacist took this as God's will and resigned himself to his son's religious vocation.

Rome, in the 1570s, was a city in transformation. For almost a century, the Eternal City underwent urban renewal: new churches, palaces, roads, monuments, fountains, and bridges dotted the vast cityscape enclosed within the medieval city walls, a transformation that would take still another century to complete. Work progressed in periods of intense activity followed by inertia: the creative pontificates of the two Renaissance popes Sixtus IV and Julius II, uncle and nephew from the della Rovere family, oversaw the establishment of the Vatican Library and the completion of the Sistine Chapel; this gave way to years of depression after the 1527 Sack of Rome; then, a new impetus began under the Farnese Paul III (pope 1534–49) and continued under his grandson Cardinal Alessandro, builder of the Gesù, in the 1560s. During the years of Ricci's Roman sojourn (1568–77), the city paused momentarily for breath, as it were, even though Gregory XIII sponsored some rebuilding, such as the Collegio Romano, before embarking upon another frenzy of architectural and artistic creation under Pope Sixtus V.

When Ricci arrived in Rome, he entered a city eight times larger in population than his native Macerata, enclosed by walls in an immense urban space that spilled over the seven hills of ancient Rome beyond the bank of the River Tiber. In spite of its immense geographical span, more than two-thirds of the enclosed city was empty, observed the French essayist Michel de Montaigne, who visited in the winter of 1580. Rome seemed to be only one-third the size of Paris in terms of population. Near the Tiber, houses were tightly packed in the center of the city; Rome was itself divided into quarters (*Rioni*), each with its own character. In one of these, the *rione* Sant'Angelo, close by the Tiber and the Theater of Marcellus, more than 3,000 Jews lived in a ghetto established by Pope Paul IV. The Spanish, French, and German nations constituted the three most numerous foreign communities, and attended respectively their national churches at S. Giacomo, S. Luigi, and S. Maria dell'anima. Others found a sanctuary from persecution: English Catholics and Greek and Albanian refugees made Rome their home. All of Italy was there: the Florentines concentrated in the V *rione* (Ponte), the Corsicans in the XIII (Trastevere), the Milanese, equally numerous, seemed more dispersed; only the Venetians did not settle in great numbers. In the midst of this urban density were scattered medieval churches and Roman monuments: the Pantheon, the Trajan Forum, the Capitoline, and the Theater of Marcellus. Close to the river, the Via Giulia, a graceful new street paved with uniform stones, led past the Farnese Palace, construction of which began under Paul III when he was still a cardinal, which became the most important palace in the sixteenth century, and is still the most beautiful Roman *palazzo* today. Across the Tiber, the menacing mount of Castel S. Angelo stood guard over the Vatican, but the papal city had yet to assume its present form. Construction on St Peter's Basilica, started in 1506, would take almost another half a century; under its new dome, designed by Giacomo della Porta, one still stood under open skies. St Peter's Square remained unshaped by the colonnades of the seventeenth-century genius Bernini; and houses on both sides of the Borgo S. Spirito obstructed a clear view to the Tiber. Beyond the dense urban nucleus, the city walls enclosed vast open spaces, as we can see from the 1575 urban plan, the *Civitates Orbis Terrarum*, prepared by the German cartographers Georg Braun and Franz Hogenberg (see Plate I). One could walk as in the country without going outside the walls. From the ancient ruins of the Palatine Hills past the Circus Maximus, a pilgrim would meditate while heading toward the Catacomb of St Sebastian on the Appian Way, the only catacomb unearthed at that time, where sometime the former cardinal nephew Charles Borromeo and Filippo Neri, both future saints of the Church, went to pray and remember the early Christian martyrs. Three other hills of Rome likewise housed few structures: the Esquiline, Viminal, and Quirinale. Most of Rome to the south and east was sparsely populated: the Aqueduct Claudiana and St John Lateran perched on the margins of the city; and from the Jesuit Novitiate Church on the Quirinale Hill, one enjoyed a magnificent view toward the city center, the Tiber, and the Vatican.

A different city for different eyes: Montaigne thought Rome 'is all court and all nobility: every man shares in the ecclesiastical idleness.' He missed the workshop-lined streets of Paris; Rome was nothing but palaces and gardens. For the English priest Gregory Martin, known for translating the Bible for English Catholics, who spent a happy sojourn in the Eternal City, Rome was all churches, convents, and hospitals. Both agreed the city staged numerous religious ceremonies: papal audiences, sermons, processions,

Lenten penances, and exorcisms displayed a vast cast of actors on the sacred stage, enacting a continuous theater of redemption directed by the Catholic clergy against the background of Rome's magnificent churches; or the fervent crowds, marching in a hundred confraternities, flogging themselves on the back, crying out at the sight of the blood-stained face of Christ on the cloth of St Veronica, gazing at the mask-like heads of Sts Peter and Paul at St John Lateran and other relics, and listening with rapt attention to the fiery sermons of repentance in churches and at street corners, in a massive display of popular devotion.

Whether it was a city of courts or churches, Rome attracted visitors like no other place in Europe. They came as ambassadors presenting their credentials at the papal court, kissing the slippers of the pope with the design of the papal arms (the first Russian diplomat from Muscovy, however, refused to perform this ritual when presented to Gregory XIII); pilgrims by the tens of thousands from every land of Europe and beyond, whose steady visit all year round turned into a torrent during the years of Jubilee, celebrated every quarter century for the general remission of sins; cultural tourists, like Montaigne, who came to gaze at churches and Roman ruins, navigating the vast city with guidebooks to ancient monuments readily available to the literate, perhaps visiting the private collections of antiquities in the palaces of the nobility, pioneers in a cultural itinerary that culminated in the Grand Tour of the seventeenth century. In addition to hospices and pilgrim homes, more than 300 inns catered to the needs of travelers. A large number of prostitutes further met the needs of the less than holy, in addition to serving their local clientele. In spite of their beauty and reputation, Montaigne complained the women charged him time for conversing, the same rate as 'the whole business', while offering little to stimulate his discursive interest. Then and now, Romans knew how to live off tourists.

This was the center of the Catholic world, battered by the storms of the Protestant Reformation, pillaged by troops serving Emperor Charles V in 1527 (a Catholic prince!), and assaulted by voices critical of the highest levels of the Roman clergy during the many sessions of the Council of Trent. But all this turmoil had ceased by the time of Matteo Ricci. With the successful conclusion of the Church Council of Trent in 1563, the Catholic world regained self-confidence, animated by a new purpose: the reconquest of souls from heretics and the conversion of heathens. Rome reasserted its role as the center of the apostolic Church, and the fulcrum of orthodox religion. At the city's gates, guards subjected all visitors to searches, as Montaigne

experienced himself, lest they smuggle poisoned books of Protestant heresies into Rome.

The papacy was the fulcrum of this assertion of orthodoxy. In 1572
Cardinal Ugo Boncompagni, a patrician from Bologna and a lawyer by
training, was elected in a swift conclave that lasted less than twenty-four
hours. A participant at the last sessions of the Council of Trent, the new
pope, who took the title Gregory, the thirteenth by that name, wanted to
imitate his predecessor Gregory the Great (reigned 590–604), who had
reformed the Church. His alliance with King Philip II of Spain indicated
unambiguously the direction this renewal would follow: a relentless struggle
with the Protestants to reclaim lost souls. Shortly after his election, Gregory
XIII struck a medal to commemorate the massacre of thousands of
French Huguenots on the Night of St Bartholomew, to the chagrin of the
Protestant world and to the private criticism of some Catholics, such as
the Cologne diarist Hermann von Weinsberg. In the same year, 1572, the
pope charged Cardinal Giovanni Morone, president of the last sessions of
the Council of Trent, to preside over a German congregation in order to
deliberate strategies for combating the heartland of Protestant heresies. In
1573, Gregory renewed the papal seminary, the German College, founded
in 1551 but which ceased operations only two years later due to a shortage of
funds. The aim of the German College, as Cardinal Morone put it elegantly,
was to prepare a Trojan Horse to be placed within the Protestant citadel of
Germany, to conquer the arch-enemy from within, by training a new
generation of Catholic clergy, learned, orthodox, disciplined, and loyal to
Rome. In the years that followed, Hungarian, English, Greek, and other
national colleges were established under Gregory's auspices. All were entrusted to the Jesuits, Catholic preceptors par excellence.

To use a representation from the times: like a human body, the Catholic
Church had fallen ill, with limbs and organs afflicted by the contagion of
Protestant heresies; the patient almost expired, but for the 'nerves and
sinews of the Church', the clergy. And if the heart of that resuscitating
body was the papacy, then the Jesuits embodied its blood vessels, pumping
life and energy to all parts of the renewed body.

Created in 1540 by the Spaniard Ignatius Loyola, the Society of Jesus,
which the young Matteo Ricci joined, was the most dynamic religious
community of the sixteenth century. Departing from traditional religious
orders, with their rules for common life, including divine offices, Ignacio
and his early companions saw themselves as preachers of the gospel. To

spread the message of Christ wherever they were called implied mobility and flexibility, for which the early Jesuits were condemned, as well as for their apparent arrogance naming themselves after the Redeemer, seemingly placing themselves above the Dominicans, Franciscans, and more established orders, who had taken their names from their founders. The first obstacles negotiated, the Jesuits quickly became educators in great demand, as their learning, doctrine, and discipline won repeated invitations from the ruling elites to establish colleges or take over defunct institutions of older religious orders. The Jesuit colleges turned into engines of growth for the Society. At Gandia, Messina, Palermo, and Cologne, the first Jesuit colleges were founded. In 1551, the Roman College, the flagship of Jesuit education, opened its doors with the inscription 'School of Grammar, Humanities, and Christian Doctrine, free'. It served as the main training institution for future Jesuits, and under the patronage of Gregory XIII, it assumed the name of the Pontifical Gregorian University. At the death of Ignacio in 1556, there were 46 colleges; by 1579, when Ricci arrived in India, a total of 144 colleges formed a vast network of Jesuit strongholds in the Catholic world on three continents. Staffed by professors, preceptors, and other assistants, and recruiting the brightest and most devout from their pupils, Jesuit colleges perpetuated the growth of the Society. The 1,500 Jesuits in 1556 became 3,500 in 1565, 5,164 in 1579; their ranks expanded to 15,544 by 1626 and climbed more slowly thereafter until reaching the peak of over 22,000 in the 1740s.

Like Rome, where Ignacio established the General Curia of his new order, the Society was a work in the making. With ever increasing members and papal patronage, the Society or the Company, as it was also called, represented the most dynamic force in the post-Tridentine Church. During the time of Ricci's novitiate, the Society counted more than 200 members in Rome, distributed between San Andrea al Quirinale and the House of the Professed Fathers at the Roman College. They constituted the second largest religious order, ceding in numbers only to the many orders in the family of St Francis, some 315 according to the report of Gregory Martin. Altogether, around 1575, there were over 1,100 male and 978 female members of religious orders, in addition to the secular clergy, in a population that stood at approximately 90,000. The Society was the rising star in this ecclesiastical firmament. Favored by the pope, one of their members, the Spaniard Francisco de Toledo, Professor of Scholastic Theology at the Roman College, esteemed as a most eloquent preacher and man of great moral virtue, held the post of Preacher at the Papal Court with only a short

interruption during the pontificate of Gregory XIII. He became in 1593 the
first Jesuit cardinal. Twelve other Jesuit preachers attended to the sermon
cycles at St Peter's Basilica, and still others preached in their own churches
and after public executions, satisfying the public's enormous appetite for
sacred oratory, in a city of religious ceremonies where rhetoric constituted a
central element in the representation of holiness. The Jesuits excelled in
sacred oratory: 'wisdom speaking copiously', as Cicero defined oratory, putting
eloquence and reason to serve the mysteries of the Christian faith. The main
Jesuit Church, *il Gesù*, construction on which began in 1568, actually designed
for the sermon with bright light and good acoustics focused on a large central
interior space, was still a model of restraint and clarity at the time of Ricci, before
its transformation in the Baroque into a monument of ornate curves, excessive
designs, and overabundant representations.

When Ricci presented himself at the novitiate, his modest possessions
consisted of an old coat, four shirts, three handkerchiefs, one towel, three
books, and some dry bread. He swore 'to observe with divine grace all the
constitutions and rules, and the way of life in the Society of Jesus, and to
be indifferent and resigned in order to reach the degree and courtesy that the
Society demands, and to be as obedient as possible to all the orders'. Receiving
him was Alessandro Valignano, Master of Novices and a nobleman from Chieti
in the Abruzzi, not far from Ricci's home country. We will hear much more
about Valignano, who would play an important role in Ricci's life. He was
succeeded by Fabio de Fabii (1543–1615), a young Roman nobleman who had
been ordained just two months earlier. In the course of the next year, Fabio
treated Ricci with kindness, which the young novice would cherish in his
memories. Later, Fabio served important posts in the Society, rising from
Master of the Novitiate to Rector of the Roman College, then Assistant of
Italy for the General, and Provincial for the Roman Province of the Society. In
January 1572, Ricci was sent to the House of the Professed (the fathers who had
taken all four vows of the Society) to practice humble house services. In May he
made his profession of faith and spent the summer at a Jesuit school in Tuscany,
which the Roman Jesuits used as a retreat for rest. In September he began his
formal studies at the Roman College.

From an original enrollment of 250 in the founding years, the Roman
College expanded in size to 1,000 students under the pontificate of Gregory
XIII. In 1572, there were more than 920 students divided into the following
classes: 60 Jesuit and 100 non-Jesuit theology students, 215 students in all for
the philosophy classes, and the rest in rhetoric, humanities, and grammar.[2]

In 1572, there were 26 scholastics, including Ricci, at the College; they were entrusted to the care of Claudio Acquaviva, a future General of the Society.[3] Forced to move twice in search of space, the College finally moved to its present site at the Piazza Collegio Romano, across from the Doria Pamphili Palace, thanks to a generous donation made in 1560 by the Marchesa della Valle, Vittoria della Tolfa, a niece of the late Pope Paul IV (see Figure 4). With some of the best minds of the Society on the faculty, the Roman

Figure 4. Collegio Romano, front façade

College enjoyed a stellar reputation. Montaigne marveled at the esteem of the Jesuits and believed 'there never was a brotherhood and body among us that held such a rank, or, to sum up, that produced such results as these men will, if their plans continue. They will soon possess all of Christendom: it is a nursery of great men in every sort of greatness. It is the one limb of our Church that most threatens the heretics of our time.'[4]

Who were the gardeners tending the seeds of greatness at this nursery of Christendom and how did they cultivate the vines of virtue?[5] The Rector of the Roman College in 1572 was Vincenzo Bonni; his successor, Ludovico Maselli, had entered the Society in 1557 with a doctorate in Civil Law, and served as Rector to the Jesuit College in Loreto prior to his appointment in Rome. The Prefect of Studies was the Spaniard Juan Ledesma, who died in 1575, but his Plan of Studies at the Roman College (*de ratione et ordine studiorum collegii Romani*) was published posthumously in 1579, and would serve as the blueprint for the authoritative 1599 *Ratio Studiorum* of the Society. Martino de Fornari and Orazio Torsellini taught Ricci rhetoric; and the German Christopher Clavius was Professor of Mathematics, of whom we will have more to say. Ricci would keep up a lifelong correspondence with his intellectual mentors Maselli, de Fornari, and Clavius, as well as with Fabio de Fabii, his spiritual mentor. The most famous professors at the time were two: Clavius, a native of Bamberg in Germany, was one of the most brilliant mathematicians of his generation, who designed a new and more accurate calendar, promulgated under Gregory XIII in 1582, to replace the Julian Calendar, and is hence the father of our modern system of time-reckoning (see Figure 5). The other was the Italian Roberto Bellarmino, an erudite theologian who first made his reputation expounding on Aquinas at the University of Louvain in the Spanish Netherlands. Called to a new chair of controversial theology at the Roman College, Bellarmino lectured on theological dispute against Protestants in the academic year 1576–7, which Ricci most probably attended. In 1599, Bellarmino was elevated to the purple, the second Jesuit to be thus honored.

After further studies in rhetoric—Cicero, Cicero, and more Cicero, 'style should be taken almost exclusively from Cicero', as the *Ratio Studiorum* admonished—Ricci started his studies in philosophy. Prescribed for a minimum of three years, the course of philosophy provided little relief from the single staple of Aristotle, honored as The Philosopher, whose texts were minutely dissected, discussed, and digested, starting in the first year with the works of logic collected in the *Organon*, proceeding in the second to Aristotle's

Figure 5. Portrait of Christopher Clavius in his study, by F. Villamena

Physics, On the Heavens, Meteorologica, On the Elements, and *On Generation,* and culminating in the third year, devoted to *On the Soul* and *Metaphysics.* Jesuit professors were admonished not to depart from Aristotle, except when The Philosopher contradicted Christian faith, and to rely exclusively on Jesuit interpretation, such as the commentaries on Aristotelian logic by the Portuguese Pedro de Fonseca (1564) and the Spaniard Francisco Toledo

(1572). Later on in his life, Ricci would demonstrate his fidelity to this education, criticizing the Chinese for ignorance of Aristotelian categories and logic, and introducing the Greek theory of four elements to replace the Chinese theory of five elements. Nonetheless, in Ricci's writings, the influence of Aristotle was less visible than that on some Jesuit missionaries after his time. It was mathematics, rather than Aristotle, that attracted the mind of the young Jesuit.

Geometry was at the heart of Jesuit mathematics, and Euclid its authority. In addition to textual explication of the ancients, Clavius, Ricci's professor in that subject, inspired students with his own original work, especially on astronomical observations and geographical calculations. In addition to textual and theoretical work, the students learned to use quadrants, armillary spheres, globes, astrolabes, and sextants; they calculated eclipses and measured the positions of the sun to determine latitudes and longitudes. In 1572, when Ricci was just a novice, Clavius and his students observed a nova, a discovery so exciting that the German astronomer was moved to write: 'I am convinced that either the nova was created by God in the eighth sphere to presage some great thing (though what this thing might be is still unknown) . . .'[6] Could it have been a sign foretelling the rise of a new star in the Jesuit firmament, a new student who would study with Clavius?

While geometry enabled the imagination of celestial space, it also facilitated the progress of cartography. The sixteenth century represented a revolution in map-making, thanks to the accumulation of nautical charts and land surveys made from many voyages of explorations by the Portuguese and Spaniards. The swiftest progress occurred precisely during Ricci's adolescence. The Fleming Gerard Mercator (1512–94), cartographer and mathematician, produced celestial and terrestrial globes in the 1560s; his method of projection used mathematical formulae to convert latitudes and longitudes into uniformly spaced straight lines, thus facilitating the representation of sea routes. His friend Abraham Ortelius, born in Antwerp, compiled the first modern world atlas. In 1564, Ortelius completed a 'mappemonde', an eight-leaf map of the world. In 1570, his *Theatrum Orbis Terrarum*, the first modern world atlas comprising fifty-three maps, was published in Antwerp. Only two years later, three Latin, and Dutch, German, and French editions had appeared in print. Unlike medieval European maps, heavy on symbolism and light on accuracy, whether in representing the earth in proximity to Eden or in depicting Jerusalem as the center of the world, these 'modern' sixteenth-century maps strove for accuracy. For the first time, the world was visible to readers; and maps presented the state of geographical knowledge. Future editions of the *Theatrum Orbis Terrarum* corrected inaccuracies, such as the west coasts of the Americas, but by and large, the Ortelius world atlas represented a splendid achievement. Expensive editions were printed in Antwerp and Rome. An excellent student of geography and mathematics, Ricci knew these works. Years later, his knowledge and enthusiasm for these subjects would serve him exceedingly well indeed.

We can reconstruct Ricci's studies from the *Ratio Studiorum*, but what was life like for the Jesuit scholar? To that we turn to *Roma Sancta*, published in 1581, which reflected Gregory Martin's experiences during his eighteen-month sojourn in Rome between the end of 1576 and July 1578. His enthusiastic encomium for the fathers of the Company echoed the fond memories of Ricci, years after the latter had left his alma mater:

Behold in one house (Roman College), there is a whole university of learning and lessons ... The Audience is so full, of Romans and Italians, of Germans and English-men ... of others out of all the cities both young and old, of every faculty and profession. ... What a goodly sight it is to see in the streets long trains of two and two, within the College a whole swarm, when after the hour they come out of diverse schools into one court together, and then new companies succeeding them in new lessons and other readers. The School is full of desks to write upon, which there is so ordinary, that he is no earnest nor daily auditor that writes not every word, if the Reader dictate[s] ... And as for the Readers, they are chosen and picked for the purpose in every faculty, very masters indeed of their faculty.[7]

Comparing the Roman College favorably with his own alma mater, Oxford, Martin waxed poetic on the lessons of divinity: some professors taught the Bible, some the questions of controversies against Protestants, some casuistry, others the whole of the *Summa Theologica* of Thomas Aquinas. Outside of lectures, 'for the commodity of the whole audience there are public disputations once a week, where one of the Readers doth moderate, and the rest sit by to urge and present the arguments of the younger opponents. This is always a notable exercise, and full of profit, with great delight, to see the grand doctors canvas a controversy before their scholars, the one urging the false part to make the other give the true answer, so to teach the hearers in all falsehood there may be probability, which, when the truth appears, is as a mist which the sun disperses and consumes.'[8]

Our English visitor, whose close friend from Oxford Edmund Campion had just joined the Society in 1573, praised the piety and charity of the Jesuits besides their learning, describing in loving details their spiritual exercises, prayers, and attendance at sacraments. Most impressed by the discretion and moderation of the fathers, Martin approved of their academic and religious schedules, which eschewed extreme physical asceticism. *Mens sana in corpore sano*: the Society provided proper medical care for their sick, planned periods of leisure into their academic schedule, and sent off their members to Tuscany at the end of the academic year to escape the oppressive Roman heat. Refreshed in spirit and body after the summer vacation, professors and students returned in autumn eager for a new academic year at the College.

Beyond this academic and religious routine, so tightly structured and thoughtfully fine-tuned by Ignatius and his successors, Ricci, like his fellow novices, was sheltered from the extreme contrasts of secular life in late sixteenth-century Rome: the world of prostitutes, criminals, and the ubiquitous beggars on one side; the luxury and leisure of the nobility (ecclesiastics included) with their palaces, servants, coaches, gardens, vineyards, and summer retreats on the other. Then, there were the days that stamped the collective consciousness: when all church bells in Catholic lands rang to celebrate the great victory of the Christian fleet over the Ottoman navy at the Battle of Lepanto, fought on 7 October 1571, not long after Ricci's entrance into the Society; or the Jubilee Year 1575, when thousands of pilgrims flocked to the spiritual capital of Catholicism.

Instituted in 1300 by Pope Boniface VIII, and celebrated every twenty-five years since 1475, the Jubilee for the general remission of sins was the major pilgrimage for the Roman Catholic Church. It was the first witnessed by Ricci. In 1575, pilgrims descended on Rome from all parts of Italy and beyond. Like the Tiber that regularly inundated the streets, pilgrims poured into Rome like a rising flood: the Trinità dei Pellegrini, a hospice founded in 1549 by Philip Neri to receive pilgrims, counted 174,467, but the total figure could easily be 400,000, more than four times the Roman population.[9] Most who came as pilgrims came in confraternities: led by their bishops and priests, they came marching with their countrymen, be it Florentines, Venetians, or Milanese, with banners flying, singing hymns and chanting prayers. In Rome, the inhabitants poured out their charity, providing lodgings and food; the nobility opened up their palaces and gardens to receive foreign dignitaries, by one count 6 princes, 9 dukes, 4 marquises, 8 counts, and 7 barons; and the clergy distributed alms, organized prayers and processions, and handed out rosaries, *Agnus Dei*, and other consecrated medallions. They visited the seven principal churches of Rome, sang hymns in Latin and in their own tongues, rejoicing in being a part of that great community that was the Church Militant, one with many diverse nations within the fold besieged, as never before, by adversaries of the faith.

The Rome of Matteo Ricci breathed the air of Catholic culture, *christianitas*, if one will: shaped by orthodoxy, right-thinking, and a hierarchy guided by the Vicar of Christ, *christianitas* represented both the continuity of Roman history from pagan antiquity to the Christian present, as well as the triumph of that present over the past. For what was sacred oratory but the use of Ciceronian eloquence to persuade and demonstrate the truth of the Christian faith? For what was Rome if not the capital of the universal Church, with Germans, Frenchmen, Flemings, Englishmen, Florentines, Venetians, Dalmatians, Greeks, Armenians, and many others congregated in their neighborhoods? And was not the Eternal City the monument of Christian triumph over pagan antiquity, when the Pantheon, a pagan temple, was consecrated as a Christian church and the Colosseum, once the site of bloody Christian martyrdom, testified in perpetual silence to the subjugation of pagan Rome? *Christianitas*, therefore, was the union of the Renaissance and Catholic renewal: it called upon the elites, educated on that synthesis of classical and Christian learning, to strive for the public good, the *res publica*, that is, the greater glory of the Catholic Church and the salvation of their own souls.

But the world of Christian civilization was fractured: Christendom no longer existed, Montaigne notwithstanding, after the followers of Martin Luther, Ulrich Zwingli, John Calvin, and many other reformers had decried the pope as Antichrist and the Roman Catholic Church as the 'Whore of Babylon' foretold in the biblical Book of the Apocalypse. 'In the place of many thousands of souls that have been led astray in Upper and Lower Germany,' so lamented the Augsburg printer Johann Mayer, 'the almighty good God... has chosen [for salvation] another people in another world, who knew hitherto nothing about Christ and his truth faith.' These were words found in the preface of a 1585 book printed by Mayer, a German account of the Jesuit Mission in Japan in the years 1577 to 1581.[10] The practice of *christianitas*, therefore, could no longer be limited to the cultivation of piety, nurtured by the simplicity of faith and the erudition of classical learning, as the Dutch humanist Desiderius Erasmus and his generation had advocated in the early sixteenth century. *Christianitas* implied action: to refute heretics, save souls, restore the world to orthodoxy, and thereby gain paradise. The theater of operations had expanded beyond fractured Christendom to the world outside Europe, wherein lay infinite gain.

Toward the end of 1576, the Portuguese Jesuit Martin da Silva arrived in Rome. Representing the Jesuit Province in India, he returned to Europe to raise funds and recruit fresh missionaries. After the 1498 voyage of Vasco da Gama, the Portuguese had made India the center of their Asiatic enterprise. Yet it was a harsh regime for empire and Church. The Portuguese wilted in the tropical heat, succumbed to new diseases, and lowered their guard against the luxuriant and exotic sensualities of the incomprehensible cultures of South Asia. In the narrow strip of Portuguese littoral strongholds that comprised the *Estado India*, with the uneasy tension between Portuguese from the motherland and those born in Asia, between Old Christians and New (the Jewish converts generally despised and suspected), and the mix of mestizos and Indian converts from different castes and ethnic groups, the Jesuits represented order and orthodoxy, a firm reminder of *christianitas* in pagan lands. Under the patronage of the Portuguese kings and viceroys, the Society of Jesus became the strongest spiritual arm of Lusitanian presence, with six colleges and sixteen smaller residences by the 1570s. But the climate also got to the fathers: most new arrivals fell ill; many died. Letters from superiors in India to the General in Rome implored reinforcements.

Matteo Ricci was moved by this appeal. He knew something about the Indian Mission. One of the professors at the Roman College, Torsellini, had written a biography and edited and published the letters of the Apostle to India, the first Jesuit missionary, Francis Xavier. Moreover, the Roman College functioned as the nerve center of Jesuit global communications: letters and reports to the General arrived from Jesuits all over the world, whether it be superiors reporting on the state of their provinces in Catholic countries, or undaunted fighters for the Catholic cause in Protestant territories, or lonely missionaries filing the latest dispatches on the front lines of spiritual conquest in distant lands. Fathers at the Roman College began to select and compile the most edifying and interesting reports for publication; the first volume of the famous *Annual Letters of the Society of Jesus* (*Annuae Litterae Societatis Iesu*) rolled off the Jesuit printing press in 1581 into libraries all over Europe. Even before the publication of this series, Ricci could read several missionary accounts from faraway missions: *The Announcements of*

Portuguese India from 1551 and 1552 by the Reverend Fathers of the Company of Jesus;[11] *New Announcements of Many Places in India and of Brazil . . . and the conversion thereof of many persons, etc.;*[12] *Particular Announcements of the Augmentation of the Catholic Church in India and especially in the Realm of Japan, with information on China;*[13] and finally, *Diverse Announcements of Portuguese India, received from 1551 to 1558, from reverend fathers of the Company of Jesus, where they concern themselves with the countries and peoples, their customs, and the great conversion of multitudes, who have received the light of Holy Faith and the Christian Religion, newly translated from Spanish into Italian.*[14] These edifying readings stirred Ricci's longing, and many others after him: to dream of long voyages through uninhabited lands, through mountains and forests in foreign countries, of maritime voyages across oceans, assaults and tortures by barbarians and infidels, sand storms whipped up by desert winds and columns of salty sea waves, of fiery and watery graves, of martyrdom and shipwreck, and the winning of eternal glory and salvation.[15] This imagination captured not only the hearts of young men: the 12-year-old Teresa of Avila, who would become the most famous female saint of early modern Catholicism, daydreamed of running off to the Moors to be tortured and martyred, before entering the convent and achieving sanctity in a far slower and more tortuous journey.

From the 1560s, a new spirit stirred the Catholic world. A generation matured, turning its back on goals cherished in an earlier time: success in this life, be it power, fame, or wealth, an endeavor that could be combined with saving one's soul. Instead, spiritual elites in the Catholic world renounced the secular world: they did not trade the active life for a contemplative life in monasteries; rather, they strove to subject all actions in life to a sacred purpose. The motto of the Jesuits summed up best this new spirit: *ad majorem Dei Gloriam*, to the greater glory of God. Notice the comparative. God may be fine in all his glory, but it was the duty of the fervent Christian to increase that glory. One acts: disputing Protestant doctrines, preaching the Catholic faith, founding religious orders, establishing schools, fighting infidels and heretics, supporting missions, constructing new churches, saving fallen women, raising orphans, visiting prisoners, and other actions that translated Catholic charity into practical social, cultural, and political actions. Again, it was actions that counted, and the more the better. 'More, more, more,' as Francis Xavier, the first Jesuit missionary, cried out to God to fill his heart to bursting with religious fervor and pious determination. 'To the greater glory of God' implies a ceaseless striving, 'more, more, more,' for holy action. Desire was all: the almost unquenchable desire for the glorification of God and the sanctification of oneself in actions. Heaven was the promised reward. And in addition to eternal salvation lay the chance for immortality in this world as well, as exemplified by Charles Borromeo, Ignatius Loyola, Francis Xavier, Teresa of Avila, and Philip Neri, who became the new saints of this restored Catholic world in the early seventeenth century.

The Jesuits embodied this new spirit. They mastered the art of holy action, simultaneously stimulating desire and controlling the passion that sprang forth from that desire. Thus, the walls of their Novices' House at San Andrea depicted instruments of torture—pincers, whips, lances, spears, swords, arrows, ropes, racks, nails, and crucifixes—by which the martyrs of the early Church were torn, lashed, pierced, beheaded, shot, hung, stretched, and crucified. Yet, to temper that ardent desire, lest the passion for martyrdom prompted indiscreet acts that bordered on suicide, the Society prescribed moderation in asceticism, proper care of the body, and the command of reason. Out of that tension, between desire and discipline, passion and restraint, burst forth an enormous energy that was capped, channeled, and directed to the numerous holy works pursued by the Society of Jesus.

Missions represented perhaps the most spectacular holy actions. Portuguese and Spanish Jesuits exercised no monopoly over this holy mission. Paolo da Camerino, Antonio Criminali, and Niccolò Lancellotti were the very first Italian Jesuits who went to India in the 1540s, leaving traces of their fervor in the pages of Jesuit relations: Criminali's martyrdom at the Cape of Comorin on the Fishery Coast in 1549; and Lancellotti's death in 1558, after years of torrid heat and repeated illness. After them, a new generation of Italian Jesuits volunteered to go overseas. Among them was Alessandro Valignano, a legend among the Jesuit novices and students during Ricci's Roman years.

Born in 1539 to a noble family in Chieti, in the region of Abruzzi, just south of the Marches and across the border of the Papal States in the Kingdom of Naples, Alessandro Valignano, tall, charismatic, and powerfully built, had served as the Master of the Jesuit novices at the time of Ricci's entrance. Unlike the younger man, who followed a classic model of Jesuit vocation, growing from an exemplary student to a fervent novice, Valignano entered the Society after a traumatic experience. Expressing the arrogance of his class and his own hot temper, the young nobleman, a student of law at the University of Padua, was arrested and imprisoned in 1562, after a young woman accused him of slashing her face with a knife. After several months' incarceration and a large indemnity to the victim, Valignano was released thanks to the intervention of Cardinal Borromeo. He left the Republic of Venice for Rome. Repentance for his former life led to a religious conversion in 1566; he entered San Andrea, the same community of which he was made superior after studies at the Roman College. In 1572, Mercurian named him Visitor of East India, representing the General in the Portuguese Jesuit Mission. In September 1573 Valignano left Rome for Lisbon and India to take up his powerful new position.[16] Among the new missionaries Valignano took with him were two natives of Macerata: Giulio Piani, born in 1537, who would serve in India and Japan, and Oliviero Toscanelli (1542–1601), a Jesuit brother, companion of Valignano in his numerous voyages, and in 1592, master of an elementary school in Macao.

No writing by Ricci exists for his Roman years. We do not know what specifically inspired him for the mission. But in the two centuries after his time, thousands of letters were written by Jesuit missionary-aspirants. Addressed to the General of the Society, the candidates for foreign missions implored in these letters, called *Indipetae* (literally letters asking for the Indies), and stated the urgency of their desires: some spoke of their missionary vocation in plain language, avowing obedience and indifference, as required by the Society; others claimed divine messages communicated in visions and dreams; still others expressed their fervent passion for the saving of souls, both their own and those of unbelievers; and a few indiscreetly betrayed their hopes for martyrdom. Did Ricci desire martyrdom? Judging by his letters and actions later in the field, Ricci betrayed no trace of the passion that inspired some to seek out a violent death. Perhaps it was a mixture of the desire for adventure, travel, and his own sanctification: 'helping others while helping yourself', to quote another Jesuit adage. Among his fellow students at the Roman College, the majority remained in Italy, contented perhaps with a more conventional career and more familiar theaters of action: Girolamo Benci (1554–1608) rose to become Provincial of the Roman Province; Giulio Fuligatti (1550–1633), Ricci's fellow student in mathematics, eventually succeeded their professor Clavius in 1587 in the chair of mathematics; and Lelio Passionei spent his later years teaching in Jesuit colleges in Modena and Mantua; these were all men remembered by Ricci oceans and years away. Others shared Ricci's desire.

In early 1577, Mercurian selected eight new missionaries at the College for the Indian Mission.[17] Six were Italians. The most prominent was the 27-year-old Rodolfo Acquaviva (1550–83), son of the Duke of Atri and nephew of Claudio Acquaviva, formerly Papal Chamberlain, presently Jesuit, and future General of the Society, succeeding Mercurian in 1581. When his uncle abdicated his influential papal post to the advantage of his nephew, a common practice in the papal hierarchy, Rodolfo refused the honor and followed his uncle into the Society. After two years of humanities at the Jesuit College of Macerata, he enrolled at the Roman College and was a theology student when called to the mission. Francesco Pasio (1554–1612), Bolognese, son of a papal judicial clerk and doctor of law, joined the Society in October 1572 and was a student at the Roman College. At 34, Michele Ruggieri (1543–1607) was the oldest of the group. He came from Apulia. Laureate in Canon and Civil Law at the University of Naples, Ruggieri had served in the Spanish government before he renounced a secular career for a spiritual one, joining the Society in October 1572 in Rome, changing his name from Pompilius to the more Christian sounding Michele. The Genoese Nicolas Spinola, born in 1549, joined the Society in March 1569 in Milan, was ordained in 1577, and nominated in Rome for the mission. The fifth Italian was the lay brother Giovanni Gerardino, a native of Ferrara who had joined the Society in 1561 in Rome. Matteo Ricci was the sixth. Two non-Italians completed the group: the Fleming Rutger Berwoutz, born in 1551, who had joined the Society in October 1576 in Rome; and Pietro Berno (1552–83), from Ascona in Switzerland, a student at the German College who had joined the Society in July 1577.

His task accomplished, Martin da Silva left Rome for Portugal in May. He took with him three of the new recruits—Pasio, Ricci, and Berwoutz—leaving the others to finish their studies and leave in November. On 18 May, the departing party received the blessing of Gregory XIII. Ricci was given permission to go on pilgrimage to Loreto and stop in Macerata to bid farewell to his family. To emphasize his sacrifice, Ricci turned down the offer. The party left Rome and headed for Genoa in the north. Following the old Roman road, the Via Flaminia, the little band of Jesuits probably hired horses from the Papal Post, for the wide and well-paved Roman road of antiquity had fallen into disrepair in so many parts along the axis Naples–Rome–Genoa that it was inaccessible to coaches and carriages. Only the section near Siena remained in good condition, as the indefatigable Montaigne observed. A few traveled by horseback; the majority walked, braving the elements and bandits that swept down on merchant convoys and treasury trains bringing the Spanish king's tax revenues from Naples to pay his troops in Genoa.

At Genoa, the Jesuits saw plenty of Spanish soldiers on another sort of Catholic mission: the repression of rebellion in the Low Countries, staged by rebels and heretics against their Catholic monarch. A decade before, the Duke of Alba had disembarked with regiments of Spanish soldiers to march north through Savoy and the Franche-Comté; the duke had long since been recalled, but Spanish troops continued to arrive on the march north. Marching under a different command, the Jesuits constituted a different service of Catholic arms, ready for other theaters of operations in the universal war against the Devil. In the 1620s, Jakob Revius, a Dutch Calvinist poet, mocked Ignatius' early military career on the occasion of his canonization, dubbing the founder of the Society of Jesus a saint canonized out of the cannons of Spanish arms.

On his first sea voyage, Ricci was 24 years old. He had not seen his parents in nine years, and he never saw them again. Neither would he return to Rome, his second home; nor would he see his family in God, the holy fathers and brothers of the Society, whose company and friendship he would recall with enormous joy and sadness a continent away. Perhaps the young Jesuit harbored no foreboding of melancholy or loss, for he was filled with the certainty and confidence of a Jesuit world, which Gregory Martin describes with these admiring words:

And as for brotherhood and mutual love, what can be greater, or how can it be shorter or better expressed, than to say, that all their houses in all the world . . . are but one house, all they among themselves are fathers and brethren and sons in respect of each other. Goeth he from Rome to Milan, from Milan to Paris, from thence to Toledo in Spain, to Lisbon in Portugal, to the East and West Indians? He is in every place at home as in the Roman College, in every place with his fathers and brethren, in every place so well that he feels no change: all rules, all orders, all conversations alike. And herein is fulfilled, that which our Savior promised to them that forsake worldly things to follow him, that they shall receive a hundredfold in this life. For one father, a hundred; for one brother, as many . . .[18]

Traveling overland from Spain, in July 1577 Ricci arrived in Lisbon, at one end of Catholic Europe and a portal into the wider world.

2

Portuguese Seas

With its back turned to the European continent, Lisbon towers over the River Tagus from its highest point at the Castelo Saõ Jorge, following the estuary with its gaze as it widens into the breadth of a lake before emptying into the infinite horizon of the Atlantic Ocean. A city of more than 100,000 in 1577, Lisbon was the third largest city in Europe, ranked only after Paris and Istanbul (see Plate II). The capital dominated the sparsely populated and mostly rural country, with a population of only 1.5 million inhabitants. A large gulf separated cosmopolitan and wealthy Lisbon from the poor hinterlands of the Trás-o-Montes or the Algarve. For the newly arrived Italian Jesuits, there was little resemblance between Lisbon and Rome, perhaps only in their hilly contours and palm trees. Graced by few Roman ruins, Lisbon was all medieval, white plastered walls and red roof tiles, with formidable fortresses and Gothic churches. Renaissance buildings, constructed in the particular Manueline style, named after King Manuel I, are more reminiscent of Late Gothic flamboyance than the proportional harmony of the Italian Renaissance. But perhaps the greatest difference was made by the sea, Lisbon being a port where merchandise and people flowed in from the whole world, among the latter Muslim war captives, African slaves, and a sprinkle of elite converts. In the late sixteenth century, one-tenth of Lisboetas were non-Europeans: the majority black Africans, both freedmen and slaves,[1] a sizeable contingent of mostly Arab and Berber Muslim war captives, and a sprinkle of Tupi Indians from Brazil. For more than a century, African slaves tilled the soil in the farms near Lisbon; they practiced handicraft in the city, and were domestically employed by all sectors of Portuguese high society, including most institutions of the Church.

After a short stay in the capital, Ricci went on to Coimbra, site of the first and most prestigious university in Portugal. There, he would begin the study of theology. In 1579, the Portuguese Province registered 550 Jesuits out of a total of 5,164 in the whole Company; almost one out of seven Jesuits was Portuguese.[2] The Society enjoyed great prestige and influence in Portugal. João III was a great patron of the new order from the time of its foundation. Like the ruling elites, the Jesuits were highly urban: they had two houses in Lisbon with close ties to the court; they were a major presence at the University of Coimbra and controlled the recently founded university at Evora.

Situated atop the highest hill in the area, the University of Coimbra still looms over the town and the Mondego, as that river gently winds and bends across verdant hills and fields. When the medieval university finally settled in Coimbra, after a move to Lisbon, it occupied the Alcáçova Palace. To increase its prestige, João III founded a royal college and in 1555 entrusted it to the Jesuits. Integrating their own College of Jesus and the new institution, the fathers dominated the arts faculty. The catalogue of the Portuguese Jesuit Province of 1585 recorded for Coimbra 32 ordained priests, 15 students of theology, 33 of philosophy, and 49 of humanities.[3] Excelling in philosophy, Jesuit professors composed commentaries on Aristotle, which became widely adopted in Jesuit pedagogy as the *Commentarii Coimbrensis*. In theology, however, a Dominican held the chair of holy Scriptures: Friar Luís de Soto-maior (1507–89), from a prominent noble family, student at Louvain and participant at the Council of Trent. Perhaps attending his lectures on the Psalms, Ricci also followed classes within the Jesuit College, attending Manuel de Gois's lectures on philosophy and Luis de Molina's on Aquinas. Most of all, Ricci and other foreigners were to adjust themselves to Portuguese ways, learning the language, mixing with Portuguese fathers, and preparing for the impending voyage. In November, the other recruits from Rome also arrived in Portugal: Rodolfo Acquaviva, Michele Ruggieri, Nicolas Spinola, and Pedro Berno rejoined Pasio, Ricci, and Berwouts. In early March, except for Berno, who would depart one year later, their superior sent the missionary recruits to Lisbon. There they would make their final preparations before embarkation and see the king.

Young King Sebastian (1554–78) had ascended the throne at the age of 3. His mother was Catarina, the sister of the Habsburg Emperor Charles V. His great-uncle, Cardinal Henry, tried to keep away Spanish influence and excluded his mother from the regency, appointing two Jesuits as the boy's educators and administrators of the royal household. Brought up in the image of a Christian warrior king, so dear to Portuguese history and national pride, the young Sebastian burned with impatience to acquire a reputation.

The great victory at Lepanto in 1571, when the combined Spanish–Venetian–papal fleet crushed the Ottoman navy, inspired Sebastian to dream of his own military triumphs and glories to rival those of his cousin King Philip II of Spain. In March, the Jesuit missionaries for India caught him in this mood, feverishly completing the final preparations for a crusade in North Africa. After the Jesuits had left on their own conquest of souls, in June Sebastian led an army of 15,000 to Morocco, where on 4 August, under a blazing African sun, he and the cream of Portuguese nobility perished in the disastrous defeat at Alcacer-Quivir.

In mid-March, Martin da Silva wrote to General Mercurian on the impending departure for India. Venting his frustration at the inability to secure an audience with the king, obsessed with a planned invasion of North Africa and negligent of Jesuit business in India, da Silva nevertheless expressed his satisfaction with the number and quality of new missionary recruits. In addition to those sent from Italy, he had picked five Portuguese Jesuits, singling out for praise Lopo Abreu and Eduardo de Sande for their knowledge of the classics and theology. Citing a papal letter permitting the ordination of missionaries departing from Lisbon before completing their requisite training, the Jesuit superiors asked Archbishop Jorge de Almeida to permit the ordination of six men: the Italians Acquaviva, Pasio, and Ruggieri, and three other Portuguese Jesuits. On 12 March 1578, the Feast of St George, the six newly ordained priests said mass at St Roque in Lisbon, taking their leave and kissing the hand of King Sebastian before their coming voyage. Da Silva reported to the General that 'I did not ordain Matteo Ricci, for he was still a youth [he was 25], and since he had never heard any lectures in theology [Ricci had followed classes in Coimbra for several months].'[4]

On the night of 23 March 1578, the fourteen Jesuits destined for India embarked in the harbor of Lisbon. Four years earlier, Valignano had embarked at the very spot, bringing with him a large group of forty-two Jesuits, mostly destined for Japan. The vessels were anchored off shore beyond the Terreiro do Paço, the area between the Customs House (Alfândega) and the Casa de Guiné e Índia, today the Praça do Comercío south of the Baixa. The ten fathers and four brothers were divided among three ships: their leader, da Silva, boarded the *São Gregorio*, together with the Italians Roldolfo Aquaviva and Francesco Pasio, another Portuguese father, and the Flemish brother Berwouts; Ricci's ship was the *São Luis*, also called 'The Captain'—the Portuguese Eduardo (Duarte) de Sande was superior of the five Jesuits on board, who included Ricci's fellow Italian and subsequent companion in China, Michele Ruggieri; the last group of four Jesuits under Nicolas Spinola embarked on the *Bom Jesus*. The careers of Ricci, Ruggieri, Pasio, and de Sande would later take them as far as China, but for the night of 23 March, the immediate journey ahead fired their excitement. In the morning, more than a thousand sailors and soldiers boarded the king's ships for the long Indian voyage.

The *São Gregorio, São Luis*, and *Bom Jesus* were among the largest maritime vessels of the late sixteenth century. Built for the long voyages to India that lasted up to six months, these Portuguese ships, called *naus*, measured some 150 feet in length and 40 feet wide; their four decks reached up to 25 feet at the main deck, with an even higher poop and forecastle. With a displacement of 1,200 to 1,600 tons and an armament of 30–40 guns, the four-mast *nau*, described as 'a mountain of wood', carried a minimum crew of 400 to 500, and contained large cargo spaces for the precious spices from Asia that made these arduous voyages so profitable and desirable.[5] While the small band of missionaries embarked, sailors busily loaded commodities (money) and victuals (biscuits, dried meat, oil, wine, and water) below deck. Granted free passage by King Sebastian, the Jesuits were privileged voyagers: each group of missionaries shared a small cabin at the stern, equipped with windows and a privy, and they brought along provisions for the voyage given by the king. Among the crew, only the captain and the pilot enjoyed private chambers; other officers shared cabins, while the men made do with a bunk and a chest in the common decks. All knew their functions: as captain, pilot, sailor, and soldier embarking on service and adventure in the name of the king, for the profit of the crown and their own coffers. The Jesuits were to serve as chaplains, for their consolation and comfort would prove necessary in the trying months ahead.

The three *naus* set sail the morning of 24 March together with many other smaller vessels, heading for Brazil, Africa, and other destinations in the Atlantic. Their flags rippling in the wind, the ships bade farewell to Lisbon in a scene best described by the poetry of Luis Camões, as the great sixteenth-century poet of Portuguese maritime explorations imagined the departure of Vasco da Gama in 1498, en route to India:

> The people considered us already lost
> On so long and uncertain a journey,
> The women with piteous wailing,

> The men with agonizing sighs;
> Mothers, sweethearts, and sisters, made
> Fretful by their love, heightened
> The desolation and the arctic fear
> We should not return for many a long year.
>   (Os Lusíadas, IV. 89)[6]

To those departing, it was rather the excitement of the journey than sorrow that animated their spirits, especially for those new to the sea, such as our Jesuit travelers. As they saw the Monastery of the Heronimites and the Tower of Belem disappearing behind the horizon, the point where the Tagus flows into the open ocean, words of Camões might well have echoed in their minds: 'We spread our wings | to the serene and tranquil breezes | and departed from the loved harbor; | and, as is now the custom at sea, | the sails unfurled, we bellowed: | 'God speed!', and the north winds as usual | heard and responded, shifting the great hull' (Os Lusíadas, V. 1).

The first euphoria over, the reality of sea voyage set in. With an excellent wind, the ships sped into the Atlantic. Immediately, many passengers got sick. Nicolas Spinola, who was on board the Bom Jesus and kept a journal of the voyage, started vomiting over the railings; he ate nothing for two days.[7] On board São Gregorio, Francesco Pasio also threw up. By the first night, as he confided to his journal, almost everyone on his ship got sick. Pasio congratulated himself on adjusting to the rolling waves in two days, while it took ten days of agony for others. This discomfort was a small price to pay for maritime travel. Even though all the islands and coasts of the Atlantic had been charted by then, and the Portuguese had the best navigational charts, a greater danger faced the Portuguese ships in the 1570s than at the time of da Gama: piracy.

In 1570, a Portuguese ship for Brazil was intercepted by French Huguenot pirates. Having overpowered the ship, the French boarded and looted the cargo. They discovered among the passengers Ignacio de Azevedo, superior of the Jesuit Brazil mission, and his new missionary recruits. The French spared the Portuguese crew but threw the forty Jesuits overboard, who became celebrated martyrs of the Society.

French corsairs lurked near Portuguese waters. A few days out of harbor, using excellent winds to full effect, the ships took their own course, and soon the three naus lost sight of one another. One day, the São Gregorio saw several small ships and prepared for battle; these turned out to be friendly Flemish grain ships. The Bom Jesus encountered real pirates: she came to the aid of a Portuguese ship that had left Lisbon together with her, chasing off two French corsairs that were about to board the hapless vessel destined for Brazil. There was to be no tragedy at sea. In fact, the three ships experienced ideal sailing all the way to the Gulf of Guinea: in four days they reached the Madeira Islands, in eight days the Canaries, and in fifteen days the Cape Verde Islands, where the winds started to diminish. Perhaps no more than a few hours' sailing from one another, the three vessels nonetheless sailed on their own toward the equator. On board, the Jesuits officiated at the mass and liturgies for Easter, hearing confession and performing the sacraments 'as if on land'.

The next stretch of the voyage was the most tedious. In late March, weather at the Coast of Guinea alternated between dead calm and sudden squalls. Days could pass without a breeze. A few years back, some ships to India had languished for thirty to forty windless days: more than a thousand died and their journey was interrupted. Luckily for our party, the sailing was slow but the ships did not stall: the *São Luis*, Ricci's ship, probably passed the equator first; the *São Gregorio* and *Bom Jesus* passed within sight of one another on 23 April, just short of a month after sailing from Lisbon. Instead of sailing directly south from Portugal, the ships now turned southwest, toward the northeastern corner of Brazil, where they would continue parallel to the coast to 20 degrees latitude before catching the strong westerly winds that would catapult them on swift currents toward the Cape of Good Hope.

Illness was the worst threat during these days of slow sailing. The first provisions had long thinned out: gone were the salted meat, dried fish, onions, and garlic; the daily ration consisted of biscuits, water, and a little wine. In any case, there was little appetite. Under the breezeless equatorial sun the water stank, the food was rotten, clothes stuck to sweaty bodies, books lost their colors, iron utensils rusted, and many were afflicted with headaches, swollen gums, and pain in all limbs. Everyone moved about languidly during the day, for 'sleep was sweating all night, stretched out on a bench with a thin mattress that smelled most foul with infinite lice, bed bugs, and other human miseries'.[8] On the *Bom Jesus*, Spinola suffered catarrh for a month; pain in his teeth and jaw deprived him of appetite, and the other Jesuits feared for his death before a recovery that the missionary attributed to God. Among the many ill with fever, one man died in great contrition, to the edification of all and the consolation of the Jesuits. The *Bom Jesus* lost one sailor, who had fallen at night from the stern; four other lucky ones were rescued on another occasion, when their rope snapped while they were hauling in a huge fish.

Fishing provided the only relief. All sorts of fish swarmed the warm waters around the equator. The crewmen caught plenty of these, which enlivened the dreary daily rations and probably restored the health of many. Others passed monotonous days hunting sharks. The men threw hooked meats into shark-infested waters, hauled up the first catch, cut up the doomed predator, threw its blood-stained head back into the water, and made a killing of the sharks attracted by the blood. Not unaware of their cruelty, the crew reflected on the similar fate of shark and human under the same circumstances, as the Jesuit Spinola noted in his journal.

It seemed the *São Gregorio* and *São Luis* fared better. No fatalities were reported. Nevertheless, impatience reigned. On board the *São Gregorio*, the Jesuits led a procession from stern to bow, carrying two relics destined for their church in Goa, namely the heads of St Gerasina, the companion of St Ursula, and the head of St Boniface the martyr, captain general of the 11,000 virgin martyrs of Cologne. At the altar set up at the bow, the missionaries recited prayers and preached sermons for the repentance of sins; from captain to page boy, all men cried out for God's mercy and benevolence. On 29 May, Corpus Christi processions were organized on board all ships, with music and the display of relics. Prayers and piety coincided with the west winds as the ships sailed east-south-east from 20 degrees toward the Cape of Good Hope.

On the dark, bright nights of the southern hemisphere, Ricci could see the South Star and constellations invisible from the hills of Rome. He would have noted with interest, as other Jesuits did, the distance sailed, the latitudes crossed, and the location of important landmarks. Lying at 35 degrees, the Cape of Good Hope represented the half-way point from Portugal to India; its passage was the most perilous part of the long voyage.

Sometime around 20 June, the *São Luis* passed the Cape without incident. A treacherous passage, this jut of land had been called not long ago the Cape of Storms (*Capo tormentoso*) by the Portuguese, who had lost many ships to the fierce squalls. Only under the reign of João III, the grandfather of the present king, had the name been changed to one of hope. On 20 June, the *São Gregorio* sighted the Cape, but swift currents and a strong wind forced the captain to turn for the open seas, lest the vessel dash against the rocky cliffs. The next day, Martin da Silva preached a sermon for the encouragement of all. Testing their resolve (and piety), a terrible squall arose on 24 June, blowing hard from the bow, the worst storm yet on the entire voyage, thought Pasio. With her sails down, the *São Gregorio* bobbed up and down for twenty-four hours going nowhere. Everyone prayed; and the Jesuits threw an *Agnus Dei* and a reliquary of St Paul into the ocean. The storm relented. The next day, a gentle tailwind eventually allowed the *São Gregorio* to round the Cape, reaching the coast which the Portuguese called Natale, near today's Durban. The *Bom Jesus* fared the worst. On 11 June, short of the Cape, she encountered a terrible gale whipping up mountainous waves that kept crashing on board. Drenched, all feared shipwreck. Fervent prayers during the next twenty-four hours seemed to have stilled the seas, when another storm, albeit smaller, arose around midnight the next day. The missionaries offered *Agnus Dei* and other reliquaries to calm the sea; the headwind turned into a tailwind, moving many to confess their sins in gratitude for God's mercy. Still on the open seas and out of sight of land, the pilot of the ship reckoned, erroneously as it turned out, that the vessel had already passed the Cape and altered the course from east to the northeast. In spite of doubts by others, the pilot persisted in his error, sailing for nine to ten days along the west side of Africa in the direction of Portugal before realizing his mistake and turning back, losing some twenty days in the process and passing the Cape only on 2 July, almost two weeks later than the other two ships.

With the Cape behind them, the sailors were not yet done with their troubles. They still had to sail into the Mozambique Channel, the large passage between the continent and the Island of Madagascar; and the stretch of sea near the Natale was known to be treacherous. Here, the *São Luis*, which had experienced the smoothest sailing of the three ships, encountered the worst squall of her voyage; the *São Gregorio* braved several squalls with favorable wind astern; the *Bom Jesus*, after a few days of fair wind, sailed into a dangerous squall, making no progress whatsoever for an agonizing twenty-five days against a strong gale. Many on board fell sick; all worried about provisions; 'charity cools', as Spinola remarked. It was also at this passage that all three ships witnessed that marvel of mariners: St Elmo's Fire. Some reported this in a matter-of-fact manner; Pasio, on board the *São Gregorio*, merely noted that the sailors called St Elmo's Fire 'the Sacred Body'. Others saw the hand of God; Ruggieri, Ricci's shipmate, had a vision of the Virgin Mary, protector of the voyage:

. . . and in that night of St Pedro Gonzalez, patron saint of mariners, in the crown of
lights the Blessed Virgin appeared above the stern mast, the mizzen mast, and the
Main topsail; there were many trustworthy people who saw this vision. In this peril,
the fathers withdrew and heard confessions from the passengers, and told them that
in these great dangers it is normal for the sailors to receive the help of the Blessed
Virgin for their salvation.[9]

If Ruggieri's words reflected the optimistic mood on board the *São Luis* and
the comfort of the divine, the journal of Spinola captured the desperation of
the *Bom Jesus* when she encountered St Elmo's Fire:

A storm arises. We all suffer terribly, as such great waves mixed with so many
crowns and lights in such a great sea. This occurred at the land of Natale, which was
not unusual, even though the sailors told me that they had never seen it on such a
great scale, and the lights were so bright that we could not see anything else, and it
seemed as if the ship were on fire, and while I have never seen or imagined such a
thing, it seemed like an appearance of hell. One would need to be very close to Our
Lord in order not to lose courage because at times it presented itself as the bridge of
death, since the sea is full of surprises, and it strengthens the resolve to face death
made before embarkation, now resigning all in the hands of Our Lord.[10]

Dejected by the gloom of death, the crew of the *Bom Jesus* redoubled
their devotion. The Jesuits organized a procession, recited litanies, preached
repentance; in tears the crew beseeched God, confessed their sins, and a few
even vowed to become clerics. Unable to proceed to the northeast, the
captain and the pilot conferred on passing beyond Madagascar for India, a
route that would increase the voyage by three months; the depleted rations
would mean many deaths. Murmurs spread when the crew learned of this.
Mutinous moods were calmed only when the Jesuits reported the danger to
the captain, and when a sudden wind astern allowed the *Bom Jesus* to sail
into the Mozambique Channel. A procession in honor of St Anthony of
Padua was organized in thanksgiving. By then, 12 August, it was too late to
anchor at the island fortress of Mozambique if the ship was to make India
before the seasonal change in winds and currents. The *Bom Jesus* continued
on course toward Goa, arriving there on 9 September after smooth sailing.

The other two ships put down anchor in Mozambique harbor on 21 and
22 July. The men on board the *São Gregorio* and *São Luis* had not set foot on
land for four months; their great joy on meeting again after Lisbon was
tinged with anxiety over the fate of the *Bom Jesus*. The Dominicans
stationed there offered a warm welcome to the traveling missionaries and
told the fathers about their own mission to Madagascar, where they hoped

to contest the domination of Islam with conversions to Christianity. The men stayed for some three weeks. Respite from the hardship of sea travel quickly restored the health of Martin da Silva, the procurator and the superior of the missionaries, who preached an eloquent sermon of thanksgiving at the Church of Our Lady of Beluarte of Mozambique. On 15 August, having taken on African slaves (300–400 on board the *São Gregorio*, perhaps the same number on the *São Luis*), the ships hoisted anchor. Keeping company, the two vessels again passed the equator on 27 August. Good wind and calm seas rendered the Indian Ocean passage a safe and uneventful one for the Portuguese crew, but eighteen African slaves on board the *São Gregorio* died of illness. On 13 September, the ships sailed into Goa, the men delighted that the *Bom Jesus* had arrived safely after all.

The six months passage prepared the Jesuits for their new missionary work. First, they faced death. The torments of waves and storms were like the torture of pagan rulers, exclaimed the Belgian Jesuit Ferdinand Verbiest one century after Ricci's voyage, in a letter sent from China to recruit more European missionaries.[11] Shipwreck and drowning thus presented the crown of martyrdom. Death was real. During the seventeenth and eighteenth centuries, approximately 15 per cent of all German Jesuit missionaries died en route, before they could make it to the Americas or Asia.[12] Second, there was illness. All Jesuits on board the *São Gregorio* fell sick at some point: everyone came down with fever, except for da Silva, who had an infected cheek. And that was on a vessel with smooth sailing. Third, the sufferings and discomfort on board strengthened the vocation of the missionaries, as Spinola wrote: 'But we suffer everything gently and easily, giving holy thanks to Our Lord, fearing nothing else, with our Lord consoling us in these miseries, remembering our pious desires with which we brought to this enterprise.'[13] And finally, the Jesuits practiced their ministry: preaching repentance, visiting the sick, giving spiritual and physical consolation to the dying, making peace between feuding parties, and strengthening the faith of those who faced storms and shipwrecks.

A robust constitution and spiritual discipline were indispensable. The missionary traveler observed on board a strict routine, as described by Pasio and Spinola. In the mornings the Jesuits devoted one hour to morning prayers and their weekly confession; they undertook spiritual exercises and penance in their cabin, a regime that included the examination of conscience morning and night. Then, they made their rounds visiting the sick, giving spiritual and physical aid. Reciting the litanies every day and often several times a day, they led the crew in hymn-singing and prayers at night in order to prevent fights. The fathers gave catechism every other day, and said mass on feast days with sermons. They tried to get the crew to forgo swearing and gambling, and led processions in times of danger, as we have seen. While the fathers undertook the spiritual duties, the brothers (Ricci among them) took on the task of caring for the sick. After Mozambique, their ministry was extended to the African slaves, giving comfort to the hapless captives destined for the slave market in Goa.

Jewel in the crown of Portuguese Asia, the city of Goa (Old Goa today) is situated on an island in a half-moon-shaped bay, separated from the mainland to the north and east by narrow rivers, while opening up westward toward the Arabian Sea. A wall on the eastern side defended the settlement against the mainland, but otherwise, Goa was open to the ocean. A city of beautiful houses and churches with many gardens, Goa resembled to travelers a 'little Lisbon' in the tropics: the whitewashed walls of Portuguese buildings glistening in the bright sun amidst palm trees and luxuriant vegetation (see Plate III). On the main street, a lively market was held every morning, except on holy days. Traders found merchandise from all of India, spices from Southeast Asia, porcelain and silk from China, and slaves from Africa. Alongside the Portuguese, the mestizos, and indigenous Indian converts, Persians, Gujaratis, Marathans, Jews, Armenians, Syrians, and Chinese mingled. Altogether, the Viceroy of India ruled over a population of 150,000 in Goa and its hinterlands, some 90,000 Christians and the rest Hindus. In spite of the great diversity of merchants, the Portuguese allowed only the practice of Catholicism in the city of Goa itself. It was the center of their civilization.

In 1510, the Portuguese captured the old Indian settlement that had belonged to the Sultan of Bijapur, and turned it into their capital of the *Estado India*. In fact, it is an exaggeration to call the Portuguese possessions in Asia a state. Their 'empire' consisted of a string of heavily fortified seaports, forming a trading network thanks to their mastery of the seas. From Sofala and Mozambique on the East African coast to Ormuz at the mouth of the Persian Gulf, from a string of fortresses on the west coast of India (Diu, Bassein, Goa, Cochin, etc.), down to Ceylon (Sri Lanka) and Malacca on the Malay Peninsula, Portuguese ships ruled the waves for most of the sixteenth century, having defeated the Ottoman and various Muslim rivals during the 1510s. Beyond the range of European cannons, Portuguese presence rapidly thinned out into the deserts, grasslands, and tropical forests of the vast hinterlands. Alternating between alliances and warfare with the local powers, the Portuguese carried on a lucrative trade, in spices, silk, porcelain, and silver, adding the Moluccas (Amboin), Macao on the southern coast of China, and Nagasaki in Japan to their network during the mid-sixteenth century.

Implanted on just a thin encrustation of European civilization in the deep Asian soil, Portuguese colonialism depended on two nutrients to keep alive: population and Christianity. The first was hard to come by. One of the most sparsely populated countries of Europe, Portugal had approximately 1.5 million inhabitants in the 1570s, compared to 3 million in England, 7 million in Spain, and 14 million in France (the most populous country in Europe). Portuguese expansion demanded manpower, as sailors on the regular fleets to Brazil, India, and East Asia, and as soldiers guarding the trading fortresses of their far-flung empire. More importantly, almost no Portuguese women ventured overseas in the sixteenth century; later, only a tiny number of orphaned girls were shipped overseas under the sponsorship of the crown. The vast majority of Portuguese men took local women; their progeny, the mixed-blood mestizos, raised as lusophone Catholics but treated as second-class Portuguese by those disembarking from the metropolitan homeland, formed the backbone of Portuguese colonialism. In Goa, Malacca, Macao, and other permanent Portuguese settlements, the male population was divided into married men and soldiers, all liable for royal (i.e. military) service. The deficit of people was made up by two other groups: slaves and converts. Highly heterogeneous, the first group comprised dark-skinned East Africans, Moluccans, and Timorese, various Indian ethnicities, and later, indentured servants purchased in south China. Just as essential for Portuguese colonialism was the convert population. In Goa, indigenous converts constituted a majority of the population, hence the importance of Christianization as the second major source for the continuance of Portuguese presence. Reflexively, the Portuguese (including the clergy) considered Christianity synonymous with being Portuguese, in speech, dress, food, and faith, with skin color and place of birth (metropolitan versus colony) serving as further markers of status.

There were simply not enough clergy to minister to the many Portuguese communities overseas and to evangelize. Shortage of manpower compelled the Portuguese to allow Italian, German, and Flemish merchants to share in their Asian commerce and profits. Likewise, Portugal called upon missionaries from other Catholic nations in Europe to assist in the harvest of souls.

Matteo Ricci and the other missionaries arrived in Goa on 13 September, the eve of the feast day of the Exaltation of the Cross. After they disembarked, the four Italian Jesuits were overjoyed to see a beautiful patch of green grass. They sat down to rest, as Ruggieri recalled with some exaggeration years later, 'for their heads were still tossing about greatly, having spent seven months in ships without ever seeing land'. The shipmates began to talk lightheartedly about God's plans for them 'in these parts'. Being the eldest, Ruggieri took it upon himself to assign tasks: all of them would be ordered to go to China, Rodolfo Acquaviva as theologian, Francesco Pasio as philosopher, Matteo Ricci as mathematician, and himself as a lawyer. After this discourse, Ruggieri smiled, entertained by 'these castles of air created in the mind', whereupon Acquaviva replied in high spirits: 'Don't laugh at this, Father, this will be so!'[14] After this, the companions continued their walk into Goa and joined the others for a warm reception at the Jesuit College of St Paul in their honor.

Four years back, General Borgia had sent a true piece of the Cross from Rome to Goa. Ruy Vicente, the Provincial of the Jesuit Province of India, officiated at Vespers and led a procession to the square before the Jesuit Church, where the travelers joined their local brethren in reciting prayers before a newly erected stone cross. The next day, Vicente said high mass to a full church, attended by the viceroy and all Portuguese dignitaries. The Rector of the College, Franciscus Monclaro, gave the homily. After mass, Father Vicente carried the relic of the Cross in a procession around the church, lowering it for all to kiss. Then the procession exited into the square, preceded by eight students of the Jesuit College, who performed a dance in honor of the new arrivals. Other students, some as young as 6 or 7, dressed up as soldiers (their later profession) and marched with arquebuses, discharging them in front of the cross in salute. After three to four days in Goa, the Provincial sent the new group to the retreat on the nearby island of Chorão, where they could refresh their spirits before receiving assignments.

Like the Portuguese Asian Empire, the Jesuit Province of India was also centered in Goa. In 1578, the Province included 257 members, making it almost half as numerous as the Portuguese Province.[15] The largest cluster was in Goa: the College counted 106 members, including the new arrivals, divided between 37 priests, 51 coadjutors, and 18 novices. Another 82 Jesuits served in other Indian locations: 34 at Bassein, 20 at Cochin, 9 at

Chaul, 14 at the Fishery Coast, and 5 guarding the reputed shrine of the Apostle St Thomas at San Tomé de Meliapor (near Chennai today). The Indian Province also had jurisdiction over other Jesuit missions in Africa and Asia. Africa proved infertile for the missions, with three Jesuits laboring fruitlessly in Ethiopia in an effort to convert the Christian Kingdom to the Roman Catholic rite. The ten Jesuits in Malacca served mainly the Portuguese community, while three intrepid missionaries manned the most difficult station in the Moluccas. Such was the harshness of jungle and natives that two Jesuits had been dismissed in 1552 by Francis Xavier for abandoning their post there; a third died a martyr in 1558; and the fourth man went mad and had to be sent back to Goa to die in 1564.[16] Much more promising were the developed countries of China and Japan: the seven Jesuits in Macao ministered to the small Portuguese merchant community and their dependants, while forty-six missionaries reaped abundant harvests in Japan. Perhaps one-tenth of the Jesuits under the Indian Province were not subjects of the Portuguese crown, most of them being Italians. All had acquired language proficiency after their long passage, as Portuguese words crept into their correspondence with the General in Rome. But unlike the Portuguese Jesuits, many of whom were content ministering to their own countrymen in the tropics, the Italian fathers longed to evangelize the indigenous populations.

Their first assignments, however, were at the College of St Paul. Vicente, the Provincial, assigned Acquaviva as Prefect of the Church and Professor of Philosophy, Pasio as minister of the College, Spinola, Ruggieri, and Ricci to study theology, and the sixth Italian in this new group, the *coadjutor temporalis*, Giovanni Gerardino, as sacristan.

His first year of theology in Coimbra truncated, in Goa Ricci followed classes in casuistry and speculative theology, listening to Eduardo de Sande, Lopo Abreu, and Laurent Pinheiro (the first two among the new arrivals) lecture on Aquinas' writings on grace, law, and the angels. The routine would have reminded him of life at any Jesuit college. Indeed, the College of St Paul, in the words of Pasio, rivaled the best built Jesuit college anywhere in Europe. A house of novices, with its own garden and chapel, had recently been constructed on the model of San Andrea in Rome, by order of the Visitor Alessandro Valignano, who was in Goa from September 1574 until just several months before the arrival of Ricci, and was now directing the mission in Japan. Decorated with magnificent altars and paintings completed by local Jesuits, the College church also housed the treasure of the heads of three saints, two of whom, as we have seen, were imported recently from Europe.

More than 900 students enrolled in the academic year 1578. The primary class with some 700 Portuguese boys learning reading, writing, catechism, and counting was the largest; the next level, the humanities, was attended by 150 external and 13 Jesuit students; the philosophy class of 19 Jesuits and a handful of external students moved to the Jesuit College in Cochin during the semester, a decision made by Vicente due to the epidemic in Goa and military clashes in nearby Salsete between the Portuguese and the Sultan of Bijapur; and finally, 20 students, almost all Jesuits, followed the classes of theology. In addition to their teaching duties, the Jesuits assisted at the City hospital by order of the viceroy, alternating with the other religious orders in Goa. They taught catechism to local boys, in the regional language Konkani for those who had learned it, and through interpreters for others still ignorant of Indian tongues. Some fathers gave spiritual comfort to those condemned to death, and regularly accompanied the victims of the Inquisition, which had jurisdiction over all of Portuguese Asia. In the autumn of 1578, the Jesuits also helped the refugees fleeing the clashes in Salsete, Indian converts fearing reprisal from the Muslim troops of Bijapur.

Still, a college life was not what many had bargained for. For that they could have stayed in Europe. For those who remained in Goa, the daily routine might have seemed anticlimactic to the heroic sea passage, remembered vividly in long letters dispatched to Europe. Spinola and Ruggieri were the most fortunate. In November 1578, after only a brief two months, they were sent to the Fishery Coast as missionaries to the Malabar Christians. Those who stayed behind, Acquaviva and Pasio, vented their frustration in private letters to the General. One manifestation of that frustration was dissatisfaction with the Portuguese. Before their departure for Portugal, their superior admonished the Italian Jesuits to be sensitive about Portuguese pride, never to say a critical word on board Portuguese ships, and to be mindful of the piety and patronage of the Portuguese crown. But some months into life at the heart of Portuguese Asian colonialism, critical voices surfaced. On 31 October 1578, Acquaviva wrote to General Mercurian, reporting on the scandalous reputation of Martin da Silva that he had picked up in Goa: suspected of sexual solicitation during confession, da Silva had been ordered by Valignano not to hear confession by women; and many in Goa were appalled that the erstwhile procurator had been admitted to the Fourth Vow as a professed father of the Company while he was in Rome.

In any event, Acquaviva eventually escaped the tedium of College and the viciousness of Goan gossip: in mid-November 1579, Ruy Vicente selected him and other Jesuits for the court of the Mughal Emperor Jalaluddin Muhammed Akbar (1542–1605), who had requested learned men of Christianity to complete the splendor and learning of his court. For three years, Acquaviva, Francisco Henriques, and João de Mesquita languished at Agra, absorbing linguistic, cultural, and political information. But seeing no prospects of an imperial conversion, Acquaviva returned to Goa in May 1583, and died two months later in Salsete during an uprising by the local Hindus against the Portuguese, fulfilling his desire to become a famed missionary and martyr.

The cross was heavier for his friend and shipmate Francesco Pasio, who wrote about the melancholy of adjustment, not so much to the intense heat and fevers of India, but the frustration of his office as Minister to the Jesuit College, for which he was in charge of the spiritual well-being of some 300 Jesuits and boarders. In a letter to General Mercurian, written on 27 October 1580, Pasio complained that it was precisely to escape from such duties that he had left Rome for India. A further spiritual cross was the Provincial, a saintly man, Pasio conceded, but fastidious, austere, rigorous, and choleric, the traits worsened after a long illness in 1577, blowing up at and shouting down subordinates at any infringement of rules or when having his will contradicted. Portuguese ways were the best ways for Vicente, reported Pasio in frustration. In the autumn of 1579, Pasio asked for permission to serve in the Ethiopian Mission, but eventually no ship departed; and in 1580, the situation became so discouraging that no mission was foreseen. His private complaints notwithstanding, Pasio enjoyed the trust of the Provincial, who made him Procurator of the Province in December 1580. For one year, Pasio dealt with all business of the Province, buying oil, wine, and a hundred sundry things, while managing the rents from properties pertaining to the Japan Mission and ensuring their safe and prompt transfer. Back to his duty as Minister of the College, Pasio finally fulfilled his missionary calling when Valignano summoned him in April 1582 to join him in Japan.

Another Italian Jesuit from the cohort of 1578 was called to a new missionary enterprise. On 12 April 1579, Provincial Vicente received a letter from Japan: Valignano ordered him to select someone gifted in languages; this candidate was chosen to learn Mandarin Chinese in Macao, in preparation for opening the Celestial Kingdom for evangelization. Valignano had in mind Bernardino de Ferraris, a Calabrian Jesuit, but he was indisposed at the moment. Making a mental roll-call, Vicente decided instead on Ruggieri, who had only been sent down from Goa to the Fishery Coast last November with a chest of law books. The Neapolitan was a Doctor in Civil and Canon Laws before joining the Society, and the Provincial hoped that Ruggieri would carry out a 'civilizing mission' as well, teaching the pearl divers and recent converts to abide by Christian and European civil law. Ruggieri's superiors thought very highly of him. Antonio Monserrate, secretary of the Province and long-time missionary down in the Fishery Coast, praised Ruggieri to General Mercurian:

Father Michele Ruggieri has left for China in order to learn the language of the mandarins, which is the most polished and elegant language of those parts, and this, with divine help, that he can commence that enterprise that the Blessed Master Francisco [Xavier] of blessed memory and other fathers subsequently, had not achieved for some divine secret. Our Lord has turned his eyes of piety toward that poor people, and by the zeal of the Father Visitor [Valignano], who has returned from Japan, and strongly determined in this undertaking. For this Father Ruggieri was chosen, as a person whose age [he was 35], virtue, skills, inclinations and other necessary qualities come together, since in the few months that he was in the Fishery Coast, he had learned Tamil with such holy zeal and fervor, that he could begin to hear confession in that language, and gave such a good name of himself that all inside and outside the house [of the Jesuits] very much regret his leaving.[17]

In another letter to the General, Vicente again emphasized Ruggieri's linguistic abilities, claiming the Italian began hearing confessions in Tamil only days after arrival, and emphasizing his virtue as another reason for the decision. Ruggieri himself, more modest and realistic, stated that he could hear confession in Tamil in just under one year.[18] In April, Ruggieri happily obeyed the command, 'for he had dreamed of this prior to arrival in India',[19] and left the Fishery Coast for Cochin, where he embarked in May for Macao (see Map 1).

Michele Ruggieri, the great hope for China; the Italian Jesuit Alberto Laerzio, who arrived with a new cohort of missionaries in 1579, wrote as much in a letter from Goa (8 November 1581): Ruggieri already knows the language and is preaching to the Portuguese merchants and other Christians in Macao, even converting some infidels, 'if Our Lord God opens the door to that grand harvest, he could enter into the country and reap stupendous fruits'.[20] Meanwhile, waiting for the Lord to knock on the door of China,

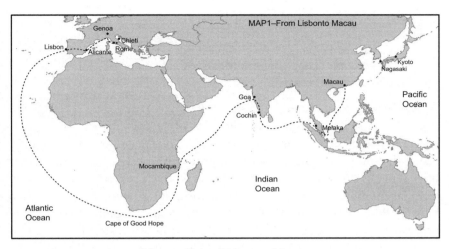

Map 1. From Lisbon to Macao

Laerzio kept company with four other Italians at the College of St Paul, two of whom, Pasio and Ricci, had spent more than three years in India.

Only at this point in our story do we hear the voice of Ricci. Like a junior colleague, 'a mere youth' in da Silva's words, Ricci kept a low profile in the background. Still only a theology student, his fellow Jesuits, more senior in rank, made no remarks about the unobtrusive young man in their letters from India. Ricci also wrote a letter shortly after his arrival, addressed to his former Latin teacher at the Roman College, Martin de Fornari. This letter is now lost. We first hear his own words in two more letters written in Cochin, dated 18 and 30 January 1580, addressed to two former teachers, the Portuguese Emmanuele de Gois in Coimbra and Fornari in Rome.

Ricci's first letter, written in Portuguese to Gois, is remarkable in its banality. Nothing of a personal note, the entire letter is a report on current missionary events, a mixture of the latest information from Goa and an echo of conventional piety. Ricci devotes most attention in his long letter to the Mughal Empire: Emperor Akbar, having met Portuguese Jesuits in Bengal, dispatched an emissary to Goa to request learned Christians for his court. Envisioning a political alliance with the mighty empire to the north, the Portuguese Viceroy welcomed this chance; and the Jesuit Provincial provided an enthusiastic welcome in the Jesuit College. Ricci reported on the selection of missionaries for this exciting grand enterprise, and echoed the common sentiments in Goa:

We are all very apprehensive, with great hopes for nothing less than the conversion of all of India, if everything goes well. But everything has its difficulties, therefore Your Reverence and others must not consider this a done deal and neglect prayers to Our Lord, for this matter concerns Moors and other obstacles which the Devil uses to obstruct similar works.[21]

At least peace was restored in Salsete with a new treaty between Goa and Bijapur, reported Ricci. He added the news of the conversion of a daughter of the deposed ruler of Bijapur, the brother of the present ruler and the actual rightful prince, now under the protection of the Portuguese. After brief remarks on Malacca and the Moluccas, Ricci related the great news from Japan: the conversion of the feudal lord, the daimyo of Bungo (called king in Portuguese sources), for which the Jesuits organized celebratory processions in Malacca and Cochin. Roman Catholicism advanced, even on the Fishery Coast, where the St Thomas Christians had agreed to subscribe to the Roman rites of Christianity, ended Ricci's triumphant report. Only a brief remark on the geography and location of the Mughal Empire faintly betrays Ricci's personal interest.

His short letter to da Fornari, composed in Italian, repeated in summary the information sent to Gois, except for news about several Italian fathers in Japan. He himself, Ricci, was teaching Latin grammar at the Jesuit College of Cochin. After Ricci's first academic year in Goa, devoted to theology, he became professor of first-year humanities at the College in September 1579, teaching Greek grammar to a dozen students, and was just about to start on Demosthenes' *Philippic* when he fell very ill. On 11 November, Vicente decided to send him to Cochin, where the salubrious air would help with his recuperation. Goa seemed an unhealthy place (swamps, sluggish rivers): Vicente reported to General Mercurian that seven Jesuits had died this year, including two students aged 19 and 18, and that Ricci had been dangerously ill.[22] Recovering his health, Ricci taught rhetoric to the humanities students in Cochin during the spring semester; on 26 July 1580, he was ordained and said his first mass. Ricci stayed on in Cochin teaching rhetoric until he was recalled to Goa by Vicente, who ordered him to resume his theological training.

On 29 November, in reply to a letter by Ludovico Maselli, his former professor at the Roman College and now the Rector, Ricci poured out his heart. He had just learned of his assignment to return to the Goan College, and Maselli's letter invoked all the warm memories of his Roman College days:

I want to say that nothing causes me as much sadness, [including] the far separation from my parents in the flesh, even if I am very carnal, as the absence of Your Reverend, whom I love more than my father. From this Your Reverend can judge how grateful I was with your letter. I do not know what sort of imaginations come to me at times, and I do not know what causes me a sort of melancholy, which seems to me to be good, and I shall have scruples if I did not have them, thinking that my fathers and brothers, whom I loved and love so much, of the college where I was born and raised, may be out of tune with me, while I hold everyone in such vivid memories, that I remember Your Reverend and the other fathers and brothers of the college with many tears, saying a goodly prayer in my misery. Nonetheless I am very happy with this second vocation and recognize the great goodness that God had given me after calling me to the Company, living with great things in that part among our fathers and brothers.[23]

One of those spiritual fathers more dear to Ricci than his own was Gian Pietro Maffei, who was sent by the General to Portugal to gather material for writing a history of the Jesuit missions in the Indies. Ricci responded enthusiastically to Maffei's request for first-hand knowledge, excusing his Portuguese letter by invoking how much he had forgotten his mother tongue. Animated with this intellectual project, Ricci showed his keen interest in humanistic and scientific learning. The best printed sources, he cautioned Maffei, are full of errors; a good historical work needs to be informed by first-hand accounts and observations. While volunteering his own experiences and the services of an unnamed Jesuit brother, 'a very good friend', who offered to check on sources for Maffei, Ricci advised waiting for the arrival of Valignano, who was expected from Japan (the Visitor did not arrive in Cochin until June 1583). Not only was Valignano an actor in the unfolding drama of heroic Jesuit missions, he was supposed to have authored a history of the Asian missions, which would be indispensable for Maffei to consult. Ricci himself had written several letters to Valignano, but these seemed to have been lost for he had not received any replies. What Ricci himself could offer, 'should Your Reverend wish', was a table with descriptions of the major places of these lands, 'with which maps and with the eclipses that I had observed and I shall be observing, which are things more certain than the things already found in print'.[24] The two greatest hopes, Ricci reported, were for the conversion of Oda Nobunaga, the Japanese warlord, patron of the Jesuits and hegemon in the civil wars that had plagued Japan for nearly a century, and Emperor Akbar of the Mughal Empire. Turning from the universal theater of Catholic missions to his own personal drama, Ricci described his illness and pedagogy with mild irony:

'As for myself, I cannot shake off this grammar.' Anticipating his return to
Goa, where the Provincial commanded him to finish his theology training,
he wrote: 'I do not know whether it will be for finishing grammar or my
life, since that place is most unsalubrious.'[25] In December 1580 Ricci was
back in Goa, where he promptly came down with fever.

Solicitous of his health, the Provincial gave Ricci no assignments other
than studies. The studious young priest devoted the entire year 1581 to
theology, coming down again with fever in the autumn months. His illness
prevented him from responding sooner to two letters from Maffei, who
asked for detailed information on the Indies. Rushing to post his letters
before the departure of the ships for Portugal, Ricci composed a reply on
1 December, recommending the biography of Francis Xavier written by
Manuel Teixeira, Rector of the Cochin Jesuit College and one-time companion of Xavier in India, a manuscript that had been sent to Rome. Ricci
counseled Maffei to turn to Teixeira, who was better informed about so
many things. Still no news about Valignano. As for his own contributions,
Ricci observed that the rivers separating Goa from the mainland were hardly
more than salt-water streams, but as to political history, he knew no names
other than Akbar. He would have to consult an honorable Muslim or a
well-educated Brahmin to find out more about Indian history. The mission
to Akbar in any case was not going as expected: more curious about western
learning than faith, the Mogul emperor was unlikely to convert; and
Rodolfo Acquaviva had already obtained permission from the Provincial
to return from Delhi. Mentioning the martyrdom of a couple of Portuguese
Jesuits in Ethiopia and the illness of many in India, Ricci fell again into
melancholy, telling Maffei of the joy his letters had brought him, hoping
that the beloved father would always continue with this correspondence.
Even though he lacked no friends in Goa, Ricci longed for his Roman days.
Mocking his own nostalgia he wrote: 'even though I am a youth I have the
nature of old men, who always praise the past. I see well that all this is my
own imperfection, and for once I shall truly entrust all cares to the hands of
Our Lord.'[26]

And the Lord saw to it that an Italian, Claudio Acquaviva, one of Ricci's
'beloved fathers in Rome', was elected the fifth General of the Society of
Jesus. On 25 November 1581, Ricci wrote to congratulate the new General,
reminding Acquaviva of the Italians in the Indian Province (there were five
in the College out of 100). After this, his third and final year of theological
studies, Ricci hoped he would be given another assignment other than

teaching the humanities, adding immediately, that this was done in obedience to God and his superior, for which he drew consolation.

Using his familiarity with the new General, Ricci presumed to give confidential advice on several matters pertaining to the Jesuits in Goa. The first was the scandal of Giovanni Battista de Loffreda, an Italian Jesuit brother who was among the recruits brought to India in 1574 by Valignano. A trained physician and a very good one it seemed, Loffreda felt his real vocation was in spiritual healing. After many petitions to superiors in Rome and Goa, Loffreda was finally ordained. But he felt slighted when his superiors restricted his priestly activities, since he was quite deaf and poor in Portuguese, and openly defiant of authority. His fellow Italians considered him emotionally unstable and an embarrassment to the Society, after Loffreda ran off into Muslim territories, only to return cursing the Company. At one point, Pasio and Acquaviva had to chain Loffreda to the dispensary, so agitated and violent was the restless man. Ricci advised Acquaviva to ignore any entreaties from Loffreda, now dismissed from the Company, who enjoyed a talent of turning his nuisance into victimhood. The second matter on which Ricci advised the new General verged on disrespect for his immediate superior and reflected the vicious gossip in Portuguese Goa. While praising Ruy Vicente as a conscientious Provincial with the best interests of the Company at heart, Ricci criticized the Provincial for recently appointing Eduardo de Sande and Gomez Vaz to be rectors of Jesuit colleges in Bassein and Malacca. This decision provoked dissatisfaction and murmur among the Jesuits in India, for the two men were 'of neophyte Jews' (Ricci using Greek words here); and since the Inquisition had condemned many New Christians to the stake in recent years, all New Christians were held in suspicion and disdain by the Portuguese nobility.

Indeed, the Inquisition had been exported to Goa, in the wake of Portuguese anti-Semitism.[27] The 1497 forced conversions in Portugal, modeled after the 1492 actions by the Spanish monarchs, inaugurated a new phase in the persecution of lusophone Jewry. A 1506 massacre in Lisbon claimed the lives of several hundred Jews;[28] under Spanish pressure, João III introduced the Inquisition into Portugal in 1536. Lured by easy wealth and looser controls in the overseas territories, many New Christians joined the adventure in the East, as successful merchants, physicians, and even Jesuit missionaries. They found in Ormuz 'white Jews' and in Cochin 'black Jews', descendants of earlier migrants from Palestine. Some New Christians might have reverted to Judaism in the lax atmosphere of Asia

before the crackdown in mid–century. Many exercised important profes-
sions. Almost all physicians in Goa, for example, were New Christians: both
dependent on and loathing them, the Portuguese ruling elites entertained
fantasies of poison plots, resulting in denunciations and autos–de–fe. Already
in 1543 the Archbishop of Goa burned the *converso* physician Jerónimo Días
as a relapsed heretic; three years later Xavier urged King João to establish the
Holy Office in India; in 1557, on the discovery of a blasphemous note in a
church in Cochin, several prominent New Christians in Cochin and Goa
were arrested and eventually shipped back to Lisbon to be burned at the
stake; and finally, in 1560, the king dispatched two inquisitors to Goa to
combat the infiltration of Jewish and Muslim errors and the relapse of
converts. The Inquisition in Goa endured until the dissolution in 1812.

From the wording in Ricci's letter, it is impossible to tell whether he
shared in the general anti–Jewish prejudice of the Portuguese or whether
he was merely informing the General of a decision by Ruy Vicente which
he considered detrimental to the interest of the Society. Indeed, Ricci
wrote: 'I believe the Father [i.e. Vicente] has done this due to the absence
of other suitable [candidates]', adding that he hoped the General would
soon dispatch qualified personnel to India. Ricci's questioning of the Provincial's judgment was poignant in that Eduardo da Sande had served as his
superior during the passage to India and would yet again serve as his superior
later in China, as their careers subsequently took them away from that
bastion of Portuguese values and gossip.

On still another matter, on which he shared his frank opinion with the
General, Ricci showed his differences with the Portuguese. A new decision
had been made this year at the College: no indigenous students, sons of
natives, could study philosophy or theology; their highest level was limited
to Latin and casuistry. 'They say they [the Indian students] become arrogant
when they learn Latin and refuse to serve in lowly parishes.' 'But all of this',
Ricci retorted, 'could be said about others who study at our school whether
in India or in Europe: it cannot be thus that we abandon teaching everyone;
the reason rather being that these indigenous people, even if they are well
educated, rarely enjoy much trust among the other white people.' It was the
tradition of the Company not to make distinction in teaching, Ricci emphasized. This new policy of exclusion would promote 'ignorance in the
ministry of the Church, in places where knowledge is so necessary, because
in any case they will become priests and curators of souls, and it is unseemly,
among so many kinds of infidels, that they become such ignorant priests,

unable to respond to an argument or strengthening themselves or others in our faith, if only because we do not want to expect miracles where they are unnecessary, and a simple Casuist cannot fit all of this.' What exercised Ricci more than anything else, and we have not seen him so passionate until now, was racial discrimination:

And the third reason, one that moves me the most, is that this people is much prostrated in our land, and nobody else would help them except for us [Jesuits]; for this reason we have shown them much love. And if they find out that the same fathers are now against them and do not wish them to raise their heads and obtain some benefices or posts equal to others, which one could obtain by studying, I doubt very much whether they would not come to hate us, and thus obstruct the main purpose of the Company in India, that is the conversion of non-believers and maintaining them in our holy faith.[29]

Ricci belonged to a minority of Jesuits who supported the admission of Indians to the Company.[30] Jesuit internationalism failed to overcome the power of Portuguese racial hierarchy and discrimination. Even Valignano had to compromise with Portuguese colonialism, explaining to Rome that Indian students lacked the high intellectual qualifications demanded of Jesuits and, even if admitted to the ranks of the Company, they would remain unacceptable for the secular ruling elites in Goa. Far from harboring a sense of European superiority, Valignano had criticized Francisco Cabral, a Portuguese Jesuit and superior of the mission in Japan, for his unkind treatment of Japanese novices and his refusal to entertain the ordination of Japanese priests. Until the suppression of the Society of Jesus in the eighteenth century, only a handful of Indians succeeded in breaching this barrier of race.

Ricci's first letters from India allow us to glimpse his intellectual and emotional maturation. Passing his twenty-ninth year in the winter of 1581, the young man from Macerata had traveled half-way round the world. His body still subject to the harshness of tropical fevers, Ricci had adapted to the social and cultural norms of Portuguese India while developing a critical eye for its injustices. We sense a quiet sadness and melancholy in his being, expressed in the effusive outpouring of nostalgia for the past, for the love and friendship of the Jesuit community in Rome, which remained his emotional home in the distant lands of the expanding Catholic world. Likewise in his intellectual endeavors—teaching Latin and Greek, a keen interest in geography, and continuing astronomical observations—Ricci remained deeply attached to his intellectual formation at the Roman College. We have the portrait of a gentle soul, a young intellectual deeply

interested in letters and science, emotional yet disciplined, obedient yet
critical. While he had not experienced direct missionary work among
Indians, Ricci could not but have witnessed the brutality and violence of
Portuguese colonial rule, while being a member of its more sublime and
spiritual manifestation. If he had stayed, Ricci might have struck out on another
path, trodden by an Italian Jesuit after his time, Roberto de Nobili, who left the
certainties of Portuguese India to live precariously among Brahmins, learn
Sanskrit, and use the language and rituals of learned Hindus to become a
guru to Indian converts. A different destiny, however, awaited Ricci.

   Around mid-April 1582, Ruy Vicente received a letter from Valignano,
instructing him to send Francesco Pasio and other Jesuits to Japan, and
Matteo Ricci to Macao. Ricci was to assist Ruggieri, his former shipmate on
board the *São Luis*, in preparing to open China for the gospel. On 26 April
1582, seven Jesuits boarded a Portuguese ship in Goa. It was a reunion:
Ricci, Pasio, and Giovanni Gerardino had embarked in Lisbon four years
earlier; now, another Italian Jesuit, the painter Giovanni Nicolao (di Nola),
joined their ranks. All except Ricci were assigned to Japan. On 14 June
1582, the ship anchored in Malacca. With a fair wind, the party departed on
3 July and sailed on smoothly into the South China Sea. Nothing compared
to the rigors of the Indian passage, this voyage still claimed its toll. Ricci fell
quite ill to the extent that Pasio worried about his health. Fortunately, on 7
August, the travelers arrived in the port of Macao.

3
Macao

C hinese records of the Ming dynasty referred to the small peninsula to the south of Xiangshan County (today Zhongshan) as Hao jing ao (Oyster Mirror Bay), a reference to the fame of the local seafood harvested where fresh and salt waters mingled; they called the cross-shaped channels formed by four small islands to the south the Shi zi men (the Gate in the Form of the Character Ten). When the Portuguese first obtained permission from Chinese authorities in 1552 'to dry their water-damaged merchandise and repair their ships' at Hao jing ao, they found but a small fishing village in the north (today the district of Mongha) and a temple at the southwestern corner of the peninsula, marking the entrance from the open seas into a natural inner harbor. Dedicated to the Consort of Heaven, *Tianfei*, the goddess and protector for south Fujianese mariners, this temple was commonly referred to by the more personable appellation of the goddess: *Ama miao* (the temple of 'Mother'). Soon, the Portuguese dropped the vocative 'A' and added their Romanization of the Chinese word 'men' (gate), for their new settlement; Macao served indeed as their gate to China (see Map 2).

Macao proved to be a haven for Portuguese traders. In the decades before 1552, the Portuguese had sailed up and down the southeastern Chinese coast, establishing bases from the north in Ningbo, Zhejiang province, south to Zhangzhou in Fujian, and on the islands of Langbaiao and Shangchuan on the Guangdong coast southwest of Macao. Colluding with Chinese merchant-smugglers, the Portuguese plied a lucrative trade between China, Japan, and Southeast Asia. It was in Malacca, which they conquered in 1511, that the Portuguese first encountered Chinese merchants. Guided by Chinese junks, the first Portuguese ship appeared off the Chinese coast in 1513. In 1517, the Governor of India equipped Fernão

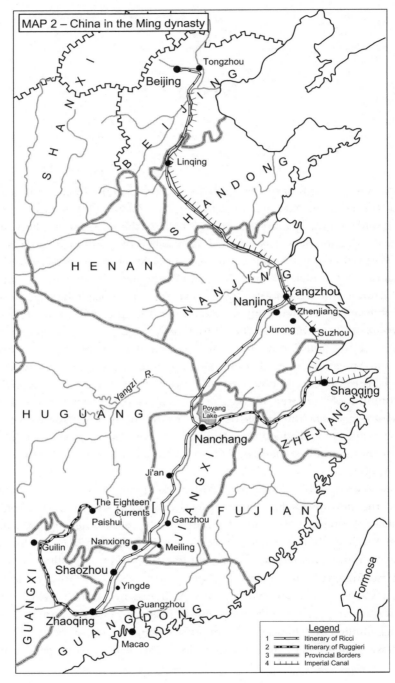

Map 2. China in the Ming dynasty

Peres de Andrade with a small fleet, conveying Tomé Pires as emissary to the Ming emperor. Gifts and bribes persuaded local Chinese mandarins in Guangzhou in 1520 to send the Portuguese delegation on to Beijing, where they bribed Jiang Bin, the high court official and imperial favorite, to secure an audience with the Zhengde emperor (reigned 1506–21) in early 1521. Unfortunately, Zhengde died shortly thereafter, to be succeeded by the Jiajing emperor (1522–66). In the ensuing purge, Jiang Bin and his faction perished. Without political backing, the Portuguese were vulnerable to the charge, raised by an emissary of the Sultan of Malacca, that the 'Franks' had seized his city and usurped his place as pretended tribute-bearers. Further-more, Simão de Andrade, the brother of Fernão Peres, had arrived off the Guangdong coast in 1518 attacking Chinese shipping, raiding coastal vil-lages, and seizing slaves, behaving as if he were off the coast of Africa. The hapless Pires was sent back to Guangzhou. There, local mandarins threw the Portuguese in jail (where Pires died), holding them as hostages for the exchange of Chinese seized by Portuguese pirates.

Although official Sino-Portuguese relations started on a discordant note, the Portuguese joined Chinese captains in the lucrative illegal maritime trade in the ensuing decades. In 1523, the Jiajing emperor sharpened the anti-maritime policy inherited from the founding of the dynasty, which forbade Ming subjects from all overseas commerce. Due to the violence of the Japanese tribute-bearing delegates in Ningpo and the piracy of the Portuguese, in 1523 the emperor forbade in addition all maritime commu-nications between China and foreign countries, official or otherwise, in effect, abolishing the tribute-bearing system, the official and only legal channel of commercial contact between China and its neighbors. Between the 1520s and 1550s, a more rigorous enforcement of maritime closure drove many Chinese traders into piracy. Coastal security became a major concern for ministers in Beijing. After a successful but costly campaign of military suppression, in 1567 the imperial court reopened maritime trade, restricting it to Yuegang harbor near Zhangzhou in Fujian. Paying maritime dues, Chinese merchantmen could sail legally to the Philippines, the Ryu-kyu Islands (Okinawa), continental and archipelago Southeast Asia; only Japan was off limits. Alongside this restrictive channel, a far larger volume of illicit trade was carried out under the protection of provincial mandarins, who benefited enormously from the profits of overseas trade.

It was one of these mandarins, the *haidao* in Guangdong, Wang Bo, who struck a deal in 1552 with the Portuguese captain-major Leonel de Sousa.[1] The *xun shi hai dao fu shi*, the full title of Wang Bo, translates literally as the Vice-Official for the Inspection of the Maritime Sector. Established during the pirate troubles of the Jiajing reign, the *haidao* in Guangdong province was the mandarin who had immediate jurisdiction in all matters dealing with the Portuguese. Charged with maritime security, the *haidao* occupied the second highest military post in the province, only after the *zongbin*, the regional commander. Charged also with the collection of maritime duties, the *haidao*, like many leading military commands, was usually entrusted to civilian mandarins, since professional military men enjoyed little trust and prestige in the imperial bureaucracy of the Ming dynasty. In Guangdong, the function of *haidao* was usually carried out by the *anchasi fushi*, the Provincial Surveillance Vice Commissioner. Their position presented the *haidao* with many opportunities of personal enrichment; hence, whatever their attitude toward the 'barbarians in Macao', they continued to advocate Portuguese interests within the provincial bureaucracy.

The agreement in 1552 between Wang Bo and de Sousa stipulated that the Portuguese were to be treated with the same protocol as the Siamese, a recognized friendly tribute-bearing country, that they could trade in Guangzhou once yearly (later extended to two semi-annual fairs), that they could use Macao as a permanent land base, and that they pay a 20 per cent duty on all imported goods.[2] In 1557, the Portuguese received permission to construct durable houses in Macao. The Portuguese gained further credit with the Ming court by assisting in coastal pacification: in 1564, they furnished 300 men to General Yu Daqiu who crushed a mutiny; in 1568, they defeated the pirate Zheng Yiben, who was raiding the Pearl River Delta; and in 1574–5 the Supreme Commanders of Guangdong and Fujian summoned Portuguese ships to help suppress the pirate Lin Daoqian. Recognizing their superior firepower and ships, Chinese mandarins came to see the usefulness of tolerating the Portuguese at their doorstep.

One more thing the mandarins appreciated about the Portuguese: these barbarians performed all official ceremonies and did not object to rituals of submission such as kneeling in front of mandarins and bowing their heads on the floor, the ritual of *koutou* (kowtow), expected of all Chinese subjects before the mandarins, and later vigorously objected to by Spanish and British emissaries. If the Portuguese seemed docile in the 1550s, their attitude was due less to awe at Ming might than to the love of profit. Thanks to Ming prohibition of direct Sino-Japanese trade, the Portuguese became the only middlemen, buying up silk brocades, raw silk, and fine porcelain in Guangzhou to ship to Nagasaki, Japan, carrying on their return voyages vast quantities of silver in the large bulk of their *naus* to feed the bullion-hungry Chinese market. In addition, the Portuguese in Macao imported sandalwood, camphor, and spices from Southeast Asia, and exported silk, porcelain, and many handicraft wares, reaping profits of more than 100 per cent in the triangular China–Japan–Malacca voyages. No wonder then that the captain-major (the *capitão-mór*) of the Macao fleet was such a desired position in Goa. Every year, the Portuguese Governor of India awarded this privilege to an individual who had performed meritorious service to the crown. The *capitão-mór* commanded all Portuguese subjects east of Malacca. During his three-year tenure, the period it took for the cycle of voyages to be completed between India, Macao, and Japan, the *capitão-mór* was the effective ruler of Macao, combining the roles of commander, captain, merchant, and diplomat. Not until the creation of a diocese in 1576 and the Senado in 1583 did the *capitão-mór* have to share power.

'From a distance it looks like a lotus leaf floating on water, and at the end of the stem is a gate', thus the first impression of Macao on the Chinese scholar Lu Xiyan, who traveled there in 1680 to study with the Jesuits.[3] We can see clearly the shape of 'the lotus leaf' in the 1639 plan by António de Mariz Carneiro—the contours of Macao being unchanged until the nineteenth century, although the city walls and many buildings depicted in these two prints had not been built yet at the time of Ricci's arrival (see Figure 6). Visible on the plan is the Gate at 'the end of the stem' (*Guanya*). Manned by Chinese soldiers, it was constructed in 1574 to provide security against the Portuguese. In the mornings Chinese workers and handlers streamed across it into Macao, hawking water, food, and all sorts of provisions upon which the Portuguese relied and returning before sunset. The Macao that Ricci saw was more modest than the city depicted in this early plan: in 1564, a Chinese record stated there were up to 1,000 dwellings constructed of wood and tile; in the 1580s, the city's residents consisted of some 1,000 Portuguese men and their dependants. Comprising the subalterns were three distinct groups: several thousand slaves of African, Indian, Malay, and Timorese origins serving as sailors, soldiers, and domestic servants; Malay, Chinese, and Japanese women who lived as companions of Portuguese men, whether as wives or consorts, together with their mestizo children; and a small number of Chinese merchants, traders, and workers attracted by the economic opportunity presented by the new community. In addition, there were Japanese Christians, a small community in the late sixteenth century,

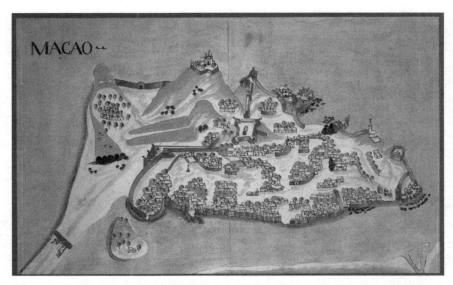

Figure 6. Macao, painting in the *Descripçam da Fortaleza de Sofala e das mais da India* by António de Mariz Carneiro, 1639. Codex 149 of the Biblioteca Nacional, Lisbon

who became more numerous and permanent after the suppression of Christianity in early seventeenth-century Tokugawa Japan. The heterogeneous population of Macao was lusophone and Christian, except for the Chinese, who were drawn from nearby villages in Guangdong and from seafaring southern Fujian, although a few had acquired the Portuguese language and cult in their dealings with these foreigners.

The Jesuits were there from the beginning. They sailed as chaplains on board Portuguese vessels, providing spiritual succor and imposing a measure of civilized behavior on unruly sailors and touchy fidalgos (noblemen). From the start, wealthy merchants sponsored the Jesuit mission, witness the close rapport between Francis Xavier and the brothers Diogo and Guilherme Pereira, and later between Melchior Nunes Barreto and Fernão Mendes Pinto.[4] Mediating disputes, disarming conflicts, and generally making peace, the Jesuits insured that the profit-seeking, alcohol-drinking, and violent Portuguese adventurers did not land them in hell. Symbolic of their central role in this small settlement with one principal street, the Jesuits established their residence on a central hill, next to the site of the fortress that would be built on the highest point of the city.

By 1582, in addition to the Jesuits, several other ecclesiastical institutions added a veneer of civility to this rough and burgeoning commercial frontier: in 1562, the hermitage of S. António, the first church, was constructed; the next year the Jesuits established a residence, and they opened a college in 1571; in 1569, the Jesuit Belchior Carneiro Leitão, titular Bishop of Nicea, founded a lepers' hospital (St Lazarus) and the Casa da Misericórdia to help widows and orphans (among the latter many Chinese girls illegally purchased by the Portuguese); in 1575 Pope Gregory XIII elevated Macao to a diocese, appointing Carneiro first Bishop of Macao, with jurisdiction over China, Japan, and Korea; construction on the cathedral (Sá) began in 1576 and that on the Franciscan church in 1580.

'There is Japan, where is born fine silver | which will to the Gospel illumination deliver.'[5] These perhaps ironic verses by Camões, who served as chief warrant officer in Macao in the years 1557 to 1560, illustrate a central truth in Portuguese Macao: God and Mammon worked hand in glove. Francis Xavier, the first Jesuit missionary, received support from the immensely wealthy fidalgo Diogo Pereira, who served as *Capitão-Mór* in 1562, in his plan to spread the gospel to China, before he died of illness on Shangchuan Island in 1552. More importantly, the expanding Jesuit mission in Japan was dependent on the Macao–Nagasaki trade, as revenues from landed properties in India and customs dues from Malacca granted by the king remained insufficient to cover expenses. In 1578, the merchants in Macao allotted the fathers a fixed share of 50 piculs of silk in the annual cargo of 1,600 piculs of raw silk shipped from Macao to Japan.[6] Subtracting expenses, the Society gained some 1,600 cruzados per year. This profit proved invaluable not only to the Jesuit Mission in Japan, but also to their subsequent operations in China as well.

None of these operations was yet apparent to Matteo Ricci and Francesco Pasio, who stayed behind in Macao after their other companions from India had departed for the more exciting Japan Mission. Compared to the grand vineyard of Japan with 45–50 Jesuits and 150,000 converts, among them several daimyo or feudal lords, Macao seemed like a puny patch of garden.[7] Before the arrival of Ricci, the small community of Macao Jesuits consisted of five: the superior Domingos Álvarez, fathers Fernão Martins, André Pinto, and Michele Ruggieri, and the brother Antonio Paez. All except Ruggieri were Portuguese. It was easy to imagine Ruggieri's delight in seeing his fellow Italians, especially Ricci, whom he had requested as companion for the China Mission in a letter written in late 1580 to

Valignano.[8] After three difficult years in Macao, Ruggieri poured out his frustrations in Italian to his countrymen: he spent hours every day learning Chinese, a most difficult language, so unlike any European grammar, so many characters, the confusion of tones, and two distinct systems for writing and speaking. Nonetheless, Ruggieri persisted in preparing himself to enter China. Hard as it might have been, learning Chinese was the easier part. Although 'this enterprise [converting China] was of such great importance', Ruggieri confided, 'we are so cold whenever we think of this'. Referring discreetly to his fellow Portuguese Jesuits, Ruggieri specified that 'some people say to him: "Why should a father lose time in learning Chinese and in this hopeless undertaking when he can serve in other occupations of the Company?"' To which Ruggieri reported that he answered in the following manner: 'Father, if I should ever desire any virtue and talent, I now desire greatly that the Lord will have mercy; for in truth, I am really not suitable for this undertaking, for I am a miserable sinner and a piece of useless dry wood. If it were only possible now to find that burning spirit of our father Francis Xavier, who had briefly followed his saintly and fervent desire to try to enter and convert China!'[9]

Ruggieri's fervor apparently silenced the objection, for he was left alone to struggle with his Chinese characters. The Portuguese fathers had their work cut out for them, let alone learning Chinese. They represented the only civilizing force in the early years of Macao, diffusing anger, preventing feuds, and making peace among the 800 to 900 rough-and-ready Portuguese merchant-adventurers. As Father Pinto put it so succinctly: 'Since these parts are so remote from justice [i.e. royal justice in Goa], and these men are so free and think so highly of themselves, in which pride played its role, the port [of Macao] is wide open for hatred and vengeance.'[10] Pinto reported that in 1564 the Jesuits prevented five to six major feuds. On one occasion, the captain of the Japan voyage had given orders to his men to fire on another Portuguese vessel commanded by a hated rival; bloodshed was avoided only when the fathers threatened the gunners with damnation. Only one of the four Portuguese Jesuits tried to follow Ruggieri's pioneering footsteps. The superior Álvarez (1535–?), who had served for nine years (1567–76) in India, dedicated his time to the fledgling Jesuit College; he eventually returned to Malacca. Fernão Martins (1545–1603) had also served in India and came in 1574 to Macao to end his career. Only André Pinto (1538–88), whose words we quoted above, and whose career spanned India, Japan, and Macao, accompanied Ruggieri in 1581 on a brief visit to

Guangzhou.[11] Like many Portuguese clerics in Asia, with the notable exception of Japan, these Jesuits considered ministry to their compatriots in Portuguese enclaves their first and often exclusive duty. Only in their pedagogic role at colleges did they engage the indigenous youth, who were raised in a Christian and lusophone milieu.

But learn Chinese he must, Ruggieri realized, if he wanted to accomplish the task assigned to him by Valignano. He was not the first European missionary with that ambition. The first Jesuits to visit the Chinese mainland were Melchior Nunes Barreto and Estevão de Góis, chaplains on board *naus*, who sailed in the summer of 1555 from Shangchuan to Guangzhou in a mission to ransom some Portuguese prisoners. In two letters addressed to his brethren in Goa and to Ignatius, Nunes Barreto gave a brief description of Guangzhou, and the looks, customs, and ceremonies of the Chinese. Observing the indifference of the Chinese toward their own religions and disregard for their own clergy, Nunes Barreto considered China a difficult mission. He saw only two strategies: an embassy to persuade Chinese authorities of their peaceful and holy intentions, and hence to gain a residence permit; and evangelizing to the people in their own language. To accomplish this second goal, Nunes Barreto ordered de Góis to stay behind in Guangzhou in order to learn Chinese. The hapless father stayed until the end of 1555 and sojourned again from June 1556 to early 1557. He made little or no progress before falling very ill and returning to Goa.[12]

About the same time in 1556, another Portuguese cleric, the Dominican Gaspar da Cruz, also visited Guangzhou for one month. In addition to generally insightful observations of Chinese society, the friar keenly observed the presence of Muslims and homosexuals. Their ignorance of the true God, wrote the Dominican, was due to the low level of natural philosophy in China, although he did wonder, on seeing a large statue of the bodhisattva Guanyin (in Sanskrit Avalokitesvara) in a Buddhist temple, whether the Apostle Thomas had not visited China from India and left behind vestiges of Christianity. The two obstacles to evangelization, according to Cruz, were the Chinese dislike of any novelties, let alone foreign innovations, and that by law, foreigners could not reside in China. The only hope was for an embassy, as the friar came to the same conclusion as the Jesuit.[13]

In 1563, the Supreme Commander in Goa sent Gil de Góis as royal ambassador. It was a good moment. The Portuguese stood in great favor with the magistrates, for in 1564 they had helped in defeating Chinese troops, who had mutinied over pay and laid siege to Guangzhou. The junks of the rebels proved no match for Portuguese gunships; after crushing the mutiny, the provincial mandarins happily received the royal embassy. Accompanied by the Jesuit Francisco Perez, Góis visited Guangzhou in November 1565 and presented a petition for the regulation of trade and diplomacy. Perez himself presented another petition, representing himself as a teacher of the laws of God, and requested permission to preach in China. Although the *haidao* spoke against it, the Administrative and Surveillance Commissioners and other high-ranking mandarins made a show of their benevolence. They liked Perez's answer that the law of the western God forbade killing and robbery, but on learning that the Jesuit spoke no Chinese (the conversation being conducted through an interpreter), they regretted that no permission could be granted.[14]

Meanwhile, the Jesuits could visit Guangzhou as chaplains of the Portuguese merchants from Macao. Father Cristóvão da Costa (1529–82) stayed there a total of three months in 1575. A young Chinese Buddhist monk, attracted by his doctrines, stole away on a Portuguese ship to be baptized in Macao. The family of the Buddhist monk complained to the mandarin, who forced the Portuguese to return the runaway, lest all commerce be stopped. Bishop Carneiro was forced to escort the Chinese monk to Guangzhou, where the young man was promptly caned by the mandarins, who gave the Jesuit bishop a scolding. The mandarins ordered that henceforth no Chinese could practice with the Jesuit fathers under penalty of death.

The next attempt to implant Christianity was undertaken by Spanish Franciscans. In 1565, a Spanish fleet under Miguel Lopez de Legazpi sailed from Mexico into Cebu in the Philippine Islands. In 1571, the Spaniards established their capital in Manila and gradually expanded their colonial control. The Fujianese merchants, a short sailing from their home ports in southern Fujian, had been trading in Luzon, and now supplied the small Spanish community with necessities and luxuries. In 1575, Sino-Spanish collaboration in suppressing the notorious pirate Lin Manhong, a danger in the South China Seas who once laid siege to Manila, ushered in a short interval of amicable relations. On the first diplomatic voyage, undertaken between June and September 1575 to Fujian, the Augustinian friars Martín de Rada and Jerónimo Marín returned with military, geographic, and economic intelligence for the Manila authorities. In de Rada's assessment, the Chinese were militarily weak and unwarlike, no match for Spanish soldiers. This bellicose stance of military and spiritual conquest by one friar reflected the self-confident belligerence of the mightiest world empire in the sixteenth century, and the recent memory of easy conquests in the Americas.[15]

Some Spanish friars, however, undertook a more peaceful approach. In July 1579, four Franciscans left Manila on a Chinese junk without official permission. After gaining Guangzhou, the friars naively entered the city hoping to gain an audience with the right authorities who would grant them permission to reside and evangelize. Encountering a Chinese interpreter, who claimed he worked with the Portuguese in Macao and was himself a Christian, the friars were led from one government office (*yamen*) to another, all the while proclaiming their desire to stay and preach the true religion. Treated kindly by various mandarins, who gave them small stipends and provisions, upon hearing that the friars came with no gold or silver and intended to beg (this was not done in China, as they were told), the friars failed to make an impression. Their ignorance of Chinese made them dependent on an interpreter, who turned out to be untrustworthy. In communication with Macao, the interpreter received a message from the *Capitão-Mór* that the Castilians were spies and must by no means be allowed to stay. The mandarins had no intention of granting the Franciscans' wish, although several showed a curiosity for their books and doctrines. The four Franciscans, Friars Pedro, Agustín, Juan Baptista, and Sebastian, were even conveyed to Zhaoqing, several days' sailing from Guangzhou, where they were summoned to appear before the Supreme Commander of Guangdong and Guangxi, Liu Yaohui. Eventually, out of money and provisions, and one of them falling ill, the discouraged friars requested to be sent home: two traveled to Macao in order to establish a Franciscan convent and the other two departed on the longer trip to Zhangzhou, where they caught a junk sailing for Manila.[16]

The one lesson to be learned from the failure of the 1579–80 Franciscan mission was this: preparations were everything. The Spanish friars spoke not a word of Chinese, even though there were Chinese residents in Luzon; they came with few provisions and no finances; and they were ignorant about the political and cultural institutions with which they had to negotiate. Michele Ruggieri was not going to make the same mistake.

The Neapolitan Jesuit realized that 'for those who want to enter China, and be accepted by the Chinese authorities and people, and not be considered barbarous and vulgar or retarded people ignorant of characters, it is necessary to know their characters and language, and not just any language, but the polished and courteous one, which even native-speakers learn from infancy with great difficulty.'[17] In other words, one has to learn not just any local colloquial idiom but the refined speech of the mandarins, *guanhua*. Ruggieri made a start at the Jesuit College in Macao, which attracted some Chinese youths from the mainland 'because they were curious to know our doctrine'. Thus was formed the first Chinese convert community. A small house adjacent to the Jesuit residence was built from alms collected from the Portuguese, to accommodate Ruggieri and his catechumens, and also to keep the Chinese away from the Jesuit College. While the Neapolitan taught these 'talented youths' Portuguese and catechism, they became his masters in Chinese. This was not an ideal pedagogic arrangement, but Ruggieri had trouble finding a proper language teacher. The Chinese workers in Macao were mostly unlettered, as were many traders. Moreover, as Cantonese speakers only a few spoke Mandarin, and with a terrible accent. Ruggieri became essentially an auto-didact. Unlike the young men, who learned Portuguese quickly, the 36-year-old Ruggieri found 'the Chinese language to be more difficult to learn than any other language in the world, and so difficult that even native speakers sometimes do not understand one another because many words have the same pronunciations and often the tones are not spoken properly'.[18] Ruggieri gave an example. To learn the Chinese word for horse, Ruggieri would draw a picture, whereupon his Chinese tutor wrote down the character and pronounced its sound. The studious pupil added that the Chinese pronunciation for horse sounded exactly like that for mother, if one did not distinguish these homonyms by tones. Even though his Portuguese brethren found his effort ridiculous, Ruggieri persisted. Time and diligence eventually paid off; God's help, for Ruggieri. The Jesuit-linguist made steady progress in reading. Quite proud of his linguistic abilities, Ruggieri claimed, rather improbably, that he had learned 10,000 Chinese characters in six months, stupefying even his own tutors.[19] By November 1581, a little more than two years into his Chinese studies, Ruggieri boasted to General Mercurian that he could recognize 15,000 characters.[20]

Although Ruggieri made feverish preparations in the little Chinese universe of his catechumen house, there was no substitute for the real thing. Above all, he hardly spoke Mandarin in Macao. In April 1580, after nine months of intensive Chinese studies, Ruggieri visited Guangzhou. It was the time of the spring trade fair. The Portuguese merchants, sailors, and their slaves, some 100 Christians in all, needed a priest for their spiritual well-being, for the fair lasted between one and three months. Sailing up the wide estuary of the Pearl River, the ships from Macao passed on the starboard side the redoubt of Humen, the strongest Chinese coastal fortress guarding the Pearl estuary; on the port side, the travelers saw small islands emerging from the water, with long dykes protecting the sandy alluvial deposits, a major reclamation project undertaken by powerful local lineages that began in the sixteenth century and would last two hundred years. All along the way, the Portuguese encountered Chinese vessels large and small in the hundreds. On many of these lived the *Danjia*, the outcast boat people despised by mandarins and settled farmers alike. Where the river narrowed opposite a large sandy bank where numerous junks anchored, the silhouette of a tall pagoda emerged from a large walled city: Guangzhou, the capital of Guangdong province and the Ming Empire's gateway to the southern seas.

The 1582 tax record of Guangzhou Prefecture showed a district centered on the walled city with 201,625 households and 584,152 inhabitants, which was likely a gross underestimate.[21] Some half of that population lived in the city of Guangzhou alone. More populated than any European city, Guangzhou was nevertheless one of the smaller provincial capitals, not to mention the northern and southern imperial capitals at Beijing and Nanjing. Suburban houses filled the embankment from the quays to the city wall, where three of the seven gates opened to the river and the south. The Portuguese entered freely into the city, to buy and sell, but when the gates closed for the night, they had to return to their lodgings on board. In this provincial capital with many government offices, the Portuguese dealt mainly with the *haidao*. Ruggieri immediately made a good impression by speaking some Chinese and performing Chinese courtesies, in order that the mandarins 'do not think we are all just traders'. He also pleaded with the mandarin that he could only properly perform religious ceremonies on land, and not on the barges. As a sign of favor, the *haidao* allowed Ruggieri to reside in a suburban house with his servant and interpreter, where the Jesuit promptly set up an altar; curious mandarins came to see the ceremonies and images of this exotic foreign religion. On Easter Sunday, after saying mass for the Portuguese merchants and their dependants, Ruggieri found his rest 'disturbed by the devil'. A Chinese man, drunk and bleeding from the head, rushed into the chapel, holding a stone in his hand and shouting that the foreign monk had injured him. A menacing crowd gathered in front of the house. The *haidao* arrived to take Ruggieri for questioning back at the *yamen*. Unable to find the injured man, who probably had wanted to harass Ruggieri into paying him off and fled when the mandarin approached, the *haidao* declared

Ruggieri's innocence to the crowd. This incident was a reminder of the missionary's utter dependence on the mandarin, and that, after more than sixty years of contact with the Portuguese, the Cantonese cultivated little good feeling toward these 'foreign devils'. During his three months stay, Ruggieri gained credit with the mandarins and literati, who came out of curiosity to visit his small chapel. They looked at Christian statues and books, asked Ruggieri questions about his doctrines, and left small donations, as was the custom when visiting Buddhist temples.

Having cultivated the mandarins, securing his *guanxi* (connections) as one would say today, Ruggieri returned to Guangzhou during the following two trade fairs. During his stay in October 1581, a new *haidao* granted Ruggieri and a Jesuit brother permission to reside in a small temple behind the official hostel for the Siamese envoys. Again, by his charisma, Ruggieri won over the new mandarin. During the audience, the *haidao* asked through an interpreter whether the foreign priest knew Chinese, to which Ruggieri replied in the affirmative. Scribbling a few characters on a piece of paper, the *haidao* handed it over to the Jesuit. Ruggieri read aloud the message: 'I am a servant of God and have no fear, and the *haidao* has never received money from the Portuguese.' Well pleased with his performance, the *haidao* praised Ruggieri in front of the Portuguese. Thus Ruggieri and his companion were lodged in a temple within the city walls while the Macao visitors could still not stay overnight on land. Immediately, Ruggieri had the statues destroyed and the temple consecrated as a Christian chapel. He commissioned a local master artisan to cast a bronze statue of Madonna and Child, which he placed in the center of the chapel to impress the unending throngs of Chinese onlookers. It was a reception of curiosity mixed with hostility: one night, the Jesuits awoke to the noise of stones landing on their tile roof. Whoever the stone throwers might have been—rowdy adolescents or xenophobes—Ruggieri simply dismissed them as the demons from the destroyed statues that had just lost their abode. In any event, the molestation stopped.

His benevolence initially bestirred by curiosity for the Chinese-speaking foreign monk, the *haidao* stopped his visits, telling Ruggieri that he could not openly show his friendship due to considerations of commerce with foreigners. In short, the *haidao* wanted to avoid any appearances of undue friendship in order to ward off suspicions of bribery. However, Ruggieri had won the friendship of a military official by the gift of a watch. During these sojourns in Guangzhou, each lasting a couple of months, Ruggieri increased his cultural and linguistic repertoire, although he still needed an interpreter.

He aroused the curiosity of the Chinese for his person and his religion, but there had been no conversions. Nor had Ruggieri secured permission for a longer stay, having to return to Macao with the Portuguese after every trading season. The breakthrough, however, came in the summer of 1582.

In 1581, Chen Rui (b. 1513) succeeded Liu Yaohui as Supreme Commander (*zongdu*) of Guangdong and Guangxi provinces. The Fujianese Chen Rui obtained his *jinshi*, the highest civil service examination degree, in 1553, and served in various provincial posts, rising to be the Grand Coordinator, the *xunfu* of the province of Huguang (roughly today's Hunan and Hubei), before being nominated to the pinnacle of his career. The mightiest mandarin in Guangdong and Guangxi, Chen Rui promptly dispatched an emissary to Macao upon assuming office: he delivered a summons to *Capitão-Mór* João de Almeida and Bishop Leonardo de Sá to appear before his office in order to answer for the fact that the Portuguese were residing in Macao without formal imperial permission. Since the Portuguese had been paying a small rent annually after 1555 to the provincial government and far larger gifts to its officials, Chen Rui's message was received and understood by the Portuguese as a not too subtle demand for more bribes. The Portuguese selected Mateus Panela, auditor, one of the highest ranking officials in the Macao administration, and Ruggieri to represent the secular and ecclesiastical authorities in this delicate diplomacy.

In April 1582, Ruggieri and Panela traveled to Guangzhou with another Jesuit, André Pinto. Before they could deal with Chen Rui, Ruggieri's party was embroiled in a confrontation between the Portuguese and the Prefect of Guangzhou, Zhou Qixiang (the *zhifu*, mandarin of the prefecture). Accusing some Portuguese of buying Chinese youths and planning to take them to Macao, Zhou threatened to arrest the wealthiest Portuguese merchants. The mandarin summoned the foreigners to an audience at a temple on the river bank. The angry Portuguese, together with the two Jesuits, appeared before the *zhifu*, who proceeded to accuse them of seven murders. During the mandarin's long harangue, which was translated to the kneeling Portuguese, Father Pinto, terrified and still weak from a recent illness, fainted. Furious, the *zhifu* ordered his men to cane the unconscious priest. At this point, Ruggieri stood up. All the Portuguese got up and drew their swords. Surprised by this defiance, the mandarin and his guards hurriedly left the temple and fled behind the city walls. Withdrawing to their ships, the Portuguese waited with arquebuses and cannons for an onslaught that never came. Later, the *zhifu* sent a conciliatory message to Ruggieri. The next day, the Portuguese returned to the city as if nothing had happened.

When the *haidao* returned to Guangzhou, having been absent during this confrontation, he was furious with the *zhifu* Zhou Qixiang, who was his subordinate by rank, and reprimanded him for causing trouble with the Portuguese. Meanwhile, the chamberlain of Chen Rui arrived in Guangzhou and wanted to have Ruggieri flogged because Pinto had not been punished. Ruggieri addressed the chamberlain in Chinese and said that he would suffer it willingly for God. The *haidao* put in a good word and Ruggieri was spared. Under escort, Ruggieri, Panela, and their retinue traveled to Zhaoqing, the office of Chen Rui.

Before narrating Ruggieri's audience with the Supreme Commander, let us follow an unexpected encounter on 2 May between Ruggieri and another Jesuit in Guangzhou: the Spaniard Alonso Sanchez (1547–93). One of the first Jesuits to arrive in the Philippines in 1581, Sanchez had been dispatched to China by Governor Don Gonçalo Ronquillo de Peñalosa on a double mission: first, to announce the 1580 union of the Iberian crowns under Philip II and to secure the sworn allegiance of the Portuguese in Macao, and second, to negotiate with Chinese officials a trading arrangement for the Filipino Spaniards similar to the Portuguese somewhere on the Fujian coast. In March, Sanchez left Manila on a frigate. Stormy seas diverted its path from Guangzhou to the Bay of Xiamen on 6 April. From there, the Spanish vessel was conducted under Chinese guard to Chaozhou. Leaving the crew behind, Sanchez and a small delegation traveled to Dongguan, where the *haidao* was exercising his duties. After presenting gifts and the official letter from the Spanish Governor, Sanchez's party was escorted to Guangzhou, where they met the Portuguese and Ruggieri. At this moment, the mandarins were preoccupied with the visit of the *chayuan*, the imperial censor, from Beijing, who had the power to report and dismiss incompetent officials. While entertaining the senior visiting official, the *zhifu* dispatched Sanchez to lodge with Ruggieri for three days; the two Jesuits enjoyed an excellent rapport, and Sanchez was full of praise for Ruggieri's learning and piety, and for his previous service as jurist in Naples to the Spanish king.[22] When Ruggieri left for Zhaoqing, he promised to put in a good word for the Spaniards.

From Guangzhou, Ruggieri and Panela embarked on barges for the 64-mile journey because larger ships could not navigate the Xijiang, the West River, a tributary of the Pearl. Heading west in a gradual ascent, the barges passed flat farmlands and towns of the Pearl River Delta before turning a bend of menacing bluffs and arriving in Zhaoqing, a large walled city and prefecture capital on the north bank of Xijiang, facing the smaller county town of Gaoyao on the south bank. The journey took three days, as we know from the account of the Spanish Franciscan Agustín de Tordesillas, who made the trip in 1578 and gave a fuller account of his audience than Ruggieri. Let us follow the friar's description of the Supreme Commander's *yamen* before turning back to Ruggieri's own records:

We were conducted to the office of the Supreme Commander, when many instruments struck up—drums, trumpets, pipes, oboes, and others that were like hornpipes and sackbuts—and they fired many chambers and arquebuses, all with such a great uproar that it seemed as if the city was going under. The soldiers of the guard hastily grabbed their weapons and everyone took his place. In front of the door is a very large patio surrounded by wooden stakes more than seven feet high, stained in black and blue, so that from a distance they appeared to be of iron. . . . [At the Supreme Commander's *yamen*] there are three doors next to one another, thirty paces in front of the audience hall of the Supreme Commander, but no-one entered through these doors. There was close to the walls and above the chair a canopy that seemed to be fixed on a very elaborate and decorated throne, and at the back of which was a table with two candles. . . . in the middle of the patio in front of the throne of the Supreme Commander was a white wall, on which was painted a very fierce looking dragon, breathing fire through its mouth, eyes, and nostrils: this picture represents the ferocity of the judge in order to stop anyone from entering the three doors at this place that are in front of the Supreme Commander or traversing the patio. Instead, there are two side entrances where those seeking an audience may enter and exit only when ordered by a man, who comes out of the door carrying a white plank on which are written some large black characters and shouts in a loud voice. Then all those who seek business enter by the right hand door and having passed the three doors kneel down in front of the Supreme Commander thirty paces removed and bow their heads on the ground, holding up their petitions with both hands and reaching forth without lifting their heads until a clerk takes the petition and gives it to the Supreme Commander, while shouting in a loud voice, upon which the petitioners withdraw quickly, head still bowed and leave by the left hand door.[23]

Presented with such a spectacle of authority, augmented for the benefit of the Macao emissaries by the additional display of several hundred soldiers, a scene more than enough to intimidate Chinese civilians, Ruggieri showed no fear. The Jesuit, clad in a short black tunic and wearing a black beret, his hair cut short but with a long beard, kneeled in front of the Supreme Commander. When Chen Rui angrily denounced the Portuguese for constructing houses and churches in Macao without permission, Ruggieri replied, on his knees, with soothing and calm words: the Portuguese had always been and were loyal vassals of the Ming emperor, and acknowledged His Excellency, the *Dutang daren* (the honorific address used by the Chinese for the Supreme Commander), as their master, for whose favor he humbly beseeched. Flattered and placated by this speech, Chen Rui ordered the Jesuit to rise and approach. Ruggieri saw an old man, dressed in the splendid uniform of a mandarin of the second rank: a silk crimson robe down to his ankles above a pair of thick black boots mounted on white lacquer; the long, broad sleeves half a palm longer than the arms, lined with decorated blue trims; in the center of the robe was embroidered, in the 'mandarin square', the chest piece, a pair of shining cocks marking his second rank, and centered in the belly with a loose belt decorated with a buckle made of rhinoceros horn; the headgear was treated with lacquer, with two long 'wings' protruding sideways, the somber black color brightened only by the jade in the center of the hat (see Plate IV).[24] Ruggieri remembered that 'I answered him with such good reasons that he calmed down and ordered the father [referring to himself in the third person] to approach him. Coming down through his throne, he showed the father much love and familiarity, touching his big beard which the Chinese all admire since they cannot grow them, having only a few strands of hair even after forty years!'[25] After the audience, Chen Rui honored the Portuguese with a banquet, attended by music and opera. Captivated by the missionary's charisma—his knowledge of Chinese, his lack of fear, and his hairy masculinity—Chen Rui became benevolent, no doubt helped by the generous gifts of cloth, crystals, and other expensive handicrafts presented by the foreigners. To present a picture of incorruptibility, Chen Rui ordered the envoys to be paid in cash for their gifts, while discreetly instructing Panela to use this money for the purchase of western goods in Macao for his personal account.

The Supreme Commander invited the envoys to a sumptuous dinner with opera entertainment. While Chen Rui questioned Ruggieri about Christian doctrines and ceremonies, and promised the foreign monk that he could have a house and chapel in Zhaoqing, Ruggieri pleaded for Sanchez and the Spaniards to be allowed to proceed to Macao. Chen Rui acceded to this request and wrote a note to praise 'the sincerity of the Spaniards in bearing tribute', but adding that there was no need for them to return to China in the future. The fifteen-day sojourn in Zhaoqing was a brilliant success; Ruggieri and Panela parted with gifts of silk brocades, silver, and Chinese books from the Supreme Commander. For the first time, the Catholic enterprise found a high patron. Ruggieri returned to Guangzhou well satisfied.

In Ruggieri's absence Sanchez had not been faring so well. After Ruggieri left for Zhaoqing, the *zhifu* imprisoned the Spaniards. To his surprise, the Spanish Jesuit found another group of Spanish prisoners in Guangzhou: a group of seven Franciscans from Manila with their retinue. Under the leadership of Martin Ignacio de Loyola, a kinsman of the founder of the Society of Jesus, the friars had slipped out of Manila without official permission. Their little frigate landed on the coast near Zhangzhou in southern Fujian, not far from where Sanchez's party had touched shore. However, unlike Sanchez's delegation, equipped with gifts and an official letter from the Governor of the Philippines, the friars came only with crucifixes and breviaries. Like the earlier Spanish party, they were con-ducted to Guangzhou under guard; but unlike Sanchez, treated as an official envoy, the friars were lodged in prisons and treated harshly. In the person of the *zhifu* of Guangzhou, the friars found a less than sympathetic mandarin. Zhou Qixiang seemed consistently hostile to the Europeans; Sanchez prob-ably had him in mind when he wrote that 'the Chinese are so arrogant that they consider themselves the cream and flower of the world, and it seems to them there is no understanding except for theirs, and no-one but they knew any laws or customs. Thus they look down on all other nations, considering them beastly.'[26] Only with the instructions of Chen Rui did Zhou Qixiang release the Spaniards, who arrived in Macao on 31 May. Although Sanchez eventually secured the allegiance of the Portuguese to Philip II, he failed in the other mission to establish Sino-Spanish diplomatic ties. His humiliation naturally shaped a negative attitude toward China, especially in his acerbic remarks about the mandarins, as we shall see in the next chapter. The Spanish friars also gained their freedom, ransomed from prison by the Portuguese.

Whatever their private misgivings about the Castilians, the Portuguese in Macao pledged their allegiance to Philip II in a ceremony on 1 July attended by all dignitaries: João de Almeida, *Capitão-Mór*, Leonardo de Sá, Bishop of Macao, Melchor Carneiro, Patriarch of Ethiopia and Bishop of Japan, and Alessandro Valignano, the Jesuit Visitor. Valignano had arrived in Macao from Nagasaki on 9 March with four young Japanese samurai, Christian converts and ambassadors to Europe for the lords of Bungo, Arima, and Omura on the island of Kyushu. This celebrated mission, the first embassy from Japan to the West, departed Macao at the end of December 1582. The Japanese youths finally reached Portugal in August 1584 and only returned home in July 1590. Their fascinating journey and sojourn, however, belong to a different story. Meanwhile, his mission accomplished, Sanchez wanted to sail for Manila but the Chinese authorities refused to release his frigate since direct voyages from Guangzhou to Manila were forbidden. Thus, Almeida and Valignano arranged on 6 July for Sanchez to board a Portuguese *nau* for Nagasaki, where he could trans-ship for Manila. A typhoon crashed the ship off the coast of Formosa, where the survivors, Sanchez included, spent some four months repairing the ship and fighting off aggressive aborigines, before returning to Macao on 3 November 1582. Spending the winter in Macao, Sanchez finally returned to Manila, arriving there on 27 March 1583.

Thanks to the Spanish Jesuit, we have a rare portrait of his fellow Italian fathers, pioneers in the China Mission. Writing several years later, Sanchez recounted his first visit to Guangzhou and Macao, and described with high praise Ruggieri as a man 'of singular virtue, great simplicity and purity, whom the Chinese love and respect'. As for Ricci, Sanchez described him thus: 'Matteo Ricci, Italian, so similar in everything to the Chinese, and seems to be one of them in the beauty of his head and in the delicacy, gentleness, and suaveness, which they value so highly, and especially in his great intelligence and memory. For besides being a very good theologian and astronomer, whom they [the Chinese] very much appreciate, he has learned in a very short time their language and many characters so that he could speak with the mandarins without an interpreter, a fact that they all admire and enormously enjoy.'[27]

In the summer of 1582, Ruggieri returned to a totally different scenario in Macao. Unlike three years ago, when he undertook the lonely task of learning Chinese, he was joined by Francisco Pasio and Matteo Ricci, compatriots and companions from India, and found the immediate presence and support of Visitor Alessandro Valignano and Pedro Gomez, en route to Japan to assume his new post as superior of the Jesuit Mission. Ruggieri himself was eager to return to Zhaoqing, but he came down with a high fever. In fact, he became so sick that the doctors bled him, which further confined him to bed for weeks. Therefore, when Mateus Panela again departed for Zhaoqing with the merchandise specified by Chen Rui (in fact, his bribe), Ruggieri was forced to stay behind. He wrote a letter reminding the Supreme Commander of his grant of residence and promised a western clock. When Panela returned to Macao, he carried an official letter from Chen Rui, permitting Ruggieri to reside in the interior and specifying the foreign monk should himself convey the western clock to Zhaoqing.

It happened that Ricci had brought with him a beautiful European clock, a gift for the China Mission from Rui Vicente, the Jesuit Provincial in India. Although Valignano hesitated, the other Jesuits persuaded the Visitor to seize this opportunity. On 18 December 1582, Ruggieri and Pasio left Macao for Zhaoqing. Valignano selected Pasio as the most capable man, even though Pasio had been busy learning Japanese after his arrival in August in preparation for his future posting in Japan. Ricci took charge of the Chinese catechumens. On the eve of their departure, Ruggieri dashed off a short and excited letter to salute the new General, his acquaintance in Rome, Claudio Acquaviva; Pasio, who also penned a letter to the General, expressed a cooler and more skeptical stance, attributing the Supreme Commander's benevolence to his greed for a western clock, distrusting the Chinese 'who normally lie and are not moved except by their own interests'.[28]

On 18 December, a Thursday, Ruggieri and Pasio left Macao by land, accompanied by two Chinese Christian boys from Macao, Balthazar and Gonzalo, and their interpreter, a convert who is known to us only by his Portuguese name of Felipe Mendes. On Friday morning, they reached Xiangshan, where they presented their business to the magistrate. On learning the Jesuits were bearing a clock for the Supreme Commander, the mandarin Feng Shengyu granted the fathers the privilege of an audience without kneeling. With the travel permit issued by Feng, the Jesuits entered Guangzhou on Monday, Christmas Eve. There, they celebrated the holy feast by saying three masses. On Christmas Day, the party boarded two small barges for the trip up the Xijiang, arriving in Zhaoqing two days after Christmas. This much hoped for breakthrough to establish a permanent residence dashed on the rock of mandarin politics, to which we will turn shortly. After barely three months, the two Italian Jesuits were forced to return to Macao.

Before this failed effort became apparent, Ricci diligently studied Chinese, hoping to join his fellow missionaries by accompanying the Portuguese merchants to the Guangzhou trade fair in March 1583 and then going on to Zhaoqing. The two letters Ricci dispatched from Macao, to Martino de Fornari and General Acquaviva, reflected his intellectual interests and sharp insights. Written on 13 February 1583, just five months after arriving in Macao, they demonstrate a remarkably astute and mature power of observation. Ricci the humanist spoke. He explained to Acquaviva the difficulties and unfamiliarity of the Chinese language, 'which is something neither Greek nor German; and in speech it is so equivocal that many words signify more than a thousand things, and there is nothing to distinguish one from another in pronunciation except with a higher or lower, in altogether four tones. And thus, when speaking, they write down what they mean in order to make themselves understood, for the characters are all different. Regarding characters: this is something incredible for someone who has not seen it and tried it like I did. There are as many characters as words and things, exceeding 70,000. . . . All words are monosyllabic. . . . The usefulness lies in that all nations that have these characters can understand one another by writing and books, even if they are of diverse tongues.' Continuing his grammatical analysis, Ricci pointed out that Chinese morphology has neither cases, numbers, gender, time, nor mood, and everything works with adverbs. The more characters one knew, the more learned one's reputation, and 'this was the reason why the sciences are not much cultivated among them', concluded Ricci.[29] In medicine, however, the Chinese were advanced and Ricci noted the presence of Chinese books on herbal medicine in the Jesuit house. Praising the Chinese for their printing, the wealth and fertility of their country, Ricci sensed that a world map would come in handy in his future dealings with them, and accordingly asked Acquaviva for a copy. Reflecting his own geographic interests, Ricci gave the coordinates of Macao as 22.5 degrees latitude and 125 degrees longitude (actually, 22.10 N and 113.33 E).

Language and science aside, there are two further points in these letters that help us understand Ricci's future behavior. First, he was remarkably frank with Acquaviva in his criticism of his fellow Portuguese Jesuits:[30]

Ordinarily in this residence of China [Macao], which is very small, there are no fathers of high quality. And may Your Reverend know that I ask you to keep this secure and not disseminate it, for I only say what I have seen, and whoever has not seen it does not know it, which is that the fathers and superior of the college here do not have much spirit, not only do they not have love for the things of conversion, but rather a certain distaste for it. . . . the three years when Father Michele Ruggieri was here represented a half martyrdom with the fathers here, who are all very holy, but understand nothing of *christianitas* nor those they deal with.

In fact, Valignano was so dissatisfied that he relieved Domingos Álvares of the rectorship of the Macao College, putting in temporary charge Pedro

Gomez, who was much more supportive of the China Mission. The dismissed Álvares accompanied Valignano back to India in December 1582. And it was Álvares who said to Ricci more than once:

that if he was to remain here as superior he would have to weed out all those youths who are studying here; and he said this not because he does not get along with us, being in fact very friendly to us, but because he is so accustomed to being in our colleges that he does not know how to love Christians.

Recalling that many of the youths were Chinese and that 'Christians' refer to converts, Ricci was in fact criticizing the introvert and exclusive mentality of Portuguese colonialism, which he had already done in India in respect to the exclusion of Indian students from theological studies at the Jesuit College at Goa. He assured the General that his 'intention is no other than to advance greatly this enterprise, which is, I think, one of the most important and of the greatest service to God today in Christendom, and considering the great good that this would be for the so many souls that are in this other world of China'.

The second point concerns Ricci's attitude toward Chinese civilization. He wrote to de Fornari that 'of the grandeur of China, it is for certain that nothing in the world is greater'.[31] Full of esteem for the literary, political, and material cultures of the Ming Empire, Ricci was nonetheless dismissive of Chinese religions, describing how 'the Chinese adore some idols, but when these latter do not grant their wishes, the [Chinese] give them a good beating, and afterwards make peace with them; they adore or honor the Devil in this way, in order he may not harm them, and thus they have very few religious cults and little respect for their priests.'[32]

Of the grandeur of China, it seemed that what most impressed Ricci in his first encounter was the political culture of the Ming Empire. Simply put, Ricci admired the grandeur, dignity, and power of the mandarins. He was not the first westerner to be awed. Many foreign visitors to imperial China before and after Ricci marveled at the power of the mandarins, including the friars Martin da Rada and Agustín de Tordesillas. The originality in Ricci's observations, which gives us an insight into his personality, lies in Ricci's repeated comparisons between the Chinese imperial mandarinate and the Roman Catholic ecclesiastical hierarchy. China was a land without noble lords, but governed by these mandarins, 'who are like gods on earth'. In their *yamens*,

they do not speak with anyone from the outside except in public either in a hall or corridor, sufficiently large like a church, and the *laoye* [literarily 'venerable lord', an honorific for mandarins] . . . is found at the end just like in a chapel, with a bench facing the front, just like an altar, and sitting in a chair with a very unusual vestment and with [a hat attached with] ears made of cloth much larger than those of horses, which are signs of their dignity, just like the red hats of cardinals. In the middle of [the hall] is a wide path well made with doors, where nobody but he can come and go. On the sides of this room are two other doors where the others enter, and many armed men stand guard according to rank either close to him or outside the door. And when one speaks to him it has to be on one's knees, more than a stone's throw away. . . . and [the mandarins] give such cruel beatings for small things that many die, and give them so lightly just like masters beat their pupils among us.[33]

The only mandarin Ricci saw in Macao was probably the *zhixien* of Xiangshan, the county magistrate, who had jurisdiction over Macao and intervened directly on occasions. Even though the *zhixien* was a minor local official, seventh out of the nine–rank mandarin system (of which we will hear more in a later chapter), he impressed Ricci with the pomp and power of his office. Showing benevolence toward the fathers, the mandarin permitted them to stand up while answering his queries about the western religion. When the mandarin traveled in the streets, men armed with weapons and placards preceded him, shouting out orders for commoners to heed his passage. Some scurried indoors, others shut their windows, all fell silent and dropped to their knees as the mandarin was borne on a sedan chair carried on the shoulders of porters 'just like the pope'. The deepest impression for Ricci was that 'these *laoye* are sons of farmers and artisans who rise to their status because of their studies of letters'. Cruelty of punishment aside, the mandarins of imperial China reminded Ricci of the Catholic hierarchy: scholarship led to the path of honor, dignity, and command, elevating an elite of letters above the common crowd through their greater learning, with ceremonies, speech, and costumes marking off their signs of distinction.

While Ricci penned his thoughts in Macao, Ruggieri and Pasio were writing a new chapter in the annals of Jesuit history. The Italians arrived in Zhaoqing on 27 December 1582. After two days Chen Rui summoned them to an audience. After the usual ceremonies, Chen Rui motioned the Italians to approach and remarked how thin Ruggieri had become (having recovered from a major illness). Getting up from his seat, Chen Rui treated the Jesuits with amicable familiarity, inquiring of them their age, and informing them that he had instructed the *haidao* and the *zhixien* of Xiangshan to show favor to the Portuguese. Then he demanded whether the fathers were afraid of demons, to which Ruggieri and Pasio replied they wanted nothing more than to have power over them. Pleased with their gifts of Japanese paper, a Venetian prism, and other small curiosities, the Supreme Commander granted the Jesuits' request to stay on land, as they still needed to prepare the clock for presentation, including making an appropriate box. Chen Rui assigned the Jesuits a set of rooms in the largest Buddhist temple in Zhaoqing, the Tianningsi, and sent them a sack of rice, a bottle of wine, some pork, chickens, and two ducks. In one of the rooms, Ruggieri and Pasio set up an altar and said their first mass in China on New Year's Day.

For the next days, the Jesuits dealt with the Supreme Commander's secretary, who was annoyed with the fact it seemed difficult to use and service the European clock without the foreign monks. Compounding the mechanical ineptitude of the literati, Pasio remarked, was the total incomprehension of western time-keeping. For the Chinese, the European clock was no more than a beautiful sound-making gadget. When the Jesuits entreated the secretary to convey their request for residence to Chen Rui, the latter was anything but encouraging. Pleased with the clock, on 5 January Chen Rui instructed his secretary to give some silver to the Jesuits, but Ruggieri replied that the clock was a gift and submitted a written petition to the Supreme Commander. Stating they had sailed tens of thousands of miles to reach China, the land of culture and learning, the Jesuits humbly begged to be allowed to reside in China in order to learn the language, customs, and ways of this great civilization, and that they would abide by its laws and never return to their lands. Cultural flattery worked. The Chinese considered the Portuguese in Macao an uncivilized and aggressive people, who showed little or no interest in Chinese civilization; clearly, these foreign monks seemed different. To the surprise of the Jesuits, Chen Rui granted their petition. In turn, he asked the foreign clerics to dress like Chinese monks. And so, Ruggieri and Pasio took off their short black robes for the long robes of Chinese Buddhist monks, which normally came in the shades of brown or a hue of blue-grey, 'in order to carry the light of Christ to the Chinese', to use Ruggieri's expression.[34]

On 8 January Chen Rui summoned the Jesuits to another audience. He promised to grant them a comfortable house, but nothing could be done before Chinese New Year, when the Supreme Commander expected visits from all the mandarins of the province. In the meantime, the Jesuits were his protégés, who continued to receive allocations of food at the Tianning Temple. During one of the rare audiences with Chen Rui, the septuagenarian asked Ruggieri whether he could exorcize a poltergeist because the

Supreme Commander owned a haunted house in Guangzhou, where he had had terrible visions. Ruggieri replied that his ministry allowed him to perform exorcism. Chen Rui was pleased, adding that he had once asked a Muslim master in Guangzhou to rid him of the poltergeist to no avail. It seemed that Ruggieri never did have the chance to exorcize the haunted house, but the poltergeist apparently departed Chen Rui's mansion in Guangzhou, and rumor started circulating that the evil spirits feared the power of the foreign monk.

The missionaries also obtained Chen Rui's permission to call Ricci from Macao, presenting Ricci as his 'brother'. A certain misunderstanding in translation helped this Jesuit subterfuge. The elated Ruggieri described to Acquaviva that they were living in an enchanted dream, for the impossible task of entering China was finally achieved forty years after Francis Xavier, thanks to the great mercy of God. Of particular consolation to Acquaviva and the Company, ventured Ruggieri, was the prospect that all three fathers who were close at the Roman College would soon be reunited in Zhaoqing half a world away.

Ruggieri hurriedly wrote to Macao on 12 February informing the Jesuits of the good news, hence Ricci's anticipation that he would travel with the Portuguese merchants in March to the Guangzhou trade fair. Back in Zhaoqing, Ruggieri and Pasio continued to demonstrate their fervor and good religious behavior, entertaining visiting mandarins who did not hesitate to show reverence to a statue of the Madonna and Child, to the delight of the Jesuits. Confidence was high. On 18 February, Pasio wrote to Gomez in Macao, requesting the Rector of the Jesuit College to send things and people; in addition to Ricci, Pasio requested liturgical vestments to carry out an exorcism, a painting of the Savior by Brother Nicolao, the Italian Jesuit Giovanni Nicolao (di Nola), and Alonso 'the Bengal', who spoke good Mandarin.[35] Optimism notwithstanding, it was doubtful whether Ruggieri had indeed succeeded in 'bringing the light of Christ to the Chinese'. In his enthusiasm, he was oblivious of the fact that the distinction between Buddhism and Christianity was by no means clear to the Chinese. A conversation between Chen Rui and Ruggieri is a case in point. During a discourse on the true God of Christianity, Ruggieri heard Chen Rui agreeing with him, saying that 'heaven' (*Tian*) indeed was omnipotent and just. Speaking past one another, the Jesuit and the Supreme Commander did not even have a common vocabulary to differentiate between Christian, Buddhist, and Confucian concepts. The difficulty of this challenge would become apparent in the next few years. In the short run, 'the enchanted dream' evaporated like dew in the morning sun.

In late February, an order from Beijing dismissed Chen Rui from his post. Chen Rui's fall from power was one in a long series of political shakeups after the death of the powerful Grand Secretary Zhang Juzheng (1525–82). An iron-willed reformer and cunning politician, Zhang Juzheng assisted the boy Zhu Yijun, who ascended the imperial throne in 1573 as the Wanli emperor (1563–1620). Acting as chief minister, who ruthlessly forced out his rivals, and as the personal tutor to the boy emperor, whom he trained with stern discipline and a heavy load of Confucian learning, Zhang Ju-zheng was the most powerful man in the realm until his death in early 1582. Although a dedicated official, Zhang made too many enemies in ruthless court and bureaucratic politics; his own extensive household also traded political influence for bribes. Long resentful of the stern tutelage of his Grand Secretary, the 19-year-old Wanli emperor decided to assert his will shortly after Zhang's death. Sensing the change in the air, officials flooded the emperor with accusations against Zhang. In early January 1583 the Censor (*yushi*) Zhang Ying submitted a memorial accusing two high man-darins of corruption: they had secured their present offices by bribing Zhang Juzheng and the eunuch Feng Bo; one of them was Chen Rui, who allegedly obtained his high post with a large bribe of precious jewels and pearls and by various illegal favors for the Zhang household during his previous tenure as Governor of Huguang province. The Wanli emperor responded by ordering the immediate dismissal of the two men.[36]

When the imperial edict reached Zhaoqing, Chen Rui sent away his two Jesuit clients, fearing critics would use his patronage of foreigners as one more accusation once he left office. As a final gesture of goodwill, the dismissed Supreme Commander gave the fathers a letter with his seal, addressed to the *haidao*, with the provision that a piece of government land be given to the Jesuits in Guangzhou to build their temple. Ruggieri and Pasio, however, were not allowed to disembark in Guangzhou and returned to Macao in March. The door of China was shut once more.

4

Zhaoqing

In the midst of deep frustration at the Jesuit residence in Macao, Chinese officers arrived. They demanded the surrender of the official document bearing the seal of Chen Rui. The new *zongdu*, Guo Yingping, upon being promoted from Grand Coordinator of Guangxi to this post, dutifully examined the papers left by the disgraced Chen Rui. This was a measure instituted by the late Grand Secretary Zhang Juzheng, in an effort to smooth the running of the cranky bureaucratic machinery. Edicts from Beijing were too often acknowledged and then quietly shelved by local mandarins. The Ming regime had become a paper administration, burdened with edicts, reports, petitions, and imperial rescripts detailing policies that remained dead letters. In 1573, Zhang instituted new procedures which required all mandarins to render accountability by a checklist of responses to all official documents. Therefore, when Guo's clerks found no report filed next to Chen Rui's grant of government land to the Jesuits, he was obliged to investigate. Guo transmitted his order to the *haidao* in Guangzhou, who, ignorant of the whole matter, passed down the order of investigation to Feng Shengyu, the *zhixien* of Xiangshan, who in turn dispatched officers to Macao.

After consultation, the fathers refused to surrender the document but agreed to return it personally to the *haidao*. Under escort, Ruggieri and Ricci traveled to Xiangshan. At the audience with Feng, the Jesuits again refused to hand over the document, provoking Feng to such anger that he threw the document onto the floor, shouting: 'What do you think a document signed by a dismissed official is good for!' He refused to grant the Jesuits a permit to travel and told them to return to Macao. Returning to their inn, Ruggieri and Ricci tried a desperate measure. They boarded a ferry for Guangzhou, without permit. Seeing 'foreign devils' in their midst, the Chinese passengers made such a commotion that the captain forced the Jesuits to disembark. Their luck changed. News arrived that Feng's father had died; by law, all officials must relinquish their posts for the three-year mourning period. The Assistant County Magistrate, Deng Shiqi, was more friendly and sent the two missionaries on to Guangzhou. There, Ruggieri and Ricci presented the *haidao* with a petition to remain in China, learn its language and customs, and teach their religious doctrines. When the latter replied that only the new Supreme Commander could grant such a request, the fathers asked for permission to reside in the 'Siamese house' while they petitioned Guo Yingping. The *haidao* refused, since this was out of the trade season; the presence of foreign monks without Portuguese merchants would arouse suspicion. Dejected, the Jesuits returned to Xiangshan, where their mood darkened even more upon reading a public notice posted on the order of the new Supreme Commander, denouncing the 'tricks' of Chinese interpreters in Macao, who had taught foreign monks the Chinese language, and encouraged the latter to agitate for residence in the interior. Guo threatened severe punishments if these annoyances did not cease. The crestfallen Jesuits returned to Macao around 10 August, having wasted a month in vain.

In their absence, Francesco Pasio left Macao. On 14 July 1583, Pasio sailed for Japan, where he made a brilliant career eventually serving as Vice-Provincial and Visitor, before being nominated as the first Provincial, when the Japan Mission was elevated in 1611 to full provincial status in the governance of the Society of Jesus. He returned to Macao only in 1612, dying of an illness in mid-July almost exactly twenty-seven years after his departure.

Ruggieri and Ricci were disconsolate for barely a week. A soldier arrived. A guard at the East Gate of Zhaoqing, this soldier had been Ruggieri's catechumen. After the fathers left, he submitted a petition in the name of their interpreter to Guo Yingping, asking the new mandarin to grant a residence to the two foreign priests. Guo's staff passed on the petition to the Prefect of Zhaoqing, the *zhifu* Wang Pan, who granted the request. 'The hour has arrived', wrote Ricci, 'when divine mercy turns his eyes to this miserable realm, and opens with a mighty hand the door shut tight to the preachers of the Holy Gospels.'[1] Ricci would soon find out exactly how divine mercy worked its way through human hands. Meanwhile, the missionaries made preparations, trying to collect enough donations, for they were determined to be financially self-sufficient; difficult enough in cash-strapped Macao, which had lost its great ship to Nagasaki from last year, the one on which Alonso Sanchez was shipwrecked. On 1 September, they left: Ruggieri, Ricci, a Chinese interpreter, their servants, led by the Chinese soldier. Ten days later, the Jesuits arrived. Ricci saw Zhaoqing, his home for the next five years.

With more than 16,600 households and a population of 47,000, Zhaoqing was a quiet and pleasant river city.[2] Devoid of the hustle of Guangzhou, Zhaoqing was famous for the natural beauty of the Seven Star Crags, a set of limestone ridges and caves around a lake to the north of the city walls. Although not a center of commerce like Guangzhou, Zhaoqing craftsmen exported ink stones and ink wells, famous throughout China. Above all, it served as an administrative center, housing the offices of the Viceroyalty of Guangdong and Guangxi, the Prefecture of Zhaoqing, the County of Gaoyeo, and regional military garrisons. A 1633 map of Zhaoqing showed the city pretty much the way it was in 1583: an elongated walled city, not quite a rectangle, parallel with the Xijiang to the south, and framed to the north by the Seven Star Crags and even higher hills in the distance. A cluster of government offices in the center of the city housed the offices of the prefecture and the county, while the *yamen* of the *zongdu* was located to the east, near the Temple to Guanyu, the God of War and Loyalty, and close to the massive East Gate, which led out to the Tianning Temple and the Prefectural School (see Map 3). Only the pagoda, the Chongxi ta, at the right margin (east) of the map, was incomplete: when Ricci arrived in September 1583 only the first storey had been constructed. All in all, Zhaoqing was a provincial town in spite of its charms: its largest Buddhist monastery, the Tianning, was modest in size and reputation even by the standards of Guangdong province; nor could Zhaoqing boast of famous Daoist temples or private Confucian academies. To the Jesuits, the intramural fish ponds and the quiet Xijiang gave Zhaoqing a backwater image in strong contrast to bustling Guangzhou, the wide Pearl River Delta, and the world beyond. It seemed Ruggieri and Ricci had walked through the high and forbidden gates of China to find themselves in a small and beautiful walled garden.[3]

Their first audience with Wang Pan went well. Through their interpreter, the Jesuits presented themselves as 'monks from the country of Tianchu' (*Tianchu guo seng*). Tianchu was the Chinese name for India; Ruggieri wanted the Chinese to identify the Jesuits with the region where once holy monks and sacred doctrines came to China. They served the 'Ruler of Heaven', continued Ruggieri through the interpreter, and had traveled for

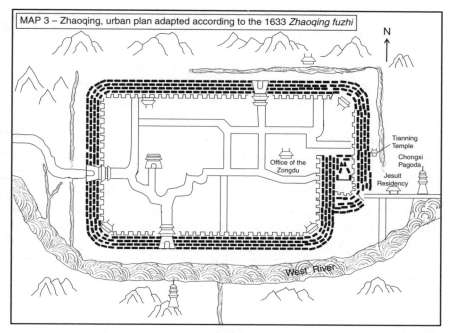

MAP 3 – Zhaoqing, urban plan adapted according to the 1633 *Zhaoqing fuzhi*

N

Tianning Temple

Chongxi Pagoda

Office of the Zongdu

Jesuit Residency

West River

Map 3. Zhaoqing

three years from the Extreme West, attracted by the good governance of the Great Ming. They desired only a quiet place far from the commerce and secular pursuits of Macao, in order to build a retreat and chapel, serving God until their death. A devout Buddhist, Wang Pan promised his benign patronage and the assignment of government land to help these foreign monks. Lest we forget, Ruggieri and Ricci, their heads and beards shaved, dressed like Chinese Buddhist monks. After all, Buddhist monks from India had travelled to Guangdong during the Tang and Song dynasties. What a magnificent encounter that after 400 years this should recur under his magistracy!

After their audience, Ruggieri went to retrieve the mobile altar, liturgical objects, and books that he had entrusted to 'an upright young man' named Chen when forced to leave Zhaoqing by the dismissal of Chen Rui. The young Chen lived near Tianning Temple and had been practicing the new rituals under Ruggieri's guidance. In Chen's house, the Jesuits saw that he had set up the altar in a small room in which were several incense burners, and behind the altar, a large scroll written with the characters 'Tian zhu'

(Lord of Heaven). Pleased with this elegant Chinese rendering of the Christian God, Ruggieri and Ricci adopted this nomenclature, which would remain the appellation of the divine in Chinese Catholicism.

The Jesuits stayed with Chen for four days before Wang Pan assigned them on 14 September their new home: a parcel of land one mile east of the city near the river bank, adjacent to the Chongxi Pagoda, in a beautiful suburban area dotted with trees and gardens. The next day, in the company of other mandarins and local notables, Wang Pan inspected the site with the Jesuits. Several men in Wang's entourage voiced their concern that the Jesuits were just the first of many foreigners from Macao who would settle in Zhaoqing. The fathers immediately assured their critics no one else would join them. Wang Pan then assigned a piece of land adjacent to the pagoda, whereupon the fathers, through their interpreter, suggested it might be too small for their needs. Wang replied the parcel was meant only for their residence; a larger plot would be chosen to build a temple. When their interpreter said the Jesuits did not adore idols but only the Lord of Heaven, Wang Pan looked visibly puzzled. He exchanged some words with his entourage and replied that it did not matter. Once the temple was built, the fathers could worship whatever god they wanted to.

Right away, the Jesuits hired workers to lay the foundation of their new house, while living next door in a temporary shelter. Their residence was a typical one-storey Chinese compound with a central hall framed by two sets of double rooms at the wings. Chongxi Pagoda, which eventually rose to nine levels, towered over the Xijiang, holding back, as it were, the energy of the swift river and safeguarding the good fortunes of Zhaoqing (see Figure 7). Be it that the Jesuits dismissed this as an example of Chinese superstition, for the inhabitants of Zhaoqing it represented the most important public work project under the magistracy of Wang Pan. An advisory committee, comprising literati and local notables, supervised the pagoda's construction. Some members were unhappy to see foreigners. After several meetings, Ruggieri diffused the tension by giving back some of the land assigned to them by Wang Pan.

In their temporary residence, Ruggieri and Ricci set up their altar to say mass, put on display a picture of the Virgin Mary, a replica of the Virgin depicted in Santa Maria Maggiore in Rome, a Venetian crystal prism, western books, and other curiosities. Every day large crowds gawked at the novelties and the exotic monks, making way only for the mandarins. So impressed was Wang Pan by the painting of the Virgin Mary and the

Figure 7. Chongxi Pagoda by the bank of the West River, Zhaoqing

prism that he moved them home to show to his domestic household. He refused, however, the Jesuits' gift of several laced handkerchiefs from Europe, behaving like an upright and incorruptible mandarin.

Once settled, Ruggieri and Ricci went to render homage to the Supreme Commander, who had approved Wang's grant of land. But Guo Yingping refused to receive them. The Jesuits never saw Guo during their stay in Zhaoqing. For the next few years, their patrons and protectors were Wang Pan and his subordinate, the Assistant Prefect Zhang Yilin. Having just established a foothold, the fathers soon ran into trouble: they spent all their money. They had to let go of the interpreter and Chinese servants, and construction on their new residence also stopped for the same reason. In December Ruggieri traveled to Macao for fundraising; Ricci and his household made do with a loan from the mandarins. For a couple of months, Ruggieri begged for largesse, which was in short supply due to shipwrecks in the Macao–Nagasaki trade. Ruggieri sold the Venetian prism for 30 taels of silver; he also obtained some help from another source. His acquaintance and fellow Jesuit Alonso Sanchez was once more in Macao. In December 1583, the Governor of the Philippines sent the Royal Factor Juan Bautista

Román and Sanchez as envoys bearing gifts for the Emperor of China; their mission was to travel on to Beijing, present gifts in the name of Philip II, and ask for the establishment of diplomatic and commercial ties. Once in Macao, Sanchez wrote to his old friend Ruggieri in Zhaoqing, stating full Spanish support for the Catholic enterprise and asking his fellow Jesuit to intervene with the Mandarin Guo on behalf of the Spanish diplomatic mission. Thus, Ruggieri's trip to Macao was not only to raise money, but also to meet with Sanchez to discuss the strategies of evangelization. Initially Ruggieri and Ricci cautioned Sanchez against an optimistic outcome: the Chinese suspected all foreigners, and considered the Spaniards an aggressive and warlike people. To their surprise, Wang Pan, to whom Ruggieri and Ricci turned, welcomed the Spanish proposal. A petition was written in the name of Wang Pan's clerk and dispatched to the *haidao* in Guangzhou. However, after Ruggieri's return to Zhaoqing in February 1584, the Italian fathers received a letter from Francisco Cabral, Rector of the Jesuit College in Macao, to the effect that the *Capitão-Mór* and other Portuguese voiced the strongest opposition to the Spanish diplomatic mission. If Sino-Hispanic ties were established, the Portuguese reasoned, Macao's unique position would be undermined by a similar concession to the Spaniards on the southern Chinese coast. And once the Spaniards could ship American silver directly to China, profits would plummet on the Portuguese import of Japanese silver, a trade in which the Jesuits had their share. Cabral, the direct superior of Ruggieri and Ricci, advised them to drop their advocacy and let the Spanish enterprise die a quiet death. The Italian fathers were only too happy to obey, for Ruggieri especially worried about the negative consequences for their new mission if the Chinese suspected their close ties with Manila.

We notice a stark contrast between Ruggieri's prudent anxiety and Sanchez's cocky confidence. In a letter to Acquaviva, dated 30 March 1584, written after his return from Macao to Zhaoqing, Ruggieri described the China Mission as 'a new and tender plant, and the slightest wind can kill it; therefore, it is necessary that in this beginning it must be tended most sweetly and delicately, and there will be a time when cultivators will be summoned for planting or for uprooting.' He worried about 'the fervor not only of our fathers, but also from other religious orders . . . who all want now to come and cultivate this plant, which . . . has not even been born yet'. With the Spanish Jesuits in Luzon in mind, he asked Acquaviva to command all Jesuit superiors everywhere not to send missionaries until a local superior for the China Mission had been appointed.[4]

Waiting more than six months in frustration, Sanchez wrote a letter on 5 July to Gaspar Coelho, the Jesuit Vice-Provincial of Japan. Affirming the fervent desire of all Spaniards in the Philippines for the conversion of China, he was nonetheless skeptical of the approach of Ruggieri and Ricci: friendship with the mandarins and peaceful evangelization. Sanchez declared that 'on the conversion [of China] by preaching, having spent several months in China and having dealt with [the Chinese] for several years in Luzon, I can say positively that it is impossible. [Some may say:] "For God nothing is impossible", but I would rather believe those there [in the Philippines] who have been dealing for twenty years and here [in Macao] for close to thirty, that everyone says the same thing and that this business [of conversion] will have to be concluded by God in the manner of New Spain and Peru.'[5]

Even though Spanish authorities in Manila considered the military conquest of China a realistic option, it is still odd that Sanchez the priest sounded more warlike than Román the royal official. In a letter to Philip II, dated 24 with a postscript of 27 June, Román expressed his optimism that they would be permitted to travel to Beijing. Unaware of Portuguese machinations and still full of confidence in Ruggieri and Ricci, who were conversant with the Chinese language and Chinese ways, Román advised the Spanish king that the only way to obtain diplomatic relations would be through the fathers, even though he himself did not hold 'any particular devotion or affection for those of the Company'. Given the wealth of China, only exquisite presents would make an impression, suggested Román: horses from New Spain, velvet, golden brocades and fabric, Flemish tapestries, Venetian glass, clocks, mirrors, gilded armor, painted lances, sharp swords, exotic feathers, robes from Milan, and wine; the whole lot costing no less than 60,000 to 70,000 ducats. He did convey Sanchez's hawkish stance: without a miracle, the Chinese, with their impossible language, could not be converted to Christianity, being a proud people disdainful of foreign ways. 'We will never in our whole lives come to an understanding with them until some minimum part of Your Majesty's power has entered into this territory and necessity forces them to learn our language, which is easier than for us to learn theirs,' Román reported further, quoting Sanchez, an enterprise for the glory of the militant Church and the reputation of His Majesty.[6]

In October, with no encouraging news forthcoming, Sanchez and Román returned to Manila. As envoy of the Filipino government the Spanish Jesuit would travel to Spain via Mexico in 1587, bringing with him the first report on the conditions of Philip's newest colonial realm. A memorandum, appended to this report and written by Sanchez, advised Philip to send an armada for the conquest of China. In it, Sanchez outlined the reasons for a 'Just War', in the interests of Christian evangelization and Spanish imperial aggrandizement. This remarkable document provoked a spirited critique by Sanchez's fellow Spanish Jesuit José de Acosta (1540–1600), and by Valignano.[7] The fact that Philip entrusted a committee in the spring of 1588 to study this memorandum while outfitting an armada for the conquest of heretical England adds an ironic footnote to our story of Jesuit evangelization in China.

If Philip had to face the North Sea gales that destroyed his armada, the danger of a strong wind that could kill off the seedling of evangelization was real enough in China. During Ruggieri's absence in the winter of 1583/4, Ricci had a nasty experience with xenophobia. Some neighbors of the Jesuits were never reconciled to the presence of the 'foreign devils'. The patronage of mandarins only increased popular resentment: both their magistrates and these foreign monks spoke only Mandarin and were ignorant of the local speech and the fierce local ways of the Cantonese. The immediate cause for hostility was the arrival of an Indian from Macao. A clockmaker and native of Goa, this dark-skinned man came to build a clock for Wang Pan, who had expressed to the Jesuits his wish to procure one. Since shipment from Europe was too expensive, it was decided to build one in Zhaoqing using foreign expertise and local material. For many years, the Cantonese had been accusing the Portuguese of buying children, an open practice in Guangdong regulated by contracts and customs but forbidden to the Portuguese. The arrival of the Goan, and the presence of the Bengali Alonso in the Jesuit residence, intensified fears, for the Cantonese despised the 'black barbarians' even more than the 'white barbarians'. Rumors of child kidnapping circulated; these dark-skinned 'foreign devils' came to take Chinese children to Macao. Some neighborhood boys entertained themselves by throwing rocks from the elevated storeys of the Chongxi Pagoda down onto the roof and courtyard of the Jesuit residence. Driven to distraction by this regular harassment, servants at the residence caught a boy red-handed and dragged him into the compound. They released the boy after a terrible scolding when some neighbors came to plead.

Two hostile neighbors saw this as a chance to get rid of the foreigners. They submitted a petition to Wang Pan, accusing the foreigners of holding the boy for three days, and put up someone to give false testimony. Ricci was conveyed to the prefectural *yamen* under guard. Unable to explain in Chinese, he anxiously prayed for divine assistance. Fortunately, Alonso the Bengali spoke better Mandarin and took the stones with him as evidence. Several neighbors also testified to the effect that the boy had only been held for a few minutes in the Jesuit compound, and the kidnapping was a drummed-up charge. When Wang Pan ordered the culprit to be caned for giving false testimony, Ricci pleaded for mercy. The matter resolved, Wang Pan dispatched the clockmaker immediately to Macao in order to avoid any more trouble. On account of this, after his return to Zhaoqing, Ruggieri informed Acquaviva that while the mandarins 'love them and are very happy with their presence . . . the common people show little affection because they do not understand our way of life'.[8]

All was not gloomy, however. For one, during his first months in Zhaoqing, Ruggieri finished revising his Chinese-language catechism, the first Christian *doctrina* in that language, initiated in Macao and four years in the making. On 25 January 1584, Ruggieri informed Acquaviva from Macao that he would submit a Latin synopsis to the other fathers of the Company to obtain approval for publication.[9] Eventually, this work was printed in late November. We will come back to it shortly.

As for Ricci, in addition to daily lessons in Chinese, he focused on his scientific pursuits, making sundials and designing quadrants for the measurement of stars. His biggest achievement was in geography. In their residence, the fathers had hung on a wall Abraham Ortelius' map of the world. This world map, an excellent specimen of advanced European cartography, never failed to elicit strong reactions from Chinese visitors, whether it was shock and disbelief or surprise and admiration. To interested visitors, Ricci explained patiently latitudes, longitudes, the equator, the tropics of Cancer and Capricorn, rapidly gaining an erudite reputation. Wang Pan suggested publishing the world map in a Chinese edition. Ricci translated all Latin inscriptions into Chinese, elaborating on the customs and history of geographical regions, using the opportunity to introduce Christian Europe, and tactfully placing China in the center of the new world map. Toward the end of November 1584, just before Ruggieri's catechism appeared in print, Ricci was ready with his map. Eventually, Wang Pan underwrote its printing and distributed copies to friends, acquaintances, and colleagues.

Things were definitely looking up. In October 1584, Ruggieri again went to Macao. The latest ship had come in from Japan, and the Portuguese enclave was again flush with money. Ruggieri returned with enough money to pay off their debts. Their new residence was near completion. It was a two-storey house constructed of brick and lime, a mixture of western and Chinese architecture, with a balcony over the entrance with a fine river view. The Jesuits hired a new tutor, a learned scholar in the Confucian classics. Most of all, their patron Wang Pan was promoted to Intendant of the West (*Linxidao*) while remaining stationed in Zhaoqing; his successor as *zhifu* of Zhaoqing was Zheng Yilin, another patron of theirs. Furthermore, fortune smiled on Wang Pan: in addition to the birth of a girl, his wife was pregnant, giving birth later to a son. People said the foreign monks were bringing good luck for the mandarin.

Wang Pan's crucial role in protecting the Jesuits is abundantly clear from the writings of Ruggieri and Ricci. Yet, he remains a shadowy figure on the stage of missionary history, which features Ricci the hero and Ruggieri the faithful companion, quite reversing the actual roles of the Italian Don Quixote and Sancho Panza, in their quixotic quest to open up China to the gospel. It is time we examine the Chinese sources and read with a critical eye the records left behind by the first Jesuit missionaries to get at the full picture partially obscured by the posthumous glorification of Ricci.

Recall the summer of 1583, when Ruggieri and Ricci received permission to travel to Zhaoqing. The roles of the soldier-catechumen and Wang Pan are recounted by Ricci, who otherwise attributed the miracle to the hand of God. But Ricci omitted to mention the reason for Wang Pan's interests in the foreign monks. According to Ruggieri, Wang Pan gave the fathers permission to reside in Zhaoqing because he was hoping for their intervention in getting a son, for he had been married for thirty years with one wife and two concubines and did not have a male heir. Within a year after the arrival of Ruggieri and Ricci, Wang Pan got his precious son, whom he took to the Jesuit chapel to make offerings to the image of Madonna and Child, entrusting his heir to her protection. Later, a second son was born to Wang Pan, who had him baptized.[10]

The Christian deity who bestowed sons: this represented an example in which the Virgin and Child, a picture of which the Jesuits exposed in their residence and whose images and statues they made gifts of, became assimilated into the Chinese understanding of the Son-giving Guanyin. Ricci recalled in his memoirs that all mandarins who came to visit them bowed and kneeled before a picture of the Madonna and Child. After a while, the Jesuits substituted instead a picture of Christ, lest the Chinese thought the

Christian God was a female deity. Clearly, the visitors in Zhaoqing confused the Virgin Mary with the Son-giving Guanyin. A discreet man, Ricci was silent on this point in his later memoirs, but at the time he recorded this success in a letter of 1586. Ricci wrote that their protector Wang Pan desired very much a male child, which he asked the Jesuits to pray for, whereupon the fathers gave him an image of the Madonna. With this success 'the rumor goes around the city that our God has given him a son'.[11] The similarities between Madonna and Guanyin confused even European missionaries, as we have seen: Gaspar da Cruz thought a statue of Guanyin in Guangzhou suggested the apostolic visit of St Thomas to China, and as we will see, the young Portuguese Jesuit Antonio Almeida would also make the same identification, when he accompanied Ruggieri on a trip out of Zhaoqing in the winter of 1585.

But we are getting ahead of our story. Let us get acquainted with Wang Pan, the shadowy but powerful patron of the Jesuits. A native of Shanyin in the Prefecture of Shaoxing, Zhejiang province, Wang Pan obtained his *jinshi* degree in 1573 and was appointed *zhifu* of Zhaoqing in 1581. He came from a region of China with a strong Buddhist monastic tradition and the practice of elite patronage for these monasteries in the late Ming.[12] The Ming elites of Eastern Zhejiang (Ningpo and Shaoxing prefectures)—mandarins, retired officials, and literati, who collectively made up the gentry—entwined their lives with Buddhism: copying religious texts, releasing living creatures, chanting sutras at monasteries under the direction of monks. A few gentry took lay vows under noted local abbots, such as under Zibo Zhenke (1543–1603). There were also many secular activities associated with Buddhist monasteries: the literati moving into monasteries as places of study, gathering at monasteries to write poetry, and building personal friendships and sharing cultural pursuits with clergy. Literary societies often met in monasteries; and it was common practice for the literati to commemorate themselves by writing poems on monastic walls. While at monasteries, the gentry also engaged in intellectual discussion with monks. Involvement by the leading gentry lineages occurred over generations.[13] The Buddhist clergy responded positively by involving themselves in turn in the social and cultural activities of the gentry. Many local abbots wrote poetry and were familiar with Confucianism. The gentry gave money to the monasteries and helped to direct their affairs by inviting abbots, interceding with government officials, providing patronage, compiling monastic gazetteers, and raising money for reconstruction. The uppermost echelon of the county gentry, well represented in the mandarinate, was predominant in the literary patronage of the monasteries. Wang Pan's patronage of Ruggieri and Ricci clearly fitted into this pattern. The two strongest patrons of the Jesuits both came from Shaoxing Prefecture: Wang Pan, the *zhifu* of Zhaoqing, later promoted to Provincial Surveillance Vice-Commissioner (*anchasi fushi*) and Circuit Intendant of the Lingxi circle (*lingxi dao*), and his successor as mandarin of the prefecture, Zheng Yilin.

The arrival of Ruggieri and Ricci coincided with a Buddhist revival in late Ming China, characterized by the activities of famous abbots and monks, monastic revival, and gentry patronage. Outside of the imperial capital Beijing, the revival was most notable in Jiangnan: the provinces of Zhejiang and Southern Zhili (Jiangsu). The key figure was the *jushi*: the lay devotee, typically male, often of elevated social status, keeping a regime of vegetarianism, sexual abstinence, and ritual observance while living 'within the world'. In the prosopography of these Buddhist lay devotees, compiled by Peng Ziqing (1740–96) in the eighteenth century, the *Jushi zhuan* (*Biography of Lay Buddhists*), there are 107 *jushi* biographies pertaining to the Ming dynasty; all except four can be dated between the Wanli reign and the end of the Ming dynasty (1573–1644).[14] The vast majority were members of the gentry; they were interested in the synthesis of Buddhism, Daoism, and Confucianism. Many *jushi* looked upon Confucianism as the learning for this world, for the *gong* (public sphere), and Buddhism as the learning for the other world, for the *si* (private sphere).

There are numerous examples of the assimilation of Christianity to Buddhism in the memoirs of Ruggieri and Ricci. First example: upon the completion of their new residence Wang Pan bestowed two wooden tablets with carvings of his calligraphy, which were hung over the front door and the entrance to the reception hall. The first read: 'Xianhua si' (Sacred Flower Temple), meaning the Temple of Lotus, the sacred flower of Buddhism; the second tablet had the four characters 'Xi lai Jing tu' (Pure Land from the West), a reference to the Pure Land of the West, the sacred abode of the Buddha in the teachings of the Pure Land School of Buddhism.

There is further evidence in the Chinese sources that Wang Pan was a devout Buddhist. The earliest extant local gazetteer *Zhaoqing Fuzhi* (Chongzhen 6th year, 1633) has an entry on Wang Pan in the section 'Famous Officials'. After listing his many public works for the people of Zhaoqing, the gazetteer lists Wang's construction projects, which included pagodas in Lishui and Gaoming counties, and the most important project, the Chongxi ta in Zhaoqing, next to the residence of the Jesuits, and adjacent to the Temple of the Living (*sheng si*) that the people of Zhaoqing built to commemorate him upon his departure from the city. Of his character, the gazetteer wrote: 'Wang Pan is ascetic, quiet, and self-contained, uncorrupt like a hermit exercising his official duties. He used to burn incense and sit quietly (*jing xo*) in meditation; [his office] was like a room for Chan meditation.'[15] The Chongzhen gazetteer also collected several literary works by Wang Pan: one poem is entitled 'Mei an' (The Plum Flower Nunnery), a Song dynasty Buddhist nunnery near the western city walls, famous for being one of the sites visited by Huineng, the Sixth Patriarch (Liuzu), the founder of the Southern School of Chan Buddhism. The poem reads:[16]

> Tired of office, with few accounts and books,
> I look for the monk in flowery greenery.
> White clouds quietly lean against my pillow
> And red leaves swirl near people.
> I love that you make your offerings in duty,
> I pity myself for not casting away my robes.
> Let us share the bright moon in our heart of Chan
> Looking at one another in the forgetfulness of return.

In two other poems, 'On the Seven Star Crags' and 'Ascending Chongxi ta', Wang Pan uses Daoist and Buddhist images, conventional and common to the literary expression of many literati of the late Ming. Visiting the limestone caves of the Seven Star Crags, Wang Pan pens these verses:[17]

> I found a deep cave with magical pills
> I beg for herbs to stay my red cheeks
> I wish to hail a stork
> To fly me up to the Immortals.

In the poem 'Ascending Chongxi ta', one finds the verse 'The sun shoots a golden wheel, scattering precious light.'[18] The term 'Golden Wheel' denotes also the 'Dharma Wheel' (*falun*), the movement of which propels the propagation of Buddhist truths.

An elegant stylist he might have been, but Wang Pan's religious sentiments and expressions were not at all unconventional for a man of his class and rank. Ricci recorded that Wang and Zheng Yilin, together with other interested mandarins, paid them regular visits, enjoying the beauty of the place where the Jesuit residence and the Chongxian ta were located, in a grove of trees next to the bank of the Xijiang, just a short excursion outside of the narrow streets of the walled city. It was in the house of the Jesuits, with their unique collection of western curiosities and their singular conversations of the Lord of Heaven, where the mandarins staged the farewell banquet for Zheng Yilin, before his journey in 1585 to Beijing for his triennial evaluation; it was then that Zheng Yilin promised to bring the missionary with him to Beijing.

All of this conformed to a common pattern of mandarin and gentry patronage of the Buddhist clergy in late Ming China. An important point to bear in mind is that by and large, the literati elites considered the clergy their social and intellectual inferiors, a fact borne out not only by the social origins of the Buddhist clergy, but also by the paucity of distinguished Buddhist monks. For this reason, those few monks who abandoned the path of imperial civil service examination, and who had achieved some initial recognition in their Confucian studies, rose to the top of the large amorphous mass of Buddhist clergy. For Wang Pan and Zheng Yilin, *jinshi* degree holders (or doctors in the parlance of the Jesuits), there were simply no Chinese Buddhist monks in Zhaoqing worthy of their interest. By comparison, Ruggieri and Ricci, in addition to their intrinsic exoticism, were more the intellectual equals of the mandarins, although their social inferiors. Francisco Cabral, who visited Zhaoqing in November and early December 1584, observed Wang Pan's friendship for Ruggieri.[19] A poem dedicated to Ruggieri, extant only in Ruggieri's Latin translation, came possibly from the pen of Zhang Yilin ('versi del mandarin Cinceo'); it recounts poetically the Jesuit's long voyage to China, braving waves and monsters, his pious devotion, and queries whether the foreign monk will grow old in holy quiescence while remembering his native soil.[20]

While implanting the first Christian mission in China, Ruggieri and Ricci were themselves being assimilated into the Chinese universe of religious representation in these early years: however strongly they stressed the unique truth of Christianity, the Jesuits—their personae, doctrines, and liturgies—were perceived by the Chinese through the lens of Buddhism. Ruggieri and Ricci presented themselves as monks from *Tianchu guo*, India, the land of Buddha; they taught salvation in the afterlife in paradise; they displayed pictures of the Virgin and Child, which was indistinguishable for many Chinese from the Son-giving Guanyin; they burned incense, recited from prayer beads, kept liturgical fasts, and possessed sacred books written in an incomprehensible foreign script, just as Buddhist sutras once were before their massive translation from Sanskrit into Chinese. True, the Jesuits insisted on the difference of their beliefs, but, similarly, successive Indian masters and Chinese schools of Buddhism in the past asserted their differences and originality. In short, during their years in Zhaoqing, Ruggieri and Ricci were seen as bearers of the newest religious teachings from India, who introduced a new school of Buddhism. We have already seen how the friendship between Wang Pan and Ruggieri fit perfectly into the pattern of gentry patronage of Buddhist monasticism. There is further evidence of this assimilation of the Jesuit mission into Chinese Buddhism. First, we will examine the catechism authored by Ruggieri, then, we will analyze the conversions made in these earliest years of Christian evangelization.

Published under the title *Tianzhu shilu*, 'A Veritable Record of the Lord of Heaven', Ruggieri's catechism was a slim Chinese book of forty-three leaves.[21] Ruggieri had labored four years on this catechism, motivated by the inadequacy of the interpreters, who failed to explain Christian doctrines to the mandarins Ruggieri had encountered; the printed text also compensated for the missionaries' lack of fluency in spoken Chinese. According to Ruggieri, Wang Pan, to whom the Jesuits presented the book, was so pleased that he sponsored a print-run of more than 3,000 copies.[22] Signing under his Chinese name Luo Mingjian, Ruggieri presented himself under the title of '*Tianchu seng* (an Indian monk)'. Ruggieri chose as format a dialogue between a monk (*seng*) and a Chinese interlocutor. In the introduction, Ruggieri argues that loving the Lord of Heaven is a natural consequence of filial gratitude; he also names gratitude for writing this booklet, to give 'truth' to the Chinese, who have shown him great hospitality, since he cannot offer them gold and jewels. The acts of the Lord of Heaven, Ruggieri tells the reader, originated in Tianchu (India) and were later propagated in the four directions. His is an easy religion, requiring no daily fasts, no Chan meditation, no need to abandon the secular life to follow a religious master; worshipping the Lord with a sincere heart is sufficient to bring blessings. The main body of the text is divided into sixteen short sections. The first four address the nature of the Lord of Heaven; section five describes Adam's fall; sections six and seven deal with the immortality of the soul and its four abodes after death; the history of redemption after Creation to the Incarnation is briefly sketched out in sections eight, nine, and ten; section eleven introduces the Credo; section twelve, the Ten Commandments; special clerical vows are explained in section thirteen; and baptism is discussed in section fourteen. The last two sections include the Ten Commandments and the Ave Maria.

While the catechism bears the authorship of Ruggieri, who had worked on it for four years, the *Tianzhu shilu* was a composite text. A crucial editorial/translator function was exercised by the tutor of Ruggieri and Ricci, a scholar (*xiucai*) from Fujian, who had been hired by the Jesuits in the early summer of 1584 and became one of the earliest converts to Christianity, receiving his baptism and the name Paul at the hand of the visiting Francisco Cabral. Although Cabral mentioned Paul as the 'translator' of this catechism, it is more accurate to think of him as the copy-editor and translation consultant of Ruggieri's Chinese text. This collaboration would explain the awkward mixture of classical and colloquial styles in the text, and perhaps the particular choice of words to represent Christian concepts. *Tianzhu shilu* is a paradox: the work contains anti-Buddhist polemics while using terms specific to Chinese Buddhist usage. Section three, which criticizes the ignorance of the Lord of Heaven in China, labels the many opinions of China 'heresies'. Those who worship 'Heaven' (Tian), a traditional Confucian concept, instead of 'the Lord of Heaven' (Tianzhu), a Christian innovation, are ridiculous, writes Ruggieri, just as if someone would kneel to the imperial palace and not to the emperor. While the Devil inhabits many kinds of idols and shrines in China, Buddhism is particularly pernicious: all Buddhist sutras are false; Ruggieri cites the *Lotus Sutra*, one of the major texts of Pure Land Buddhism, and ridicules its advocacy of sutra recitation. If mere sutra recitation brings rebirth in paradise, Ruggieri reasons, then only the rich can attain paradise for they alone could buy the sutras. Elsewhere, when he discusses the immortality of the human soul, Ruggieri again attacks the Buddhist idea of rebirth, especially the reincarnation of humans in animal bodies. And yet, in addition to styling himself a *Tianchu guo seng*, a title which could only signify a Buddhist monk to the Chinese, Ruggieri uses explicit Buddhist terms in his text. Narrating the Incarnation, Ruggieri used the word 'hua' (transform), a term employed in Buddhist texts to denote the transformation of Buddhas and boddhisatvas into their myriad representations.[23] This sentence is followed by one that describes Jesus descending upon the earth to teach his doctrines. Here, Ruggieri uses the verb 'jiang', conjuring up for Chinese readers the familiar idea of the porosity between heaven and earth, with deities descending to teach, punish, love, and marry mortal humans, and in the contrary direction virtuous human individuals rising to the heavens in acts of apotheosis. The virgin birth was narrated in a style reminiscent of the stories of miraculous births ascribed to famous personages in Chinese history.[24] Ruggieri used the words 'chu jia' to denote entering the religious life in Christianity, a term that Chinese readers understood to mean leaving one's family to become a Buddhist monk.[25] In the text, Ruggieri consistently used the words *seng* (Buddhist monk) to denote himself, and *si* (Buddhist temple) to refer to Christian churches.

This paradox aside, Ruggieri's catechism manages to convey in a very succinct form the major tenets of Christianity: an omnipotent and omniscient God, creator of heaven and earth, invisible but real, perfect and just, who rewards virtue and punishes sin after death; the creation of the universe in seven days 5,550 years ago; the European cosmology of nine heavenly spheres; the nine orders of angels and Lucifer's rebellion; the fall of Adam and the revelations of God's laws, first through Moses and the Ten Commandments, then through the Incarnation of Jesus; the stories of Noah and the Flood, Lot and the destruction of the sinful cities; the difference between the vegetable, animal, and human soul; the immortality of the last, and its abode in hell, limbo, purgatory, and paradise after death; the Virgin birth; the death and resurrection of Jesus; the Ten Commandments enumerated and explained, and the description of baptism and the washing away of sins.

All of this was familiar matter from the catechisms of Catholic Europe. More original were Ruggieri's adaptations to his Chinese audience. The Lord of Heaven rules in the celestial court just like the emperor rules in Beijing, Ruggieri writes. And just as he, who has only been in Guangdong province, knows there is an emperor in Beijing, on account of the order and hierarchy of mandarins and administrations, so too reason deduces from the natural order of the universe and teaches the existence of an omnipotent deity. Arguing specifically against neo-Confucianism, Ruggieri states that 'heaven and earth are not self-generated'. Other examples: When glossing the First Commandment, Ruggieri attacks fortune-telling, nature worship, and beliefs in dreams and omens, all common practices in Ming China. When glossing the Fourth Commandment, he stresses the concordance between Confucian ideals of filial piety and social order and that implicit in Christianity. Glossing the Fifth Commandment, Ruggieri praises China as a peaceful country, where people go about unarmed, thus avoiding the sin of killing. Explaining the Sixth Commandment, Ruggieri condemns polygamy, a prevalent practice among elite males in traditional China.

According to Ruggieri and Ricci, Wang Pan was pleased with this new work and sponsored a print-run, but he refused to honor it with a preface. Not surprisingly, both Jesuits ascribed a significant role to the catechism in winning converts, who were attracted to the religion of the foreign monks not so much by the critique of Buddhism in the *Tianzhu shilu*, but rather by the affinities between Christianity and Buddhism. It is time we examined the process of conversions, which was after all the sole purpose of the missionary enterprise.

The very first baptism administered in Zhaoqing was to a dying man. The fathers found a pauper on the streets, took care of the terminally ill man, and baptized the grateful poor soul before he passed from this miserable world. The next baptisms, the results of proper instruction, took place during the visit of Francisco Cabral: the neophytes were the young Chen, already acquainted with Ruggieri in 1582/3 and the author of the term Tianzhu as we have seen, and the scholar-tutor of the Jesuits, Ruggieri's collaborator on the Chinese catechism, a native of Fujian province and hence a stranger in Zhaoqing like the Italians, who departed for Beijing for his civil service examination shortly thereafter. Other than these three, Ruggieri and Ricci baptized about twelve converts by October 1586; Ricci wrote: 'Until now we have no more than a dozen Christians, most of them penitents, which in the Chinese context means people who do not eat meat or fish.'[26] Adherence to this strict vegetarian regime, called *shou chang zhai* (keeping the long fast), distinguished the most fervent Buddhist laypeople from the mass of worshippers, the latter refraining from meat and fish only on the first and the fifteenth of every month, and on special Buddhist feast days. In sum, the earliest converts under Ruggieri and Ricci all came from fervent Buddhist devotees; their conversion to Christianity represented not so much a repudiation of 'superstitions' for the 'true religion', as the Jesuits saw it, but rather liturgical and doctrinal substitutions, which preserved a deep structure of emotional and psychological continuity for the neophytes. Furthermore, it was the persona of the Jesuit as 'Indian monk' that facilitated this substitution. To understand this process, we will turn to the career of Ruggieri, the senior priest in the Jesuit China Mission, the pioneer in Chinese studies, who brought Ricci into the enterprise.

5
Ruggieri

With hindsight, it is easy to forget that Ruggieri was in fact the founder of the Jesuit Mission in China, the pioneer in learning Chinese, and the author of the first Christian work published in the Chinese language. In the historiography of the Catholic mission, Ruggieri is remembered only as someone who 'prepared the way for Ricci, who introduced him to China, and then fade[d] away in silence from the scene', to use the words of Pasquale D'Elia, the erudite editor of the *Fonti Ricciane*.[1] Like an older actor in Chinese opera who yielded to a younger and more talented player, Ruggieri eventually retired from the theater of Jesuit missions, his mask and persona replaced by those of the new dramatic star. Amidst the thunderous applause for Ricci, it is time to remember the achievements of the older man.[2]

Unlike Ricci, who would adopt the persona of a Chinese scholar, as we will see in Chapter 6, Ruggieri remained true to his ascribed role as the 'foreign monk'. We have seen that he published the first catechism under his Chinese name, Luo Mingjian, and the title *Tianchu guo seng* (Buddhist monk from India). Ruggieri's identification with the role of the eminent monk was also reflected in his poetry. Seeking to emulate the Buddhist clerical elites (who in turn emulated the Confucian literati, their patrons), Ruggieri composed classical Chinese poetry. Thirty-four poems penned by Ruggieri have recently come to light, and ten of them use Buddhist terms, from the self-identification of Ruggieri as *seng*, to using the commonplace Buddhist terms lotus leaves, moon, and Tianchu. Let us hear the unusual voice of the foreign monk-poet:

Two Poems written while in residence at the Tianzhu si for Some Gentlemen:[3]

> On a small barge I set sail from the seashore,
> And came to China after a three years' voyage;
> Like autumn water my mind is always clear and bright;

Unlike the bodhi tree I am in need of enlightenment.[4]
If you do me the honor to allow me to stay,
Forthwith shall I take up my abode.
And if you ask me about the things of the Western paradise,
My explanation is not that of Buddha Sakya.

Yet, Ruggieri was not just any average Buddhist monk. He was an erudite and exotic monk, whose company the mandarins enjoyed. During one of the banquets when Wang Pan, Zheng Yilin, and their colleagues visited the Jesuits in their charming residence by the river, an occasion to send off Zheng to Beijing for his triennial evaluation, required of all magistrates above a certain rank, Ruggieri presented Zheng with a picture of the Madonna and Child. So impressed by the picture was Zheng, he spontaneously promised Ruggieri that he would take him in his entourage to Beijing. Later, more cautious counsel prevailed—it would be unseemly for a mandarin to bring foreigners to the imperial capital on his own initiative—and Zheng assured Ruggieri instead that he could travel to Shaoxing, the hometown of Zheng and his superior Wang Pan.

Eager for the chance to open a new residence, Ruggieri accepted the offer also for another reason. Appointed Provincial of India, Valignano had dispatched two Portuguese Jesuits, Duarte de Sande and the 28-year-old Antonio Almeida, to reinforce the China Mission, the former as the new superior. They arrived in Macao on 31 July 1585. Ruggieri and Ricci obtained permission for their new superior to travel to Zhaoqing, and later license to reside. To allay local fears that more foreigners from Macao would settle in the city, and in consideration of the small size of their residence, the Jesuits were only too glad for a chance to expand their operations. In early November Ruggieri traveled to Guangzhou. There, he met up with a brother of Wang Pan, a silk merchant from Zhejiang, and helped him unload his merchandise at a good price with the Portuguese traders from Macao. There also, Ruggieri made a rendezvous with Almeida, for whom he had obtained permission to travel as his disciple, and who had arrived from Macao on 12 November, bursting with enthusiasm for evangelization and knowing hardly any words of Chinese.

On 20 November the party departed Guangzhou. The entourage and the merchandise they bought in Guangzhou traveled on several barges on the Beijiang, the North River that provided the major artery of communications in interior northern Guangdong. Although one of the barges caught fire, causing the loss of the personal merchandise of Wang Pan, nobody was hurt. After a leisurely pace of seventeen days on the North River, during which Ruggieri wrote a Chinese poem on a rainy day, to the admiration of their Chinese companions, the party arrived at the northern boundary of Guangdong, where they disembarked to pass over the Meiling, a low ridge separating the provinces of Guangdong and Jiangxi, and the major inland pass connecting China's subtropical south to its central provinces. While servants loaded merchandise onto the back of mules, coolies carried merchant Wang and his monkish associates on sedan chairs up the well-paved but steep path of the Meiling. Ruggieri, a bit on the hefty side, required four men instead of two to carry him across the highest point of the ridge. Descending into the valleys of Jiangxi, the party embarked on three new barges on the River Gan. Passing many walled cities in a fortnight, they reached Nanchang on 17 December. From the capital of Jiangxi province, the party sailed on to Chindezhen, the famous center of Chinese porcelain, whose products were known all over the Portuguese and Spanish empires. After Merchant Wang had made his purchase, the party headed east into Zhejiang province, arriving in Shaoxing after a journey of two months.

This journey made a deep impression on Ruggieri. His memories of it represented the most vivid passages in the journal he wrote after he had left China. In addition to the excitement of travel, accentuated by discovering the novelties of other parts of the vast empire, Ruggieri was pleasantly surprised by their encounters. The people outside of Guangdong seemed to be less wary of foreigners, wrote Ruggieri, and they treated the Jesuits with better respect than in Zhaoqing and just like everyone else, a sentiment echoed by Almeida, who remarked that 'once we got out of Guangdong province, there does not seem to be this amazing anxiety [we used to have], especially since everyone treated us with great respect'.[5]

This respect and amicability extended to an encounter with Buddhist monks. In the last leg of their journey in Jiangxi, just before entering Zhejiang province, on 5 January 1586 Ruggieri's party stayed for three days at Gaoling. Ruggieri remembered: 'A lot of people came to see them, who were convened by a protector of the idols and who was performing rituals in his temple.' This 'idolater', a Buddhist monk no doubt, asked the Jesuits to come to him, where Ruggieri and Almeida saw

many altars with vestments, and many fathers dressed in caps and silk dalmatics reciting prayers and performing their ceremonies. They [the Buddhist monks] received them [Ruggieri's party] with great love and ate with them at a banquet and showed the fathers particular love and reverence. Our fathers [i.e. Ruggieri and Almeida] gave them some copies of the catechism in their language, in which the falsity of the idol is confuted; and it seemed to all of them that this was a most excellent doctrine. And thus our fathers see how the demon imitates the ceremonies of the holy Catholic Church as a mimic in that Father Antonio d'Almeida, the companion of Father Ruggieri, would easily have been deceived into thinking that the painted lady holding the dragon and the moon under her feet could have been the image of the Queen of Heaven, had not Father Ruggieri told him that she was the only daughter of the Emperor of China by the name of Cunn, and that all around in the temple were hung many paintings of miracles, with eyes and feet of silver and gold, such as one would see in the famous churches dedicated to Our Lady in our Europe.[6]

Arriving in Shaoxing, Ruggieri and Almeida met the fathers of Zheng Yilin and Wang Pan, who were respectively 80 and 70 years old. Ruggieri attributed the warmth of the hospitality to their prayer intercession for a sick servant of Merchant Wang, who quickly recuperated during the trip, earning the Jesuits the reputation of wondrous intercession. Old Patriarch Wang played host to the foreign monks, housing them in the lineage hall, a commodious building with tablets of all ancestors, a public space of the extended Wang lineage. Ruggieri and Almeida were assigned two rooms in the compound, with an entrance to a canal in the back and a door to the front street.

Surrounded by rivers that flowed into the city through a network of canals, Shaoxing reminded Ruggieri of Venice. The capital of the ancient state of Yue, Shaoxing was a center of commerce and culture, with a population of over 100,000 in 1586. Like Zhaoqing, Shaoxing also served as an administrative center, housing the prefectural magistracy by that name (*zhifu*), and the county magistracies of Shanyin and Huiqi (*zhixien*). Unlike Zhaoqing, Buddhist monasteries dotted the urban and suburban space; one of these, the Little Nengren monastery, excelled in Chan meditation and provided hospitality for the many pilgrims traveling to the Island of Putoshan, entirely devoted to Guanyin and one of the most popular pilgrimage sites in all of China.

The arrival of two exotic foreign monks was immediately reported by the chief Buddhist abbot to the magistrate. Xiao Lianggan, the *zhifu* of Shaoxing, summoned Ruggieri and Almeida to an audience; impressed with Ruggieri's demeanor, he invited both to a banquet and confided in Ruggieri that he wanted a son. According to Ruggieri, Xiao and his wife came to pray before an image of the Madonna. It worked; Madame Xiao was pregnant in

a few months. This success aside, the Jesuits enjoyed gracious hospitality and
invasive curiosity: so continuous was the stream of visitors that the two
priests found little time to say mass and recite their daily prayers. Everyone
seemed pleased with the foreign monks, including a high mandarin on a
three-year mourning leave in his hometown, who invited the Jesuits to a
banquet and asked Ruggieri for prayers on behalf of his deceased mother. So
pleased was the retired mandarin with Ruggieri that he promised to take
him to Beijing after his period of mourning. This was most probably Sun
Kuang, who had resigned from his post as Vice-Director of the Court of
Imperial Sacrifices (Taichang ci) in Beijing when his mother died in 1584.
The Suns were one of the most prominent families in Shaoxing, distinguished by four generations in imperial service. Sun Kuang's grandfather, an
imperial censor in Nanchang, had died resisting the rebellion of a Ming
prince in 1519 (see Chapter 7); his father had served as Minister of Rites in
Nanjing; his brother and two half-brothers all achieved high mandarin
posts. Since Sun Kuang and Wang Pan succeeded in the *jinshi* examination
in the same year, the two local elite families formed a close bond. Sun
Kuang composed a poem in honor of the Elder Wang's seventieth birthday;
and the father of Wang Pan, no doubt, was proud to show off his western
monks to Sun Kuang. Although Sun Kuang never took Ruggieri to Beijing,
a decade later he would play a key role in promoting the ascent of Ricci.[7]

The Jesuits' social success failed to translate into making converts. One
reason was Ruggieri's mediocre spoken Chinese. In spite of reading proficiency and the ability to compose classical Chinese poems, Ruggieri never
acquired fluency in the spoken language; be it tone deafness or natural
reticence, he was the first of many students of Chinese more expert in text
than in speech. During the six months of their sojourn, the two fathers
gained exactly one convert: the septuagenarian Patriarch Wang, the father
of Wang Pan, a devout Buddhist, who received baptism in spite of the
strong opposition of his family. No wonder that Almeida wrote: 'One life
was not enough for the conversion of China, but ten thousand lives!'[8] It was
this old man who brought a 15-year-old relative to the Jesuits. The teenager
was said to be possessed by spirits (*ran gui*), being lackadaisical and catatonic.
Ruggieri had a different diagnosis: 'it seemed that he had been reduced to a
half-wit and made insentient by too much studying.'[9] The teenager Wang
was just one of many young men reduced to depression and melancholy by
the strenuous preparations for 'examination hell', the major determinant of
social success in traditional China. Young Wang stayed with the fathers.

After Ruggieri instructed the youth in Christian doctrines, he entrusted him to the care of Almeida 'who instructed him with much love and taught him to assist at mass and finally curing him of all his madness'.[10] On other occasions, Ruggieri refused to intervene when called to save other possessed persons, in order 'not to lose credit, because these persons were really mad and not possessed'.[11]

In the spring of 1586, Ruggieri received a letter from Wang Pan, asking the Jesuits to return to Zhaoqing. The memoirs of Ruggieri and Ricci disagree on the reasons for this letter. It was unclear whether Wang Pan recalled Ruggieri and Almeida because his kinsmen complained (they had opposed Patriarch Wang's baptism), or whether Wang felt anxious that the new Supreme Commander, who had just been nominated, would rebuke him for granting too much license to these foreigners. In Shaoxing, Ruggieri and Almeida waited for the return of Zheng Yilin from Beijing, and together, they returned to Zhaoqing, arriving in August 1586. Recalling his adventures in Zhejiang some years later, Ruggieri remembered the time fondly, recalling at length the graciousness and hospitality he had encountered. In contrast, toward the end of his life, Ricci dismissed the interlude as a failure due to the linguistic deficiencies of his fellow fathers. This discrepancy reflected a growing tension between the two men, perhaps resulting from a changed mood at Zhaoqing. After Ruggieri's return, Wang Pan distanced himself from the Jesuits. He asked the fathers not to pay him the usual courtesy call on the first of each lunar month and demanded they remove the frontispieces bearing his calligraphy that graced the entrance to their residence. On one occasion in the midst of other mandarins, Wang Pan pointedly ignored the foreign monks. We do not know the exact reasons for this change of behavior. Perhaps it had something to do with Ruggieri's visit to Shaoxing, or it was caused by Wang's anxiety for his close association with these foreign monks in a time of heightened xenophobia in Guangdong (more on this later). In any case, the symptom of this estrangement expressed itself in an episode recalled by Ruggieri: once Ricci told their patron Wang Pan the exact latitude and longitude of his hometown and was surprised to find that Wang 'was very angry and reprehended [Ricci] for knowing such things'. Missionaries must not be seen by the Chinese to know or describe their country or provinces, Ruggieri concluded, as they would otherwise be suspected of harboring evil intentions of conquest.[12]

While Ruggieri returned to a less hospitable Zhaoqing, Almeida returned to Macao. Meanwhile, Ricci carried on under the authority of his new superior, Duarte de Sande, one of the two Jewish converts who had been nominated rectors of Jesuit colleges in India, appointments denounced by Ricci to the General. If Ricci harbored awkward feelings, he was too discreet to commit them to paper. The documents are silent on their relationship. Once back, Ruggieri became restless again. On the advice of a friend, Ruggieri obtained permission to travel as a pilgrim to Mount Wudan in Huguang province, one of the most famous holy sites of Daoism. Accompanied by a Christian servant and his Chinese tutor, Ruggieri set out first for Guangxi. At Guilin, the provincial capital renowned for its beautiful limestone landscape, he was cold-shouldered by the Grand Coordinator Wu Shan. Turning next to the Prince of Gui, a prince of imperial blood enfeoffed in Guangxi, Ruggieri proffered gifts in the hope of obtaining his patronage. When Wu Shan learned of this, he ordered the foreign monk to leave Guilin immediately. Taking pity on him, the chief eunuch of Prince Gui arranged for Ruggieri to go to the village of Baishui, a fief of the prince in Huguang not far from Guangxi. There, Ruggieri languished for some time until recalled by Duarte de Sande. This trip lasted two months and had accomplished nothing.

Meanwhile, Wang Pan heard of Ruggieri's treatment by the mandarins in Guangxi. Further weighing on him were repeated complaints from mandarins in Guangzhou about the connections between the fathers in Zhaoqing and the Portuguese in Macao. When the Guangdong provincial governor Wu Wenhua received a promotion to Nanjing, Wu Shan from Guangxi was nominated to succeed him, the same mandarin who had driven Ruggieri from Guilin. Anxious for his own position, in November 1587, Wang Pan told the Jesuits to return to Macao, promising to recall them at some future date. Thunderstruck, the three Jesuits beseeched their patron with tears and entreaties, moving Wang to the following solution: Father Duarte returned to Macao; Ruggieri and Ricci stayed in Zhaoqing; and Wang issued a public proclamation to the effect that the foreign monks had built their residence with their own money, that they had contributed nothing to the construction of the Chongxi Pagoda, contrary to rumor, and that they had lived peacefully in Zhaoqing and promised not to bring in any more foreign monks.

As the Chinese saying goes, 'hardly has one wave subsided before the next arises'. This time, trouble came from within the small Christian community. A poor convert from Guangzhou by the name of Cai Yilong (Martin) befriended two converts in Zhaoqing, father and son, who were attracted to Christianity in part by the reputation of the Jesuits as alchemists and worked for the fathers as interpreters. Rumor circulated that the foreign monks never lacked money, a fantasy fed by the Portuguese purchase of mercury in Guangzhou and their importation of Japanese silver. The father, Lu Yuchong, questioned Cai Yilong, who claimed to be close to Ruggieri, whether the Jesuits indeed knew the secret of turning base metal into silver. Cai assured his co-religionist that Ruggieri had promised to pass on the secret, and beguiled greedy Lu into feasting and clothing him, and even buying him a wife. This went on for three to four months with Lu getting more impatient with Cai. Knowing the game was up, Cai went to Ruggieri and borrowed the Venetian prism, on the pretext of showing it to relatives, and fled to Guangzhou, where he hoped to get a good price for the exotic stone. The victims of the trick went to Ruggieri and revealed the whole story, lamenting they had lent Cai their savings. Twice, Ruggieri went to Guangzhou, but Cai was in hiding. Matters came to a head during a visit by Wang Pan and other mandarins, who demanded to view the prism. The fathers had to reveal the theft. Wang then dispatched his men to Guangzhou, who found the hideout of Cai and escorted the trickster back to Zhaoqing prison.

Desperate to save his skin, Cai got some associates to distribute handbills in town accusing Ruggieri of seducing a married woman. He bribed Luo Hung to present a formal grievance against Ruggieri, to the effect that upon returning home from a trip, Luo suspected his wife of adultery and beat her into confessing the crime. The case was adjudicated by magistrate Zheng Yilin, who quickly declared the innocence of Ruggieri. The accusation by Luo Hung (contrived by Cai) simply lacked any credibility: on the date of the supposed adultery, Ruggieri was traveling in Guangxi. Moreover, in the judgment written by Zheng, which the Jesuits copied as an appendix in their Chinese–Portuguese dictionary, the magistrate declared that

Since Luo Hung has never had any dealings with Luo Mingjian [Ruggieri], why would he denigrate his own wife and accuse the foreign monk? Moreover, the South Gate [where Luo lived] is far from the monastery. How can a monk wearing foreign clothes and speaking a foreign tongue go there for liaison without being seen by people along the way? Even if he got there in stealth, he could hardly avoid being heard by neighbors. It is difficult for criminals to escape: he would have been captured and delivered to the magistracy or blackmailed, and not waited to be denounced by a long absent husband . . . And since now Luo Hung does not appear before the magistracy to face the accused, it is clear that Cai Yilong has made the accusation under a pretended name for vengeance, and therefore he is guilty.[13]

Zheng sentenced Cai to a caning and prison, where he died. Once more, calm was restored to the Jesuit Mission.

Throughout these trials and tribulations, Ruggieri maintained an unfailing cheerfulness in his correspondence and in his subsequent memoirs. A different mood seemed to have descended on Ricci, like the heavy, moist, and hot air of southern China. His letters from 1585 and 1586 reveal an individual who felt isolated and melancholic, resigned and lethargic. It was not that Ricci felt lonely: other than Duarte de Sande, the Jesuit residence housed another twelve persons—servants and catechumens dependent on the Society's budget. It was not that he could not communicate, for by 1585 he spoke Chinese well enough that he dispensed with an interpreter, and 'wrote and read fairly well [Chinese] books'.[14] Telling his companion in the Roman College, Giulio Fuligatti, about their adaptations to local ways, Ricci wrote that 'I have become a Chinese . . . in dress, appearance, in ceremonies and in all external things we have become Chinese.'[15] For this reason, as Ricci explained to Acquaviva, 'many say that they [the Jesuits] were almost like them [the Chinese], which is not insignificant in such a closed and proud nation'.[16] And it was not that the consolation of their holy work was denied to them, for in these years the Jesuits made a modest harvest in souls. Ricci wrote of the septuagenarian Nicolai, a fervent convert, who persuaded his extended family to receive baptism, to the joyous tears of the missionary;[17] or Paul, another 'man of penitence, who has refrained from eating meat, fish, eggs, milk for many years in penance, and having seen and read the catechism [Ruggieri's *Tianzhu shilu*], brought his idols and books to be burned, and kneeling before us and kowtowing on the ground begged us to make him a Christian'.[18] Small though the Christian community might have been, some twenty in all, it was a beginning, a seedling, to use Ruggieri's metaphor. Yet, a sadness prevailed in these reports of missionary activities which Ricci addressed to his erstwhile companions in Rome.

Only 33 years old, Ricci already sounded like an old man in his letter to Ludovico Maselli, one of his professors at the Roman College. After reporting on the events and curiosities of the mission, Ricci concluded the letter in protesting to Maselli that:

Even though I am very happy in this place, where obedience has placed me, I cannot help but shed many tears, when I remember Your Reverence, and the golden time that I had spent with you. Since it will be easy to understand how different it is for me now to be in the midst of a people inimical to God, whereas I stood in the caress of Your Reverence and of the other fathers and brothers, who were most dear to me. I console myself in hoping that God will not allow me to fall into any precipice, or that he will lend me his shoulders, after he had taken me away from the maternal nest and made me fly so far away. It seems that I will finish my earthly existence, in the few days that God will grant me, in accommodating myself and loving this land as much as I can.[19]

To his former professor, Ricci might have been putting on a brave face ('I am happy in this place, where obedience has placed me'); to his fellow student, Giulio Fuligatti, Ricci expressed his true feelings, in a letter written only two weeks after that to Maselli. Acknowledging a recent letter from Fuligatti, Ricci thanked his correspondent for awaking the memory of his beloved companions in Rome, 'whose memory helps me a great deal in this sterility, and has refreshed in me some of that good fervor which was formerly born amongst them'.[20] Excusing himself for mixing in Portuguese words and expressions, and for forgetting elegant Italian expressions, Ricci explained that he mixed languages so much that when he wrote in Italian, 'I know not whether it was German or another language. And all would certainly forgive me for this, since I think I have become a barbarian for the love of God.'[21] Finally, Ricci asked his friend to pray for him, 'since I find myself so tepid where it is necessary to go with great fervor, such that I have gained very little in these parts due to my unworthiness'.[22] In the last letter from Ricci extant from Zhaoqing, dated 29 October 1586 and addressed to Maselli, Ricci ended with these words: 'I am, praise be to God, well in body, but not happy with myself, for this is a very grand enterprise, and I wish Your Reverence would recommend me particularly to the Lord.'[23]

The tribulations of 1587 could only have added to Ricci's malaise. Although the case of adultery ended in the vindication of Ruggieri, Lu Yuchong and his son, who had been tricked by Cai Yilong, had not recovered their money, and eventually grew resentful of their employers, the Jesuits. When Ruggieri traveled to Macao at the end of 1587 to allow Duarte de Sande a chance to get back to Zhaoqing (since only two priests were allowed at any one time), the two Lu, who failed to receive monetary satisfaction from the fathers, posted bills in their neighborhood denouncing the illegal residence of de Sande. More nasty was the assault on the Jesuit residence. The flooding in the winter had damaged the dykes on the Xijiang. During the repair work, a gang of workmen started to vandalize the gardens and orchards nearby, on the pretext of looking for wood and other material. When they tried to enter the garden of the Jesuit residence, the ruffians were startled to find a tall and strong African, a servant of the fathers, barring their entrance. Several Indian servants rushed to reinforce the defense. Intimidated by the dark-skinned strangers, the gang retreated out of harm's way. When the inhabitants failed to pursue them, the gang was emboldened and rained stones on the Jesuit residence, breaking windows, knocking down tiles, and damaging the walls. De Sande and an interpreter hurried out the back to alert the magistrates. Fearing an assault, Ricci told the mob they could enter the courtyard of the residence and take whatever material they needed. Strangely, the violence stopped. The men gathered wood and other material and departed without further violence. By the time soldiers arrived, the residence had sustained serious damage. The next day, Ricci asked Zheng Yilin to post a notice on their door, forbidding further attacks. This was not the last time Ricci faced physical danger during his years in Guangdong. Anxious at the latent and overt hostility of the local population, Ricci never quite overcame his distrust of and discomfort with the Chinese masses. Unlike some later Jesuits and mendicant friars, Ricci never developed into an evangelical preacher to the people, being quite content in the company of educated elites like himself, as we shall see in the following chapters.

Yet again, the Jesuits were dependent on the goodwill of the mandarins. Duarte de Sande returned to Macao, where he would continue to exercise his function as superior. He would only return for one more brief stay in China in the summer of 1591, and died in Macao on 4 November 1596.

Meanwhile, at the end of July 1588, Valignano was back in Macao, having arrived from Europe and India with his Japanese youth. Learning of the difficulties in Zhaoqing during the past years, Valignano decided that the best way to secure a firm foundation for the Catholic mission was dispatching a papal envoy to Beijing. Only a diplomatic effort at the highest level could possibly overcome the disdain of the Chinese literati for foreign ways and the xenophobia of the populace.

In spite of his Chinese publications, Ruggieri could not shake off the reputation of being a bad linguist. When Valignano decided in the autumn of 1588 to ask the papacy to send an embassy to Beijing, an idea first suggested by Ruggieri in 1581,[24] he selected Ruggieri; because, in the words of Ricci, 'Father Ruggieri was already old, and could not learn the Chinese language, I [referring to Valignano] choose this good occasion to send him to Europe.'[25] But at 45, Ruggieri was hardly old. Somehow, he seemed to have lost the confidence of his fellow missionaries. Valignano also repeated the same reasons for transferring Ruggieri out of China in a letter to General Claudio Acquaviva, dated 23 November 1588:[26]

Father Michele Ruggieri has worked a lot in this mission and now is going to Rome because it is a chance to give him some rest, especially since he is already old and burdened, and with the workload so heavy, he will get more burdened. And he is leaving here because he does not have good pronunciation of the language; and for this reason Your Paternity should excuse him from returning here, then this mission is not for old and tired men.

Since Valignano did not know Chinese, he must have formed his judgment based on information furnished by Ricci. Clearly, Ruggieri was not held in high regard by his confreres. Already in early 1584, Valignano has selected the Portuguese Duarte de Sande to be the superior of the China Mission, a man more prudent than Ruggieri. Similarly, Francisco Cabral, Rector of the Jesuit College in Macao, thought Ruggieri unsuitable as superior of the Chinese Mission and wrote to Acquaviva that Ruggieri, although very virtuous, 'is more simplistic than necessary and somewhat fainthearted' ('he mais simplex de necessarijo e algun tanto pusilanimo').[27] Compared to Ricci, who made a brilliant first impression, Ruggieri did not cut a good figure.

While Ruggieri was preparing in Macao to leave for Europe, in Zhao-qing, Ricci remained the only westerner after the departure of de Sande. For more than half a year, he managed on his own. The Jesuit residence continued to be a destination of exotic attraction, enhanced now by the addition of a large mechanical clock; its hands and chimes charmed visitors no end. In August, Valignano sent Antonio Almeida to assist Ricci. Shortly thereafter, new troubles arose. On 3 September, a petition reached the mandarins in Zhaoqing. It originated in Guangzhou. Ming law stipulated annual banquets for all virtuous old men, to be hosted by the local ma-gistrates. This year, the ancient honorees submitted a petition to Cai Mongshui, the Provincial Surveillance Commissioner, the *anchasi*, stating their fears of the foreign barbarians in Macao: having established their hold on Chinese soil, the foreigner monks had installed themselves in Zhaoqing and claimed to have built a pagoda, and more of them clamored to enter China and seek permission to send a tribute mission. They feared lest good

government and peace would be undermined by this infiltration of foreigners and their alliance with rebellious elements. The petitioners were clearly
disturbed by repeated attempts by Spanish friars to settle in China. In August
1586, the Franciscan Martin Ignacio de Loyola, who had already failed once,
traveled to Guangzhou with two other friars; all were once again expelled to
Macao in 1587. Also in late 1586 and 1587, Spanish Augustinians and
Dominicans opened new churches in Macao and tried in vain to gain access
to the Chinese interior. Through the chain of magistracies, this petition
arrived in the office of the Zhaoqing Prefecture. Zheng Yilin, the *zhifu* and
Jesuits' friend, was absent in Beijing for his triennial evaluation; his associate,
Fang Yingshi, the *tongzhi*, was sympathetic, told Ricci that Guangzhou had
no business meddling with his jurisdiction, and advised Ricci to compose a
rebuttal. The missionaries had been fortunate so far. But what if a hostile
magistrate held office? A diplomatic overture at the highest level seemed all
the more urgent.

On 20 November 1588, Michele Ruggieri left Macao on a Chinese junk
for Malacca. On a mission to plead for a papal embassy to the Ming court,
unsuspecting that his superior Valignano had already decided he was not to
return with the papal legation, should such a mission be approved in Rome,
Ruggieri carried with him a letter. This diplomatic note, written in Chinese,
was composed by Ricci and a Chinese scholar in Zhaoqing: addressed by the
pope to the Wanli emperor, entitled 'Tianchu Guo Jiaohua huang zhi
Daming Huangdi shu' ('Letter from the King of Morality in India to the
Emperor of the Great Ming'), this letter, which was never delivered, since
the mission failed to materialize, asked the Wanli emperor to allow papal
monks to preach their faith in the Ming Empire. But the text used Buddhist
terms to denote the pope and Catholic priests, thus giving the impression
that the papacy was located in India.[28] This curious diplomatic note made its
way eventually to Paris, where it was discovered and published, more
recently in a sanitized modern Chinese version, which removed all
Buddhist terminologies and replaced them anachronistically with modern
Catholic terms.

After twenty days of sailing, Ruggieri reached Malacca. After a month, he
boarded a Portuguese galleon, which was crowded and dirty. The worms,
disease, and bad weather brought back familiar and unpleasant memories.
His ship finally arrived in St Helena, where it met up with other Portuguese
galleons. Ruggieri enjoyed meeting a fellow Italian Jesuit, Monelato Penati,
who had been a missionary among the Tamils. The six Portuguese ships that

met up in St Helena came from Brazil and India, and they were shadowed by an English fleet. There was great fear on board of the English pirates and heretics. Eventually, the Portuguese decided to make a dash and risk combat. The convoy sailed against contrary winds for seventeen days until provisions ran out. Some thought of returning for victuals, but were dissuaded by the danger of running into the English ships. Then, favored by a tailwind and a contrary one against the English, the Portuguese ships sailed into Lisbon harbor on 13 September 1589.

For three months Ruggieri rested in Lisbon to recover from the voyage. He was the guest of Philip's governor, the Cardinal of Austria, who asked him for information about China. Catarina, the Duchess of Braganza, also honored the China missionary with an audience. Traveling on to Madrid, Ruggieri met the king's ministers before being granted a two-hour audience with Philip II, which was a signal honor. Philip expressed his curiosity about China and marveled at the Indian servant that Ruggieri brought along. Although Philip wanted Ruggieri to linger at his court, he allowed Ruggieri to travel to Rome for the greater good of the mission. By way of Valencia, Genoa, and Naples, Ruggieri finally arrived in the great heat of Rome during the summer of 1589. Graciously treated by all, he was received by Sixtus V and several important cardinals, all expressing great interest in converting China, especially Don Vergilio, nephew of the papal cardinal, who wished to become a China missionary himself, if his uncle gave permission.

The planned papal diplomacy came to naught. Before any actions were undertaken, Sixtus V died in August 1590. The new pope, Urban VII, reigned for only ten days after his election. During the long conclave that led to the election of Gregory XIV, Ruggieri returned to his mother house in Naples. And although the new pope summoned Ruggieri to Rome, Gregory was too distracted by the religious and political crisis in Europe. In France, religious civil wars were raging, and the papacy was compelled to deal with a legitimate but heretical contender for the throne, Henry of Navarre, who eventually agreed to convert to Catholicism and became Henry IV. Philip II, whose patronage was indispensable for Catholic diplomacy to China, suffered enough vexations from the English Protestants and the Dutch rebels. Everywhere, the cries of war drowned out the speeches of diplomacy; and Catholic conquest by the sword took precedence over persuasion by Christian rhetoric. Soon, six years had passed, and China remained just a distant memory, vivid only in the journal that Ruggieri composed, in answering a command from General Acquaviva, his adventures, personality, and experiences relegated to yellowing folios filed away in the vast archive of the Society of Jesus.

Half a world away, Christianity progressed at a snail's pace. Ricci baptized eighteen people during his last year in Zhaoqing. Among the neophytes were the first women converts, several abandoned infants, and a young man scared out of his wits when he traveled at night through a cemetery in the hills. His parents brought him to Ricci after Daoist priests had failed in their exorcism. Judging him not possessed, Ricci rubbed sacred objects on the 'indemoniac'; when the young man recovered, his entire family converted. A more visible sign of success was the popularity of the Jesuit residence. It developed into a proto-museum for the Chinese, similar to the curiosity cabinets and treasure chambers of early modern Europe. Crowds came to gawk at the grand clock, western oil paintings with their strange perspectival techniques, engravings and prints, astronomical and mathematical instruments, western books bound in leather and stamped with golden letters; the more refined visitors examined books on cosmography and architecture, marveled at the geographical novelties depicted on the wall map of the world, and even questioned Ricci about the contents of the books: the countries, politics, customs, and religion of the West. The Jesuits, especially Ricci, served as curators of this fascinating collection of curiosities; their residence was one of the highlights for cultured visitors to Zhaoqing.

Many refined visitors were mandarins. They traveled to Zhaoqing to pay courtesy visits to the Supreme Commander of Guangdong and Guangxi. A continuous flow of mandarins from the two provinces sailed to Zhaoqing on the Xijiang, disembarking at the pier, which was just a short walk from the Jesuit residence. The occasions were many. Every promotion and transfer, every Lunar New Year, each birthday of the Supreme Commander, other feast days, and important official business all brought mandarins in their barges to Zhaoqing, and these exalted officials in sedan chairs to the Jesuit residence. The Jesuits kept a record of their notable visitors. As these mandarins moved into other provinces and higher offices, the Jesuit Mission acquired future patrons and friends. Bit by bit, the Jesuits built up their *guanxi*, their personal network, crucial then and now to advancement on the ladder of success in China. In his memoirs, Ricci listed some of the most prominent men. We will meet them as the time comes. One of them would become a close friend, Qu Rukui, son of a famous minister, who would play a significant role in the next chapter of Ricci's life.

Just as the comings and goings of mandarins structured the life of the missionaries, the procedure of the imperial bureaucracy brought to an end the first Jesuit residence in China. As we have seen, Ruggieri and Ricci depended on the patronage of the Prefect Wang Pan during the first three years of their residence. We have also seen that after Wang Pan's promotion to *lingxidao*, Intendant of the Western Circle, he distanced himself from his foreign protégés. In January 1588, Wang Pan exited altogether from the stage of Jesuit history. Promoted to Provincial Administration Vice Commissioner for the province of Huguang,[29] Wang Pan departed Zhaoqing as a 'good magistrate'; the people created a living shrine to commemorate the many good works of their 'father and mother magistrate'—the remodeling of the Prefectural school, water works, the construction of the Chongxi Pagoda, and the general benevolence of a mandarin who considered the welfare of his charge and not his own gain the primary mandate of his office. The Shrine to Wang was established next to the Chongxi Pagoda, adjacent to the Jesuit residence.

In the shuffle of bureaucratic promotions, the *xunfu* of Guangxi, Liu Jiezhai, was nominated to succeed Wu Shan, who died in office only several months into his tenure. This new Supreme Commander of Guangdong and Guangxi enjoyed a certain reputation, 'second in incorruptibility, only after Hai Rui', thus the comment in the *Veritable Records of the Ming*.[30] Hai Rui, Censor in Nanjing, had just passed away in November 1587. This eccentric, upright, and stern official was famous for his forthrightness, virtue, and uncompromising principles, and his death left behind an impoverished household. Other mandarins might have praised Hai Rui for his incorruptibility, but they were reluctant to follow his impecunious example. 'Hai Rui Number Two' Liu might have been, but Ricci had harsh words for him, describing the new mandarin as 'a cruel, ambitious man, a friend of money'.[31] In light of what happened between the two men, Ricci's judgment is hardly surprising.

Whether a hypocrite or an upright man, Liu Jiezhai was afraid of ghosts. He refused to move into his official residence because his predecessor had died in office. While residing in neighboring Wuzhou waiting for his new residence to be constructed, Liu Jiezhai heard of the Living Shrine for Wang Pan and the beauty of the Jesuit residence. He too desired a Living Shrine, to be located right next to Wang's. In April 1589, Liu Jiezhai ordered the *lingxidao* Wang Shiyu to investigate the foreign monks in Zhaoqing on their extensive contacts with Macao and on their seduction of the people with their novel doctrines; if these charges proved accurate, they were to be removed to Macao or to Nanhua, the largest Buddhist monastery in Guangdong. It was unseemly for foreigners to reside in the same city as the Supreme Commander.

When advised by the sympathetic Fang Yingshi, the Associate Prefect, Ricci wrote to Valignano in Macao advising compliance. But the fiery and dominant Valignano instructed Ricci and Almeida to fight the eviction. It was clear to local mandarins, however sympathetic they felt toward the Jesuits, that resistance to the Supreme Commander was futile. On a trip to Macao, Ricci obtained Valignano's consent: it was better to transfer the residence to another site in China than to lose a foothold altogether. There remained the question of compensation. The Jesuits spent some 600 taels of silver on building their residence, and Liu was offering 50–60 taels in recompense. Ricci refused to accept; and Liu refused repeatedly to grant the foreign monk an audience. During the impasse, the fathers received an unexpected visit from Liu Jiezhai, who was sending off an imperial censor from Beijing. At the last moment, the visiting mandarin expressed a desire to see the European curiosities. The visit went off with the usual courtesies, but it did not mean the retraction of Liu's decision, as Ricci hoped in vain. In August, Liu Jiezhai reprimanded Fang Yingshi, who had been delaying the order to expel his Jesuit protégé. Now, the Supreme Commander instructed that the foreigners were to be sent back to Macao and not allowed to stay in China. The offer of 60 taels was final.

The Jesuits had no choice but to summon their flock for a final farewell. Some seventy weeping Christians came to their residence. Ricci and Almeida left some images and liturgical calendars for the leaders of the community, admonishing them to gather for prayers and promising to return. To the poorer Christians, the fathers gave away furniture and other items too cumbersome for transport. Heavy in spirits, Ricci went to the office of Fang Yingshi to present the keys of the house. Once again, Fang asked Ricci to accept the 60 taels of silver. Ricci declined and wrote a note to that effect upon Fang's request, receiving one in turn from the magistrate testifying to the good conduct of the Jesuits. The two missionaries and their servants then boarded a barge and sailed for Guangzhou.

Ricci and Almeida had to stay in Guangzhou in order to wait for the *haidao* to return for official permission to travel on to Macao. The next day, they were surprised to see a fast boat from Zhaoqing, with a message summoning them to return. Their spirits lifted by this unexpected turn of events, the Jesuits heard rumors for Liu's change of mind: some said his wife had a dream of the foreign gods; others whispered the high mandarin feared the retaliation of the Portuguese. The truth was simple: Liu Jiezhai feared for his reputation when Fang Yingzhi reported on the negotiations with Ricci and showed his superior Ricci's note refusing the money. As 'Hai Rui Number Two', Liu simply could not afford to hurt his reputation by seizing the Jesuit residence without the foreigners accepting any compensation. A Living Shrine befits a good magistrate, not an arbitrary official. Hence, the fast boat, the message of recall. Once again, Ricci explained to Fang Yingzhi, the unwilling intermediary in this whole affair, that the house of God was not for sale. Fang told Ricci to see Liu.

At the audience, Ricci took with him an interpreter, not that he needed one, but for show. After kowtowing, Liu Jiezhai summoned Ricci to approach his desk. In a benevolent manner, Liu asked Ricci why he had refused the money meant for his voyage back to his home country. Ricci replied he had all that he needed; friends and fellow monks would extend their hospitality. 'Even so,' Liu countered, 'it is bad manners to refuse what I have offered.' Ricci said calmly, 'Since Your Excellency has expelled me from this land as a bad person, after I have lived here so many years in peace, there is no reason to accept your gift.' At this, Liu burst out in rage. He stood up and shouted, 'How dare you not do what the Supreme Commander commands!' Turning to the trembling interpreter, Liu cried, 'The reason for all this is this scoundrel who has put him up to it!' He commanded his guards to put the man in chains. The frightened interpreter fell on his knees and clamored that he had nothing to do with this. Undaunted, Ricci continued to speak calmly: 'The interpreter is not responsible; it is I who did not want to. There is no reason for Your Excellency to be angry, for you do not have to show your goodwill by giving me money, which I have little need for, but by sparing me the perils and dangers of the maritime voyage that I had endured once. Even if you do not wish I stay in Zhaoqing, I beseech you to grant another location in China, where I can finish the few days that remain in my life.' Still angry, Liu failed to understand everything Ricci said at first. A guard knelt and repeated Ricci's words. Liu seemed mollified. His anger placated, Liu told Ricci it was not his original intention to expel them to Macao. He promised to send Ricci to another location within his jurisdiction, with the exception of Zhaoqing and Guangzhou. Ricci named the town of Nanxiong in northern Guangdong, just on the boundary with Jiangxi. Liu advised Ricci to look into first the possibility of settling in the monastery of Nanhua or the nearby town of Shaozhou. At this, the audience ended amicably, thanks to the brilliant diplomacy of Ricci. Both sides saved face. While defending his dignity, Ricci managed to placate the powerful magistrate by appealing to Liu's benevolence, expressing his own abject position (perils of sea travel, the few days left in his life), and offering a face-saving solution of little cost to Liu. 'Almost a Chinese', Ricci certainly knew the ways: direct confrontation yielded little or nothing, especially in dealing with those of superior powers; flattery and flexibility paved the way for success in negotiations. Ricci would have made a successful mandarin.

Ricci came out of the *yamen* and saw the consternation on the face of Fang Yingzhi, who had heard the shouts. Their relief at the solution was enhanced by meeting Lu Liangzuo, a magistrate in Shaozhou on an official visit, who had an audience with Liu Jiezhai, now full of praise for the foreign monk. At the sight of Ricci, after Fang's introduction, Lu was dumbstruck for a moment. He then told the two men his wife had had a dream last night in which she saw strange gods, not the usual statues on her altar. That was indeed an omen prior to meeting this strange, foreign monk. Magistrate Lu invited Ricci to travel with him, but Ricci had to attend to a few last things. Once more, he met and consoled the Christians. For the last time, he paid a round of visits to all the mandarins in Zhaoqing, including one to Liu Jiezhai to show his gratitude. On 15 August 1589, the feast day of the Assumption of the Virgin Mary, Ricci and Almeida left Zhaoqing in high spirits, so different from just a short while ago. They looked back at Chongxi Pagoda towering over the bank of the river, and just beyond a glimpse of their first home in China, the images of the past dissolving like reflections of Zhaoqing in the water as their barge sailed beyond the sight of the city.

6

Shaozhou

After eight days on the river, Ricci and Almeida arrived on the banks near Nanhua monastery. Nestled in low-lying crisply green hills alongside a whispering brook, the monastery, founded in AD 502, was made famous by Huineng (638–713), the Sixth Patriarch of Chan Buddhism. A native of Guangdong, the uneducated Huineng, a disciple of the Fifth Patriarch in northern China, received the mantle of dharma succession before returning home to found the School of Sudden Awakening in Chan Buddhism. After its apogee in the Tang and Song dynasties, Nanhua monastery went into a long period of decline. In spite of the unbroken succession of leading Chan Buddhist abbots, Nanhua monasticism reached its nadir between the late fifteenth and the end of the sixteenth centuries. According to a history of the monastery, compiled in the early seventeenth century by the reforming abbot Hanshan Deqing, the influx of laypeople— farmers, shopkeepers, and other fortune-seekers—from the late fifteenth century was the cause. Over time, the land around Nanhua, previously all monastic property, came to be alienated: some was sold to land-hungry peasants, some was occupied by powerful local clans. Right outside the monastic gates, a whole street of commerce developed; the various shops included butchers and gambling houses that offended Buddhist sensibilities. Hanshan Deqing, one of the great Buddhist reformers of the late Ming dynasty, visited Nanhua in 1596. He described scenes of dilapidation and disrepair, a vast and almost empty monastic compound: most of the monks, indistinguishable from the laity, lived in the outside village, some even with wives and children, intermingling freely with laypeople. Only a handful of monks and the abbot still resided in the monastery, guarding the central hall, the Hall of the Sixth Patriarch, where the incorruptible body of Huineng radiated the last aura of Buddhist sanctity.

Still, Nanhua was impressive. It remained the most famous monastery in South China (see Plate V). On the bank, the Jesuits found several Nanhua monks waiting for them. Having been alerted by Viceroy Liu Jiezhai, the monks put on their best faces, while worried that perhaps these foreign monks were entrusted to reform their way of life. Ricci told Almeida to wait with their baggage and servants at the boat and followed his Buddhist hosts up the path toward the monastery. He had already decided not to stay in Nanhua. Since its foundation, the Society of Jesus was an active religious order, finding its spheres of action in cities and courts, and eschewed hermetic monasticism. Eager to show Ricci the treasures of Nanhua, the monks led him through the triumphal arch into the compound, touring the House of Arhats with statues of the four heavenly kings, refurbished only in 1580, then passing into the open-air courtyard before the Hall of Three Treasures, where two tall cypress trees, reputedly planted by Huineng himself, shaded the August sun. Behind the Hall of Three Treasures, the largest structure in the monastery, with its green tile roof, red beams, and golden characters, lies the inner sanctum of Nanhua: the Hall of the Founder, where the incorruptible body of Huineng is kept, with his personal items: a mendicant bowl, an iron walking stick, a ruby prayer bead, a jade ring for the mantle; other monastic treasures included two imperial decrees from the Tang and Yuan dynasties granting favors to the monastery, and three golden-lettered sutras bestowed by higher powers. This was not all. There were other halls and buildings, dedicated to Guanyin, the Fifth Patriarch, and other deities, and rooms for lectures, Chan meditation, and sutra reading. The pagoda, built in the Tang and restored in the Ming, towered over the precinct; from its top floors one could see the Bell Tower and the Drum Tower. Furthermore, wells, bridges, pavilions, unusual rock formations, caves, shrines, and inscriptions graced the hills beyond the monastic walls. All in all, Nanhua was a most pleasant site and a beautiful monastery.[1]

Ricci was indifferent. He only wanted to get away. Paying no attention to the explanations of his guides, he hurried through the various sites like a modern-day tourist eager for the next scenic stop. Puzzled by his behavior, the monks were offended when Ricci refused to show any respect in front of Huineng's body. What kind of monk was this! they probably asked themselves. Good riddance, they thought, when Ricci insisted on continuing to Shaozhou, refusing the monks' hospitality for the night. The bitterness of his expulsion from Zhaoqing must have added to his distaste for Buddhist monasticism. He had no reason to know that his nemesis, Viceroy Liu

Jiezhai, was a patron of Nanhua, who would grant a request for monastic renovations, which were carried out in the winter of 1590/1. To commemorate the occasion, Liu composed an essay, carved on a stone stele, in which Liu praised that:

There is no lack of mutual inspiration between Chan and our Confucian learning. We Confucians say that human nature is good, and that nothing is superior to human nature; they say once you know your heart and understand your own nature, you can achieve instant enlightenment. . . . the principles of the Southern School implicitly agree with our learning. Violent scum and recalcitrant shrews ignore the words of sages and virtuous laws, but they scramble to bow to Buddhism once they hear the Chan teaching of cause and effect, hence Chan is an auxiliary for us Confucians.[2]

In his eagerness to get away, Ricci reached Shaozhou even before Almeida. Imagining a propitious new start, Ricci eagerly absorbed things he heard: the town was double in size to Zhaoqing (it was not), and the inhabitants spoke better Mandarin (which they apparently did); the truth being that it was just another provincial city of no great renown. Shaozhou, known today by the name of Shaoguan, sits at a pivotal site in northern Guangdong. A railway junction on the Guangzhou–Beijing line, Shaozhou is the gateway from Guangdong into Hunan and Central China; another road, a more ancient route, heading to the northeast, cuts across the low-lying Lingnan ridge and links the south with Jiangxi province and eastern China. Squeezed in an elongated neck of land between two river bends and at the confluence of three rivers, the city is located in the wet lowlands of the meandering oxbows, surrounded by jagged and low hills. The surrounding landscape is beautiful, graced by waterfalls, phallic and animal formations of limestone and red sandstone, and mist; the climate, a high humidity characterizing the winter cold and summer heat, and city air trapped between hills, is less than salubrious (Map 4).

In 1589, the walled city of Shaozhou was the administrative capital of the prefecture of the same name and the county magistracy of Qujiang. In the late sixteenth century, some 7,500 households and 45,000 people lived within the city; the population of the entire prefecture hardly exceeded 100,000.[3]

At Shaozhou, Ricci explained to magistrate Lu Liangzuo his refusal to lodge at Nanhua: as educated foreign monks, they preferred urban life and sociability with the literati; moreover, they practiced a different cult from that of Buddhism, a statement confirmed by the Buddhist monks from Nanhua who accompanied the Jesuits, confirming the foreigners' complete lack of interest in their cults and their refusal to honor the relic of the Sixth Patriarch. Magistrate Lu agreed to grant Ricci and Almeida a piece of land

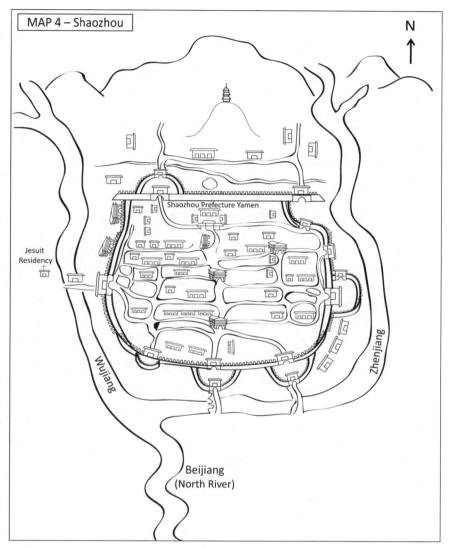

Map 4. Shaozhou

that belonged to Guangxiao monastery located across the Wu River to build their residence. In the meantime, the Jesuits and their servants stayed in a set of rooms in Guangxiao si.

Exhausted by the stress of their last days in Zhaoqing and their recent travels, both Ricci and Almeida fell ill, although both recovered without

major medical intervention. Fortunately, help was on its way. En route to
Shaozhou, Ricci had dashed off a letter to Macao, informing his superior of
the change of fortunes. In late November, three months after their arrival,
Ricci and Almeida welcomed two Chinese from Macao sent by Duarte de
Sande. Huang Mingsha (c.1569–1606) and Zhong Mingren (1562–1621)
were born of Chinese parents, the former in Macao and the latter in
Xanshui, a small town just north of the Portuguese enclave. Baptized at a
young age in Macao, the two Chinese youths studied at the Jesuit College
and imbibed the Luso-Christian culture of Macao. Fluent in Portuguese
(more so than in classical Chinese), Huang and Zhong were known in Jesuit
records as Francisco Martins and Sebastian Fernandes. Sebastian had a
younger brother, Zhong Mingli, baptized as João, who also studied with
the Jesuits in Macao. Unlike the African, Indian, and Malay servants of the
Jesuit Mission, subalterns of the Portuguese, who performed everyday
physical tasks, Huang and Zhong, or Martins and Fernandes, were spiritual
workers and represented the first of many 'sons of Macao' (filhos de Macao), a
term used in a Jesuit record, Christians either of Chinese stock or of Sino-
Portuguese parentage, entirely educated in a lusophone and Christian
environment, and who served in the China Mission as members of the
Society of Jesus. During the first year, Ricci tutored Martins and Fernandes
in classical Chinese and Latin, in preparation for evangelical work. On 1
January 1591, he accepted them as novices of the Company. In their
Chinese personae, Huang and Zhong rendered valuable services, whether
in running essential errands between the interior missions and Macao or in
operating incognito, for no external appearance marked them off from the
Cantonese, 'their brothers in the flesh'. Other than these novices, Macao
also sent reinforcement in the person of an Italian priest, Francesco de Petris,
who arrived in Shaozhou on Christmas Eve 1591. There will be more on
him later in the narrative. For now, let us meet Qu Rukui (1549–1612), a
key figure in Ricci's subsequent success, who became a lifelong friend of the
western missionary.

Qu Rukui met Ricci in Zhaoqing. He recalled their first encounter in a
preface written in 1599 for Ricci's treatise *On Friendship*:

In the Yin chou year of Wanli [1589], I, the ineloquent, was visiting Mount Luo
fou [near Guangzhou]; on the occasion of visiting Viceroy Sir Liu Jiezhai, I met the
Venerable Li [Ricci's Chinese name was Li Madou] in Zhaoqing. The moment I
saw him, I was struck by his look of distinction. And when Sir Viceroy moved Li
to Shaozhou, I happened to be passing through Nanhua Monastery and again

encountered him. Thus, I studied mathematics and astronomy with him for two years before departing.[4]

A chance meeting, but that was not the whole story.

A native of Changshu, near Suzhou, roughly half-way between Shanghai and Nanjing, Qu Rukui, literary name Taisu, hailed from a famous literati-mandarin family. His father, Qu Jingzhun (1507–69), obtained the highest score among the 300 elite candidates in the 1544 capital civil service examination, and placed number two in the palace examination. He rose in rank to Left (First) Minister of Rites in Nanjing, and served as editor-in-chief of several prestigious imperial book projects, including an edition of the Encyclopedia compiled under the Yongle reign (early fifteenth century). As a Hanlin academician, a forthright man, and an elegant stylist, Qu Jingzhun enjoyed a high reputation among his mandarin peers. Four sons from three wives were born to this high mandarin: one died young; two, Ruzi (1548–1610) and Rushuo (1565–1623), followed their father's path of success in examination, although they never rose to the same exalted mandarin rank; Ruzi, the oldest son, also acquired a distinguished reputation as a major lay intellectual and supporter of Buddhism; only Rukui was absent from the roster of fame. In fact, Qu Rukui, Ricci's admirer, was struck from the family lineage; his name is not even mentioned in his father's biographical entry in the dynastic history of the Ming dynasty.

A black sheep of the family, Qu Rukui later told his story, which Ricci summarized in his memoirs:

This one son [of Qu Jingzhun] was even more brilliant than his brothers, and if he had continued his studies, he could have easily gained high offices and honors. But in the prime of his youth (his father, who had held him in restraint, having passed away), he was led astray. Among his bad inclinations, he wanted to learn the art of alchemy, losing thousands of taels of silver in the process, including his patrimony. Reduced thus to poverty, he left his home with his wife and servants, wandering about China, living here and there, wherever he could find mandarins who were his friends or those of his father. He lived well enough on the gifts he received from them, or from people who wanted him to secure a favor from the magistrates, this being a way of life among the gentry.[5]

Qu Rukui, in other words, was living off his father's reputation and the network of *guanxi* that got things done in mandarin society. That was the occasion of his visit to Viceroy Liu Jiezhai in Zhaoqing, a friend of his father, and to Huang Shiyu, the *linxidao*, who was from his hometown, in the hope of some favor and patronage. Besides Ricci's distinguished airs, Qu Rukui was no doubt attracted by the Jesuits' reputation as alchemists, experts in the fabrication of silver, a dubious renown that had led to the accusation of adultery, in Ruggieri's case, as we have seen in the last chapter. Frantic attempts to save the mission, and the preparations for departure, cut short any time for friendship to develop. After Ricci left, Qu Rukui stayed on in Zhaoqing, but ignored by the viceroy, he decided to depart as well. In Shaozhou, Ricci quickly disabused Rukui of his alchemical notion. Nevertheless, Qu fell under the charisma of Ricci, and became fascinated by western mathematics and astronomy. He took a room in the same Buddhist monastery that was the missionaries' temporary residence, and beseeched Ricci to accept him formally as his disciple. From the start, Qu Rukui turned out to be a brilliant student of European science and gradually got interested in European religion.

This, in short, is Ricci's narrative of his early association with Qu Rukui. But that was also not the entire story. The real story of Qu Rukui's youth, hidden from family records and revealed by Rukui to no one, not his master Ricci, not his friends, was only unearthed in recent historical scholarship.[6] In the early 1570s, Rukui, a dashing young man in his twenties, had seduced his sister-in-law. This scandal was all the more odious since it occurred within the three-year mourning period of his father's death. The object of his adulterous attention was the wife of his half-brother, the eldest son Ruzi, daughter of the retired Nanjing Minister of Works, Xu Shi, a colleague and friend of his late father. A woman in an arranged marriage between amicable and prestigious literati families, young Xu was doomed to unhappiness. Her husband Ruzi was described by contemporaries as 'very short in stature like a dwarf', measuring somewhere between four feet four and eight inches. A contemporary portrait depicts him as a thin-faced and less than handsome man. Unattractive physical features aside, Qu Ruzi was a devout Buddhist, who preferred celibacy to passion. His Buddhist beliefs reinforced by Confucian filial piety, Ruzi carried things to extremes and refrained from intercourse with his wife during the three years of ritual mourning. A scandal in any event, this adultery was especially odious in a Confucian society that prized proper family relations above all else. When the liaison came to light, Qu Ruzi repudiated his wife. Retired Minister Xu sent an assassin after the seducer and only relented when Rukui proclaimed his guilt in front of the outraged father; in the Qu family, Rukui's name was deleted from the lineage record; he left Changxu in shame.

At Shaozhou, Qu Rukui threw himself wholeheartedly into his new studies. After easy introductory lessons in western arithmetic, Rukui was the first Chinese to learn European cosmology and Greek geometry. On the first subject, Ricci used the textbook by his Roman professor, Christoph Clavius, whose *Commentary on the Spheres of Bosco* represented the most widely read cosmological text until the seventeenth century. In the textbook, Clavius provided detailed explanations and commentaries on the succinct treatise by Johannes de Sacro Bosco, a mid-thirteenth-century astronomer and professor at Paris, who described an earth-centered universe with fixed stars moving on solid spheres, a synthesis of Greek astronomy and Christian doctrines. On geometry, Ricci lectured on Euclid's *Elements*, teaching Rukui three-dimensional geometry. In time, Rukui was making sundials, measuring heights and distances, and knew all about spheres, astrolabes, quadrants, clocks, and other European instruments.

At 40 and 37 years old, Qu Rukui and Matteo Ricci were not just disciple and master, but friends in mid-life who glimpsed reflections of brilliance and an independent spirit in one another. Their elective affinity led from mathematics and science to ethics and religion. Between lessons in cosmology and geometry, Master Ricci discoursed little by little on Christian doctrines: the existence of an omnipotent God, the creation of the universe, the making of humankind, sin and redemption, and the moral precepts of Christianity. Disciple Qu stayed away three to four days; he returned with a small treatise listing all the difficulties he encountered in Christian doctrines. Astounded by the questions, which seemed to anticipate the major themes of Christian theology, Ricci composed a response so reasonable and persuasive that Qu Rukui was ready to accept the western faith. One impediment, however, stood in the way. With his wife, who had recently died, Rukui had only one daughter. He had taken a concubine, hoping to have a son; but he hesitated to marry her due to her low birth. In 1591, his first son, Shigu, was born. In time, both father and son would receive baptism, as we shall see.

At Shaozhou, daily life for the mission repeated the pattern of Zhaoqing: cultivating the goodwill of the mandarins, facing the hostility of the common people, and evangelizing and ministering to a small Christian flock. Having Qu Rukui as disciple boosted Ricci's prestige among the local elites. He hobnobbed with the ruling elites: Xie Taiqing (*zhifu* of Shaozhou), Liu Wenfang (*zhixien* of Qujiang), Huang Men (like Qu Rukui also a Changshu man and his former tutor), and Wang Yinlin (literary name, Yuzha), *zhixien* and *tongzhi*, magistrate and assistant magistrate of neighboring Nanxiong

County), and finally, Su Daiyong, magistrate of Yingde County to the south. In years to come, several of these men would play a role in furthering Ricci's career, spreading the word of his fame, erudition, and publications, as they advanced on the ladder of mandarin promotion.

Su Daiyong extended an invitation to visit Yingde. Every occasion the mandarin visited Shaozhou, he paid courtesy to Ricci and entreated him to visit his district, only three to four days by boat to the south on the North River. At first reluctant, anxious over Viceroy Liu's reactions, Ricci was convinced by these words. The father of Su Daiyong, 72 years old, who was visiting his son, desired fervently to meet the foreign monk. As a child, Old Man Su had his fortune told: at 60 he would remarry, and at 70 he would meet a distinguished man from a foreign country, a harbinger of good fortunes. For years Father Su dismissed the predictions; one wife was enough for him. Alas, at 60, he lost her and remarried. Thus, when he heard of the fame of the foreign monk Li Madou, he asked his son, the magistrate, to arrange a meeting.

Qu Rukui accompanied Ricci on this trip. A friend of Su Daiyong, he also did not want to miss any lessons with Ricci. The party stayed in Yingde for three to four days enjoying the warm hospitality of Magistrate Su. Father Su was delighted to meet Ricci and listened to his expositions of Christian doctrines. The old man asked immediately for baptism, but the Jesuit thought a bit more instruction was in order. Ricci promised to continue catechism instruction in the old man's hometown of Ningdu, near Ganzhou in Jiangxi, and gave him a medallion of Christ to wear around the neck. With Magistrate Su as their host, the party visited a local scenic spot a short distance south of the walled city: Bilou Cave, a subterranean stalactite lake, in the midst of a limestone forest. There, they met Wang Yinlin, Assistant Magistrate of Nanxiong, who was showing the local scenic highlights to a high mandarin, a Censor from Beijing. Magistrate Su arranged for a banquet and musical entertainment for the outing. Qu Rukui composed a long seven-character poem, 'A Song of Bilou', to commemorate the occasion. After verses describing the ascent of steep paths, 'their walking sticks pointing like dragons into the air', Rukui wrote that 'the western monk (xi seng) could also ascend in flight'. This first description of Matteo Ricci in a Chinese text intrigues with Rukui's verses celebrating the banquet. With libations set up amidst cascading water, cool breeze, flickering light, and floating clouds, Rukui expounds on the dharma (fa) before the 'Old Dragon', while the foreign monk looks intently without uttering a word. We do not know whether Qu Rukui was referring to the doctrines of Buddhism or Christianity with his word 'fa'; the 'Old Dragon' was likely a reference to Old Man Su. And Ricci, the 'foreign monk', sat in enigmatic and intense silence.[7]

Disciple he might have been, but Qu Rukui interceded with the magistrates on behalf of Ricci on important occasions. A little over a year after settling in Shaozhou, Antonio d'Almeida fell gravely ill, his health ruined by extreme ascetic mortification of the flesh and the damp cold of winter. At the end of 1590, Ricci sent one of the Macaoese Jesuit brothers to take Almeida to Macao for medical treatment. At Chinese New Year, Ricci displayed on the altar of the church a depiction of the Madonna and Child, and the apostle John, a framed painting from Mexico. While this novelty attracted many curious visitors to the Jesuit residence, it also provoked a nocturnal attack. One night, a gang threw stones on the tiles of the Jesuit house. When the servants of the residence went out to investigate, they were set upon and beaten up, returning with torn clothes and light injuries. When Qu Rukui found out, he wanted to alert Prefect Xie Taiqing right away. Ricci hesitated, reasoning that he was hoping to request permission for Francesco de Petris to travel from Macao as Almeida's replacement; he was anxious not to appear too demanding. Qu Rukui insisted: the culprits would be emboldened if Ricci failed to notify the authorities. He himself alerted the Prefect of the assault. Enraged, Xie summoned the two *lijia*, the neighborhood heads who were charged with maintaining security by the magistrates, gave one a bastinado, and demanded they arrest the culprits. That was an unenviable task. The two men knew the identities of the culprits: the toughs were all neighborhood youths; some came from important families. Not wishing to antagonize their neighbors, the two *lijia* did nothing until two servants of Ricci happened upon one of the young men and brought him by force to the *lijia*. Afraid they would be turned over to the magistrate, the family of the youth pleaded with Ricci, who decided to demonstrate Christian charity by forgiving the assault. Thus, the two *lijia* reported to Magistrate Xie that they were unable to determine for certain the identities of those who had committed the assault. Angered by this report, Xie ordered a severe beating for one man and threw the other in jail. More fearful of the magistrate's ire than their neighbor's disapproval, the two men revealed the names. The chief culprits fled. Ricci pleaded with Xie. And Qu Rukui succeeded in getting a travel permit for a Jesuit father from Macao.

Instead of de Petris, it was Duarte de Sande who traveled in July to Shaozhou with the safe-conduct. As superior of the China Mission, he wanted to inspect conditions at first hand, but as Rector of the Jesuit College, he could only be absent for three months. Still convalescing, Almeida yearned to return to his mission post. Shortly after his return, the still enfeebled Almeida fell feverish. Francisco Martins, the Chinese brother, nursed the sick priest, since Sebastian was also bedridden with fever. From time to time, Ricci came to relieve Brother Francisco, and consoled the Portuguese missionary that he was dying within the Company and in the mission field, for the good of his soul. After seven days, Almeida died on 17 October, at the age of 34. Moved by Almeida's great devotion in his last days, Martins wrote a long letter to Duarte de Sande reporting on the saintly death. Among the things Almeida left behind, Ricci found seven little books, spiritual diaries, which recorded the young Jesuit's spiritual journey. Ricci gave two of these to Francisco Martins for edifying reading. At the news of the death, several mandarins came to give their condolences, as did the monk-official and chief Buddhist monks of the city. The Chinese disapproved that the Jesuit household wore white mourning garments for only a few days, notwithstanding the explanation that the passage of a priest, already dead to the world, from the vale of tears to his eternal reward was not an occasion for mourning. Since Chinese customs forbade intramural burials, Almeida could not be buried next to the church. And since Ricci did not wish to see his fellow Jesuit entombed on a hillside outside of town, which was the custom of the Chinese, the body of Almeida rested in his coffin within the residence for two years before it was shipped back for burial in Macao. In this, at least, the Jesuits kept their death rituals in conformity with Chinese practice.

On 8 December 1591, Francesco de Petris set out from Macao. Ricci began once more to train a younger colleague in the language, customs, and learning of the Chinese. In the spring of 1592, Liu Jiezhai passed through Shaozhou on his way north. He had been promoted to Vice Minister of Revenue in Nanjing.[8] Ricci took de Petris to pay a courtesy call, and Liu reminisced with Ricci on the old days at Zhaoqing. Courteous on the surface, in his heart Ricci had not extended Christian forgiveness to the viceroy. Later in the year, Liu was dismissed from office. He died at home, peacefully, according to a biographical collection published in 1622, badly, according to hearsay passed on by Ricci, who told the anecdote of the old man asking in vain for some water, while his sons and nephews argued over the division of his property.[9] 'It seems that God wants to show that even in this life he can punish the injustice that was inflicted on the fathers in

Zhaoqing,' commented Ricci. Liu Jiezhai had turned the Jesuit residence into a Living Shrine for himself, desecrating the temple of God with 'statues of idols'. Like the Chinese he so resembled, Ricci also knew how to harbor bitterness in his heart while showing all suavity and urbanity to the world.

Ricci's bitter memory faded with the experience of success, thanks to his friendship with Qu Rukui. Sixty miles and three days journey to the east of Shaozhou and close to the border with Jiangxi province lies Nanxiong, a thriving commercial town, where northerners came to do business in Guangdong. There, Qu Rukui told one of his associates, the 60-year-old Guo, all about the teachings of the foreign monk Ricci. A successful merchant employing some forty workers, Merchant Guo was a devout Buddhist for most of his adult life. Keeping a permanent Buddhist vegetarian fast, Merchant Guo was adapt at Chan meditation and all Buddhist rituals. Yet, spiritual consolation seemed to have eluded him. Hence, Merchant Guo visited Ricci in Shaozhou. His fervent desire to learn things about the afterlife and the soul greatly edified Ricci. After several days of intense catechism, Ricci baptized Guo, giving him the name of Giuseppe. As a former devotee of Chan meditation, Guo was the first Chinese Christian to practice the *Spiritual Exercises* of Ignatius Loyola under the guidance of Ricci. Guo stayed with the Jesuits for one month before business recalled him to Nanxiong.

One day, during Guo's stay, the old merchant came to Ricci in tears to bid farewell, saying he was going to die. Startled, Ricci inquired: 'You are not yet old and in good health. How do you know your time is up?' Guo explained: 'When I was fifty-five, I met a master in astrology, who told my fortunes and made predictions for the next five years. Although the good things he predicted did not necessarily happen, all the bad things came true. He told me I shall die before the middle of the fourth month in my sixtieth year. Well, this month I had a dream and saw various bad omens. Hasn't the augury been proved? Alas! Only at sixty do I get a son; and who will take care of this crying baby? I am so sad!'

Ricci sighed. He stamped his foot in frustration and tried to comfort the pitiful old man: 'There is nothing more empty and wrong in this world than the predictions of astrologers and the things we see in dreams.'

Guo countered: 'You see the signs, how can you not believe?'

Ricci explained that while there might have been coincidences, most predictions were wrong. Good and bad fortunes, he continued, resulted from right and wrong, acts which fell within our control. Human will was stronger than the stars. To avoid evil, one had to forsake evil and turn to virtue. For those who refused to repent and still hoped to be spared punishments, even if astrologers might allow it, the Lord of Heaven would not consent! Ricci then used the moral teachings of Confucianism to strengthen his point: did loyal officials and pious sons recoil from death and danger in serving their country and families in crisis, or did they first consult astrologers? Exposing fortune-tellers and astrologers as frauds, Ricci asked why they did not enrich themselves first if they were so clairvoyant, instead of preying on the credulity of the ignorant and anxious. Similarly, dreams were absurd; even if a few seemed true, they were not real.

Still not wholly convinced, Guo said: 'In the past I had never believed in astrologers, but all the things predicted by this master during these past five years came true. How can it be coincidence?'

Ricci sighed: 'Do you know how these misfortunes in the past years came about? He told you and you accepted it. If he told you nothing, you would not believe, and no misfortune would have happened. So, the fact that you asked him to tell your fortune has caused you misfortune.'

Startled, Merchant Guo asked: 'Why?'

Ricci said that after he came to China, he was appalled by the popular credulity in astrology, fortune-telling, and geomancy. But if Guo was willing to listen to him, he could save his life. To an expectant and eager Guo, Ricci explained that the human heart was the central organ in the body, and the worst affliction on the heart was fear itself. If one believed in predictions of good fortune, one would rejoice, even if rejoicing could not produce the good things of life. However, if one believed in prediction of misfortune, one would worry; and anxiety led to illness, hence fulfilling the prediction. Ricci then used the metaphor of someone walking on a narrow strip of wood. If the wooden strip was placed on flat ground, nothing would happen, but if it were balanced at a high point, the walker would assuredly fall. Reinforcing his psychological analysis, Ricci added a story about a physician who told a prisoner he was bleeding when he was not, and the man died from his belief without suffering any wounds. Finally, Ricci invoked the authority of the Confucian classics, citing sentences from the *Spring and Autumn Annals*, the *Yiqing*, and from the *Shuqing* to argue that divination, as it was practiced in antiquity, was used as a last resort to decide between two options in statecraft and had nothing to do with fortune-telling.

This conversation demonstrated Ricci's enormous powers of persuasion. Having stated his argument by brilliant reasoning, Ricci cited the ancient

Chinese classics as unassailable authority and used vivid and interesting examples from the West, drawing from his large repertory of humanistic texts, from Graeco-Roman antiquity to the Christian past. In future years, Ricci would develop this rhetoric to perfection. Toward the end of his life, when Ricci recorded this episode in his book, *Jiren shipian, Ten Discourses of the Man of Paradox*, he recalled that not only did Merchant Guo father a second son at the age of 64, but he was still alive and well in his late seventies.[10]

At Lent 1592, which coincided with Chinese New Year (*c.* 12–14 February), Ricci took Francisco Martins on a visit to Nanxiong to baptize Guo's only son. The Jesuits stayed with Qu Rukui and paid a courtesy visit to Wang Yinlin, the Assistant Magistrate, who was in charge of Nanxiong in the absence of the *zhixien*. When Magistrate Wang returned the visit the following day, showing Ricci great courtesy, it was a signal for all the notables in Nanxiong to rush and meet the distinguished guest. The street in front of Qu Rukui's house was crowded with sedan chairs and carriages. Here, we have the Matthew principle in action ('more blessings will be given to the blessed'): in China, once a relationship is established with some notable person, other connections with power-holders will come; once the entrance to the majestic mansion is opened, all the doors to inner courtyards, gardens, corridors, and chambers will open. This pattern of success, so sweet to the missionary, would be repeated in coming years when Ricci ascended the ladder of social success in Ming society, moving from provincial backwater to provincial and imperial capitals.

Of equal comfort to Ricci was the visit to Merchant Guo, where many people, 'lesser in dignity but superior in virtue', to use Ricci's pithy formulation, came to hear him discourse on salvation. Ricci spent days talking, sometimes until midnight, and hardly had time to eat or say prayers. At the end of an intensive week of catechism, Ricci baptized six catechumens, who showed the greatest understanding of Christian doctrines, including a brother and some relatives of Merchant Guo. He also baptized four young sons of the neophytes. There would have been many more baptisms, Ricci informed Claudio Acquaviva in a letter written on 15 November, had the Chinese not believed, erroneously, that to receive baptism meant forsaking home and family, becoming a religious hermit, just like becoming a Buddhist cleric. Nevertheless, this represented a major coup of Christian triumph, for the Jesuits had made only six to seven converts in Shaozhou after their arrival, and a couple of these came from afar, including a cousin of the Chinese Jesuit brother Sebastian Fernandes (Zhong Mingren). By Christmas 1592, the

mission counted twenty-two converts, of whom ten were those baptized in
Nanxiong. Ricci observed that most of the people in Merchant Guo's coterie
hailed from other provinces. He concluded that 'it is true what they say that
in other provinces of China there are many more people who believe in the
immortality of the soul and try to procure their salvation'. To the General,
Ricci expressed the hope that once they got out of Guangdong into other
provinces, they would make many more conversions.[11]

Not wishing to leave the inexperienced Francesco de Petris alone for too
long, Ricci returned to Shaozhou. Under Ricci's mentoring, de Petris
advanced quickly in Chinese. By mid-November, as he informed General
Acquaviva, de Petris could speak and read enough Chinese to receive visitors
by himself. An astute observer, de Petris analyzed in detail the major
impediment to conversion in China: the prevalence of polygamy. It was
impossible to persuade the notables to convert, for almost all elite men took
concubines. De Petris asked the General for permission to baptize those men
who kept a vegetarian fast and did not reside with their wives or concubines.
This contradiction between Christian morality and Chinese social practice
would run as a constant theme in the history of the Christian mission.

One midnight in July, the inhabitants of the Jesuit residence woke up to
loud noises. Thinking to scare off the thieves, the fathers and their servants
headed toward some dark shadows in the garden, and were startled to find
about twenty intruders armed with choppers, torches, and other weapons.
In the mêlée, two servants received serious wounds. The intruders also cut
de Petris in the head with a chopper. Without a single weapon and out-
numbered, Ricci ordered his men to retreat behind the corridor and
attempted to lock the door leading to the inner compound. Sliced in the
hand, Ricci and his men could not hold the door. They fled into their rooms
and barred the doors. A young student went upstairs and started throwing
tables onto the intruders below. Climbing out of a window, trying to get
help, Ricci fell and injured his foot. Unable to move, he shouted loudly to
alert the neighbors. No one came. Alarmed by the commotion and by the
violence they had caused, the intruders quickly fled in the direction of
Guangxiao monastery.

The next morning, the Jesuits reported the armed assault. The magistrate
suspected the neighborhood, since nobody came to the aid of the Jesuits. He
arrested some men, put one under judicial torture, and got a confession: the
intruders, bad youths in the neighborhood, had lost money gambling and
thought they could rob the Jesuit residence; several of them were culprits in

the stoning incident last year. The magistrate further arrested a dozen youths. In spite of the petitions of their relatives and Ricci's plea, he sentenced the ringleader to death, and various prison terms and bastinados for the gang members and the *lijia*. In between the many judicial sessions, which Ricci had to attend, he was bedridden with his injured foot. Meanwhile, Magistrate Wang from Nanxiong sent herbal medicine; and a military officer posted troops to safeguard the residence. Convinced there would not be another assault, his enemies now sufficiently intimidated, Ricci worried about the harsh sentencing; an execution would nourish vengeance.

The stress was enormous. It showed in a spate of letters written by Ricci in mid-November, in the middle of the trials. After receiving a letter from Fabio de Fabii, his Master in the Novitiate, with whom he had not been in contact, Ricci expressed his great joy that de Fabii, 'occupied by so many important matters at the capital of the world [could] still remember vividly this poor one, who is doing less than nothing here, at the end of the world'. The letter from Rome was a great consolation for Ricci, who 'stood in this desert so far from his spiritual fathers'. Summarizing his adventures after his departure from Rome, Ricci stated that to recount 'all that we have suffered because of this people [the Chinese] in the six or seven years that we have been here would be much longer than the limit of a letter'. Ricci then recounted the accusation against him of kidnapping children, the worse one against Ruggieri, leaving out the specific charge out of discretion, the many suspicions of spying, the denunciation by the elders of Guangzhou, the assault on their house, and the daily insults on the streets of Zhaoqing. Then came the ultimate tribulation, the expulsion from Zhaoqing. And although the people of Shaozhou seemed more benevolent, Ricci had already lost his companion of three years, Almeida; and both he and his new companion de Petris had been injured in a recent assault. How Ricci wished that 'if it pleased his divine majesty, all of this would end with a felicitous death, like the one of Rodolfo Acquaviva...'[12] But like so many missionaries, Ricci's fate was to suffer the 'white martyrdom' of exile and hard work, not the glorious shedding of blood.

Indeed, Ricci had death on his mind. He was reminded of mortality and exile by a letter from Geronimo Costa, his boyhood friend from Macerata, also a Jesuit, informing him of affairs at home, including the recent death of his grandmother Laria. He received the news sometime after the assault, still bedridden with his badly twisted foot, and had not said mass for many days.

But now, 'remembering with great tenderness the love she showed me when I was a small boy, and for a time when she raised me like a second mother', Ricci wrote in a letter to his father Giovanni Battista, he forced himself out of bed to say three masses for her soul. In this letter, Ricci excused his failure to write every year. He had written a very long letter after leaving home, but had not received any letters from home in all these years in China. And even though his friend Costa kept him abreast of news at home, not a single letter from his father Giovanni Battista or his brother Antonio Maria had come into his hands.

Words from home would have comforted him in his mission, trying to 'lead back to their creator this people who are so far from the path'. The Chinese are a 'people with great aptitude but very little interest for their salvation'. As for himself, Ricci asked for prayers from his father and brothers. And for them, Ricci 'pray[s] to God, that full of years and good works, they will go and enjoy eternal happiness', adding that 'although we live in life so far from one another, may we be worthy of being together at the eternal tabernacle after death, since in the end this miserable life is so short that it matters little whether we are together or apart'. Ricci told his father that it was his wish his mother frequent the Jesuit church, and closed the letter reminding his father of preparing one's life for eternity: 'If there is one thing that I desire to see you about, it would be to speak with you about this matter.' Ricci signed his letter 'Your most loving son in the Lord'.[13]

The magistrates in Shaozhou sent Ricci to Zhaoqing in early December, where the *anchasi*, the Provincial Surveillance Commissioner, had to confirm the sentencing. Ricci used the opportunity to exhort his Christian flock, and baptize five children who had been born to the converts after his departure. While in Zhaoqing, Ricci received a letter from Valignano, who had arrived in Macao from Nagasaki, summoning him for a conference on the state of the mission.

During the month-long stay in Macao, Ricci briefed Valignano extensively on the China Mission and recuperated from his injuries. Ricci was also overjoyed to see Oliviero Toscanelli, his fellow Maceratan, a Jesuit brother and traveling companion and assistant to Valignano. The Portuguese doctors, however, could do little for his foot. Valignano, who always had a good impression of Ricci, judged him to be someone 'of great talents, judgment, and prudence, with good literary distinctions, virtuous, and a very good worker, who is now already serving our Lord, and in time, hopefully, even much more'. And even though Ricci had no administrative experience, Valignano considered him capable of governing a college or a residence.[14]

In February 1593, Ricci returned to Shaozhou. The culprits were still languishing in jail and their families were afflicted. Their only hope was for a reprieve. Ming law stipulated that all death sentences in the country had to be confirmed by the Ministry of Justice in Beijing. Autumn was the season for executions. Relatives of the condemned anxiously awaited the arrival of the Imperial Censor, the *chayuan*, who possessed final authority. On 3 October, more than fifty of them swore to fight the sentences. They composed a petition, addressed to the *chayuan*, complaining that the presence of the foreigners from Macao was the direct cause of local disturbances, and that their expulsion would restore peace. After several mandarins refused to accept their petition, they found a magistrate willing to pass on their grievance to the *chayuan*: Assistant Prefect Guan Gu disliked the Jesuits and was apparently a political rival of some mandarins who were friendly to Ricci.

When Ricci learned of this grievance, he conveyed a message to his enemies: they would only make matters worse for the fact of the assault was indisputable; it was Ricci who had been pleading for leniency on behalf of the condemned. At this, the complainants withdrew their petition. Ricci was true to his word of Christian charity. Thanks to his intercession, the *chayuan* commuted the capital punishment and prison sentences to twenty bastinados for each of the condemned. The enemies of the Jesuits, however, were not impressed when Ricci turned the other cheek. The day after the release of the imprisoned men, more than 200 went to see the *chayuan*. Accompanied by Assistant Prefect Guan, they demanded to submit a petition for the expulsion of the Jesuits. Already preparing to leave Shaozhou, the *chayuan* refused to receive the crowd. Such an important matter cannot be left to the point of departure, the *chayuan* chastised the petitioners, but must be submitted at the beginning of the inspection. He left Shaoshou on 28 October. The implacable hostility of his neighbors, 'their ingratitude', to use Ricci's words, was one of the most unpleasant shocks in his life.

Anno horribilis. On 5 November, Francesco de Petris died. It was all very sudden. In robust health, de Petris was only 31 years old. He came down with fever. To the others, it seemed like routine illness. But de Petris sensed death. After Ricci had heard his confession, de Petris got up from bed, placed his arms around Ricci's neck, and in words choked back with tears, asked Ricci to stay with him for a bit longer. Stunned by this, Ricci was momentarily at a loss for words. He then consoled the younger companion, saying the illness was not fatal, that he need have no fear. But de Petris replied: 'I know what it is; there is no avoiding it.' This lugubrious scene was not helped by the presence of Almeida's coffin in the residence; for two years, Ricci had been waiting for a resolution from Macao concerning the burial of Almeida. De Petris apologized to Ricci that his death would cause even more trouble, for Ricci would have two dead bodies to deal with. A few days after this conversation, de Petris died.

Ricci's melancholy was compounded by the double loss in two years. He seemed genuinely fond of his younger countryman. Francesco de Petris was born in the village of Farfa outside of Rome and enrolled as a young pupil at the Roman College. His life resembled that of Ricci's in many ways. De Petris joined the Society in 1583 as a young student of 21. In 1585, he and other Italian Jesuits escorted the four Japanese Christians on their return trip to their home country. After a long stay in India, the party arrived in Macao on 28 July 1588. Expecting to join the Jesuit Mission in Japan, de Petris had already learned some Japanese during the long voyage. But in Macao, Valignano chose him instead for the China Mission. He stayed on to study Chinese while the Japanese departed for Nagasaki. Finally, with the death of Almeida in 1591, he was chosen to be Ricci's companion in Shaozhou. Similarly to Almeida, de Petris learned Chinese from Ricci, from the first characters and phrases to studying the canonical Confucian Four Books (*Great Learning*, *Golden Means*, *Analects*, and *Mencius*) and one of the Five Classics. All that effort wasted. Unlike Almeida, whose constitution was weakened by excessive asceticism, de Petris was robust. Ricci thought he had great talents, and praised his prudence, piety, and modesty: 'beloved by everyone in the house.' These years in Shaozhou were the hardest years in his life.

Once more, the death of a companion reminded Ricci of home. He wrote to his father on 10 December: 'for some years now I have not received letters or news from home. Either you have not written, or the letters are lost in transit; but I have not forgotten to remember you in my poor sacrifices. If it is not too much trouble, it would gladden me to know how you are and whether everyone is alive.' Telling his father of the death of de Petris, his second companion in four years, Ricci wrote that 'if one should look at me with the eyes of the world, I am without doubt abandoned; but, considering the Lord is our help, it seems to me I have never been happier in my life.' One consolation for Ricci in his melancholy was his command of the Chinese language, which allowed for great sociability. The major regret for Ricci was that he could not leave Guangdong to start a new residence, which had been his hope in preparing Almeida and de Petris for solo missionary work.

An end, a beginning. The Jesuit superiors in Macao had finally made preparations to transport the caskets of Almeida and de Petris for burial on Christian soil. They promised to send Ricci a new companion. Even though the China Mission was sown with 'seeds of tears', its reports more of tribulations than edification, as we read in Ricci's letter, the seeds for an abundant harvest were indeed sown in these difficult years. The need to train Almeida and de Petris in speaking, reading, and writing Chinese meant that Ricci, once more, applied himself intensively to the Confucian classics. During his stay in Macao in the winter of 1592/3, Valignano concurred with Ricci on the desirability of establishing a second Jesuit residence and bringing in the two Portuguese Jesuits, João Soerio and João da Rocha, who were assigned to study Chinese in Macao by Valignano. Ricci faced another important task: to prepare a new Chinese catechism to replace the *Tianzhu shilu* composed by Ruggieri, 'which did not succeed as well as expected'. Even though de Petris still hoped in November 1592 that Ruggieri would soon return with a papal delegation to China, it was clear the Jesuit Mission needed a fresh approach. The seven years at Zhaoqing yielded no more than eighty converts; and fewer than thirty baptisms in the five years in Shaozhou. Slowly, Ricci developed a new vision, a program, and a new catechism, that aimed at the conversion of the literati and mandarin elites. Throughout 1593 he was hard at work on his Confucian classics; in Ricci's words, he 'hired a learned master and in my old age I have become a school boy'. Responding to Valignano's command, Ricci set out to translate the Confucian *Four Books* into Latin, and by December, he had finished three of the four works.[15]

The new vision entailed nothing less than the complete repudiation of Buddhism. Recall that in all these years, the Jesuits had lived in China dressed like Buddhist monks: bald heads, shaved beards, Buddhist robes, introducing themselves as 'monks from India' (*Tianchu guo seng*). Developed by Ruggieri, who seemed very comfortable in this adopted persona, this identification with Buddhism, in large part imposed by Chinese expectations, had never sat well with Ricci. 'It is impossible to persuade the Chinese [we] are anything but *heshang* [Buddhist monks], since we do not marry, we recite prayers in a chapel, doing everything their *heshang* do,' complained a frustrated Ricci.[16] The first clear sign of the break was Ricci's visit to Nanhua monastery in the summer of 1589: he refused to stay there, even overnight, and showed no interest or respect for any Buddhist relics and rituals. Settling into Shaozhou, not only did Ricci again make no effort to accommodate himself to the Buddhist monks at Guangxiao monastery, he seemed to have antagonized them, for they numbered among the enemies of the Jesuits involved indirectly in the night assault of July 1593. This new vision, the repudiation of Buddhism and the appropriation of Confucianism in Christian evangelization, grew over time with Ricci's experiences. But we can recognize a key moment: Ricci's visit to Nanxiong in February 1592. Describing to Acquaviva his visit to Magistrate Wang, the great courtesies, the pomp and circumstance, the banquet, and the honors, Ricci recounted how he traveled not on foot but in a sedan chair, carried on the shoulders of porters, 'just like their people of substance, on whose authority we are very much dependent in these parts, because without it our work will bear no fruit among the gentiles; and the names of foreigners and clerics are so vile in China that we need have recourse to this and other similar inventions to show that we are not clerics as vile as theirs.' Besides, using a bit of sophistry, Ricci justified these honors since the streets were so crowded and if he did not travel in sedan chairs, he could simply not get through the gawking crowds.[17] Recall also that in Nanxiong Ricci was staying with Qu Rukui. It was his friend, scion of a great mandarin and literary family, who advised Ricci to distance himself from the Buddhist persona, on account of the inferior social status of the Buddhist clergy. Over time, in Shaozhou, Ricci was no longer referred to as *xi seng* or western Buddhist monk but *daoren*, man of the Way, or *yiren*, extraordinary man, in other words, an indeterminate master of esoteric doctrines, a man of cultivation and mystique, a term that the Chinese understood as those with special powers who could not be classified as Buddhist monks, Daoist priests, or Confucian scholars. With his expertise in mathematics and astronomy, his library of western books and western scientific instruments, Ricci, the Master of the Way, was worthy of the attention of Confucian literati. In time, his new persona as *daoren* and *yiren* opened more doors to higher places, for the Chinese elites were fascinated with the magical and extraordinary powers of these *yiren*, as many an entry in local gazetteers would testify to the intense curiosity of late Ming society.

The *daoren* of the West welcomed his new companion sometime in late spring and early summer. Like Ricci, the Tuscan Lazzaro Cattaneo entered the Novitiate of San Andrea in Rome; together with Ricci, 'by and by [they] make all the re-creations of Rome' in Shaozhou. A consolation indeed for Ricci, who had lost four companions in his twelve years in China, two to death, the third, Ruggieri, returned to Rome, and Duarte de Sande, assigned to Macao. With Cattaneo, Ricci could share dear memories of Rome, the formative years of his life, as he confided to Fabio de Fabii in a letter of 15 November 1594:[18]

And thus the things of the first years of the Company are those which have stayed especially in my memory and which are most profoundly rooted in my heart . . . and let me confess to you the truth: with all the things that have befallen me in the midst of this people in so many years, if I had been without the memory of the things that God had shown me, when he took me from my family and showed me the mountain of the religious life, I would have found myself in much greater danger than those that I was in.

Catteneo actually knew the late de Petris, for both had traveled from Rome to India in the entourage of the Japanese Christian samurai. Whereas de Petris continued on to Macao, Cattaneo stayed behind in India, serving as superior of the Jesuit Mission on the Fishery Coast in southern India before being assigned to Macao and China in 1593. Blessed with musical training and a good ear, Cattaneo, after the usual period of struggle, quickly acquired a good pronunciation of Mandarin Chinese and devised a western system to notate Mandarin tonal differences. Ricci himself made further progress in classical Chinese. By October 1594, Ricci felt confident in classical Chinese composition. He had made advances in the Confucian Canon far beyond where Ruggieri had reached. It was an excellent decision to employ a Confucian master. Prior to the resumption of intensive work in 1593, Ricci did not have a Chinese master for seven or eight years. With his new master, Ricci listened to two lectures daily and practiced composition. He began to write 'a new work of our faith, full of natural reason, which will be distributed throughout China once it is printed'.[19] How well it succeeded was probably beyond Ricci's fondest wish, a story we will narrate when the time comes. His literary progress compensated perhaps for the meager harvest in souls: only five or six baptisms in 1594, although one of them was his Chinese teacher. Resigned that the seeds he had sown would only be harvested by others, Ricci nonetheless confided to his friend Girolamo Costa, 'human imperfection would be more consoled if one sees the fruit of one's labor'.[20] At least, 'the Enemy of Humanity', the

Devil, had been unable to extinguish the little hearth of Christianity in Shaozhou. Ricci found consolation in the death of his opponent, Magistrate Guan Gu; with Prefect Xie Taiqing off to Beijing for his triennial report, it left Magistrate Guan, Ricci's friend, as senior mandarin in Shaoszhou.

Once Ricci escaped from the Chinese expectation of Buddhist monkhood, he could consider adopting the persona of a western Confucian scholar, *xiru*, or a western literati, *xishi*. In November 1594, Ricci visited Valignano in Macao in order to seek formal permission for the change of Jesuit identity in the China Mission, a decision that he had obviously come to some time before. With the blessing of the Visitor, Ricci and Cattaneo exchanged their Buddhist robes for the long, silk robes and tall four-corner hats of Confucian scholars. They also let their hair grow because 'shaving off your beard and hair in China is a sign of the sect of idolaters [Buddhists], and no-one who shaved himself does not adore the idols', justified Ricci.[21] By the summer of 1595, the two Italians had a full head of hair and beards down to their belts.[22] Dressed in their silk robes and four-cornered hats in their visits to the mandarins, Ricci and Cattaneo began to perform the ceremony of the *xiucai*, Confucian students, and were pleased to be received as such.

In the midst of these changes came a promising sign. In mid-1594, Wang Zhongming, Minister of Rites in Nanjing, stopped in Shaozhou on his way to his hometown of Dingan on Hainan Island. Apprised of the reputation of Ricci, Wang paid the Jesuit a visit. Impressed by Ricci, especially by his knowledge of mathematics, Wang promised Ricci that he would sponsor the latter on his return journey to Nanjing. The imperial observatory was located in the hills of Nanjing; and the Minister of Rites had jurisdiction over the Directorate of Astronomy: Ricci was perfect for the task of emendation of the calendar.

But by the time of Wang's return from Hainan, Ricci was no longer in Shaozhou. Another powerful mandarin had taken the Jesuit under his protection. The paths of Wang and Ricci would cross again, when the Minister of Rites sponsored Ricci's next step on the ladder of success. Meanwhile, Ricci found another powerful patron, someone whom Ruggieri had most likely met in 1586 during his sojourn in Shaoxing (see Chapter 5). In April 1595, Sun Kuang and his family passed through Shaozhou.[23] Promoted to the rank of Vice Minister of War, Sun was urgently summoned to Beijing to deal with the messy diplomatic debacle in the wake of the 1592 Japanese invasion of Korea. Sun Kuang had a son aged 22, who had recently failed his examination for the degree of *xiucai*. The father worried about his only son, who had fallen into a deep depression; no medical remedies seemed effective. Ruggieri's exploits with the melancholic and 'possessed' student in 1586 had apparently not been forgotten. Once in Shaozhou, Sun sent an officer bearing gifts and an invitation to the Jesuit residence. Ricci and Cattaneo hurried to Sun's barge. There, after polite conversations about the West, the father broached the subject of his son. Ricci replied that he was unable to cure the young Sun's spiritual affliction in a day or two, but if the Minister would permit him to travel with his son into Jiangxi province, he could dispense greater spiritual care during the journey. Sun Kuang readily agreed and ordered the magistrate in Shaozhou to issue travel permits for Ricci. Since departure was imminent, Ricci had only one and a half days to prepare. He took with him João Barradas and Domingo Fernandes, two Catholic Chinese youths from Macao sent for probation before admission to the Society, and two trusted Chinese servants. The two Chinese Jesuit brothers, Wang Mingsha and Zhong Mingren, stayed behind in Shaozhou, for Wang was bedridden with illness and the other indispensable in helping Cattaneo, still

Figure 8. A view of Zhuji Lane, part of the road from Nanxiong to Meiling traveled by Ruggieri and Ricci. Photo by author

Figure 9. Meiling Pass, gate at the top of the ridge. Photo by author

struggling with the Chinese language. On 18 April 1595, the party set sail toward Nanxiong. There, they disembarked and traveled on land through the Meiling, the watershed between the North River and the Gan River, and a range of hills that separated Guangdong and Jiangxi. Upward the party advanced, on sedan chairs, mule backs, and on foot, a journey undertaken ten years earlier by Ricci's former companion Michele Ruggieri. Half-way toward the summit, on a road lined with trees and served by inns, ran a stretch of steps paved with stones. Constructed in 716 during the Tang dynasty, the Way of Meiling permitted travelers, soldiers, and merchants a smooth trek, plodding on in both directions with their mules and single-wheel pushcarts, packed with merchandise and luggage (see Figures 8 and 9). Ricci admired the beauty of the road, letting fly his memory to 1577, when he and his companions struggled on the Via Flaminia, which seemed so ill paved and poorly maintained, compared to this road that led to his future.

7
Nanchang

The three years Ricci spent in the provincial capital of Jiangxi province were the turning point of his career. For one, they occupied the middle of his China years: in April 1595, when Ricci left Shaozhou in haste, he turned his back on the twelve apprenticeship years of bitterness and frustration in Guangdong; when he departed Nanchang for good in the summer of 1598, he would look forward to almost twelve years of triumph. His letters tell the whole story. Of the 54 extant letters written by Ricci, 11 were posted from Nanchang. In three short years, Ricci dashed off 11 letters to his superiors, friends, and family, including the longest letters he had ever written. Compare this epistolary activity to the 16 letters from the twelve years in Guangdong and the 18 letters from his nine years in Beijing, and we get a sense of the excitement of a fresh opening. Indeed, at Nanchang Ricci entered deeper into the inner corridors and chambers of Ming society. In Jiangxi, Ricci experienced the heartland of late Ming intellectual revival, meeting leading Confucian scholars, attending sessions at private academies, and gaining a scholarly reputation with his first Chinese publications. In Nanchang, Ricci penetrated further into the circles of power, establishing relationships with Ming princes and high mandarins, and witnessing at first hand the imperial civil service examination, that machinery of elite formation in traditional China. Eventually, his successes in Nanchang catapulted Ricci to greater heights of fame in the two Ming capitals.

Even at the end of his life, Ricci had the most vivid memories of Jiangxi. How could it have been otherwise? There, he came close to death.

We left the voyagers climbing the Meiling. At the summit, where a Buddhist monastery stood, Ricci saw rolling plains and hills stretching to the horizon, and lying at the foothills, Nan'gan, the first city in Jiangxi, where they embarked on new barges. Knowing Chinese ways, Ricci cultivated the secretary and majordomo (*guanjia*) of Sun Kuang, promising a valuable gift to the mandarin. Through this intercession, Sun Kuang invited Ricci for a meal on his barge and satisfied his curiosities about the customs, religion, and learning of the West. As for Ricci's wish, the Minister discouraged the Jesuit from going to Beijing or Nanjing; foreigners could simply not settle down without imperial permission. Sun Kuang suggested his home province of Zhejiang, but Ricci feared that the Chinese of coastal provinces would be especially hostile to foreigners. Even the suggestion of Nanchang failed to impress Ricci. Along their way in Jiangxi, so many local mandarins welcomed the passing Minister en route that Ricci hardly had time to administer spiritual counseling to the troubled son. The missionary enjoyed the sight of soldiers, lined up in their thousands on the banks of the river, discharging their arquebuses in honor of the Vice-Minister of War, a ceremony organized by the Grand Coordinator, *xunfu*. After Ganzhou, the barges entered a treacherous stretch of water: the Eighteen Rapids, with their swift currents, rocky shoals, their twists and turns. To Ricci's bemuse-ment, Sun Kuang, the great mandarin, like all travelers, made offerings at a Buddhist temple to pray for safe passage. At the second rapid, Tianchu tan, a barge carrying Sun's wife and concubines dashed against a rock. It did not sink, but the luggage was ruined by water pouring into the hulk. Ricci and his men helped the frightened women and children onto his barge. Await-ing a replacement from Ganzhou, Ricci and one of the Macao boys, João Barradas, ceded their places and boarded another. Suddenly, a strong wind arose. Before the sailors could adjust the sail, the barge tipped on its side. Ricci and others were thrown into the water. Unable to swim, Ricci was already commending his soul to God when his hand grabbed a rope that was tied to the barge. Pulling his head above water, Ricci and all others struggled onto the half-submerged barge. But João Barradas was missing. Sailors searched for him, but the boy was not found, living or dead. Fond of the boy, who confessed weekly and would have made an excellent candidate for the priesthood, Ricci fell utterly dejected and even doubted the wisdom of continuing the journey. Only the thought that young João was enjoying his eternal reward gave Ricci some comfort.

When the fleet of barges reached Ji'an, a storm arose. Fearful of watery auguries, Sun Kuang decided to proceed by land to Beijing. Since this entailed greater expense, he thought of sending Ricci back to Shaozhou. Aware of the mandarin's intention, Ricci approached Sun's secretary,

whom he had befriended en route, and dangled a prism, promising it as a gift
if the Minister would bring him to Beijing. Thinking it a precious jewel, the
secretary arranged for Ricci to proceed to Nanjing by boat according to the
original plan, traveling with a couple of servants who guarded the heavier
baggage of Sun Kuang. While Sun and his entourage drove off in thirteen
carriages, followed by more carts carrying their luggage, and hundreds of
servants and soldiers on horseback, Ricci and his servants, escorted by two
men from Sun's household, continued on the river.

Their next stop was Linjiang. A further day's sailing, Ricci stopped at the
small town of Zhangshuzhen (today Qingjiang), famous for being the
hometown of four imperial censors, whereas the entire province of Guangdong could boast of only one.[1] Here, Ricci paid a visit to Liu Wenfang, the
magistrate of Qujiang, a friend of the Jesuits. Liu was on his way back from
Beijing after his triennial evaluation. Putting on his best silk robe, Ricci
visited Liu and was happy to be received with better courtesies than those he
was used to in Shaozhou. Explaining his hair, beard, and scholarly robes to
magistrate Liu, Ricci said: 'Our profession is of letters and we are men who
teach the law of God and other things. Since we did not know how to speak
Chinese nor did we know her customs when we first arrived in Zhaoqing,
we fooled ourselves into wearing the habits of Buddhist monks, from whom
we are totally different for we profess different doctrines.'[2] Ricci was
delighted his explanations were accepted without fuss, and began to feel
comfortable underneath his Jesuit silk.

On 29 April, eleven days after leaving Shaozhou, and passing what seemed
an infinity of sampans and boats, Ricci arrived in the provincial capital
Nanchang. Together with some of his fellow travelers, Ricci came inside
the city walls and visited the famous Daoist Temple, the Tiezhugong, the
Temple of Iron Column, so called because legend has it that a Daoist sage had
used it to defeat a river dragon and saved the city. In his first encounter with
Daoist priests, Ricci noted they wore their hair and beard long. A large
crowd had followed Ricci from the boat's landing to the temple. Domingo
Fernandes, the Macao youth, told the crowd that Ricci was a learned scholar
from the West. In front of a giant statue of the Daoist sage Xu zhen jun, the
onlookers urged Ricci to kneel in reverence. Ricci responded that he did not
recognize the statue. The Chinese answered all the mandarins showed
reverence. When Ricci refused, the crowd still tried to persuade him, fearing
the offended deity would punish the foreigner. Some even wanted to force
Ricci on his knees, for his own sake, and only desisted when one of the sailors

on his boat said the foreigner adored no idols. At that they dispersed. Disturbed by the experience, Ricci resolved never to visit another temple in China. While Ricci returned to the barge, the servants of Sun Kuang made calls on the friends of their master, chief of whom was Huang Jilou, a great physician, who knew the *zongdu* of Jiangxi and all other top mandarins. He would turn out to be a good contact for Ricci.

From Nanchang, a traveler had two choices: to sail eastward toward Zhejiang, the route taken by Ruggieri in 1586 which led to little success, or to sail into Lake Poyang, the direction Ricci took, whence he traveled down the Yangzi, past Jiujiang and Anqing, on his continuing quest for recognition. Ricci noted the many walled towns on both banks of the Yangzi, recording the latitude and longitude of the principal ones, the great variety of fish and cereals, and observed 'the incredibly great multitude of boats, [a fact] impossible to convince anyone who has not seen them, and the sheer amount of logs floating down with the current, to the point as if the river was clogged'.[3] For this reason, the western visitor also observed the deforested landscape, totally denuded of trees except for bamboo, all that timber transformed by human labor into the multitudes of three- and four-mast ships sailing up and down the Yangzi.

On 31 May, six weeks after leaving Shaozhou, Ricci stepped ashore at the southern imperial capital, the ancient city of Nanjing. Ricci scarcely got to know the thriving metropolis, once the heart of imperial power and still the cultural center of the country, for his stay was cut short to two weeks.

Taking lodgings outside the city walls, Ricci was wandering about the city during his first days plotting his next step when he was recognized by a friend of his Guangdong acquaintances. This man alerted the fifth son of Liu Jiezhai, who, unlike his father, was well disposed toward Ricci and had visited the Jesuit twice in Shaozhou. It was Fifth Son Liu who invited Ricci to banquets and made introductions. Eager to get the right contacts, Ricci even left his calling card with the Zhu family, whose son, Zhu Zhifang, had scored first in the year's metropolitan examination and was honored as the *zhuangyuan*, the top-scorer in the entire country for the triennial examination candidates. Then Ricci heard about another former acquaintance who had made it big in Nanjing. This was Xu Dayin. Ricci took this to be a sign from God. A native of Xuan cheng in Anhui province, Xu passed most of his bureaucratic career in Nanjing, except for a brief stint as Assistant Commissioner (*shenyi*) of Guangxi, a post that took him on several trips to Zhaoqing. Like many mandarins, he met Ricci, and received gifts—a sphere, a globe, and a clock—from the western monk. In 1592, Xu Dayin visited Ricci in Shaozhou, while traveling to his new post in Nanjing. By 1595, when Ricci arrived in the southern capital, Xu held the post of Vice-Minister (*shilang*) of Works.[4]

Heartened by this news, Ricci put on his best robe and brought along a valuable gift for the visit to the Vice-Minister. It took the astounded Xu Dayin a moment to recognize Ricci, no longer the western Buddhist monk, but dressed in a silk scholar's robe, wearing a long beard and a four-corner hat. Quickly recovering his composure, Xu Dayin offered the smiling and expectant Ricci tea and the usual courtesies. Then, Ricci showed Xu Dayin the travel permit granted by Sun Kuang and told Xu Dayin how pleased he was to see an old friend, who might help him gain a residence permit. At this, Xu Dayin uttered a loud sigh: not a wise move to come to Nanjing, especially to visit him, admonished Xu, especially in these days of war, when Chinese troops were fighting the Japanese invaders in Korea. Ricci must return to Guangdong, warned Xu, now in a raised voice. A residence permit for a foreigner in the southern capital was out of the question. Xu lectured Ricci for half an hour, at times bordering on rudeness. He ordered his clerks to summon Ricci's landlord and advised Ricci to leave the capital. Escorted by his host out the door, Ricci got the distinct impression that Xu was anxious about being seen with a foreigner. Embittered, Ricci concluded, 'from the great friendship that we had with this mandarin, we can understand how little trust we can place in the words and promises of the Chinese, because if this powerful mandarin, considered a virtuous and sagacious man in China, treats me in this way for fear of the other mandarins, we can well imagine what the others will do, who are less powerful and more hostile to us'.[5] Disappointed, he returned to his residence to find the family of his landlord trembling in fear, for clerks from Xu's office had already summoned the landlord.

At the audience, Vice-Minister Xu gave the poor man a scolding and threatened punishment for illicit liaison with a foreigner; the landlord must evict Ricci at once. Some acquaintances counseled Ricci to ignore the threat, but Ricci, dejected, took this to be a sign 'that this time the Lord does not want [him] to remain in Nanjing'.[6] Deeply humiliated by Xu's rejection, for Ricci had told all his acquaintances in Nanjing of his friendship with the powerful mandarin, he could only save face by leaving. What were Xu's motives? A contemporary biography described Xu as an upright and austere mandarin, parsimonious in spending public funds and alert in avoiding any occasion for self-enrichment.[7] Clearly, Xu thought association with Ricci would damage his reputation. Ricci might have donned Confucian robes, but he was still a Nobody in the field of bureaucratic power.

With a heavy heart, Matteo Ricci embarked in Nanjing on 16 June 1595 to sail up the Yangzi. The twelve-day boat trip to Nanchang lulled the Italian missionary into a pensive mood. He had been in Nanjing just two weeks, but it was almost thirteen years in all that he had spent in China. His dejection was all the deeper for his hopes had been dashed from the high expectations of his recent experiences.

After ten days on water, as the boat approached Nanchang, having crossed Lake Poyang, Ricci fell asleep, worn out by the years of labor that seemed so burdensome after this unexpected reversal of fortunes. Ricci dreamed:

Close to the metropole of Jiangxi, he was quite pensive all day about things to be done, and an unknown man appeared to him in a dream, who said to him on the roads: 'And you go about with the intention of extinguishing the ancient religion of this realm and replacing it with a new one?' The father, who at this time took great care not to disclose to anyone his intention of disseminating our holy law, said: 'Oh, you must be God or the Devil to know this.' He replies: 'I am not the devil, but God.' The father immediately prostrated himself at his feet, since he had met the one whom he had desired to meet for lamenting, and said: 'Lord, since you know my intention, why do you not help me?' And he began to weep at his feet. Then the Lord began to console him and said to him he would be favorable to him at the courts.[8]

Another version of this dream had God pointing to Beijing and Ricci then successfully entering the imperial capital.

Water and ways: Ricci was literally at a crossroad in his life. Would more than a decade of labor float away with the Yangzi, as the poet Su Shi (Su Dongpo, 1037–1101) laments in the 'Ode of Red Cliff': 'The Great River floats east | its waves wash away | oh, how many heroes of the past thousand years!' And would a determined Italian missionary, who had risked nine months of oceanic waves to sail from Lisbon to Macao, be cast aside in a provincial backwater by the ebb and flow of mandarin politics? Ricci knew the answer when he awoke from his sleep. For Ricci's dream in Nanchang was a prophetic and foundational dream: it prophesied God's grace in bestowing success upon Ricci in Nanjing and Beijing, and it drew a parallel between the founder of the China Mission and the founder of the Company of Jesus.

Almost sixty years before (1537) when Ignatius Loyola and two of his companions decided to give up their missionary dream of preaching in the

Holy Land and offer instead their services in Rome, the future founder of the Company of Jesus saw a vision of God the Father and Christ while praying intensely in a church a few miles from Rome. This vision at La Storta, briefly told in Ignatius' *Autobiography*, was recalled in more detail by one of those companions, Diego Laínez, the future successor to Ignatius as second General of the Company:[9]

We were traveling to Rome by way of Siena, when our Father—since he had many spiritual sentiments, especially in receiving the holy eucharist, which he asked for everyday, it being administered either by Master Pietro Fabro or by me, who said mass daily, and he not—said to me that it seemed that God the Father was impressing these words in his heart: 'I will be propitious to you in Rome.' And not knowing what this signifies, he said: 'I don't know what will become of us, perhaps we will be crucified in Rome.' On another occasion he said that it seemed that he saw Christ carrying the cross, and the Eternal Father said to him [Christ]: 'I want you to ask him to be your servant.' And so Jesus asked him [Ignatius] and said: 'I want you to serve this way.' And therefore, in taking on great devotion to this most holy name, he wanted to name the congregation the Congregation of Jesus.

God was indeed propitious to Ignatius in Rome, supporting him in the midst of 'intense persecutions' after his arrival in 1538, and crowning this achievement with the foundation of the Society with papal approval in 1540. Ricci's dream words, 'il signore a consolarlo e dirgli che nelle Corti lo favorirebbe', merely rephrased into indirect discourse God's words to Ignatius, 'Ego ero vobis Romae propitius.' Modeling himself after the first Jesuit, Ricci, in his own writing, imitated the style in the foundational sources of the Society: Laínez calls Ignatius 'il Padre', and likewise Ricci refers to himself in the third person, 'il Padre', in his memoirs, *The History of the Introduction of Christianity in China*. Even the so-called persecutions suffered by Ignatius in Rome in 1538 foreshadowed the brief but intense persecution suffered by Ricci in 1600, when he was finally permitted to visit Beijing as an envoy from the West, on which trip the Eunuch Ma Tang accused Ricci of practicing magic upon seeing the crucifix in the Jesuit's luggage (see Chapter 9).

A classic 'wish-fulfillment', to use Freud's formulation, Ricci's dream in Nanchang contained multiple meanings: calmed by the long journey on water, Ricci's subconscious (his intention, *disegno*, revealed to no one in China) was affirmed by a divine promise, a prophecy, uttered in words similar to the foundational vision of the Society of Jesus. Just as Ignatius founded the Company that became the bulwark of Catholic renewal after the Protestant Reformation, Ricci was promised by God the role of founder of the Christian Church in China as a faithful son of that Company of missionaries. In all these senses, the dream in 1595 is singular: it occurred almost in the middle of Ricci's long career in China (1582–1600) and prefigured his ascent to Nanjing and Beijing, his triumph, glory, and a death remembered in the annals of Chinese and Jesuit histories. Ricci's dream is singular in another sense as well: it is the only dream narrated by Ricci in his long memoir; and it is the only dream described by any Jesuit missionary in China about himself in almost 200 years.[10]

On 28 June, Ricci set foot again in Nanchang. He probably disembarked outside the Guangrun Gate, behind which lay the Temple of Iron Column, where he had visited only a month ago. Ming Nanchang was a large walled city shaped almost like a square with the lower left corner missing just at Guangrun Gate, the point where the Gan River flowed into the walled city, forming three large lakes in its eastern precinct. Embraced by two arms of the Gan River, Nanchang turned to water, with three of its seven gates facing the main arm of the Gan. Palaces, government offices, temples, and houses were packed tightly within its walls; the 1587 census counted 76,705 households and 167,098 inhabitants, four times the size of Zhaoqing, or 'twice the size of Florence', according to Ricci.[11] Not only was the city of Nanchang the capital of Jiangxi, with the usual arrays of provincial offices, including a large examination hall, it also housed the next two levels of local government, serving as the site of the Nanchang prefecture (Nanchang fu), and the two county magistracies of Nanchang and Xinjian. The various sub-provincial magistracies governed a large chunk of territory. In addition, the city served as the headquarters of several military commands. To top it off, three palaces occupied large parcels of land within the city wall: these belonged to hereditary Ming princes, younger sons of former emperors and their descendants who had been enfeoffed in the provinces; by the late sixteenth century, the palaces in Nanchang belonged to the princes of Jian'an, Le'an, and Yiyang (see Map 5).

Ricci noticed the difference from Guangdong, 'a barbaric and uncivilized place', he quipped.[12] There is much less mercantile bustle, he observed, 'and the nature of the people is more moderate and contented with less . . . The people are inclined toward piety, and many of them fast all their lives.' Everything seemed better in Nanchang to the Jesuit: 'The people are better: they look better, they are more noble, there are more literati, and the people are more courteous and considerate; the houses are better, the streets are

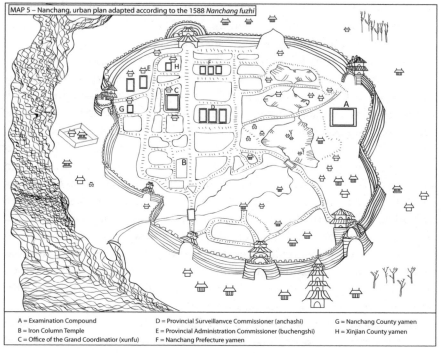

MAP 5 – Nanchang, urban plan adapted according to the 1588 *Nanchang fuzhi*

A = Examination Compound
B = Iron Column Temple
C = Office of the Grand Coordinatior (xunfu)
D = Provincial Surveillanvce Commissioner (anchashi)
E = Provincial Administration Commissioner (buchengshi)
F = Nanchang Prefecture yamen
G = Nanchang County yamen
H = Xinjian County yamen

Map 5. Nanchang

wider and straighter . . . there are more ceremonial arches, which the mandarins erected; there are many more of them and much better made than those in Guangzhou . . .'[13] Ricci also noted the presence of private academies, where scholars gathered to discuss 'things of virtue'.[14] Indeed, Jiangxi province was one of the centers of late Ming intellectual life and mandarin power: it had more private academies than any other province, a total of 294 out of 1,946 academies in the Ming dynasty; it supplied one of the highest numbers of *jinshi* degree holders. 'And if the Portuguese write very negatively about the lack of courtesies in China,' Ricci informed General Acquaviva in Rome, 'you should know that it does not apply to all of China, but only to the province of Guangdong and others like it.'[15] In the 1595 metropolitan examination, Ricci wrote in another letter to his superior Duarte de Sande in Macao, Nanchang alone furnished seven or eight *jinshi* among the final 300 candidates, whereas the entire province of Guangdong produced only five or six;[16] Zhang Wei, who served as one of the grand secretaries between 1591 and 1598, was a native of Nanchang;[17] and the city was closely associated with the leading figure of late Ming intellectual life, the official and philosopher Wang Yangming (1472–1529).[18]

A native of Yuyao (modern day Shaoxing), Zhejiang, the same home-town as Sun Kuang, Wang served in various government posts until his promotion to Grand Coordinator of Jiangxi. In 1519, he suppressed the uprising of Prince Zhu Chenhao, during which Sun Kuang's grandfather, the Censor Sun Sui, was killed as one of only two officials in Nanchang who refused to submit to the rebellious prince. During his tenure in Jiangxi Wang Yangming also built schools, revived defunct private academies, and promoted Confucian learning. However, since Wang opposed the teach-ings of the Song dynasty scholar Zhu Xi, whose doctrines were declared orthodox in the early Ming, he was ostracized for a long time by many mandarins and scholars. Eventually, Wang's teachings prevailed, thanks to the influence of his many disciples. In 1584, the Wanli emperor permitted sacrifices to Wang Yangming in Confucian temples, the highest honor for a scholar, setting his statue alongside those of Confucius, Mencius, Zhu Xi, and other sages of the Confucian tradition.

Staying low for several days, Ricci had Domingo Fernandes inquire whether there were acquaintances of his from Guangdong. This turned out unpromising, and Ricci blamed his young subaltern 'who had little talent for what was necessary and for other things'.[19] After several days, Ricci decided to visit physician Huang Jilou. Eager to make a good first impression, Ricci donned silk robes and wore a tall scholar's hat, in the style of Su Dongpo, the famous poet of the Song dynasty, and was carried in a sedan chair to Doctor Huang's residence. Apprised of the arrival of a remarkable foreigner in the entourage of Sun Kuang, Huang Jilou received Ricci courteously. A man eager for novel conversations, Huang was charmed both by things western, Ricci's gift and discourse, as well as by the foreigner's knowledge of Chinese texts. Being the physician to the powerful in Nanchang, Doctor Huang provided invaluable contacts. He invited Ricci to a banquet, attended also by Ming princes and their relatives. 'With the doctor's friendship,' Ricci admitted, 'my reputation began to circulate and grow in the city, and they regard me not only as a great scholar who could have gotten the *jinshi* degree . . . having studied all of the six Confucian classics, but they say I also know other great sciences, which they do not know in China. In this reputation, I think I have been helped greatly by what our friend [Qu Rukui] had been telling the others.'[20] Ricci only wished he could repay Qu's good graces by making Qu into a Christian, when and if it served God. Soon, Ricci started to receive many distinguished visitors, whom he introduced to western mathematics and astronomy, impressing them furthermore with his photographic memory, by reproducing on a blank piece of paper Chinese characters shown to him and written in no particular order.

Much has been made of Ricci's prodigious memory. The literati in Nanchang also marveled at the foreigner's ability to recite whole passages from the Confucian classics, and were stunned by Ricci's feat in reciting in reverse order any particular passage requested. Surely a miraculous formula explained this remarkable memory. Almost daily, literati came to Ricci asking to be taken as disciples, some offering lucrative payments for the secrets of his mnemonic sciences. Pleading he had yet to settle in Nanchang, Ricci promised he would soon satisfy their entreaties. Imagine a shortcut to success in the civil service examination, freeing thousands of scholars from the struggle to memorize scrolls and scrolls of ancient texts. Flattered by the extraordinary attention, Ricci summarized western mnemonic methods in his second Chinese work, *Xiguo jifa* (Western Mnemonics), which was composed at the request of Viceroy Lu Wangai, as we shall see.

This short treatise, comprising six brief chapters, introduced a spatial method of memorization, the so-called 'memory palace'. Actually, the *Xiguo jifa* was a disappointing book, for it proved useless for the many eager Chinese readers. In essence, this book of Western Mnemonics used spatial imagination for classifying Chinese characters, a method that only made sense for non-native Chinese speakers. Its methods represented Ricci's own long experience in memorizing Chinese characters: how these could be broken down according to radicals, sounds, and meaning for easier comprehension. His methods made sense only for students unfamiliar with the non-phonetic nature of Chinese, who needed a visual aid for breaking down and classifying the complex shapes of Chinese characters. Ricci's Chinese readers, who had learned their characters from a tender age, already recognized these characters; Ricci's method was useless for them. Take for example Ricci's explanation in chapter 2, 'Applying the Method':

To learn mnemonics, one has to place in sequence the visual images of things and events in specified places; therefore we call this visual mnemonics. Suppose you want to remember the four chacters '*wu*' (military), '*yao*' (to want), '*li*' (profit), and '*hao*' (good), you have to imagine a room with four corners for storage, using the southeastern corner as the first site, the northeastern as the second, the northwestern as the third, and the southwestern as the fourth. You take the character '*wu*', which looks like a warrior holding a spear ready for battle, and another man restraining him by the wrist, thus forming the image of '*wu*', and you place it in the southeastern corner. You take the character '*yao*', imagine it as looking like a Muslim girl of Central Asia, forming the character '*yao*', and you place it in the northeastern corner. You take the character '*li*', imagine it to look like a peasant holding a sickle harvesting in the fields, forming the character '*li*', and you place it in the northwestern corner. You take the character '*hao*', imagine it to look like a young girl, playing with a baby she is holding, forming the character '*hao*', and you place it in the southwestern corner. Once you have placed the four characters in these four sites, if you want to remember them, recall the room and find them in their different corners, and you will recall their images and remember the characters.[21]

This was only the most basic step. In chapters 4 and 5, Ricci introduced far more complicated and elaborate methods of spatial placement, to facilitate remembering whole sentences and paragraphs.

The trouble with Ricci's method, as one Chinese student observed, was that 'these precepts are the true rules of memory, but one already needs good memory in order to use them'.[22] Moreover, Ricci's linguistic excursions into the etymology of Chinese characters struck readers either as naive or absurd, making sense perhaps for foreign students of Chinese, but not to Chinese literati steeped in a long tradition of historical phonetics and etymology. *Xiguo jifa* found little reception: only one edition was printed and few copies disseminated.

Like the Chinese characters he recalled, figures from his past also popped up in no particular order. In Nanchang, Ricci encountered Li Chunhe, who had served for one year in 1589 as Assistant Prefect (*tongzhi*) in Shaozhou. A native of Nanchang, Li was visiting his family en route to another post; he promised to help Ricci secure a residence permit and referred him to a cousin, a *xiucai*. Meanwhile, the Grand Coordinator, Lu Wangai, who had heard of the fame of the Jesuits during an earlier posting in Guangxi, sent an officer to inquire whether the foreigner in his jurisdiction was indeed the same person. Going to the audience in his best robes, not knowing what to expect, Ricci was much relieved when Lu Wangai asked him to rise from his knees. Magistrate Lu told the missionary that he had heard of the latter's learning and virtue. During the hour-long audience, Ricci recounted his journey from Shaozhou in the entourage of the Vice-Minister of War and his visit to Xu Dayin in Nanjing, omitting the unpleasant details, properly impressing Lu with his high contacts. Conversing on matters astronomical and mathematical, Ricci also showed Lu a Venetian prism, which so delighted the magistrate that he sent it back to the inner chambers for the enjoyment of his female household. When asked about his future plans, Ricci replied he intended to return to Guangdong, to which Lu suggested he should rather stay in Nanchang, a far nobler place. Ricci was very pleased with the audience. His friend Doctor Huang, obliged by a precious gift from Ricci, and who was treating the magistrate's son, had also put in a good word, telling Lu about Ricci's knowledge in making sundials, his stupendous memory, and his exotic collection of prisms, western books, and world map. Thus, Magistrate Lu asked Ricci to make a sundial for him and to compose a mnemonic guide in Chinese for the use of his three sons, who were studying for the examinations. Thanks to this opening, Ricci made the rounds, visiting all the other mandarins in Nanchang. In two short months, he had succeeded in establishing himself among the elites of the city.

Foremost among the elites, in status if not in power, were the Ming princes of Jian an and Le an. The enfeoffment of younger sons in the provinces was established by Zhu Yuanchang, the founder of the Ming dynasty, After the early fifteenth century, these imperial princes no longer held effective power, being barred from military command and the civil bureaucracy. Equipped with their own mini palaces, they languished as wealthy landlords, forbidden to visit the imperial capital except by order of the emperor, and generally restricted to their places of enfeoffment. Younger sons of these enfeoffed princes in turn received lesser ranks. Over the course of time, some branches died out; others were abolished; and all received stipends from the government. By the end of the dynasty, the imperial lineage grew to huge proportions, no fewer than 627,424 men and women with imperial blood by a count in 1624, consuming the lion's share of the annual government revenues.[23] Deprived of any function in society, some provincial princes amassed fortunes, indulged their senses, and behaved like lawless petty tyrants; others cultivated the arts, patronizing poets, priests, and esoteric 'men of the way'; a few, such as Prince Zhu Chenhao, tore at the leashes of provincial confinement, intolerable when measured against their ambitions and abilities, and plotted rebellion, as we have seen. Prince Chenhao was the fifth-generation descendant of the seventeenth son of Zhu Yuanchang, enfeoffed as the Prince of Ningxiang. After the abortive rebellion, Zhu Chenhao was forced to commit suicide, and his title was abolished. There were other black sheep of imperial blood of lesser rank in

Nanchang, who committed lesser crimes: in 1583, three cadet members of the Ruichang line (the title was abolished in 1519 after the rebellion) handed in fraudulent claims for stipends; in 1591, several younger sons of the late Jingjiang prince terrorized the city, beating up commoners and even a mandarin, and were demoted to commoner status or put under house arrest; in 1592, in a vendetta against a commoner, several cadet members of the Ruichang line were convicted of robbery, violence, and rape, and were sentenced to imprisonment as commoners.[24]

The princes of Le an and Jian an did not resemble their lawless kinsmen. Both men descended from younger sons of the main branch of the Ning-xiang line. Already an old man when he met Ricci, the Prince of Le an, Zhu Duogang, succeeded to the title in 1561. Devoted to scholarship, in 1584 he had requested the emperor to bestow a set of the *Four Books* and *Five Classics*, and a name for the academy he sponsored.[25] The Prince of Jian an, Zhu Duojie (d. 1602), whom Ricci got to know well, succeeded to the title in 1573. He, too, was a man of cultivation.

As always in China, high connections opened doors. Doctor Huang introduced Ricci to these princes, one of whom had a daughter of Qu Rukui, Ricci's good friend, as his daughter-in-law. As usual, friendship was sealed by banquets and the exchange of gifts. The Prince of Le an gave Ricci some lengths of expensive silk, a pair of silk shoes, and a book painted with a scene of their banquet; in return, Ricci presented a European book with illustrations of Christian saints. For the Prince of Jian an, Ricci gave expensive and exotic presents: a sundial carved out of black marble, marking the twenty-four seasons of the Chinese calendar, the hours of sunset and sunrise, a sphere, a world map, pictures and glass, and two books printed on Japanese paper, one entitled *Description of the World* and the other Ricci's very first Chinese book, *On Friendship* (*Jiaoyou lun*).[26] And because the prince showed 'an inclination toward the next life', and his conversion 'would represent a great beginning since many would follow his example and our holy faith would expand greatly in China', Ricci also gave Prince Jian a painting depicting St Stephen in prayer.[27] So delighted was he with the painting, the prince had it elaborately mounted and entreated Ricci to become his permanent house guest and religious master, an offer politely refused by the Jesuit, who had set his eyes on a far grander prize.

Jiaoyou lun was more than 'an exercise in Chinese composition', the description Ricci used in a letter to Claudio Acquaviva. Written in response to a query on friendship in the West by the Prince of Jian an, who enjoyed making a new friend, the virtuous and learned westerner, Ricci composed the short treatise in several days in early December 1595. The text consisted of 100 maxims or aphorisms concerning friendship culled primarily from Greek and Roman authors, the main ones being Plutarch, Aristotle, Diogenes Laertius, Cicero, and Seneca. Ricci most likely selected the majority of the maxims from a text, *Sententiae et Exempla ex Probatissimis Quibusque Scriptoribus Collecta* (Maxims and Exemplars Compiled from Writers Worthy of Approval), compiled by the Portuguese humanist and Dominican Andreas Eborensis (1498–1573), and widely available in the libraries of Jesuit colleges. Others he recalled from memory.

The very first aphorism defines friendship: 'Although my friend and I have two bodies, we have but one mind.' But friendship is more than just pleasure in the company of an alter ego, it satisfies our deepest need for material and spiritual mutual help, and is the joy of humanity. Friendship must be based on sincerity, loyalty, and material disinterest; Ricci included many aphorisms to illustrate how true friendships transcend the divide of wealth and poverty, fortune and bad luck. Above all the foundation of friendship lies in virtue. To that effect, Ricci selected many maxims to illustrate this point:

Only when virtue and will are alike, can friendship be strong; to make friends is like curing an illness, for the physician truly loves the sick but hates the disease. For the sake of curing the sick, he injures the body and feeds bitter medicine. If a physician cannot tolerate illness in a sick person, how can a friend tolerate the evil in a friend? Admonish him, admonish him! Do not worry about his displeasure in hearing, do not fear the stubbornness of his head; if there is more pleasure than virtue in friendship, it cannot last; if a person's friends are as numerous as trees in a forest, you know he has great virtue. If a person's friends are far apart like the morning stars, you know he has little virtue; a friendship that turns to enmity when there is a conflict of interest is due to the absence of righteousness in that friendship. If a friendship is righteous, both good times and bad times can be shared.[28]

Many of these maxims sounded familiar to the Chinese, who enjoyed their own aphorisms of friendship. But Ricci included six aphorisms from Greek history (three concerning Alexander the Great) to give his Chinese text an exotic flavor. *Jiaoyou lun* was an instant success, for it echoed, by design, the Confucian views of friendship, which we will examine shortly. In form, it resembled generally the most important text in the Confucian Canon, the sayings of Confucius as recorded by his disciples, compiled in the *Analects*; the teachings of the Great Sage, too, were uttered in short maxims and aphorisms for the most part, gems for repeated readings and reflections. Ricci kept a copy of his manuscript, which he translated into Italian, and annotated the Chinese characters with Italian sounds. Acquaintances borrowed the text; many copied it; a friend, probably Su Daiyong, mandarin in Ganzhou, formerly serving as *tongzhi* in Yingde, Guangdong, paid for a private printing in 1596 without Ricci's knowledge. Ricci's first Chinese work went through at least five editions; the text acquired prefaces from learned scholars and mandarins as Ricci's own circle of friends expanded ever wider. For the 1599 edition, his friend Qu Rukui wrote a preface, in which Qu stated that since antiquity the Chinese had always treated foreign visitors with the appropriate ceremonies of friendship, as diverse peoples were themselves attracted to China by the splendor and virtue of its civilization. And just as the Han dynasty penetrated the northern deserts and the Tang dynasty visited maritime neighbors, Qu continued:

Only under our great Ming Dynasty, splendorous like the midday sun and surpassing all epochs, with sacred emperors succeeding one another, and their virtue growing without limit, does a profoundly virtuous man such as Lord Li [Ricci] come to visit, in admiration of our civilization. He wishes not to make a name for himself, but to be ranked among the people, reciting the sacred commands [of the Confucian Canon], respecting imperial law, wearing the belt and headgear of a scholar, making sacrifice in autumn and spring, observing in his own person the moral principles, and practicing the proper respect for the truth.[29]

It is interesting to note that Ricci signed his work *Da Xi yu shanren* (Man of the Mountain of the Great Western Region). Ricci used the term *shanren* in the sense of scholars who dwelt in the mountains, far from the bustle of urban commerce, hence the derivative meaning of hermits or eremites. In the Ming, the title was often adopted by literati artists who either achieved no high official status and held no office or who had retired from insignificant posts but were able to befriend officials who could employ them for their own literary projects, or patronize them by promoting their works or referring them to other patrons.[30] Clearly, Ricci had a subtle understanding of his delicate new position in elite society.

By portraying the West in a positive light, Ricci also flattered the Chinese, for friendship, between peoples and cultures, consisted in the mirror images of the 'I' and alter ego, between friends of two bodies but one mind. In *Doctrine of the Mean*, one of the texts in the *Four Books* of the Confucian Canon, friendship is defined as one of the five basic human relationships, together with those binding the ruler and his official, father and son, elder and younger brother, husband and wife. Similar to Ricci's representation of western friendship, Confucian scholars also understood moral virtue as the foundation of true friendship. They knew by heart Confucius' maxims in *The Analects* on virtue and friendship: 'Zi Gong asked about friendship. Confucius said: "Give good advice and guide [friends] on the path [of righteousness]," and further, "There are three kinds of beneficial and three kinds of harmful friends: friends who are straightforward, friends who are sincere, friends who are broadly learned, they are beneficial; friends who dissimulate, friends who flatter to please, friends who argue stubbornly, they are harmful."' Indeed, these maxims would form the basis of Ricci's friendship with an eminent Confucian scholar.

Zhang Huang (1527–1608), the foremost scholar in Nanchang at the time, was already a venerable man of 70 when he met Ricci. A teacher to Ricci's good friend Qu Rukui, Zhang Huang had heard many good things about the virtuous western scholar. Through the good graces of Doctor Huang, Zhang Huang indicated his interest in meeting Ricci. The younger man paid a visit to the venerable older scholar, and the two hit it off right away. After several visits and long conversations, Zhang Huang found Ricci such a kindred spirit that he called Ricci a younger brother. Ricci impressed Zhang Huang with his bearing and learning, not only with his European erudition, but his knowledge of Confucian texts. And thus the circle around Zhang Huang, 'who are used to treating everyone with great arrogance, come to treat the Father with much humility and courtesy', observed Ricci wryly.[31] Despite his irony, Ricci liked the literati at the academy and was happiest in their presence.[32] In turn, Ricci admired the old scholar for his erudition and virtue, particularly for his hostility to Buddhism. And even though 'he was not a mandarin', Ricci remarked, 'or better said, he made a profession of not wanting to be a mandarin, everyone treated him with great honor and courtesies'.[33] Having many disciples and honored by all the mandarins, Zhang Huang enjoyed a generous government stipend. A living sage beyond the vulgarities of power and wealth, Zhang Huang served as a model of emulation; this was the apex of what Ricci could hope to achieve in a society that was not his own.

On the banks of the East Lake within Nanchang, Zhang Huang had constructed a lecture hall (Cixi tang), where he presided over learned gatherings. In addition to the standard themes of discussion at these colloquia—the nature of virtue and morality, human conscience, and natural knowledge, all commonplaces in the Confucian classics—Ricci introduced the subject of Christianity, using rational arguments and western books as authority. His lectures on western astronomy and mathematics, in particular, fascinated the academicians. 'Truly for them I can say I am another Ptolemy,' Ricci observed ironically, 'since they know nothing.'[34] Writing to Acquaviva, Ricci said, 'if China were the whole world, I should be without doubt the greatest mathematician and natural philosopher, for the things they say are ridiculous, and it is a wonder how little they know, since everyone is dedicated only to moral philosophy and elegance in speaking and writing'.[35] Contemptuous of the literati's ignorance of astronomy, Ricci dismissed their lack of technical expertise (they could only make inclined equinoctial clocks) and their ridiculous view of the universe (Heaven is round and liquid, earth is square and solid). While Ricci and Zhang disagreed on many things—the origins of the universe, the existence of an omnipotent God, the punishment of hell and the reward of heaven—they also shared a fundamental belief in the ethical ordering of society and the leading role of elites schooled in virtue. No doubt, the colloquia at Cixi Hall reminded Zhang Huang of two aphorisms in *The Analects*: 'Practicing one's learning, is that not a pleasure? Meeting a friend from afar, is that not a joy?' 'Through texts and learning, a cultivated man (*jun zi*) makes friends; and he relies on friends to progress in virtue (*ren*).'

Even though Ricci was reticent on this point, his conversations with Zhang Huang represented a pivotal moment in the search for harmony between Christianity and Confucianism. For a couple of years, Ricci was engaged in the intensive study of Confucian texts. By now, his purpose had progressed beyond perfecting his command of the language to understanding Confucian thought from within, and to finding points of correspondence with Christian teachings. Catholic doctrines would also be dressed up in a Confucian gown, much like Ricci the Jesuit in scholar's robe, for Chinese taste. A careful reading of *Tianzhu shiyi* (*The True Meaning of the Lord of Heaven*), Ricci's celebrated dialogue composed during his years in Nanchang, reveals key themes that echo the ideas of Zhang Huang. Ricci himself described their intellectual exchanges:[36]

I have had already several disputations [with Zhang Huang], as a result of which he marveled at the fact that I argue based on the doctrines and argumentations from their own texts. One day Old Master Zhang came to me and concluded that there is nothing more to say about the doctrine that I had presented of heaven and hell, which they deny, not having any value without the moral virtue and the goodness of this life, an embarrassment really, except for one sentence written by a great scholar of the past: 'If there is paradise, good people will go there; if there is hell, evil people will deserve it.' And this one sentence ended our disagreement.

The sentence that brought Ricci and Zhang to agreement came from the *Chujian lu* of Yu Wenbao, a Song dynasty scholar who flourished around 1240. Actually it was more a case of agreeing to disagree. Zhang Huang emphasized the hypothetical: if heaven and hell indeed existed, he would agree with Ricci that the good and bad would go their separate ways. By no means did Zhang admit to the existence of these Christian places. However, in Ricci's memory and recording of this exchange, the hypothetical nature of Zhang's first utterance was gradually transformed into a tacit agreement in his letters and finally to the admittance of the Christian doctrine in *Ten Discourse of the Man of Paradox*.[37] Nonetheless, the fact that this citation, and many similar ideas, appeared in *Tianzhu shiyi* reflected the importance of these discussions in the formation of Ricci's ideas.

For this reason, we will turn to the thought of Zhang Huang and his place in late Ming intellectual history, and emphasize the points of correspondence with Ricci's intellectual agenda. They are: first, a return to the ancient texts of the Confucian tradition in order to reconstruct a Confucian orthodoxy untainted by latter exegesis and by ideas of Buddhism and Daoism; second, the search for harmony between the study of nature and self-cultivation, the advocacy of a unitary program of introspection, self-discipline, and the study of texts and nature; and finally, the practice of moral knowledge in daily life, as exemplified by learned societies and colloquia.

Unlike the vast majority of scholars, who devoured the Confucian classics only in order to succeed in examinations, whose vision for power and prosperity remained focused and undistracted by the moral precepts in the books they read, Zhang Huang never sat for the civil service examination and never held an official post. He was that rare breed in late Ming society: a pure scholar. A posthumous biography written in 1611 by his disciple Wan Shanglie described the auspicious portents for the birth of this Confucian sage.[38] His father, who fervently desired a son, had two dreams: an old man in the Milky Way, knowing his wish, admonished him to accumulate ethical merits; in the second dream, he saw a baby sitting with dignity in the moon. Indeed, the boy Zhang Huang had an air of grave dignity. He never uttered a vulgar word; a model student, he drew portraits of Confucius, Mencius, and other sages; and he was moved by suffering, particularly by a debtor who was chained up for three days without sustenance. Losing his father and a beloved younger brother as a young man, Zhang Huang resolved to renounce fame and fortune and dedicate his life to study and reflection.

In his search for life's meaning, Zhang Huang focused on the study of the *Yijing*, 'The Book of Changes', an esoteric divinatory book of diagrams and texts compiled in the early Zhou dynasty (1122–256 BC), but believed in traditional China to have been composed by the mythical figure Fu Xi, one of the earliest legendary rulers of China in the third millennium BC. From the *Yijing*, Confucian scholars developed a theory of the universe: that it was self-generating out of primordial matter, combining the elements of yin and yang, symbolizing the nature of earth and heaven, and of all things living and insensate in the world; that its forces, ever waxing and waning, opposing and complementary, govern human life; and that all things in the universe, including humankind, share in the same universal substance. This vision of a unitary universe implies a unified and righteous way in all things: in the construction of order in the world, in good governance, in maintaining proper family relations, and in the moral cultivation of the self. For Zhang Huang, there was no substantive difference between star gazing, herbal medicine, and moral philosophy, for all knowledge was one. For this reason, Zhang Huang was particularly impressed by Ricci's command of astronomy. He included excerpts of Ricci's work in his compilation of important works, *Tushu bian* ('Anthology'), and wrote: 'I recently met Qu Taisu (i.e. Qu Rukui), who visited Guangdong and saw a monk, who called himself *huloba* (i.e. European), a great expert in calendar and mathematics. When he sailed the seas, all he had to do was to observe the quadrant, and he would know not only the hour and position, but also the distance to the four directions of the compass.'[39] What impressed Zhang Huang even more was that this remarkable astronomer was also a man of great virtue. It happened once that Ricci complained to Zhang Huang about the throngs of visitors, who left him little time for study and self-cultivation. The famous Confucian scholar advised the Jesuit to instruct his servant to announce his absence when he did not wish to be disturbed. Ricci replied that would be a lie. Zhang Huang objected that this hardly qualified as lying. But Ricci stated that as a man dedicated to the service of God, he must always tell the truth, no matter the occasion. These words of self-promotion made their round in Zhang Huang's circle, and Ricci came to be honored as the man who never lied.

We can glimpse the central ideas of Zhang Huang's thought in the Eight Point Program of Study he wrote in 1592 for the Bailu dong shuyuan, the White Deer Grove Academy.[40] It contained his stress on self-discipline and moral introspection, his focus on ancient Confucian texts, and his rejection of the late Ming syncretism with Buddhism, all significant themes that would feature in Ricci's *Tianzhu shiyi*.

Located in Lushan, the scenic mountain north of Nanchang, White Deer Grove Academy, founded in the Song dynasty and restored by Wang Yangming during his tenure as Governor of Jiangxi, was one of the most prestigious private academies of the Ming dynasty, thanks to its historic association with Zhu Xi and Wang Yangming, the two greatest figures in neo-Confucian thought. In 1592, Zhang Huang was appointed president of the academy (*zhudong*). He composed an Eight Point Program, probably given as an inaugural lecture for the students, which we will summarize below.

One. The root of all learning is to confirm one's will for virtue . . . While many people are endowed by Heaven at birth with abilities and talent, without will, their mind would succumb to wealth, career, and sensual pleasures . . . With the will to virtue, one's mind turns to the things of heaven and earth, and for the continuation of the lost teachings of past sages.

Two. The main aim of learning is to gain friendships that will help us in the path to virtue . . . Our will has to focus on the acquisition of virtue (*ren*), and not be lost in luxurious enjoyments or the success and failure of examination . . . This day, we gather in this hall, a day to make friends, to help one another in virtue, and to learn together the entrance into sagehood. You should all reflect silently within yourselves, to find evidence for what you know, to question your doubts in order to gain understanding, and to raise for discussion difficult passages in canonical texts or aphorisms from previous scholars that you have come across. You should question one another with equanimity, accept criticisms with humility, correct one another who are competitive, lazy, or commit faults in words and deeds.

Three. The way into learning is to observe the physical world and one's mind . . . For the world, the country, our bodies and our minds, our knowledge and wishes, they are all one . . . All things in heaven and earth are but one body . . . In recent days, there are those who speak of innate moral knowledge, *liangzhi*, thinking that only what we know presently is useful for innate moral knowledge, and that this represents sudden enlightenment . . . They forget that only by washing out gravel could one get real gold, and that an overflowing pond must be cleaned before one could return to the source. How can one even say that learning of the self does not involve knowing the physical world?

Four. The shield of learning consists in the anxiety to uphold rules. The ancients feared the commands of Heaven, they respected virtue, and feared the dereliction of duty . . . If you keep to the rules with care, your spirit would be constrained by your sharpened consciousness, focused and unified, as if God on High (*Shangdi*) has come upon you . . .

Five. The foundation of learning is piety and honesty . . . Even Confucius, who was the greatest sage sent by Heaven, said that he had not even followed one of the four virtuous ways. To ensure that acts match words is indeed the characteristic of a man of moral cultivation. We who wish to emulate Confucius, how can we not strive to achieve this?

Six. The inspection of learning consists in punishing wrongs, controlling desires, and correcting our faults. Goodness is infinite, humanity has many faults, the desire to commit wrongs is difficult to eradicate, and we are easily moved by sensual lust. (Zhang Huang illustrated this point by analyzing the nature of change in two hexagrams (*qua*) in the Trigrams of the *Yijing*.)

Seven. The ultimate aim of learning is to fulfill our human nature and destiny . . . Everything that has been mentioned refers to the principle of human nature and destiny. Why? All things are one. If you can truly study things and understand, then all acts and words of piety represent manifestations of this one thing. The proper relationship between human beings, *ren*, is human nature and destiny, and represents another name for this one thing.

Eight. The authority for learning lies in researching Antiquity and exhausting the meaning of the classics . . . Are not the *Six Classics* and the *Four Books* the legacy and teachings of ancient sages? But those who speak of learning today forsake the laws of past sages, and despise the constraints of Song scholars. In everything, they rely only on their own mind, engage in rootless and self-referential discourse, advocating instant moral enlightenment, setting up their own schools, claiming that an illiterate commoner could join the rank of sages. They state either there are no ancient texts worth reading, or boast that the *Six Classics* are merely footnotes of their own mind. And thus, everyone utters heterodox discourses, insults the words of sages, turns away from the way of sages, to the point where they can hardly be saved! There are some in our own time, considered the most brilliant minds, men who devote themselves to the Learning of the Mind (*xin xue*), often abandoning their families, going with their companions to a never-never land . . . practicing their silent meditations and seeking to prove their own inner truths. If you mix up the three teachings [of Confucianism, Buddhism, and Daoism] into one, in fact you are treating the works of our sacred school as nothing but rubbish and dirt!

As a third-generation disciple of Wang Yangming, Zhang Huang's ideas showed the mark of the great master. The key concept in Wang's philosophy was *liangzhi*, innate moral knowledge; the individual should not rely on any external authority in his search for the truth, but should look within himself to discover his own innate moral knowledge. Wang believed strongly in the natural goodness of humanity: 'In the original substance of the mind there is no distinction of good and evil. When the will becomes active, however, such distinction exists. The faculty of innate knowledge is to know good and evil. The investigation of things is to pursue virtue and eradicate evil.' Likewise, Zhang Huang echoed Wang's teachings on the oneness of the universe: 'Man is the mind of the universe. At bottom Heaven and Earth and all things are my body. Is there any suffering or bitterness of the great masses that is not disease or pain in my own body?' Furthermore, the disciples of Wang Yangming believed that sagehood was attainable by mortal men, and that the unity of human nature with all things entailed a moral duty to cure the sick body of the world, to relieve suffering, and to help one's fellow humanity.

In the standard classification of Ming learning advanced by the late Ming scholar Huang Zongxi (1609–95) in *Mingru xue an* (*Records of Ming Scholars*), Wang's disciples could be divided into three geographical groups. Zhang Huang belonged to the Jiangxi group, the so-called Jiangyou School (School of the Right Bank of the Yangzi). The key figures were associated with the Fugu shu yuan (Restore Antiquity Academy) in Ji an. Incidentally, one of Ricci's stops in his trip of April 1595, Ji an provided more successful candidates for the *jinshi* degree than any other prefectures during the Ming dynasty. Zou Shouyi, Ouyang De, Nie Bao, and Luo Hongxian, the leaders of this group, targeted their teachings at the elites and the emperor. They believed the maintenance of moral virtue required a lifelong effort, and practical external action as well as inner cultivation. Some of them were also highly critical of the two other schools of Wang Yangming disciples, namely the Zhejiang and the Taizhou schools, for giving too much weight to Daoist and Buddhist meditation, and for pandering to the masses. Hence, the attack on syncretism by Zhang Huang fell squarely within the traditions of the Jiangxi school. The gibes in Zhang Huang's speech at the White Deer Grove Academy referred to two contemporary leaders of the Taizhou school: He Xinyin (1517–79) was an advocate of sagehood for the illiterate masses; and Li Zhi (1527–1602), who abandoned his wife to pursue enlightenment as a Buddhist monk, and flouted social norms by accepting unmarried young women as disciples. Both men caused uproar by challenging orthodox Confucian social norms; both men died in prison. Ricci would have an occasion to meet the brilliant and eccentric Li Zhi.

On 24 December 1595, Ricci welcomed João Soeiro (1566–1607) and Francisco Martins (Huang Mingsha). The Portuguese Soeiro had joined the Society of Jesus in 1584 and left Europe in the company of the Japanese

Christian samurai. After working in Mozambique and Goa, he was sent to Macao. Brother Martins accompanied him from Shaozhou to reinforce Ricci. With these new arrivals, Ricci's thought turned to securing a firmer footing in Nanchang. Once again, he approached Lu Wangai with a sundial and the book on mnemonics, as previously requested by the mandarin. On the matter of residence, Lu referred Ricci to the Prefect (*zhifu*) Wang Zuo. Not knowing Ricci personally, at first Wang Zuo reacted coolly to Ricci's petition, wanting to settle him in a Buddhist monastery outside the city walls. Anxious not to revert to the status of a Buddhist monk, Ricci renewed his entreaties with Lu with still more presents. As it turned out, a favorable word from Lu Wangai was more than enough. It was far better for the mandarins to give verbal protection to the foreigner Ricci than to issue a written document; informal patronage afforded a safeguard for disclaiming responsibility in case something went wrong. Thus, in late June, exactly one year after Ricci's return to Nanchang from Nanjing, using what little money was forwarded from Macao, he purchased a modest house close to the Prefect's *yamen*, in spite of the objection of the heads of his neighborhood. This came not a moment too soon, for Ricci was responsible for a household of two Jesuits plus an additional eight to ten servants and disciples, including the convert Ignacio, a young man who had received baptism in Shaozhou against the strong opposition of his father and who ran off to join his western master once he heard that Ricci had settled in Nanchang.

While settling down during 1596, Ricci took up again his work on the new catechism, begun in Shaozhou and interrupted by his move to Jiangxi. By October, Ricci had probably finished a first draft, which he passed around to Chinese friends, to solicit suggestions for stylistic and textual revisions. No doubt, Ricci's participation in Zhang Huang's monthly colloquia sharpened his thoughts, as we have seen. But Ricci was a victim to his own success. He scarcely had time to rest, let alone write. All day long, he received visitors. There was hardly time to eat. Every week brought two to three dinner invitations, sometimes two on the same day. All this popularity exacted a price, especially on Christian feast days, when Ricci had been fasting all day, then going to banquets for hours of conversations on an empty stomach, often eating a late dinner of vegetables (he refrained from fish as the Chinese thought this was not really fasting). His work, which was eventually completed after his move to Beijing, was published in 1603 under the title *Tianzhu shiyi*. Meanwhile, the catechism which this text was meant to replace, Ruggieri's *Tianzhu shilu*, with its references to

Buddhism, was judged no longer acceptable by Valignano and de Sande, who ordered the woodblocks destroyed.

Day by day, Ricci's reputation as a great scholar increased. Many came to his door: most wanted to learn mnemonics, some requested instruction in mathematics, others in alchemy but their ranks grew thinner over time, and still fewer those asking for religious instruction; all addressed him as master. Turning away the alchemists, Ricci agreed to instruct the others, refusing their offers of money and the title of master. Time was not yet ripe for the harvest. 'As yet, we do not want to force them to become Christians,' confided Ricci in a letter to Giulio Fulgati, 'and we are satisfied with laying the foundations for a grand work, when His Divine Majesty opens the way.'[41] For Ricci, pedagogy was preaching, and scholarship salvation, for his conversations, 'even though they do not explain all the mysteries of our holy faith, they all lay down the fundamental principles, namely that God is the creator of heaven and earth, that the soul is immortal, that good and evil will be rewarded and punished, all things unknown and not believed until now by them; and they listen with such satisfaction and with such tears, that very often they burst out spontaneously in verses of praise.'[42]

Two things were clear, Ricci wrote to Acquaviva: given official permission to preach the gospel, they could make millions of converts in a short time; without official permission, they could suddenly lose the little they had achieved. Still obsessed with entering Beijing, Ricci hoped for the long awaited papal embassy, remembering his former companion Ruggieri. If this failed to materialize, Ricci hoped for intercession through his elevated connections: the imperial princes or the three sons of the Grand Secretary Zhang Wei, who were all his friends.

Full of optimism during his three years in Nanchang, Ricci looked toward the future, ameliorating his melancholic nostalgia for the past. The only discordant note came in the autumn of 1595, when a letter from his friend Girolamo Costa informed Ricci of the death of his parents (which was not true). In a tone of sad resignation, Ricci wrote to his brother Antonio Maria: it had been many years since he had had word from home, and even though his friend kept him informed, he prayed that Antonio Maria would 'write in detail about all our brothers, cousins, and sisters, what each person is doing, how they are, who is living well and who is not, in order to console me and to help them in my poor prayers'. Ricci congratulated his brother on obtaining a benefice in the cathedral chapter of their hometown, but warned that if comfort and wealth should bring spiritual harm, it would be better to live as a mendicant. Now that their father was gone, Ricci enjoined his brother to keep watch over their younger siblings, to guide them in the right path, to act as their father. As for him, 'I am already old, very busy in this China, where I have been many years and where I think I will finish my life.' Ricci asked his brother not to think that he 'live[d] in misery so far from our country and among a barbaric people for the love of God because heaven and the angels, citizens of our true country, which is heaven, are always with us and accompany us in every place, and already in this world we have a secure deposit of goodness, which we will enjoy in the next'.[43]

Ricci himself was accumulating a large deposit of reputation, both in China and in the West. The story of his success began to make the rounds in all the corners of the Catholic world, from Japan, to India, to Europe. He had become the leading expert on China. In October 1596 Ricci sent a *Description of China* to Rome, a text which probably served as the basis for the first of five books in his life work, *History of the Entry of Christianity into China*.

A sharp and often acerbic observer, Ricci offered vivid images of late Ming China. To his friend and former companion in the Roman College, the Jesuit Lelio Passionei, Ricci described in detail the imperial civil service examination, which he witnessed in Nanchang. Even though China was governed by an emperor, 'it is rather more a republic than a monarchy, since no relative of the emperor . . . holds any office in the realm . . . The government of the realm is entirely in the hands of the literati.'[44] After describing the disdain for the military and the low status of military officers, Ricci explained that all mandarins were chosen through examinations.[45] The first degree, the *xiucai*, was awarded annually by Education Intendants (*tidu xuedao*), who examined candidates in different cities. The second degree, the *juren*, was decided in provincial examinations, held every three years on the ninth day of the eighth lunar month (it fell on 19 September 1597 in Nanchang). Only some 4,000 candidates out of some 30,000 *xiucai* in the province of Jiangxi earned the right to sit in this examination after passing a preliminary examination. Thousands of anxious young scholars (some not so young) descended on the provincial capital, accompanied by servants and family. On the day of the examination, they filed into the large examination hall, a walled compound divided into 4,000 tiny cells, each equipped with a desk and chair, only after a thorough body search to prevent cheating (see Plate VI). Guarded by soldiers and supervised by mandarins dispatched from other provinces, the candidates sweated long hours composing essays on assigned topics. Once done, scriveners copied their original papers so that the grading officials could recognize neither name nor hand-writing. A fourfold grading process narrowed the 4,000 examinations down to 190, double Jiangxi's quota for the *juren* degree. The mandarin examiners selected the fortunate 95-degree candidates, with each essay ranked from one to ninety-five according to excellence. Then the essays were matched with the originals, and the names of the new *juren* were posted on a large bulletin board, amidst scenes of despair and elation. The following year, all holders of *juren* degrees were entitled to participate in the metropolitan examination, held in Beijing, for the ultimate *jinshi* degree. Of the thousands of hopefuls, only 300 succeeded in each selection, with all ranked in a hierarchy of distinction that determined their first assignment in the large imperial bureaucracy.

Keenly consciousness of rank, Ricci noted in Nanchang he was hobnob-bing with vice-ministers (*shilang*), prefects (*zhifu*), and top provincial offi-cials in the executive and judicial branches (*buzheng shi si* and *ancha shi si*), and mandarins of the full third and full fourth ranks, unlike the lowly bureaucrats he used to socialize with in Guangdong, the county magistrates (*zhixien* and *tongzhi*) of seventh and eighth rank.[46] His obsession with rank and status seemed to indicate Ricci was thinking like a member of the Chinese elite. He certainly behaved like one. During a banquet in Nan-chang, Ricci met a mandarin, formerly the magistrate of Xiangshang Coun-ty with jurisdiction over Macao, then Prefect of Hainan Island, who gave Ricci the supreme compliment by saying to the other mandarins that there was nothing foreign about the Jesuit, except for his face.

The more Ricci behaved like the Chinese elites, the more successful he became. The more his reputation augmented, the greater his self-confidence in knowing the superiority of the West. In several letters from Nanchang, Ricci analyzed the reasons for his success, the foremost being his superb knowledge of the Confucian classics, made more impressive by his stupen-dous memory, which the literati had not expected in a foreigner; equally important was his superior knowledge of mathematics and astronomy. In September 1596, a solar eclipse occurred. Ricci had predicted it months in advance. His Chinese friends were perturbed by the inaccuracy of the prediction issued by the Imperial Directorate of Astronomy. Ricci explained to them that the extent of eclipses depended on the particular site of observation: an eclipse was not the same phenomenon seen from different vantage points. We have seen earlier his acerbic and contemptuous remarks on the state of Chinese astronomy. Ricci's feeling of cultural superiority extended to other fields: 'It is evident that we are superior to them [the Chinese] in many things, as we see in our painting, tapestry, books, discourses, the science and instruments of mathematics, weapons, musical instruments, expensive vestments such as velvet, brocades, woolen drapery, and an infinity of things. With all this, it seems they should be submitting to us and be more humble. I think also that in jurisprudence we can teach them something.'[47] To his professor Clavius, who had sent him his latest book on astrolabes, Ricci replied that he had shown it to Chinese scholars, 'who were astounded by the variety of illustrations'.[48]

Perhaps all these expressions of superiority, vindicated by success and triumphs, allowed Ricci to vent his profound bitterness from the past. Explaining the change of missionary tactics to Duarte de Sande in August 1595, Ricci wrote:[49]

It is not our intention to go after honors, but in this land, where the law of Our Lord has never been known, the reputation and credit of the preachers of this holy doctrine, and to a certain extent the reputation of the law itself, depend on accommodating and acting externally like the Chinese. And now we see how it is important because until recently we have been behaving with external humility and were considered to be Buddhist monks; we were always treated as lowly sorts and nobodies, and could never establish connections with mandarins and other people of note. And now, with this transformation, we have established connections with them and are treated with much honor and courtesies. To safeguard us from the evils of this honor, which we are beginning to receive, Our Lord has made us spend twelve years in Zhaoqing and Shaozhou, suffering so many dishonors, humiliations, insults, and so many persecutions enough to build a good foundation, for in all this time we were treated and held as the scum of the earth. Our Lord, who gave us strength to persevere through so many tribulations, may he give us the same grace so that we will not be destroyed by these honors.

8

Nanjing

In his smooth silk robe, hobnobbing with princes, mandarins, and literati, 'nothing foreign about him, except for his face', as one mandarin remarked, we might easily forget Ricci was a Jesuit. Indeed, beyond Ricci's network of local friendships, invisible to his friends in Nanchang, lay a far greater loyalty to that international Company of missionaries. On 1 January 1596, Ricci swore the Fourth Vow of the Society: beyond the vows of poverty, chastity, and obedience sworn by all Catholic religious, the Jesuits cherished a fourth vow of special obedience to the pope, promising to serve in whatever missionary assignment the supreme pontiff should declare. The professed, as those fathers who take the Fourth Vow are called, form the elite within the Company, for they alone are eligible for positions of leadership. That charge came soon to Ricci. In August 1597, Valignano appointed Ricci superior of the China Mission, subject in theory to the authority of the Rector of the Jesuit College in Macao, but enjoying in practice great autonomy as Ricci was now the senior man and the leading expert in Chinese affairs. In Nanchang, Ricci headed a house with some ten inmates, and oversaw as well the residence in Shaozhou. It was a far cry from the early days, when Ricci was the junior companion to Ruggieri; in 1597, he acted as superior to three priests, two Chinese brothers, and more than a dozen Chinese servants. Soon, his charge would expand even further.

Recall the journey of Michele Ruggieri in 1588 back to Rome. In spite of Ruggieri's failure to secure a papal embassy to the Chinese emperor, Valignano was obsessed with the idea of securing the highest political protection for the fragile China Mission, no doubt inspired by the great success enjoyed by the Jesuit Mission in Japan, under the patronage of feudal lords who had converted to Christianity. From Macao, Valignano prepared and forwarded to Ricci gifts for just such an embassy. But for Ricci, even with his contacts, this proved a daunting task. The Prince of Jian an, whom Ricci approached, flatly refused to help: Ming law barred all feudatory princes from unauthorized travel to Beijing; any act perceived as political intervention could only bring suspicion and censure from the imperial court.

Again, help showed up where least expected. An acquaintance from his past, Wang Zhongming, former Minister of Rites in Nanjing, who had stopped in 1594 in Shaozhou while traveling to his hometown on Hainan Island, had promised to use Ricci's knowledge in mathematics for the emendation of the imperial calendar. Recalled to his post after the prescribed period of parental mourning, Wang Zhongming passed through Shaozhou. On instructions left by Ricci, Lazzaro Cattaneo paid the mandarin a visit and reminded Wang of his earlier promise, informing the mandarin that Ricci was now in Nanchang. Traveling quickly, Cattaneo and a new Portuguese missionary, João da Rocha, arrived in Nanchang two days ahead of Wang. Alerted of this new opportunity, Ricci made preparations. He paid Wang a visit, upon the latter's arrival. Telling the mandarin of his ardent desire to offer gifts of tribute to the emperor, Ricci showed Wang the precious commodities he had received from Macao: two European clocks, a painting of the Savior, and a Venetian prism. The last item Ricci presented as a gift to persuade Mandarin Wang; to this Ricci added the overwhelming gift of a clock to clench Wang's goodwill.

In a sanguine mood, Wang Zhongming promised to take Ricci not only to Nanjing, but on to Beijing, where he was heading to present gifts for Emperor Wanli's birthday on the seventeenth day of the eighth lunar month. A quick decision was made. Leaving the two Portuguese fathers Soerio and da Rocha in Nanchang, Ricci took along two old companions, Cattaneo and the Chinese brother Sebastian Fernandes (Zhong Mingren), as well as the young Macao Chinese You Wenhui (1575–1633, baptized Manoel Pereira). Having studied with the famous Jesuit painter Giovanni Nicolao, one of Ricci's companions in the 1582 voyage from Goa to Macao, You Wenhui later joined the Society and became Ricci's companion in his last years, from whose brush comes the only authentic portrait of the legendary missionary.

After a short journey, Wang's party arrived in Nanjing by boat on 25 June 1598. Ricci, of course, knew this route well. Unfortunately, he arrived at a bad moment, just like his first visit. In 1595, the Japanese invasion of Korea had overshadowed Ricci's first visit to the southern Ming capital; now, the breakdown of peace negotiations, and a second invasion of Korea by

Hideyoshi, sowed even greater suspicion on all foreigners. Nanjing was in fear: Japanese spies had been arrested, and officials admonished all inn-keepers not to accept suspicious persons. Unable to find lodgings on land, Ricci and his party sweated on the barges. He paid an exorbitant sum to a famous Chinese scholar, who composed an elegant memorial to accompany his tribute gifts. But the *tongzheng shi*, the official responsible for transmit-ting all memorials from Nanjing to Beijing, refused to accept it. Since Wang Zhongming was traveling to Beijing to present birthday gifts on behalf of all the Nanjing ministries, and since he was the patron of this foreigner, the *tongzheng shi* refused to take on any responsibility, lest he himself got into trouble. Such truculent moods affected even the sanguine Wang. He wanted to send Ricci back to Nanchang. But indebted to Ricci for extrava-gant gifts, Wang resolved to banish his anxieties. Taking the faster land route, Wang set off for Beijing, while arranging for Ricci and his com-panions to travel by boat as members of his household.

An invitation delayed Ricci's departure. Unbeknownst to him, an ac-quaintance of Ricci from his Shaozhou days, the Subprefect of Nanxiong County, Wang Yinlin (Yuzha), had privately published Ricci's *Map of the World*. In 1598, Wang Yinlin had risen to the rank of *zhifu* of Zhenjiang, an important port and fortress on the Yangzi a little distance downstream from Nanjing. To his superiors and colleagues in the mandarin world, Wang had given reprints of the *World Map* as presents, albeit without Ricci's name. One copy ended up in the hands of Zhao Kehuai, the *xunfu* of Nanjing (the Southern Zhili Province) and Wang's immediate superior. Charmed by the map, Zhao wrote a preface, had it reprinted, and distributed copies as his own gift, including one to Wang Zhongming, to congratulate his old friend on his reappointment to the Ministry of Rites in Nanjing. Having seen a similar map in Ricci's possession, Wang Zhongming consulted with the Jesuit and was proud to discover that he was indeed the patron of the author of a famous world map. Wang Zhongming wrote to inform Zhao, who promptly issued an invitation for Ricci to visit him at his magistracy, located in the little town of Jurong, 25 miles to the southeast of Nanjing. Zhao's invitation arrived the day before the Jesuits' scheduled departure. Charging Cattaneo with the trip to Beijing, Ricci set out for Jurong, where he spent eight to ten days in intense and pleasant conversations on mathematics, Europe, and Christianity with Zhao Kehuai, who showed unusual rever-ence to a picture of Christ, setting it up on a table to offer incense and salutations. Unable to detain Ricci further, Zhao sent a party to escort the westerner to the Yangzi, where Ricci took passage on a fast boat to travel north on the Grand Canal.

Travel agreed with Ricci. After leaving Nanchang, Ricci noted the distances between towns and the geographic locations of cities; now, on the Grand Canal, Ricci noted the details of life along its route, observing scenes along the major supply line for the northern capital, where hundreds of slow barges transported rice, vegetables, fruits, silk, porcelain, and other products from the fertile and rich provinces south of the Yangzi to the austere north, where fast boats carried urgent couriers and perishable foods, brutal eunuchs and important mandarins, pushing past other traffic lined up at the sluices with threatening shouts and ostentatious banners. At every sluice, hundreds of workers on both banks stood ready to pull the heavy boats on thick ropes wound around their tattered clothes and bulging shoulders. At every town, inns, eateries, and shops catered to travelers, soldiers, and workers. In the summer of 1598, Ricci also saw numerous barges loaded with logs, cut from the mountain forests of remote Sichuan province, all for reconstructing buildings in the imperial palace destroyed by recent fires. Somewhere on the Grand Canal, Ricci caught up with his party. Along the route, the Jesuits had a first taste of the arbitrary and avaricious power of the palace eunuchs, empowered and dispatched by Emperor Wanli as tax farmers, who terrorized the country with their cruel and corrupt demands.

On 8 September, the feast day of the Virgin Mary, the Jesuits arrived in Beijing. They had disembarked in Tongzhou, the terminus of the Grand Canal, and had proceeded by land for the short distance to the capital. There, out of the dusty brown soil, loomed the mighty city. Beijing was a veritable fortress: impregnable outer walls higher than those of any European city, in width more than twenty feet thick, shaped the rectangular capital; a second wall protected the Imperial or Forbidden City; all along the parapets, watch towers, and city gates soldiers stood guard. Ricci disliked Beijing. Dust everywhere. The streets were unpaved. There was little water. When the northern winds swept down from the Mongolian Desert, they whipped up the dust like so many small twisters, blowing in the face of people, who went about the city covered with black hoods to protect their eyes from the sand that got into everything: clothes, chambers, and beds. When it rained, the streets turned to mud. Unlike the southern cities, in Beijing there were no rivers, streams, or canals to sail on, no sedan chairs to wander about the tree-lined and stone-paved streets. The poor walked.

Those who could afford rented horses. This form of transport, plentiful though expensive, had the disadvantage of pollution: horses defecated, as did the camels from the caravans of Central Asia and the donkeys driven into town by peasants selling their produce. A foul smell engulfed Beijing. In the winter months, the winds served up a revolting mixture of sand, desiccated feces, and coal dust, the latter from the ubiquitous heating material used in northern China, dug from the surface of the land. Wood was long gone. The hills to the north and west of Beijing had been deforested for more than a century before Ricci. After the capital was transferred from Nanjing to Beijing in 1421, the population of the former forlorn frontier town quadrupled within half a century; the great demand for fuel quickly denuded the hills around Beijing.

In this arid, cold, and dirty city, a mighty capital of a powerful empire, and yet a frontier fortress, Ricci stayed for two months. This was indeed the capital of Great Cathay, Cambaluc, described in the book of the Venetian traveler Marco Polo, thus concluded Ricci. His dislike echoed the sentiments of many Ming literati, who hailed from the softer climate, waterways, and green towns of the south. During his first month, Ricci and Cattaneo stayed with Wang Zhongming, but the latter's effort to secure contact for Ricci with palace eunuchs failed. Although they seemed to like the gifts of the Jesuits, the eunuchs deemed it unwise to introduce foreigners to the capital in these dangerous times of war. After a month, by decree, Wang Zhongming left the capital. Spending the money sent to him for this purpose from Macao, Ricci rented a private house. But he failed to make any contacts. His mandarin acquaintances avoided him. The eunuchs spoke only the language of bribes, for which the money from Macao was far from enough, and mostly about the Jesuits' alchemical reputation, which Ricci was unable to live up to.

Ricci had enough. The problem with Beijing, he concluded, 'was that this emperor was very cruel with the eunuchs of his palace, and had them caned to death for the smallest offence. And nobody bestirred himself for any external business, if there was no occasion of gaining money. Likewise, the mandarins harbored the same intention, that is to demand money from those coming from the outside seeking business at court, to make the provincial mandarins, who had robbed clean the provinces and the cities, cough up large sums of money. So it seems that this city is a veritable Babylon of confusion, full of all kinds of sins, with no-one interested in justice, piety, or his own salvation.'[1]

The Jesuits left Beijing in early November, having secured a good price on the empty barges returning to the south. It took their boat a month to arrive in Linqing, just over the provincial border in Shandong. By then, the waters of the Grand Canal were frozen. They were forced to winter in Linqing. Impatient to return, Ricci charged Cattaneo with the care of the gifts, the baggage, and the travelers, and hurried back to the south with one servant. He was determined to seek out Qu Rukui, his disciple and good friend from the days of Guangdong.

After leaving Ricci in Shaozhou, Qu had returned to Suzhou. From his hometown, Qu wrote a few times to Ricci in Shaozhou and Nanchang, suggesting his master might settle there. There Ricci hastened. In this 'Venice of the East', with its canals, bridges, and urban gardens, famed for its urban and feminine beauty, Ricci learned that his friend was lodging in a Buddhist monastery in nearby Danyang. At the end of 1598, the old friends met again. Qu Rukui offered Ricci his own bed, sleeping instead on the floor, while the two reminisced on the past and discussed the future. Worn down by his journey, and the stress, Ricci fell very ill. But in a month, Qu nursed him back to health. Suzhou it will be, the two concluded: such a beautiful city, a center of commerce and culture, where the Qu family counted among the notables. The two would travel to Nanjing to ask for a letter of patronage from Wang Zhongming to be presented to the mandarins in Suzhou. But first, the friends celebrated Chinese New Year, which fell on 27 January in 1599, in Zhenjiang, where they met up with another old acquaintance, the magistrate Wang Yinlin, who organized an official escort for Ricci and Qu. On 6 February, the friends arrived in Nanjing. They took lodgings at the Cheng en si, a Buddhist temple constructed in the 1450s. Located close to the southern city gate (today the Zhonghua men) near the Qinhuai River, the temple stood in the midst of the entertainment district of Nanjing, famous for its taverns, teahouses, restaurants, and parlors of courtesans.

The friends paid Wang Zhongming a visit. Feeling guilty, perhaps, for his failure to secure Ricci a better hearing in Beijing, Wang played the gracious host, inviting the westerner to his official residence for the evening of the Lantern Festival, the fifteenth day after Lunar New Year, where they watched the sky above Nanjing lit up with a spectacular show of fireworks.

To succeed one needs 'heaven's timing, local advantage, and human harmony', as the Chinese proverb goes. Ricci had all three. The timing was right. The Korean War was finally over. The Japanese warlord Hideyoshi had died on 18 September 1598. War weary, the invasion army returned to Japan, not before a final defeat by the Sino-Korean navy. Nanjing, and all of China, was in an ebullient mood. For human harmony, Ricci enjoyed the friendship of Wang Zhongming, who introduced the westerner to his colleagues at the other Nanjing ministries; Ricci was also in the company of Qu Rukui, whose father had been a famous figure in Nanjing and who knew almost everyone of note. Day after day, streams of visitors paid courtesy at their rooms in the Buddhist temple. As for local advantage, Nanjing was unparalleled.

Political power might have moved north with the imperial court in 1421, but Nanjing remained the cultural and social capital of the Great Ming. Three rings of fortifications protected the grand southern capital: an extensive outer wall, constructed from earth interspersed with brick strongholds, a middle wall encompassing large spaces and sixteen gates, and the proper city walls, constructed between 1365 and 1386 by Zhu Yuanzhang, the founder of the Ming dynasty. This last ring of city walls measured more than twenty miles, making them longer even than those of Beijing. Unlike the rectangular layout of the northern capital, the Nanjing city walls hugged the landscape, incorporating rivers and hills into its defense. Rising from the banks of the Yangzi in the west and north, the walls skirted Lake Xuanwu and hugged the hills to the northeast (the Ziqinshan and the Zhongshan) before turning south to take advantage of a tributary of the Yangzi to anchor the southern walls. No fewer than thirteen gates, some with a capacity to house thousands of troops, guarded the capital with its population of over 780,000. Coming from a hill town with formidable walls, Ricci was properly impressed and would describe the walls of Nanjing in detail.

No less impressive was the functional division of urban space. The Imperial City, enclosed by its own walls, sat beneath the northeastern hills and occupied the eastern part of Nanjing, together with the offices of the ministries and other government bureaus. Encompassing some high grounds and facing the Yangzi, the northern quarters formed the military stronghold where the garrison was stationed. As we have seen, the southern district, named after the Qinhuai River that flows through its streets, was the entertainment center. Crowded into the urban space were altars to heaven and earth, the Drum and Bell Towers, palaces of blood-line princes and hereditary dukes, offices of regional and local magistracies, the Directorate of National Education (the *guozi jian*), and the official Confucian academies. Numerous Buddhist and Daoist temples dotted the city and outlying hills. Here and there, ancient monuments reminded visitors that in different guises, the city had served as the capital for six dynasties and several regional kingdoms in China's past. Of special interest to Ricci, on the Jiming Hill to the north was situated the observatory of the Imperial Directorate of Astronomy; the Muslim Bureau, which the Ming had inherited from the Mongol Yuan dynasty, was located outside the southern gate (the Jubao Gate, now the Zhonghua Gate) and its observatory situated on the hill behind Yuhuatai (see Map 6).

This center of power was no more, after the imperial court moved north. Uninhabited, the imperial palace lapsed into faded glory and disrepair. Only a rump of the imperial bureaucracy remained: manned by a skeletal staff, the six ministries were no more than prestigious sinecures, a pale reflection of the real power wielded in the ministerial corridors of Beijing. Nevertheless, Nanjing retained its leading role as a cultural and consumption capital: all the products and riches of Jiangnan flowed into the city; all the talent of the country congregated here. From its provincial hinterland and from neighboring Zhejiang and Jiangxi provinces, where the lion's share of

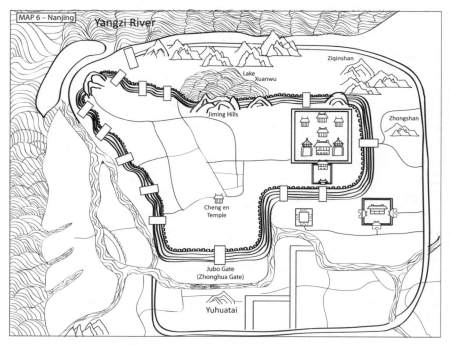

Map 6. Nanjing in the Ming dynasty

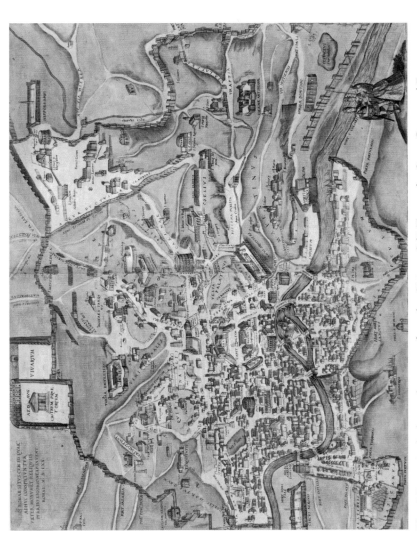

Plate I Rome in the late 16th century, from the *Civitates Orbis Terrarum* by Georg Braun and Franz Hogenberg (1575), provided by the Hebrew University of Jerusalem and the Jewish National Library

Plate II Lisbon in the late 16th century, from the *Civitates Orbis Terrarum* by Georg Braun and Franz Hogenberg (1575), provided by the Hebrew University of Jerusalem and the Jewish National Library

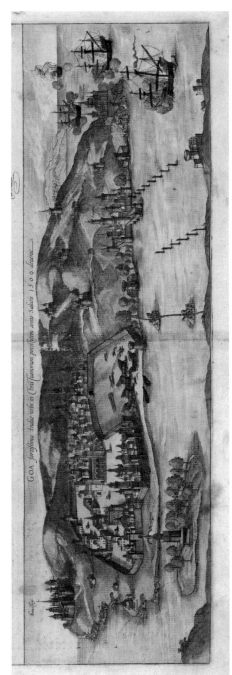

GOA. *foraffima Indiæ Indiæ urbis in Christianorum poteftatem anno Salutis 1 5 0 0 . deuenit.*

Plate III Goa in the late 16th century, from the *Civitates Orbis Terrarum* by Georg Braun and Franz Hogenberg (1575), provided by the Hebrew University of Jerusalem and the Jewish National Library

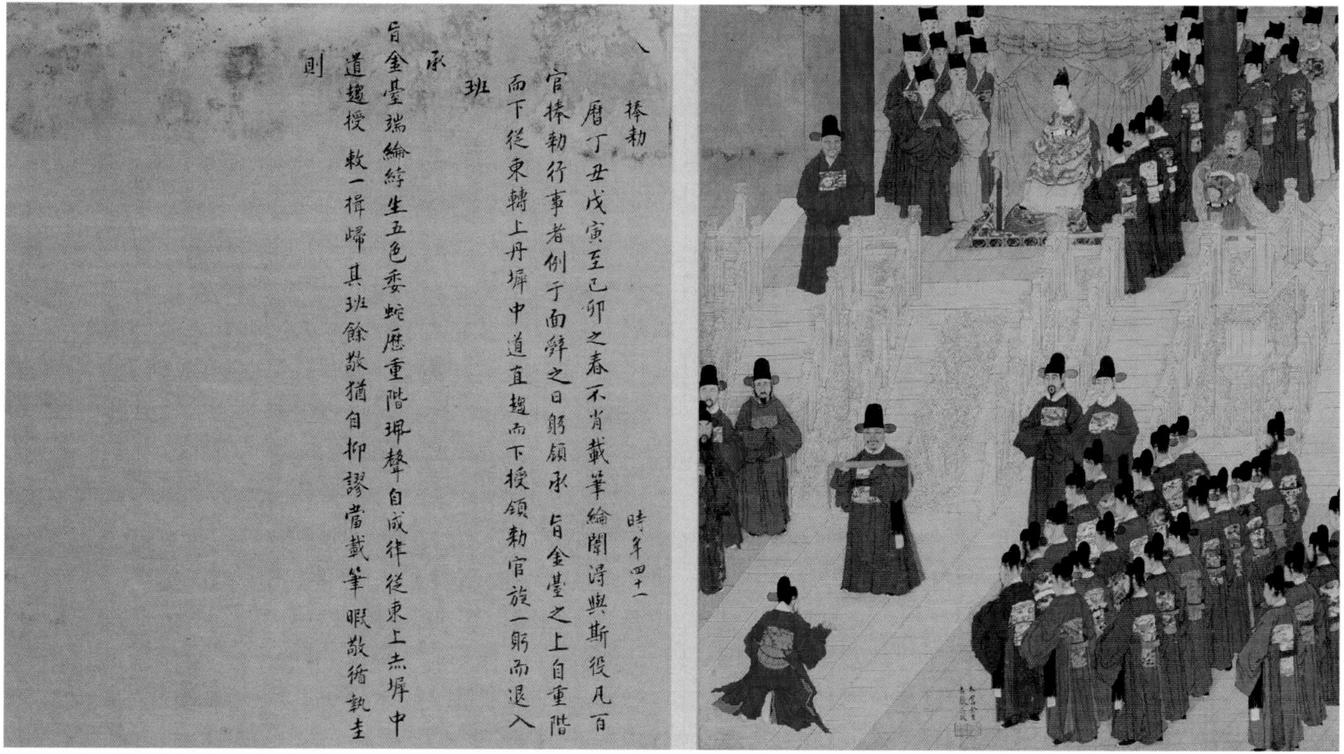

Plate IV Portrait of Ming mandarins, a scene from the life of the Ming mandarin Xu Xianqing. Palace Museum, Beijing

Plate V Nanhua Monastery, main entrance. Photo by author

Plate VI Candidates in the Imperial Civil Service Examination Hall, a scene from the life of the Ming mandarin Xu Xianqing. Palace Museum, Beijing

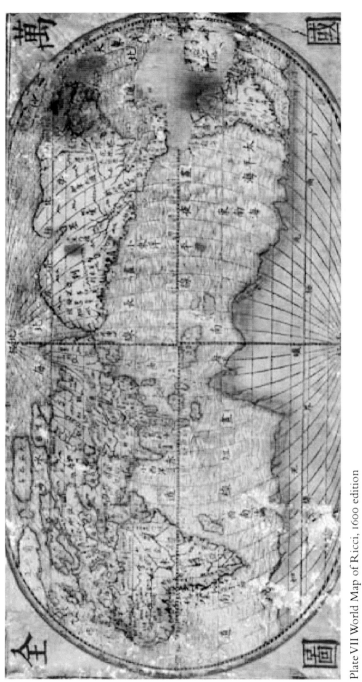

Plate VII *World Map of Ricci, 1600 edition*

Plate VIII Portrait of the Wanli emperor

Plate IX A Ming painting of the Forbidden City in Beijing

Plate X Nicholas Trigault, portrait by Peter Paul Rubens, Metropolitan Museum of Art, New York

successful examination candidates and famous literati hailed, Nanjing drew its human resources. A secondary capital it might have been, but Nanjing offered much more of a pleasant life than the harsh climate and uncertain politics of Beijing.

Wang Zhongming urged Ricci to settle in Nanjing, as did many visitors who offered advice and references to potential real estate. Meeting unexpected success, Ricci gradually changed his mind about Suzhou; his friend Qu Ruikui spoke no more of it, happy in the knowledge that Ricci would go far in the southern capital. In time, Ricci moved out of the monastery and rented a commodious house before eventually buying a large residence. Although Ricci spent only fifteen months in Nanjing (6 February 1599 to 18 May 1600), he achieved more in that short time than in any other period of his long sojourn in China. Like a pebble thrown into a pond, Ricci's reputation rippled in wave after wave of recognition. More solid in renown than before, having published *The World Map* and two Chinese treatises in Nanchang, and having returned from a tribute-bearing journey from Beijing, Ricci found Nanjing the largest body of water so far in his China sojourn, a sea of social networks that could float or sink a career.

In his memoirs, Ricci recorded many names from the far larger number of people he had encountered: aristocrats, mandarins, literati, scientists, and converts. Among the highest ranked, Ricci was received by the Duke of Wei, Xu Hongji, descendant of General Xu Ta, who fought alongside the dynastic founder, Zhu Yuanzhang, and by the Marquis of Fengcheng, Li Huan, the top military commander in Nanjing. A curious meeting also took place between Ricci and Feng Bao, chief of the eunuchs in Nanjing and, before his disgrace in 1582, one of the most powerful men in the country. Forty years ago, as companion to the young heir apparent, the future Wanli emperor, Feng Bao acquired vast influence. Even after ascending the throne, the teenage emperor regarded Feng Bao with a mixture of affection and awe, calling him 'Big Companion'. Unlike most eunuchs, Feng Bao was an educated man, who appreciated music and literature. Appointed Director of Ceremonials, Feng Bao was the head of the thousands of eunuchs in the Inner Court. By cultivating the Empress Dowager Ci Sheng, a mother beloved and feared by the young Wanli, and allying himself with Zhang Juzheng, the new and ambitious Grand Secretary, Feng Bao controlled communications between the Inner Palace and the court, making himself into a powerbroker for the first decade of Wanli's reign. As Wanli matured under the strict supervision of his mother and

Grand Secretary Zhang, he chaffed under the restraints of his strict moral upbringing. One night, the 18-year-old emperor, under the influence of two trusted eunuchs and intoxicated, went on a violent rampage and injured two boy eunuchs who belonged to the household of Feng. Chief Eunuch Feng reported this to the empress dowager, who threatened to dethrone the rambunctious Wanli, until her son, in tears and kneeling, promised repentance, an act formalized in an edict of apology to his court, forced upon the deeply humiliated young man. Wanli never forgave Feng Bao. After the death of Zhang Juzheng, he dismissed Feng Bao from office. Only the memory of happier times with his childhood companion saved Feng Bao's life. Instead of execution urged by several censors at court, Wanli demoted Feng Bao to Nanjing and ensured a comfortable retirement by a generous stipend, after confiscating the enormous wealth accumulated by the powerful eunuch during his years of power.[2]

In 1599, Feng Bao, an old man of 70 and long out of power, was curious to meet Ricci. Sharing the disdain of the mandarins toward the eunuchs, Ricci was reluctant, especially since Feng's attendants insisted the westerner utter obsequious compliments. Ricci refused. He greeted Feng with the usual courtesies he used for mandarins, but since Feng was almost deaf, one of his attendants repeated Ricci's words and added the desired compliments. Nevertheless, the audience went nowhere. Feng Bao desired a prism as a gift. Ricci answered that it was reserved for the emperor. The eunuch replied that the emperor possessed many larger ones. They parted and never met again. Long out of power, Chief Eunuch Feng Bao had not forgotten the pomp of past glory. For the Jesuit missionary, the encounter further reinforced his negative image of eunuchs, who were used by Wanli to extract mining and other extraordinary taxes and were becoming a plague on the country.

Some fell from power, others were destined for higher offices. Among the mandarins introduced to Ricci by Wang Zhongming was Ye Xianggao (1559–1627), the Vice-Minister of Rites, Wang's immediate subordinate. In 1607, Ye was promoted to Minister of Rites in Beijing and the Grand Secretariat; from 1608 to 1614, and again between 1620 and 1624, he served as the Senior Grand Secretary; after his retirement to his native Fuzhou, he became the patron and protector of a new generation of Jesuit missionaries in his native province.[3] Another Nanjing mandarin Ricci met who would be promoted to higher office in Beijing was the Hanlin academician Yang Daobin, who became a Vice-Minister of Rites in Beijing.

Among the literati and the scientists (the two were not mutually exclusive categories in traditional China), Ricci met some of the leading intellectuals of the late Ming. In terms of political employment, some had served in the imperial bureaucracy and left out of disillusionment, others still held office, and still others belonged only to the world of letters. In terms of intellectual affinities, we may divide them into three groupings: the first group met Ricci due to his literary fame and his friendship with Qu Rukui; others gravitated to Ricci because of their interest in mathematics and astronomy; and a last group, many of them Confucian literati with strong Buddhist commitments, engaged Ricci in philosophical and religious discussions.

In this veritable market of culture and ideas, Ricci wandered, 'dressed in clothes . . . completely in the style of the literati, which is quite honorable, and wearing a square beret in the shape of a cross, quite similar to our priestly berets'. And thus, Ricci proceeded to dispute against the teachings of Buddhism and Daoism, while praising those of Confucius, 'who, ignorant of the things of the other life, had only given doctrines of living a good life in this present world, and of governing and conserving the peace of the realm and the republic'.[4]

But not all literati, though schooled in the common Confucian Canon, were enemies of Buddhism and Daoism. Intellectually, the Ming literati were as diverse a group as their fashion, as the Nanjing native Gu Qiyuan, a student of Ye Xianggao, would remark in his 1617 collection of vignettes about life in the southern capital, *Leftover Conversations from the Guest Seat* (*Ke zuo zhui yu*). In his anecdote on men's head- and footgear, Gu writes:

Fashion in the southern capital was still austere before the reigns of Longqing and Wanli . . . In recent years, they tend to the new, the curious, and the odd. There are many names to the headgear of the literati: the Han style, the Qin style, the Tang style, the Zhuge Lian style, the Daoist style, the Su Dongpo style [this was Ricci's beret], the Wang Yangming style, the Jiuhua style, the Jade Platform, the Carefree style, the yarn hat, the Huayang style, the four-open style, the Warrior style. Some attach jade ties to their hats, others a jade-flower vase attached with two large jade rings. For the Daoist, Jiuhua, Carefree, and Huayang styles, there are front and back flaps that flutter with the wind. The stitches are lined with golden thread. The fabrics are silky, meshed, or dyed; other than simple yarn one also uses horse-tail yarn and dragon-scale yarn; they come in sky-blue or sky-green. For those headgears woven from horse tails, there is a difference between the single and the double threaded. In our day, we have indeed reached the summit of luxury and conspicuous consumption for fashion![5]

Compared to some of these dandies, Ricci no doubt cut a modest and austere figure.

Let us meet the first group of literati Ricci encountered through his friendship with Qu Rukui, who were known for their literary achievements. The most prominent was Li Xinzhai. Like Qu Rukui, Li Xinzhai also made a living from his fine calligraphy and elegant compositions. Initially wary of Qu, whom he feared as a competitor using the reputation of the remarkable westerner, Li Xinzhai warmed to Ricci after Qu Rukui introduced the two in order to forestall any animosity. Telling Li that his presence in Nanjing was only temporary and only to help Ricci find a house, Qu Rukui turned Li Xinzhai into an ally for the Jesuit. Likewise, Qu introduced Ricci to his friend Zhu Shilu, who held the post of Supervising Secretary of the Office of Scrutiny for Personnel (*li ke gei shi zhong*), a famous poet and calligrapher, who admired Ricci for his book *On Friendship*. It helped that Zhou was a native of Jiangxi, where Ricci had spent three years and published his encomium on friendship.

A second group of literati interested in mathematics and astronomy gravitated toward Ricci since the westerner, in his own modest words, was 'another Ptolemy'. Ricci's judgment that 'the Chinese knew nothing [of astronomy]' and that the Ming literati were 'dedicated only to moral philosophy and elegance in speaking and writing', while exaggerated (see Chapter 7), contained a kernel of truth. Indeed, mathematical and astronomical knowledge in the Ming dynasty had fallen behind the achievements of the medieval period under the Song and Yuan dynasties. There was a social and political explanation to the general lack of interest in natural philosophy among the Ming literati. Mathematics was not a subject in the imperial civil service examination and hence irrelevant to social advancement. Astronomy, on the other hand, was shrouded in political privilege: knowledge of the stars, and the secrets of heaven it revealed, belonged to the most arcane and protected sphere of statecraft, invisible to the commoner. Nevertheless, there was a growing concern in sixteenth-century China to recover the knowledge of past astronomical and mathematical achievements, which explained, in part, Ricci's great reputation with the literati.[6]

Among his first students in Nanjing were two disciples of Li Xinzhai, one particularly skilled in mathematics. But Ricci's best student was one Zhang Yangmu, a disciple of Wang Kentang. A Hanlin academician and son of the famous mandarin Wang Zhao, Kentang had resigned from office and returned to Nanjing. Interested in natural philosophy and particularly learned in medicine, Wang Kentang was keenly aware of the deficient state of astronomy. Due to his age and residence in Zhenjiang, Kentang was unable to come to Nanjing, sending his student Zhang Yangmu in his place. In all of this, Qu Rukui, Ricci's friend and first disciple, served as a teaching assistant, having already translated the First Book of the *Elements* of Euclid during his time with Ricci in Shaozhou.

Among the many astronomical ideas introduced by Ricci, some were novel and represented a more accurate picture of the heavens, others reflected the limitations of the Ptolemaic-Aristotelian cosmology current in late sixteenth-century Europe, only a decade away from the invention of the telescope by Galileo and his challenge to the traditional earth-centered view of the universe. In terms of scientific progress, the introduction of Euclidean or three-dimensional geometry represented a major break-through. Ricci was able to teach his Chinese students the process by which lunar and solar eclipses could be predicted, and demonstrate the reason by which one could deduce why the sun was a larger celestial body than the moon. With the help of his students, Ricci, an expert technician, made various astronomical instruments both for pedagogic as well as for propaganda purposes: astrolabes (for measuring angles), quadrants (for measuring heights in surveillance), celestial spheres with the earth in the center (showing the equator, equinoxes, solstices, the ecliptic, the polar circle, and the meridian), and sundials, both horizontal models and those that could be mounted on walls, marked with celestial signs and the twenty-four Chinese seasonal terms. Many were produced as gifts, which quickly spread the fame of the western astronomer in Nanjing.

Ricci's expertise provoked anxiety. At the Directorate of Astronomy, the imperial astronomers, whose task consisted only in nightly observations and recordings of stellar positions, feared that the foreigner would jeopardize their meager stipends and job security. Discreetly, they contacted Ricci's students, who boasted their master was such an important man back in his own country that any office at the Directorate would be below his dignity. Assured of their rice bowls, the mandarins paid Ricci a courtesy visit. Their lack of scientific curiosity left a bad impression on Ricci, who dismissed them as 'men of little spirit and knowledge'. However, our Jesuit astronomer was much more impressed by their instruments. Returning the courtesy visit, Ricci toured the Imperial Observatory on top of Jiming Hill, located within the northern city walls close to Lake Xuanwu (see Figure 10). This was an eye-opening experience for Ricci, who saw beautiful astronomical instruments, cast in bronze, grander than any he had seen in Europe. Four in particular impressed him: a celestial globe larger than the embrace of three men, marked with meridians and latitudes (lines showing right ascension and declinations), set on a cube with a door allowing an astronomer to enter within, though seemingly unfinished since no constellations were marked; an equatorial armillary sphere with a diameter of two arms' length, showing

Figure 10. Nanjing, Ming city walls, with a view of the pagoda of the Jiming Temple in the background

the poles and the horizon circle, marked by 365 degrees, and in the center, instead of the earth, was inserted a sighting tube that could be moved to observe any sector of the sky; a gnomon four to five arms' length in height, set on a stone slab, for measuring the solstices and equinoxes; and the largest instrument of all, an equatorial torquetum, consisting of three to four circles showing the equinoxes and the vertical circle, with carvings of gradations that could be detected by touch in the dark night sky. These instruments were eloquent testimonies to the genius of the great Yuan astronomer Guo Shoujin (1231–1316), whose unsurpassed astronomical knowledge and star catalogue had been lost by the time of the Ming dynasty.

Ricci had a fragmentary knowledge of Chinese astronomy. It was not his fault. The failure to accumulate astronomical knowledge in China impeded scientific progress. While Ricci could demonstrate more accurate predictions of eclipses and explain astronomical phenomena in a theoretically more systematic way, he did not grasp some fundamental differences between the European and Chinese astronomical systems. While European astronomy, following the Greeks, focused on the ecliptic, measuring the heavens and the passage of time by the sun's path (i.e. the ecliptic path of the earth around the sun), and representing the latter by the twelve zodiacal signs, Chinese astronomers fixed their gaze on the Pole Star and measured time by dividing the heavens into twenty-four lunar mansions (constellations), based on their observations of the movements of stars around the North Pole.

Two works by Ricci in Nanjing illustrate precisely the ambivalent nature of Ricci's scientific pedagogy: it introduced advanced ideas and techniques to China while maintaining an assumption of western superiority based on erroneous knowledge. The first work is an updated and vastly expanded edition of the *World Map*, first published in Zhaoqing, and the other is a booklet, *On the Operations of the Four Elements*.

The second edition of the *World Map* (the Chinese title was *Kunyu wanguo quantu*) presented a vastly greater amount of geographical knowledge than the 1584 Zhaoqing edition (see Plate VII). In addition to presenting sharper, more accurate contours of the continents, Ricci provided detailed notations for various regions and countries of the world. The biggest innovation, however, was the incorporation of western astronomical knowledge into cartography. At the four corners of the new *World Map* Ricci drew four circles: two represented the globe viewed from the North and South Poles; the third presented the Ptolemaic view of the cosmos, with

the earth at the center of nine concentric spheres, where the planets are
fixed in place; and the fourth shows an armillary sphere, showing the polar,
equatorial, ecliptic, and equinoctial circles. Finally, two tiny diagrams
explain the equinoxes and the solar and lunar eclipses. This revised edition
of the *World Map* was printed not only in the format of a large flat sheet, but
also mounted on a globe; it made a huge impact and was reprinted many
times during Ricci's life and after his death.

The second work, *On the Operations of the Four Elements* (*siyuanxing lun*), was
written to refute the Chinese theory of Five Elements, and later incorporated
as a chapter in the larger work *Qiankun tiyi* (*A Theory of Heaven and Earth*),
published in 1601 after Ricci's move to Beijing. Written as a dialogue between
himself and a Chinese interlocutor, this work possibly represented the conversations during his astronomical lessons. The Chinese theory explained the
interactions among the five elements of metal, wood, fire, water, and earth as
essential to all natural phenomena. Criticizing this theory as erroneous, Ricci
advanced instead the theory of Four Elements developed from the Greeks, in
which air, water, earth, and fire constituted all matter.

The interest of this short treatise lies not in the substitution of the Graeco-
Renaissance theory of matter for the Chinese one, but in Ricci's rhetoric of
persuasion, a method which would also characterize his most famous work,
the *Tianzhu Shiyi*, a treatise on philosophy and theology published later in
Beijing. To advance his arguments, Ricci resorted to both Aristotelian logic
and ancient Chinese classics. Defining *xing* (operation) as an act from a pure
essence, Ricci casts doubt on the Chinese theory: although water, fire, and
earth represent pure essences, metal and wood are compound elements and
cannot constitute fundamental elements. The Chinese, in Aristotelian
terms, confused substance with accidents: only air, water, fire, and earth
represent substances, whereas metal and wood are accidents of material
operations, produced by the interactions between fire and earth (for
metal) and water and earth (wood). To mitigate his critique, to save face
for the Chinese, Ricci declared that:

When I read accounts of the Creation from the ancient legends of Tang and Yue,
and the *Chen Mo* of *Xia Yu*, I observe that these five things are listed together with
grains as the six essential supplies for the people. There was never any talk of water,
fire, metal, wood, and earth as elementary operations or as the essence of all matter.
Only the scholars from latter times (*hou ru*) claimed water gave rise to wood, wood
to fire, fire to earth, and earth to metal, and then expanding to say that wood is born

of water, fire from wood, earth from fire, and metal from earth, and water from metal. This theory is hardly persuasive.[7]

In other words, in science as in religion, the ancient Chinese had the correct understanding, all errors were made by later Chinese scholars. Ricci was doing nothing other than demonstrating to the Ming scholars the correct ideas of their own ancient sages. After explaining how the four elements govern the character of celestial bodies, the four seasons, and the four fluids of the human body (from Greek medical theory), Ricci used the occasion to attack Buddhist theories of nature. Convinced by the master's discourse, the Chinese interlocutor uttered to himself: 'The five operations and six essentials from our antiquity thus refer to the uses of the four elements. Our literati have confused these terms, failing to distinguish between substance and accidents. That must not be!'[8]

Yet the Chinese student was puzzled about Ricci's location of the four elements: 'Teacher, you say fire is concentrated underneath the ninth heaven [the sphere of the sun in Ptolemaic cosmology], this is a new discourse, never known in China. I would like to know by what reason your esteemed country has come to this view?'[9] Ricci's reply reflected the mixture of the correct and erroneous that was characteristic of this encounter of Sino-European astronomy. Demonstrating the sun's much greater mass than that of the earth, a fact unknown in traditional Chinese astronomy, Ricci went on to repeat an error in Ptolemaic cosmology. Among the reasons he cited to support the location of fire in the ninth sphere, Ricci explained: 'the shooting fires one sees at night look like falling stars, but they are not stars, rather streams of smoke rising from the earth that get ignited when they reach the locus of fire. From antiquity there are a fixed number of stars that form constellations and cannot be diminished. If stars fall from the sky every night, how can we maintain their number and their constellations? Would the celestial stars not all die? Since celestial matter never decays, how can it fall?'[10]

Ricci was unaware that ancient Chinese astronomers had observed supernovae, variable stars, and comets, including several sightings of Halley's Comet between 87 BC and AD 1066, many centuries before Halley's own observation in 1682. Frozen in the solid, fixed planetary spheres of Ptolemy, the orthodox astronomical doctrines of the West, Ricci dismissed ancient Chinese astronomy, ignorant of the Chinese theory of the universe as an infinite empty space and their meticulous recordings of falling stars.

The rigid celestial spheres, as it were, held up a doctrine of creation, placing Man and the earth at the center of the created world, with concentric planetary spheres turned by the Prime Mover, God. While all astronomical systems seek to recognize celestial regularity through measurement, in order to devise calendars for the periodic division of light from darkness, the warm season from the cold, they are also enmeshed in specific cultural imperatives. The Christianized cosmology presented by Ricci to the Chinese, derived from Ptolemaic astronomy and Aristotelian logic, aimed for the permanent and the demonstrable, for the cosmic manifestations of divine authority. Chinese astronomy, in contrast, focused on observing, recording, and perhaps forestalling the celestial changes that govern human affairs, for the purposes of divination.

Like the ancient Greeks, and Renaissance practices condemned by the Catholic Church, the Chinese made little distinction between astronomy and astrology. There are several anecdotes in *Conversations from the Guest Seat* by Ricci's contemporary Gu Qiyuan that illustrate this mentality:

Once a friend remarked: If the fourth star of the North Polar constellation [The Great Bear, Big Dipper or Ursa Major] is dim, it means the mandarins in the realm are powerless. This interpretation is different from ancient divination. There are seven stars in the Northern Pole, the first four form the bowl, the fifth to seven the handle. The first star is named *tian shu* [celestial pivot, alpha], the second *xuan* [celestial template, beta], the third *ji* [celestial armillary, gamma], the fourth *quan* [celestial balance, delta], the fifth *yu heng* [jade sighting tube, epsilon], the sixth *kai yang* [opener of heat, zeta], and the seventh *yao guang* [twinkling brilliance, eta]. *Shu* signifies heaven, *xuan* earth, *ji* human, *quan* time, *yu heng* sound, *kai yang* melody, *yao guang* stars. According to Master Shi [this refers to Shi Shen, an astronomer of the fourth century BC, author of a star catalogue and a book on astronomy], the first is the orthodox star in charge of the virtue of yang, and is the sign of the Son of Heaven [the emperor], the second is the star of law in charge of justice in the nether regions, and signifies a female ruler, the third is the public star in charge of disasters, the fourth is the star of suppression in charge of celestial justice and suppresses injustice, the fifth is called the killing star that dominates the center and aids the four sides, and kills the culpable, the sixth is the star of danger in charge of the five grains in the celestial granary, the seventh is the star of followers or response in charge of military affairs. He also says: the first dominates heaven, the second air, the third fire, the fourth water, the fifth earth, the sixth wood, and the seventh metal... Zhang Heng [the Han astronomer famous for his star catalogue, AD 78–139], writes: if the Son of Heaven fails to respect his ancestors and the spirits, then the first star will become dim or change color; if [the emperor] builds lavish palaces and cuts through hills, then the second star will become dim or change color; if he loves not the common people, and arbitrarily increases taxes and exactions, then the third star will become dim or change color; if he gives commands contrary to the season and the way of heaven, then the fourth star will become dim or change color; if he neglects his proper duties and indulges in his senses, then the fifth star will become dim or change color; if he fails to encourage agriculture, inflicts arbitrary and excessive punishments, and dismisses sage counselors, then the sixth star will become dim or change color; if he fails to pacify the barbarians of the four directions, then the seventh star will become dim or change color . . . If these seven stars are bright, the country will prosper, if they are dim, the country will perish.[11]

Given the exact correspondence between celestial and human affairs in traditional Chinese assumptions, a good astronomer could also divine the future. Gu recorded three stories about these erudite scholars in the hidden arts. The first was one Wang Qi, 'an expert in astronomy, divination, and stellar numerology', who came to Nanjing in the reign of Cheng Hua (1465–87), who predicted the fortunes and disaster that befell the careers of mandarins.[12] The second was the astronomer Zhou Gongxian, who became the head of the Directorate of Astronomy in the reign of Jiazheng (1522–66), and enjoyed a reputation as someone who could tell by his gaze the exact position and brightness of a star. But his books on mathematics and the calendar were already lost by the time of Gu Qiyuan.[13] The third man, Cui Zijun, a relative of the famous scholar Jiao Hong, skilled in numerology, predicted that Jiao Hong would score the very top in the Metropolitan Examination of 1589.[14]

Ricci condemned astrology and prognostications, listing these as some of the numerous superstitions among the Chinese, who believed in fate and sought to know and control their fortunes. In contrast, the European astronomy he taught, although flawed in its Ptolemaic earth-centric doctrine, presented a different methodology, using geometry to demonstrate the size, distance, and angle of heavenly objects, and the explanations behind the eclipses. In spite of his frustration that only the first book of Euclid was available in Chinese (the full translation only appeared in 1608), Zhang Yangmo, Ricci's best student, learned all he could from the western master. In time, he transmitted the new knowledge to his Chinese master, the Hanlin academician Wang Kentang, who had sent him to Ricci in the first place. Later, in his own publications, Wang would recapitulate Ricci's use of geometry to demonstrate the larger body of the sun over the earth, commenting that 'the westerner Li Madou [Ricci] says: the sun is bigger than the earth. Although this shocked most people, who remain incredulous, it remains a fact that cannot be disputed.'[15]

If the cultural imperative of Chinese astronomy was to predict human affairs, Ricci aimed to propagate the Christian faith with his astronomy lessons: the correct knowledge of the heavens ultimately served to know the one, true Creator, and to confound the erroneous theories of creation and the universe by rival religions. We have already alluded to Ricci's attacks on Buddhist theories of the universe in his work *On the Operations of the Four Elements*. Ricci made no secret of this. Knowing Ricci's intention of eradicating Buddhism, his student Zhang Yangmo told his master that 'it [was] not necessary to refute the doctrines of the idolaters; focus only on teaching mathematics.' 'Once the Chinese know the truth of heaven and the material earth, they themselves will see the falsehood of the idolaters' books,' concluded Ricci. With disdain, he commented further: 'The authors of this sect [of Buddhism] are not satisfied with doing theology and teaching so many falsehoods of the other life, they also want to philosophize and discourse on astrology and cosmography.'[16] 'Indeed, it comes to pass that many who have learned our science of mathematics reject the laws and doctrines of the idolaters, saying that if they say so many errors about natural things and about this life, there is no reason why one should believe what they say about supernatural things and of the other world.'

Ricci had plenty of things to say about the natural and supernatural, for there was a large group of Ming literati who were devotees of Buddhism. They included some of the most erudite scholars and original thinkers of the late Ming—the historian and philologist Jiao Hong and the philosopher Li Zhi were among them. To win them over from Buddhism would represent the most difficult challenge to Ricci. We will now turn our attention to Ricci's interaction with this third group of literati during his sojourn in Nanjing.

Jiao Hong (1539–1620) was the brightest star in the brilliant literary firmament of Nanjing.[17] A native of the city, Jiao Hong grew up in a military family, where his father, a mid-level officer, was a devout Buddhist. Jiao Hong compensated for earlier failures in the imperial civil service examinations by scoring first place in the 1589 Metropolitan Examination and obtaining the honorific title of *zhuangyuan*. Appointed to the Hanlin Academy, Jiao Hong gained a reputation as champion and tutor to the Eldest Prince, Zhu Changlo, son of the empress. But the Wanli emperor procrastinated in declaring Changlo his heir apparent, favoring instead the son of his beloved Consort Zheng, Zhu Changxun. Such a move would

have been against imperial tradition. For years the emperor and his mandarins were locked in confrontation: officials submitted repeated memorials
in favor of the Eldest Prince and admonished the emperor to remember
dynastic tradition; Wanli generally ignored his officials, but was occasionally
provoked to acts of dismissal, demotion, and punishments of caning. The
impasse over the imperial succession paralyzed the court during the 1590s;
only in 1601 did Wanli bow to public opinion and declare Changlo the heir
apparent. Immensely frustrated at the mandarins' opposition to his imperial
will, Wanli refused to meet his officials in daily audiences and became more
and more a recluse in the Inner Palace, a seclusion intensified by his obesity
and ill health. Such was the background to Beijing court politics, as yet
invisible to Matteo Ricci.

Admired for his fervent championship of the Eldest Prince, Jiao Hong was
also a prolific author and editor, who wrote on history, the Confucian classics,
Daoism, Buddhism, poetry, phonology, and etymology. His outspoken personality and his elevated position around Prince Changlo caused envy and
resentment among some colleagues. In 1598, two of them criticized Jiao Hong
for his failure to detect unorthodox statements in nine successful provincial
examination papers in the Beijing Prefecture, where Jiao Hong had served as
Deputy Examiner. The emperor, who already disliked Jiao Hong, demoted
him to a provincial post in Fujian. In 1599, Jiao Hong resigned and returned to
his native Nanjing, arriving the same year as Ricci.

Ricci might have discarded his Buddhist persona, but he failed to escape
the Buddhists. How could he? There were more Buddhist institutions in
Nanjing than in any other Ming city: 8 large, 38 mid-size, and 130 smaller
temples were recorded in a city where Buddhism found many fervent
devotees among the common people and the mandarin-literati elites.[18]

Like Zhang Huang, eminent Confucian and Ricci's friend in Nanchang,
Jiao Hong was also a third-generation disciple of the great Ming philosopher
Wang Yangming. Unlike Zhang Huang, Jiao Hong belonged to a different
tradition of Wang followers, the Taizhou school, which looked for a
synthesis of Daoism, Buddhism, and Confucianism, and whose teachings,
it may be recalled, were roundly criticized by Zhang Huang (Chapter 7).

The urge to synthesize, to refuse differentiations, to see the relativity of
the One Truth, is manifest in many of Jiao Hong's writings. He criticized
orthodox Confucians for their moral censure, and lamented Mencius'
intolerance toward Yang Zhu and Mozi, Warring States thinkers branded
as unorthodox by this greatest disciple of Confucius. Similarly, Jiao Hong

brilliantly pointed out that Zhu Xi, the great Song neo-Confucian scholar, only criticized Chan Buddhism precisely because he felt threatened by the truth of its teachings. An eclectic author, Jiao Hong wrote on *Zhuangzi*, the great Daoist text, on Buddhist sutras, as well as on a large variety of more 'orthodox' Confucian topics.[19] The following text is representative of Jiao Hong's thought, and is interesting as it refers to the publication of a Buddhist sutra that links us back to Ricci. The occasion is the engraving of the *Huayan Sutra*, an early medieval Chinese Buddhist text that was based in part on translating the Sanskrit *Avatamsaka Sutra*, a title that means a ring of flowers or garland. The instigator of the project was Qu Ruzi, Buddhist devotee, famous scholar, and cuckolded husband, since he was half-brother to Qu Rukui, Ricci's first disciple (see Chapter 6). Jiao Hong, famous for his style, wrote a preface to this new edition of the *Huayan Sutra*:

The *Book of Rites* says that following nature is the Way (*dao*), and cultivating the Way is teaching. Although the teachings of sages are different, cultivating the Way in order to recover one's nature is unitary. The true and great men of antiquity existed alongside the gods and spirits. It was different when the sages purified and hid their hearts in secret, while sharing the fortunes and sufferings with the common people. When the Great Merciful One [Buddha] recognized his body was but dream and illusion, and his heart but dirt and earth, he held himself above the heavens and people as a model in order to show the wondrous, perfect, and true Self to ten thousand generations. Is this not identical to the teachings of China's sages? I have recently read the *Huayan Sutra* and learned that the ancient sages took different paths toward the same goal. Thus all doubts should be removed. The perfect teachings of Huayan state that in nature there is no self; there is no nature that is not dharma; one dharma is no different from another; there is no dharma that is not nature, meaning there is no need to abandon the world and our heart. Therefore, non-action is revealed in the world of action; and when non-action is revealed, the dharma cannot decay. Those who can accomplish this, how is it different from those who purify and hide their hearts, while sharing the sufferings with the common people?[20]

Then, Jiao Hong comments that the last chapter of the *Huayan Sutra*, 'Entering dharma-dhatu (*ru fa jie pin*)', enumerates fifty-three persons who became bodhisattvas, only a few of whom were monks. Hence, everyone can become a Buddha; everything leads to enlightenment. Jiao Hong continues:

Raising your foot, you enter the realm of dharma. Lowering your head, you practice Buddhist devotion. In cleaning, washing, conversing, you understand the teachings of the gentlemen; in eating, drinking, and daily life, you taste *The Doctrine of the Mean*. Confucian, Buddhist: they are different, and they are the same.

Therefore, the self, Buddha, and all phenomena belong to the one dharma. Reason and practice arise from the same self.

Using a metaphor from *Zhuangzi*, Jiao Hong describes the truth as an ocean, without origins or end. He concludes:

After reading this sutra, I know that the *Six Classics*, the *Analects* and *Mencius* are simply Chan meditation; and [the ancient emperors and sages] Emperors Yao and Shun, the Duke of Zhao, and Confucius were actually Buddhas.

Although abhorred by more traditional Confucian scholars, Jiao Hong's ideas were not uncommon among the intellectuals of the late Ming. One who shared his thoughts was his best friend Li Zhi, the radical Confucian philosopher turned Chan Buddhist, considered by some to be a genius, by others a seducer of youth and women, a heterodox and subversive thinker.

Li Zhi (1527–1602) was born in the port of Quanzhou in Fujian province.[21] The center of medieval China's maritime trade, Quanzhou merchants sailed as far as the Persian Gulf. One of them was a forefather of Li Zhi, who married a Muslim woman. Islamic traditions apparently continued in the household, until Li Zhi's generation. After obtaining the *juren* degree in the 1552 local examination, family poverty forced Li Zhi to abandon hopes for further studies and success. For more than twenty years, he struggled to raise his family on the meager income of a low-grade official, serving in various capacities as an educational mandarin in Henan, Beijing, and Nanjing. His was a harsh life. Of four boys and three girls, only his eldest daughter survived to adulthood. Meanwhile, Li Zhi had lost both his father and grandfather. By the time Li Zhi got his first break, when he was appointed Prefect (*zhifu*) of Yaoan in Yunnan in 1577, a post that provided a comfortable stipend, he had lost all worldly ambitions. After his initial three-year appointment, Li Zhi resigned office.

Retirement did not mean resignation. Far from it. Li Zhi thought very little of most people and regarded himself very highly. He wrote in 'An Encomium to Myself' that he was a person 'impatient in character, haughty in presentation, vulgar in writing, obsessive in heart, straightforward in action, aloof in friendship, warm in meetings, eager to find faults with others, and no pleasure in their strengths; and when he dislikes someone, he cuts off all ties and wishes them ill'.[22] Most of all, Li Zhi despised the hypocrisy and incompetence among the mandarins, which was the main reason why he left the imperial bureaucracy. When a scholar once mocked him asking whether he was acquainted with Lin Daoqian, the notorious pirate (see Chapter 3), because both were Fujianese, Li Zhi retorted by praising the pirate as a true leader of men, whereas the mandarins and literati reaped his scorn:

Huh! When all is quiet, the only thing they know is to make courtesies. They sit immobile all day like clay statues, telling themselves they are real saints and sages because they have no evil thoughts. Those who have learned a little evil would lecture on conscience (*liangzhi*), while secretly hoping for a higher office. In a crisis, they all stare at one another, pale as ghosts, denying any responsibility, wishing only to save their skins.[23]

His most sarcastic remarks were reserved for the Confucian literati. Li Zhi despised them for their hypocrisy: they lack any understanding of the ultimate concerns of life and death; ignorant, vacuous, odious, the highest they can achieve is a hollow reputation. The highest achievement for a Confucian was to die for reputation: 'thus one knows the horror of Confucian learning.'[24] For Li Zhi, most scholars were despicable, for

they openly lectured on morality, while secretly scheming for wealth; dressed in the elegance of scholar's robes, they behaved like dogs. Why do so many speak, lecture, and accept disciples? They want to be rich! But smart people can get rich without scholarship, only the mediocre have to resort to scholarship. Thus, today, the untalented, the unlearned, the do-nothings, and the ignorant, who aspire to great wealth, have no choice but to discourse on ethics and scholarship. Today, those who truly wish to discuss ethics in order to find the transcendental teachings of Confucianism, Daoism, and Buddhism, and to avoid the sufferings of wealth, they have no choice but to shave their heads and become monks.[25]

True to his word, Li Zhi sent his wife and daughter to Quanzhou. He shaved his head, donned Buddhist robes, and declared himself a Buddhist master. Even in choosing this alternate path in life, Li Zhi created ever more contradictions. An acerbic critic of the literati, Li Zhi lived as a guest of the Geng family in Hubei, a powerful gentry lineage that had furnished famous mandarins and literati. Yet he quarreled incessantly with his patron, who was scandalized by Li Zhi's flouting of all moral conventions: visiting brothels, discussing philosophy in the inner chamber of a young woman, and generally posing as a bad influence for younger scholars, many of whom admired the originality and daring of the old man. Both in act and in words, Li Zhi aroused the irk of the ruling elites. Asked to leave the Keng household, Li Zhi readily found other influential supporters, who helped him establish a small monastery, where he acted as an unlicensed abbot. Traveling to solicit donations and see friends, in 1599 Li Zhi visited his best friend Jiao Hong in Nanjing, where he met Ricci, one of the few people he found impressive.

It was indeed Li Zhi who gave us the sharpest and most interesting portrait of Ricci. Describing the Jesuit to a friend, Li Zhi writes:

You asked about Ricci: he is a Westerner from the Extreme West, and traveled for over one hundred thousand *li* to reach China, sailing at first to south India, where he first learned of Buddha . . . When he reached Guangzhou and the South Sea, he found out that our Great Ming Realm has had the virtuous kings Yao and Shun, and the sages Zhou and Confucius. He lived in the south and in Zhaoqing nearly two decades, reading every book of our nation, asking teachers to help him note the pronunciations and meanings of the words . . . so that now he is fluent in speaking and writing our language, and following our rituals. He is a most urbane person. He is most intricate and refined in his interior (*zhong ji linglong*), and very plain and modest in his exterior; and listening to scores of people debating nosily, he can follow and recapitulate their arguments in order. I have never seen anyone more impressive. People are either too critical or too flattering, either showing off their brilliance or coming across as too dull. But I have no idea why he is here. I have met him three times already and still do not know his intention in coming here. Perhaps he wants to study our Confucian learning, but surely this is a stupid guess, which probably does not reflect his real intention.[26]

Li Zhi's brilliant insight into Ricci reflected not only his own intelligence, but also the reason why the westerner was so attractive to him and to his friend Jiao Hong: here was an extremely subtle and intelligent man, original, non-conformist, who was deeply interested in the things not of this world. It is interesting to note that Li Zhi's adjective (*linglong*) in describing Ricci's character echoes the term for the armillary (*linglongyi*) at the Nanjing Observatory. The term suggests artifice, intelligence, subtlety, intricateness, and complexity. Indeed, these qualities suggest the personality of the Jesuit, whose writings reveal so little of himself.

In Ricci, Li Zhi recognized a kindred spirit: an original mind, a solitary path. In parting, Li Zhi composed a poem for Ricci:[27]

> Leisurely descending from the Northern Pole,
> marching with pleasure toward the South,
> leaving your name in temples,
> marking the maritime journey in wondrous mountains.
> Behind your head lie one hundred thousand *li*
> as you gaze at the city with nine walls.

Have you seen the light of the country?
The midday sun is shining brilliantly.

Li Zhi left Nanjing for his monastery in Hubei. Recall Li Zhi's description
of Ricci: 'listening to scores of people debating nosily, he can follow and
recapitulate their arguments in order.' This referred to an actual event, a
banquet, a moment of glory for Ricci, when Li Zhi might well have been
present.

The host of the banquet was Li Ruzhen, a retired official at the venerable
age of 70, with a reputation of great virtue and a large following of disciples.
A devout Buddhist, Li Ruzhen invited Ricci for a meeting through their
mutual friend Qu Rukui. Taken aback by Ricci's frank criticism of Buddhism, which the westerner compared to a half-rotten apple, Li Ruzhen
thought the Jesuit understood little of Buddhist doctrines. Shortly thereafter, at a colloquium among the literati, Li Ruzhen spoke on the superior
teachings of Buddhism. A Vice-Director in one of the bureaus of the
Ministry of Works (*yuan wai lang*), Liu Guannan shouted out in anger:
'How can you belittle the teachings of our sage Confucius and praise the
superiority of these foreign doctrines of Buddhism!' Venting his anger
further, Liu Guannan told Li Ruzhen that even a westerner like Li Madou
(Ricci), whom he knew only by reputation, praised the virtuous teachings
of Confucius and criticized the falsity of Buddhism. Li Ruzhen replied that
he had indeed met the westerner, who seemed ill informed about the whole
matter, and that he would teach him better the doctrines of Buddhism. At
this, the colloquium ended; and Liu Guannan left in a huff.

A few days later, Li Ruzhen invited Ricci to a banquet. Ricci guessed Li's
intention: he did not wish to get into a confrontation; moreover, it was the
Lenten fast. Ricci politely declined. However, Li Ruzhen repeated his
invitation. Qu Rukui, also a guest, persuaded Ricci to change his mind
since it would have been rude to turn down three repeated invitations.

When Ricci and Qu showed up, they found some twenty to thirty
invitees at Li Ruzhen's house. The guest of honor was the most famous
Buddhist cleric in Nanjing, the Abbot Xuelang Hong'en.[28] A native of the
city, Hong'en, whose family name was Huang, took the Buddhist title of
Xuelang (Snow Wave), after the mountain in Zhejiang where he first
practiced the monastic life. At the age of 13, Hong'en accompanied his
father on a visit to the Bao en Temple, where they listened to a sermon on
the *Lotus Sutra*. At the point in the text where the sufferings in life were

compared to living in a house on fire, the teenager felt a sudden stir. He secretly cut his hair. When it was time to leave, Hong'en gave a tuft of his hair to his father, and asked that it be entrusted to his mother as a memento. His father broke out in tears, but the boy merely looked calmly at the man, with whom he had just severed all ties of the flesh. Legend has it that the apprentice monk showed great talent from the start: his eloquence and innate understanding impressed everyone. Taken under the wings of the Abbot of Bao en Temple, Hong'en matured into the most famous Buddhist monk in Nanjing, known not only for his great learning in many Buddhist sutras, but also in the Confucian classics and literature. In time, Hong'en himself inherited the mantle of abbotship.

At the time when Hong'en met Ricci, in March/April of 1599, he stood at the apex of his reputation. A brilliant speaker, Hong'en had given lectures on Buddhist texts for thirty years. Putting aside arid commentaries, Hong'en returned to the sutras themselves: with a cup of tea and an incense burner, Hong'en sat and discoursed; or he would lecture while walking amidst the audience, using the natural scenery around him as metaphors for the finer points of Buddhist doctrines. An expert on the *Hua yan Sutra*, Hong'en enjoyed enormous reputation as a great Buddhist intellectual, who understood the ideas of inter-causality and the interpenetration of all phenomena, the difficult central concepts in the Hua yan school. In 1598, the top of the pagoda at Bao en Temple collapsed. Constructed of crystal and topped by copper, the pagoda was one of the most famous Buddhist monuments in Nanjing. Abbot Hong'en led several hundred monks and went around the city to solicit funds. The campaign was a resounding success.[29] Li Ruzhen had obviously invited Abbot Hong'en to teach Ricci the doctrines of Buddhism.

Both sides were ready for the verbal combat. Ricci knew Hong'en was 'sufficiently different from the other Buddhist clerics because he was a great poet, intelligent, and learned in the doctrines of all the sects'.[30] After introducing his guests to one another, Li Ruzhen seated Hong'en next to Ricci, who immediately felt 'the great arrogance wrapped in the torn and vile robes that [Hong'en] wore'. A man with a high forehead, bright eyes, square cheeks, and a large mouth, Hong'en was an imposing figure. He demanded to speak about religion with Ricci.

Ricci replied: 'Before we discuss anything, I would like you to tell me what you think of the first principle, the creator and lord of heaven and earth and of all created things, whom we call Tianzhu, the Lord of Heaven.'

Hong'en explained: 'Yes, there is indeed such a creator of heaven and earth, but he is not a great being, for all human beings are equal to him.'

Here, Hong'en was referring to a central teaching in the Hua Yan School, which argued that the Buddha existed already in human nature, and that all persons had the potential to become Buddhas.

Irritated by Hong'en's self-satisfaction, Ricci provoked him: 'Can you do the same things as this creator of heaven and earth? Otherwise, it is just empty talk!'

Thinking no doubt of the doctrine that all natural phenomena exist only due to human consciousness, Hong'en replied with confidence: 'Yes, I can create heaven and earth.'

Ricci cut in: 'I don't want to burden you with creating another heaven and earth. I pray you, just create another fire-pot like the one here.'

Hong'en shouted: 'It is ridiculous for you to ask this!'

Shouting even louder, Ricci retorted: 'You should not have promised something you cannot do!'

At the shouting, the other guests came over. According to Ricci, who recorded every word of this exchange, they all thought he was right.

Calming his spirits, Hong'en started to explain to Ricci the fundamental teachings of Buddhism.

'I have heard you are a great astronomer. Do you know mathematics?'

'Yes, I know something about it,' replied Ricci.

Hong'en pursued his line of attack: 'When you speak about the sun and the moon, do you go above to the heavens, where the planets stand, or do these planets come down to your heart?'

Ricci explained: 'I do not go up to heaven, nor do the stars come down to earth. When we see something, we form a figure and species of the thing we have seen. Afterwards, when we want to think and speak of it, we look inside our own minds at these images we have formed.'

'Ah ha!' Hong'en stood up and exclaimed: 'Just as you yourself have created anew the sun and the moon, you can therefore create all other things.'

'The images in the mind are not the sun and the moon,' Ricci disagreed, 'they are only figures, and are very different from the sun and the moon. And if one has not first seen the sun and the moon, one would not have been able to form these images, not to mention creating the sun and the moon.'

Using the mirror as a metaphor of the mind, Ricci explained that no one would confuse the reflection with the actual objects of the sun and the moon. Relying on the Thomistic principle of sensual knowledge, Ricci asserted a philosophy that argued for the real existence of physical phenomena: all created things are visible, and by the sensual perception of the visible created order, the intellect can apprehend the invisible creator, God.

It is interesting that Ricci should use the metaphor of a mirror, which was a favorite metaphor as well with Hua Yen masters. The inter-causality and interpenetration of all things, they explained, can be likened to a set of mirrors placed in different positions to a burning flame: the reflections and the reflections of the reflections resemble an unending chain of causations that negate a first principle, the original flame, only seemingly a real essence because of the limited subjectivity of human consciousness. At the moment, Hong'en failed to think of this reply; and Ricci noted with satisfaction, in his memoirs, that most sided with him, to the irritation of a fuming Hong'en. To forestall an escalation in the verbal battle, the host Li Ruzhen came over and took Hong'en to a different part of the dining hall.

The banquet began. As a foreigner, Ricci was given the place of honor, seated at a place directly opposite his host at the large round table. The conversation turned to human nature, a debate that first animated the thinkers of ancient China. Some guests took the position of Mencius, who wrote that human nature is good and only ignorance, and the lack of education, led to evil deeds. Others argued the position of Xunzi and the thinkers of the Legalist School, who saw law and discipline as the only measure to restrain the human propensity to selfishness and evil. A third group ventured that human nature was neither intrinsically evil nor good, but puzzled as to what might explain the differences in human behavior. Throughout this debate, which lasted over an hour and several servings of dishes, Ricci sat quietly, thinking to himself that the literati 'knew not logic, nor the distinction between the moral and the natural, still less the corruption of human nature by original sin, and the grace of God'.[31] His fellow diners understood Ricci's silence differently: perhaps their debate was too subtle for a foreigner, who failed to follow a noisy discourse in a foreign language. Out of courtesy, someone turned to Ricci and asked for his opinion. Ricci had been waiting for this moment. He first summarized in some detail the arguments and positions of the opposing parties, which stunned everyone. Then he added: 'Nobody can doubt that the Lord of Heaven and Earth is of the highest good. If human nature is so feeble that one doubts whether it is good or evil, how can Master Hong'en just now say that human nature is the same as that of God, the creator of heaven and earth? Who can doubt whether this nature is good or evil?'

One of the guests stood up and applauded Ricci. He turned to Hong'en and asked: 'What do you think of this?' The Buddhist abbot tried to laugh this off, not wishing to respond. Ricci and other guests pressed him. Hong'en cited Buddhist texts and authorities, but Ricci refused to acknowledge authority. He wanted to argue by reason. Ultimately, Hong'en expressed the opinion that God is neither good nor bad, for a thing can be sometimes good, sometimes bad. Here, Hong'en based his argument on the central idea of Mahayana Buddhism, the doctrine of Emptiness, that is, no phenomenon possesses a permanent and unchanging essence. All things—life, death, happiness, sufferings—are constituted by a combination of circumstances and causes, which are constantly in flux, hence, the inherent meaninglessness of good or evil. At this Ricci countered by saying the sun's nature is light, not darkness. Rejecting Buddhism's doctrine of Emptiness and relativity, Ricci argued the principles of Aristotle, a philosophy based on the distinction between substance (essence) and accidents. Most of the guests were with Ricci, so we read in his memoirs. Although we have only a one-sided record of this intellectual encounter between Buddhism and Christianity, two things were clear: it created a stir among the literati in Nanjing, 'all of Nanjing was talking a lot about this debate', in Ricci's words (and in Li Zhi's, as we have seen); and it shaped the Jesuit missionary's polemic with Buddhism. The arguments in this debate with Hong'en would later form parts of chapter 7 in Ricci's masterpiece *The True Meanings of the Lord of Heaven*.

Shortly after the famous banquet, sometime in April 1599, Ricci purchased a large house for the Jesuit residence. It was Liu Guannan who got Ricci his deal. This mandarin, who was so irate with Li Ruzhen's pro-Buddhist discourse, had a haunted house on his hands. Built as a residence for public officials, the large house, situated within the inner city walls close to the southern gate, was uninhabited. Several former mandarins who had lived there moved out hurriedly, citing ghosts and demons. No one would buy it on the private market. Inspecting the property, Ricci saw sword marks on columns left by unsuccessful Daoist exorcists. Liu offered the property at a loss, happy to recover a fraction of the public cost, and accepted payment on credit since the Jesuit had insufficient cash to pay for it in full. Ricci was eager to buy the centrally located house, especially since Cattaneo and the others had finally arrived in Nanjing. This haunted house was possibly the one described by Gu Qiyuan: the former office of the Inspectorate of Schools, located inside the southern gate, where an inspector and his wife, pacing under the moonlight, suddenly saw dozens of young scholars dancing on the steps. Frightened out of their wits, they moved out, and hence nobody ventured within its walls even in broad daylight.[32] Other than a bargain, the house was built on higher ground, an advantage not to be discounted in a city prone to flooding. In June 1586, it rained for fourteen days. The streets were under several feet of water and the only means of getting through the western gates near the Yangzi was by boat, as Gu Qiyuan recorded in his book of vignettes.[33]

Attracted by Ricci's growing reputation, mandarins and literati came to see Ricci, 'like madmen'.[34] There were so many visitors, Ricci wrote, 'on occasion, I do not have time to eat'.[35] At no point did Ricci confuse this sociability with real success: the Chinese merely came to experience a great object of curiosity—the famous westerner; when Ricci 'spoke to them of the miraculous work of God in the West, they looked stupefied'.[36] With a firm sense of realism, Ricci replied to his Macerata friend and fellow Jesuit Girolamo Costa, who had inquired about news of some great conversion:

Know that I and all those who are here dream of nothing else day and night. For this we have left our country and dear friends, and are dressed in the clothes and shoes of China; and we speak, eat, drink, and dress in nothing but the manners of China. But God does not yet wish to see more fruit from our labor, even though the fruit of our achievements can be compared or even surpass those of other missions, and it seems that we have done wondrous things. This is because our time in China is not yet one of harvest, nor even of sowing, but of opening wild forests and combating wild and poisonous snakes. By the grace of God others will come and write of conversions and the fervor of Christians.

Hard as this pioneering work might be, Ricci was optimistic about evangelization, for he believed that

China is most different from other lands and peoples in that the people are learned and interested in the arts and not war; they are intelligent, and now, more doubting of their own religions or superstitions than ever before. Thus it will be easy, as I clearly intend, to convert an infinite number of them in a short time.

The only obstacle, Ricci cautioned, was the distrust of foreigners among the Chinese, a fear of rebellion that prevailed with the emperor and the ruling classes. Hence, when Christians congregated, suspicion arose. Therefore, the most urgent task was 'to gain credit with this people and allay all suspicions, and then proceed with them to conversion'. Fortunately, the Jesuits had distinguished themselves from all previous foreigners by their learning and reputation, Ricci added, 'and some, glory be to God, consider us as the greatest saints who have come to China in a miraculously long journey'.[37]

Ricci, indeed, was impressive. Gu Qiyuan, the author of the vignettes of Nanjing life, met the Jesuit and left this description:

[Li Madou, i.e. Ricci, was a] European from the Western oceans. He has a pale face, a curly beard, and deep-seated eyes the color of bright yellow like a cat; he knows Chinese. He came to Nanjing and resided to the west of Cheng Yang Gate, telling everyone the way (dao) of his country is the worship of Tianzhu, the Lord of Heaven. This Tianzhu is the creator of heaven and earth. In painting, it is depicted as a little boy held by a woman, called Tianmu (heavenly mother). This painting was done on a copper board, and the figures look alive, with the bodies, arms, and hands raised above the board; the concaves and declines on the faces make them no different from real people. People ask: 'How do you paint this?' He replies: 'In Chinese painting, one paints the visible (yang) but not the invisible (yin), therefore, the human figures look flat, without contrast. The painting of my country uses both yin and yang techniques, and therefore you have contrasts in the faces and round-ness in arms and hands. For the human face, if it faces the light, it is painted bright and white; if it faces sideways, the side facing the light is white, whereas the eyes, ears, nose, and mouth that do not face the light are painted dark. The figure painters of my country understand this method, and can therefore erase the distinction between painted figures and real people.' He has brought many printed books from his country, all printed on white paper on both sides, with words running horizon-tally. The paper is like the cotton paper from Yunnan nowadays, thick and sturdy, and the ink is very fine. Sometimes there are illustrations of people and buildings, which are fine as hair. The binding is like the Song folded style, with lacquered leather on the outside for protection, whereas the edges are lined with gold, silver or copper, and the pages are painted with gold both on the top and bottom. You open the book, and every page looks new; you close the book, and it looks like a plate painted in gold. There is a self-sounding clock, built out of iron, wound with wires, hung up with wheels turning up and down incessantly, and sounding the times. There are many similar instruments, all finely fabricated . . . He has written Tianzhu shiyi and xilun, with many novel sayings, but is most skilled in astronomy and mathematics.[38]

Later, Gu Qiyuan also met João da Rocha, who went to Nanjing in late 1600 to replace Ricci; he thought this 'disciple' of Ricci was by no means as smart and intelligent as the master.

Having established their small residence, the Jesuit missionaries became the caregivers for a new Christian community. The first Nanjing convert was an old man of 70, a Mr Cheng, a retired military officer. His son, Cheng Qiyuan, who would later obtain the degree of military jinshi in 1604 and had a successful military career, followed in the elder Cheng's footstep.[39] Father and son were baptized Paul and Martin; most members of their large family followed suit and became the first Christians in Nanjing.

Encouraged by his success, Ricci was thinking once more about Beijing. He needed reinforcements: personnel, money, and gifts for the emperor. In August 1599, Ricci sent Cattaneo to Macao in order to secure support. In January 1600, Cattaneo returned with additional funds and gifts, and another missionary for the China vineyard, the Spaniard Diego de Pantoja.

Having secured a travel permit from his friend the mandarin Zhu Shilu, Ricci was prepared once more to proceed to Beijing, ostensibly to offer tribute to the emperor, in reality to obtain imperial protection for the Catholic mission. Ricci left Catteneo in charge of the Jesuit residence and Christian community in Nanjing; he took with him Pantoja and the two Chinese Jesuit brothers, Sebastian Fernandes (Zhong Mingren) and Manoel Pereira (You Wenhui).

Through Zhu Shilu, Ricci secured two rooms on a ship under the command of the eunuch Liu Cheng, who had been dispatched as a tax-intendant to Suzhou and Hangzhou. Liu was returning to Beijing with several boatloads of brocade and now, also, an official western tribute-bearer, with his gifts of clocks, paintings, and books for the Wanli emperor. On 18 May, 1600, Ricci set sail once more on the Grand Canal. With his 'pale face, curly beard, and deep-seated eyes', had Ricci already seen his destiny in the stars above Nanjing, as he headed for his final destination?

9

Beijing

M atteo Ricci almost did not make it to Beijing. At first, the voyage went well enough. Carried by the crest of success, the 48-year-old Ricci set sail with his small group of younger men: Zhong Mingren, aged 38, who had followed Ricci for ten years from Shaozhou, Nanchang, to Beijing, and back; You Wenhui, only 25, and already a good painter; and Diego de Pantoja, born in 1571 and freshly arrived from Toledo, the first Spanish Jesuit to join the China Mission.[1] Thanks to Zhu Shilu, the Jesuits and their servants were graciously received by Eunuch Liu Cheng, who refused payment for their two commodious rooms. During these pleasant days, Pantoja practiced on the clavichord, which he had learned from Cattaneo in Nanjing, in preparation for presentation of the musical instrument to the emperor; he also continued his Chinese lessons with Zhong Mingren and practiced conversation with a 10-year-old servant boy, a native of Nanjing, whom Eunuch Liu had purchased and given to Pantoja. Laden with silk from Hangzhou and Suzhou for the emperor, these government barges, dubbed *ma chuan* or horse boats, combined speed and comfort. Still, the Grand Canal was clogged with water traffic, much of it official, and many boats jostled for the lead in passing the numerous sluices along the way. Showing the famous westerners and their exotic instruments to every mandarin at every gate station, Eunuch Liu obtained preferential treatment; and by late June his little flotilla had reached Jining in Shandong, where the Director of Canal Transportation held office.

The Governer, Liu Dongxing, a man of 60, was eager to receive Ricci. Liu's son had met the famous western scholar in Nanjing, and told his father all about the remarkable man and his wonderful doctrines of salvation, tales confirmed by Li Zhi, a close friend of the mandarin, who was, serendipitously, visiting the Elder Liu when Ricci arrived. At the mandarin's mansion, Li Zhi greeted Ricci like an old friend; and the three men conversed on things of the West and the afterlife. Returning the visit at the barge, Liu saw a picture of the Virgin Mary, flanked by Christ and John the Baptist. Later, Madame Liu told her husband of an earlier dream, in which she saw the bodhisattva Guanyin attended by two boys. Mulling over this augury, Liu took Ricci's hand and said: 'I want to go with you to paradise.' Moved by their warmth and sincerity, Ricci hoped he could convert both men one day, but that was not to be.

On 3 July, they arrived in Linqing, where about one year before, Cattaneo was forced to winter after the Jesuits' first abortive attempt to settle in Beijing. There, they fell into the hands of Eunuch Ma Tang. As tax-intendant, Eunuch Ma provoked deep hatred through his corrupt and cruel rapacity; in 1599, rioters killed thirty-seven of Ma Tang's men and burned down his office. Yet, the eunuch received the full backing of his even more rapacious master, the emperor, who wanted to squeeze every silver coin from his subjects. Rejecting the gifts presented by Eunuch Liu Cheng, Ma Tang refused passage to Liu's barges. Anxious for the delay, lest he be punished, Liu offered Ma Tang a more presentable bribe: there were westerners in his charge, bearing unique and valuable gifts for the emperor; and should Eunuch Ma intervene on their behalf, he might stand to receive an imperial bounty for his efforts. Sensing an opportunity for advancement and self-enrichment, Ma Tang promised he would visit.

Alerted and alarmed, Ricci sought help from an old acquaintance, the Commander of Military Affairs in Linqing, Zhong Wanlu. A native of Qingyuan, Guangdong, Zhong had first met Ricci in Zhaoqing; they renewed their friendship in 1599 when Zhong was assigned to Nanjing. In Linqing, he had been expecting Ricci. Knowing the power of the eunuch tax-intendants, Zhong Wanlu cautioned Ricci it would be impossible to escape Ma's clutches; better to dissimulate friendship and play along. Not to be trifled with, the grand eunuchs were intelligent men first recruited as youths from humble backgrounds. Obsequious and subservient, despised by mandarins and literati, and subjected to the cruelty and whim of the emperor, many lusted after power, once entrusted with any position of authority, and lorded it over mandarin and commoner with equal cruelty.

Ma Tang was pleased with the western presents, which he saw on the barge. Eunuch Ma offered to transmit the westerner's memorial to the emperor. With measured courtesy, Ricci refused, citing his many mandarin acquaintances in the capital. The eunuch laughed. The emperor hardly read memorials from mandarins, but replied quickly to all his memorials, boasted Ma Tang. He ordered his men to transport the Jesuits' luggage to one of his own boats. Having abandoned his passengers and won the goodwill of Ma Tang, Eunuch Liu hurriedly departed.

Ricci and his men spent almost a month in Linqing. They were treated well enough. Ma Tang even invited them to a banquet, followed by performances of Beijing opera and acrobatics. Zhong Wanlu also helped. His frequent visits with Ricci reminded Ma Tang that these foreigners were not without powerful friends. Several times Ma Tang hinted at bribes, but Ricci feigned innocence. At the eunuch's request to move the tributary gifts to his palace, Ricci cited the perils of transit damage, and the necessity of their presence in daily maintenance of the mechanical clocks. Ma Tang left it alone, for the time being.

After a new memorial was written, on 31 July, Ma Tang sent the Jesuits to Tianjin, where they arrived on 8 August; he himself followed in mid-August. After one month, an imperial edict asked for an itemization of the tributary gifts. Ricci prepared a list, which was submitted in time for Wanli's birthday, which fell on 23 September in 1600. Contrary to Ma Tang's expectations, the emperor did not summon the westerners. Eunuch Ma began to worry whether he had incurred imperial disfavor by sponsoring the westerners.

Winter arrived. Before the Grand Canal froze over, Ma Tang had to sail back to Linqing. Eunuch Ma moved the Jesuits to a temple inside the city walls and kept the tributary gifts under official storage. In their dirty and cold rooms, the missionaries received an unexpected visit from Ma Tang. The pompous eunuch arrived with the commander and a large retinue of soldiers. An angry Ma Tang accused Ricci of hiding precious gems and not reporting all members of his household. The soldiers opened and searched the luggage. They found nothing of value. Ma Tang was furious. Then, a soldier discovered something in the personal possession of Pantoja. He showed it to Ma Tang. It was a wooden crucifix with the life-like nailed figure of Christ oozing with blood. Stupefied, Ma Tang shouted loudly: 'This is an instrument you had made to kill our emperor; people who have these artifices are evil!' Upon seeing the crucifix, the other Chinese recoiled and stared with disgust at the westerners, the purported author of such cruelties. Calmly, Ricci responded. 'He did not want to say this was the true God' because it would have been difficult to explain this mystery to 'these ignorant people and at this time'. Moreover, Ma Tang would have dismissed such an explanation as an excuse. Choosing his words carefully, Ricci explained: 'Don't imagine this is what you think it is. It is in fact a great saint of our country, who had wanted to suffer the pains of the cross on our behalf. For this reason, we have sculpted and painted him in this manner, in order that we will always behold him and be grateful.' Hearing this, the commander said it was still not good to have a human figure like this.

Ma Tang was not convinced. The search continued and the soldiers found other crucifixes and paintings of the Crucifixion. The eunuch began to calm down. These objects could not all have been tools of witchcraft. Ma Tang and the commander motioned Ricci and Pantoja to sit down. First, Eunuch Ma made a great show of returning to Ricci a bag of more than 200 silver ducats, the Jesuits' travel funds, expressing his honesty, to which Ricci dissimulated great gratitude. Then, Ma Tang ordered his men to make an inventory of the more than forty items confiscated from the Jesuits, including a couple of ivory reliquaries and a silver chalice. Ricci asked for the reliquaries, but Ma Tang ignored him. When Ricci anxiously implored the return of the chalice, a sacred vessel for offerings to God, not to be touched by unconsecrated hands, he explained, Ma Tang ordered the chalice to be brought to him. Turning the chalice over in his hands, Eunuch Ma mocked Ricci: 'Why do you say this cannot be touched, huh?' Controlling his anger, Ricci said to Ma Tang, in a voice of displeasure: 'Take this bag [of silver coins], which weighs more than double of the chalice, and return what we need for our ministry.' Hearing these words, the mandarin intervened. He asked Ma Tang to return the chalice for it was not the money that seemed to matter for these foreigners. Even Eunuch Ma took pity and returned the chalice.

Ma Tang returned to Linqing and the Jesuits were left in peace. They passed the days anxiously waiting for news, fearing all that was achieved in the past years would vanish in one go. Prayers did not help. At the end of 1600, Ricci sent two servants to Linqing: one was given a beating and sent back by Ma Tang; the other was secretly received by Zhong Wanlu, who admonished his Jesuit friend that things looked very bad, for Ma Tang wanted to submit a memorial accusing the westerners of using witchcraft to kill the emperor. Destroy all crucifixes, save your lives, flee to Guang-dong—these were the only words of advice for a disconsolate Ricci. Zhong Mingren, who slipped away to Beijing with letters of Ricci to his mandarin friends, also returned empty-handed. Nobody was able or willing to help.

Suddenly, in January 1601, an imperial edict arrived, instructing the westerners to proceed to the capital with their gifts. It seemed that one day the emperor remembered something about a 'self-sounding clock' and asked for it; the attendant eunuch reminded the emperor he had not responded to the memorial of Ma Tang and the westerners were still waiting in Tianjin, hence the sudden edict. By then, the Jesuits had been shivering for ten weeks in the cold temple and it was more than eight months after their hopeful departure from Nanjing. Reluctantly, Ma Tang ordered the return of the gifts and the westerners' possessions. The latter included Ricci's mathematics texts, which Eunuch Ma had confiscated, citing the prohibition of divinatory books in Ming law. Fortunately, the soldier who fetched the possessions from the warehouse was illiterate and unable to read Ma Tang's sealed injunctions. Without these western books, Ricci's ministry by science would have been hampered in Beijing.

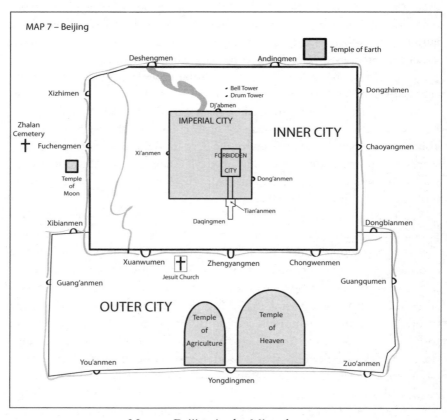

Map 7. Beijing in the Ming dynasty

Traveling by horses, the western tributary mission entered the imperial capital on the eve of the Chinese New Year, 24 January 1601 (Map 7). The gifts were solemnly conveyed to the palace. These consisted of:

- three paintings, a small modern one representing Christ, a modern one representing the Virgin Mary with the Child Jesus and St John, and an old portrait of the Virgin, a copy of the picture in the Borghese Chapel of the Church of Santa Maria Maggiore in Rome,
- a breviary with gold-lined pages,
- a crucifix decorated with relics, pearls, and glass of different colors,
- a copy of Abraham Ortelius' *Theatrum Orbi*,
- a large mechanical clock made of iron and decorated with dragons, and a smaller one, the size of a palm, made of shiny metal and decorated with carvings,
- two prisms,
- eight pieces of mirrors and glass vases,
- a clavichord,
- a rhinoceros horn,
- two sand clocks,
- European belts, fabric, and coins.

On seeing the portrait of Christ, Wanli exclaimed: 'This is a living Buddha!' Spooked by the lifelike portrait, with his searching eyes, the emperor sent this painting to his mother, the Empress Dowager Ci Sheng (née Li), a devout Buddhist. Also unnerved by the three-dimensional painting, Ci Sheng had it deposited in the imperial treasury; she was however much attached to the Madonna and Child, the picture at S. Maria Maggiore, and offered daily incense and prayers before this novel representation of the Son-giving Guanyin bodhisattva.

Emperor Wanli (see Plate VIII) was most curious about the western mechanical instruments. Frustrated that the clocks would not chime, he ordered Ricci and Pantoja to enter the outer precincts of the Forbidden City, where they could instruct four eunuch mathematicians in the proper tuning and maintenance of the clocks. This having been accomplished, the emperor wished to hear western music performed on the clavichord. Pantoja, groomed for the occasion, became master to four eunuch musicians;

and Ricci translated eight European songs into Chinese, using the words *Shangdi* (God on High), *Tian* (Heaven), and *Tianshen* (Angels) to hint at the Christian message. These lessons occupied more than a month, during which the Jesuits lodged in a house outside the Forbidden Palace, under strict surveillance from the men of Eunuch Ma Tang, who still wanted to reap some benefit from his sponsorship. Bored by his daily passivity and frustrated by the continuing criticism over his handling of the succession (see Chapter 8 and later), Emperor Wanli took an unusually keen interest in these foreigners, who protested their lack of interest in office and desire only for a quiet abode in Beijing. Not wishing to depart from his refusal to grant audiences to his mandarins, Wanli ordered two court painters to fashion portraits of Ricci and Pantoja, the results of which 'resembled neither myself nor my companion', as Pantoja confided in a letter. In any event, when the emperor viewed the portraits, he supposedly exclaimed: 'Oh, they are Turks (*hui hui*)!'[2]

During the days of music lessons, when Pantoja was preoccupied with his eunuch pupils, Ricci attempted to establish contacts with his mandarin friends in Beijing, none of whom returned his letters. His frustrations were compounded by the close surveillance by Ma Tang's men, who forbade him to pay a visit to the Minister of Rites, Yu Jideng, who had jurisdiction over all foreign tributaries. The only contact Ricci made was with the Censor Cao Yubian, who visited Ricci because he admired the westerner's reputation for honesty and righteousness. The two would become friends over the next years.

One day, a dozen *yamen* clerks stormed into Ricci's house. They had been dispatched by Mandarin Cai of the Ministry of Rites, Director of the Hostel for Barbarians (*Xiyi guan*). Displeased that the westerners had presented their tributes to the emperor through Eunuch Ma Tang, and not through the proper channels of the Ministry of Rites, Cai had issued a summons. At first, thinking the clerks were trying to blackmail him for money, Ricci refused to go with them. The clerks then tied ropes around the necks of Zhong Mingren and You Wenhui. Ricci and his men were locked up in their rooms. Hearing of this, Ma Tang's men rushed to the rescue: they broke the lock and accused the clerks from the Ministry of stealing gifts for the emperor, scaring the intruders into a hasty retreat. Seizing the chance to escape Ma Tang's clutches, Ricci insisted on obeying the summons. The next day, Ricci and a eunuch appeared before Mandarin Cai. The eunuch admonished Cai not to intervene and threatened to present a memorial to the emperor. Consulting his colleagues, Cai stood his ground. The eunuch left, leaving Ricci to be interrogated. To the irate mandarin Ricci explained: they had been seized by Ma Tang while traveling; how could a foreigner resist the injustice of such a man when many high mandarins were afraid of him? Moreover, after their arrival in Beijing, they were summoned daily to the court and under constant surveillance. He had lived in China for many years, Ricci pleaded, and had already visited Beijing and should not be considered a foreigner anymore. Hearing these words, Cai, initially severe, responded with encouraging words: Do not be afraid of the eunuchs; he would send a memorial to the emperor. Meanwhile, Ricci and his men could stay in the *Xiyi guan* at the government's expense.

The Hostel for Barbarians consisted of a large walled compound, divided into hundreds of rooms to accommodate the many tribute-bearers from Central, East, and Southeast Asia to the Ming court. More commerce than diplomacy, the tributary system was instituted in the early fifteenth century to satisfy the vanity of the emperor. Every three to five years, groups of Turks, Arabs, Mughals, Persians, Mongols, Tibetans, Koreans, Ryukyians (from modern day Okinawa), Siamese, Burmese, Javanese, and Malays traveled to Beijing bearing tribute. With a few exceptions, such as jade from Central Asia, most of these tributary gifts were of little value. Their expenses in China all paid for, and their symbolic submission rewarded handsomely, the foreigners returned loaded with silk, porcelain, and rhubarb, the last a powerful laxative in Chinese medicine that fetched a high profit in western markets. With the exception of the Koreans, who were the most assimilated to Chinese culture, the foreigners were treated with formal courtesy but little respect. The name of their official residence tells the story: The Hostel for Barbarians. None of the rooms came furnished; the guests slept on straw, guarding their 'gifts' and animals; and aside from the occasion of tribute-presentation and their departure, all were kept locked in the compound during their sojourn, with the notable exception of the Korean emissaries.[3]

Here, Ricci and Pantoja stayed for three months (March to May 1611). Cai treated them with uncommon courtesy, assigning the westerners a furnished room. In early March, a few days after they had moved in, Ricci and Pantoja, together with other tribute-bearers, were escorted to the imperial palace (see Plate IX). Passing through gates guarded by soldiers and elephants, they appeared before Huangji palace, where the throne was set on a carpet, flanked by the insignia of imperial authority, shielded by a curtain of fine copper threads, and approached by steps of marble.[4] On this occasion, as had become the routine of a do-nothing emperor, Wanli was absent. After kneeling and bowing to an empty throne, to the loud chant of the mandarin directing the ceremony, the foreigners were received by Zhu Guozuo, the acting Minister of Rites, who stood in for the mortally ill Yu Jideng, and returned to their walled compound.

Prisoners in all but name, the Jesuits befriended the other inmates. Some Muslims told the missionaries of a Christian community in Gansu province in northwest China: they had fair skin; the men wore long beards; they ate pork and worshipped images of Jesus and Mary. Ricci showed great interest in what must have been the remnants of the once flourishing Nestorian community in China.

After Ricci's visit to the throne, Zhu Guozuo sent his men to question the westerners. The Jesuits stated their intention: they wanted to remain in China and preach the doctrines of their God. Ricci submitted a prayer book and a copy of his work for inspection. According to bureaucratic procedure, Zhu submitted a memorial, in which he excoriated Eunuch Ma Tang for abrogating to himself the proper jurisdiction of the Ministry of Rites, in collusion with the westerners. The memorial reads:

In *The Statutes of the Great Ming* (*Da Ming Hui dian*), only the country of Sri [author: this refers to Sri Lanka and the Coromandel coast of India, called Sri or *Xi yang*, Western Ocean in Ming records] is mentioned, and not the Great Western Ocean (*Da Xi yang*), hence there is no way to know the truth [of Ricci's claim]. Moreover, he has lived here for twenty years before bearing tribute, which is different from those coming from afar in admiration and bearing tribute. The pictures of the Lord and Mother of Heaven he presented are improper; he has bones of fairies in his luggage. If they were really fairies, they could of course fly away, how can there be bones left over? This is exactly what Han Yue of the Tang dynasty referred to as evil and dirty matter [author: Han Yue opposed the presentation of Buddhist bone relics, which he dismissed as 'evil and dirty matter']. It should not be introduced into the Forbidden City. Furthermore, these tributary gifts were presented without having been examined by my ministry: the reprehensible intervention of that eunuch [i.e. Ma Tang] and my own fault cannot be excused. Furthermore, having received a summons to come to my ministry, [Ricci] did not comply and remained in a Buddhist residence. Your servant cannot understand his intention. I beg that a gift equal to the tributary presents be bestowed, and that Li Madou [Ricci] be given a headgear and belt in accordance with tributary rules, and be ordered to return post haste, and not to reside secretly in either capital and mingle with eunuchs, in order to avoid further trouble and the confusion of ignorant commoners.[5]

Contrary to procedure, the emperor did not respond to the memorial. Later, Ricci heard from a eunuch that Wanli was displeased with the memorial: 'Are they perhaps robbers to be seized like this? We see what the Minister of Rites will do.' This memorial was not the only one that irritated the emperor. For two years, Yu Jideng, the Minister of Rites, now mortally ill, had been submitting one memorial after another, urging Wanli first to declare his eldest son the heir apparent, and then to arrange for the crown prince's marriage. Such was the frustration Yu felt at the emperor's inaction and resistance that he fell gravely ill. Consequently, any memorial from the Ministry of Rites irritated the Wanli emperor. And so he did nothing. One month passed. Some mandarins criticized the Ministry of Rites for keeping Ricci a virtual prisoner; others disapproved of Zhu's recommendation to expel the westerners; many speculated Ricci enjoyed connections with the eunuchs; and all knew of Wanli's displeasure. Zhu Guozuo submitted a second memorial, in which he avoided criticism of the eunuchs and softened his tone regarding the westerners. The emperor kept silent. The truth was that Wanli wanted the westerners to remain in Beijing, if only to service his beloved mechanical clocks, a desire ardently shared by the eunuchs entrusted with their maintenance, fearing for their own necks should something go wrong with these curiosity items. But procedure dictated the emperor could only respond, and not initiate, in matters pertaining to foreigners. Unnerved by the imperial silence, Zhu Guozuo submitted another three to four memorials, each time softening his tone and adding praises for the westerners; he even recommended assigning Ricci and Pantoja to Jiangxi or another province in the south. But the key words, Beijing residence, were missing. Still no word from on high. Meanwhile, urged by many mandarins, who wished to meet the remarkable westerner, Director Cai gave Ricci permission to leave and return at will to the Hostel for Barbarians. He even supplied a horse and groom (to report on Ricci's activities). One of the first mandarins Ricci visited was Censor Cao Yubian, who was fast becoming a friend and admirer. In May, Censor Cao pulled rank and told Director Cai he was wrong to keep the westerners in the Hostel. Soon after, Cai allowed Ricci and Pantoja to choose their own abode in the city, and promised to supply them and their servants with provisions, in accordance with their status as foreign emissaries.

Their livelihood assured with a modest but prestigious imperial stipend, which eventually amounted to 72 taels a year, the Jesuits went to work. Ricci continued his successful mode of proceeding: networking, making friends, all in high places, learned conversations, and writing books. During the second half of 1601, Ricci established a work pattern that would last until his death: he received visitors from the top echelons of Ming society; he conversed with them on the customs and laws of the West, and where appropriate introduced Christian doctrines; he made sundials, globes, quadrants, and other astronomical instruments as gifts for his Chinese inter-locutors; and he went about to endless rounds of banquets, to more con-versations and networking. It was exhausting work. An elaborate etiquette governed elite socializing: the presentation of *cartes de visite*, properly styled; the donning of silk ceremonial robes; the presentation of status-appropriate gifts; the obligation of return visits; and, above all, the ability to engage in intelligent and elevated conversations, without ever seeming vulgar or indiscreet. In the circles he dealt with, it was impossible for Ricci to refuse an invitation without offence. He seldom ate at home. Often, he had to attend three or four events daily, even during days of fasting. In his spare moments, Ricci said mass, recited prayers, supervised the Jesuit residence, and directed the other Jesuit residences in Nanjing, Nanchang, and Shao-zhou by correspondence. It was a routine that gave little leisure.

Between June and December 1601, Ricci made a number of influential friends. From Ricci's own writings and extant archival documents, we can reconstruct the general picture of his intense socializing and the specific contents of many conversations. Little by little, Ricci conveyed knowledge of the West to the Ming elites and in the process accumulated valuable social capital that proved indispensable for investing in the foundation of the China Mission.

An anonymous manuscript in Chinese, entitled *Shi ke wen da* (Answers to Visitors' Queries), today in the French National Library, gives us a vivid description of the hectic social life Ricci must have experienced. It dates from the early seventeenth century, and was written by a Jesuit missionary as a language/social primer (possibly by Ricci himself). The textual dialogue, a composite of many actual ones, begins with a scene of scholars visiting one another in the capital. It describes a very busy host (Ricci?), visitors leaving their calling cards, and return visits; it records in detail the polite conversa-tions, which begin with the usual courtesies such as expressing the admira-tion of someone's fame and their writings. After formal greetings and questions as to the native place, which the Chinese still use as a primary identification of the self, the conversation turns to one driven by the curiosity of the Chinese visitors about the West. The conversation goes something along these lines:

How many countries are there in the West? Do they go to war with one another? What do the officials wear: do they wear mandarin robes with round collars and mandarin headgear? What do the common people wear? How do they wear their hair? Do the men tie their long hair in a bun on top of their heads? Do men grow beards? Are western women beautiful? Do they bind their feet? And what kinds of shoes and jewelry do they wear? How do people marry, through marriage brokers, parents? Do people remarry? How big is your esteemed country? Are there prostitutes? [Here, the missionary answers: yes, but they are few in numbers and not tolerated in the cities;[6] the Chinese visitor chimed in approvingly that this was precisely the custom in antiquity.] How long is the journey from the Great Western Ocean? How are western ships constructed? What are the dangers of sea travel? Are there sea monsters? How many people can travel in a ship and what do they eat? How many countries has the esteemed Westerner passed through on his way to China? There are questions about Africa and India: on food, customs, material culture, and languages. Is China the middle of the world? [Here, the Jesuit interlocutor had to disappoint his visitor and replied that the equator was the middle of the world.] Why did the venerable western master not take the land route to China? [The answer is that Muslims made it difficult to travel.] The Chinese and the westerner conversed at length about Chinese porcelain and European glass, after which the visitor's curiosity turns to the salaries for officials in the west. The Jesuit missionary astonishes the Chinese visitor with the astro-nomical salary of a prime minister in the West, some 60,000 to 100,000 taels of silver, in Chinese denomination, or 75,000 to 125,000 in silver pesos or half in golden ducats, impressive sums indeed for the Ming mandarins, whose fixed salaries ranked the lowest in all the Chinese dynasties.[7] Are Western officials greedy? Are there civil service examinations? How does one get appointed an official? Can one sit for a subject in military science? The Jesuit answers no to this, but adds that one can study medicine, and the subject of the humanities is the learning of the Lord of Heaven. The conversation turns to astronomy, fortune-telling, Western medicine and pharmacy, before the Chinese visitor, indelicately and characteristically, asks about money: How do your friends send money? The missionary answers that the money was sent via Guangzhou, to which the Chinese visitor confesses that he never believed the rumor that the esteemed westerner used magic to transform mercury into silver. The subject of alchemy leads to the monetary system in Europe, which in turn leads to poverty and charity. Are there bandits? How are they punished? How does one construct houses? What styles? What material? Are there hereditary rulers in the West? Are there cities and fortifications? From the latter topic the conversation meanders to European weaponry and horses before ending with several disparate subjects: tribute-bearing, palaces, geomancy, and lions.[8]

One can imagine Ricci, the gracious and brilliant conversationalist, repeating once again the story of the West and the tale of his journey to the Realm of the Great Ming.

Ricci socialized with the highly ranked but powerless—relatives of the emperor and empress—as well as with the powerful but less prestigious—military commanders. But above all he moved in the circles of the governing class, the high mandarins. Most were officials in the capital; others came from Nanjing or the provinces on business. We will meet the most prominent ones shortly. An object of intense curiosity, a visit with Ricci became the newest social fad among the elites in Beijing. 'We can say that all sorts of weighty people come and visit,' concluded Ricci. 'But the little people', the Jesuit missionary observed, 'are afraid to come to [our house], even though the door is always open, just like those of any resident in the city. And it seemed that nobody there who had any authority did not appreciate having a conversation with the fathers or have the fathers come to their houses.'[9] The common people, as we shall see, Ricci would leave to Pantoja. Let us now meet Ricci's grand mandarin friends.

The grandest of his new friends was Shen Yiguan, a native of Ningpo, Zhejiang. A member of the Grand Secretariat, which served as the highest body of councilors for the emperor, Shen became the senior Grand Secretary in 1603 before his enemies at court intrigued his dismissal in 1606. A devout Buddhist, Shen Yiguan was no Buddha and showed little mercy in the vicious and deadly game of court politics, as we will see in the next chapter. To Ricci, however, Grand Secretary Shen acted with great magnanimity, praising Christianity for its practice of monogamy and its social discipline, and showering Ricci with gifts of money and silk. After their first meeting in late 1601, Shen continued his friendship, which gave the Jesuits powerful political patronage in Beijing.

Another devout Buddhist was Li Dai, the Minister of Personnel. Intensely preoccupied with the afterlife, the 70-year-old minister engaged Ricci in discussions of life and death, which gave the Jesuit an opportunity to discourse on the transitory nature of human existence. At their first meeting, Li Dai inquired after the westerner's age. Ricci replied: 'I have already lost five decades.' Puzzled, Minister Dai asked: 'Does your religion reverse having and not having?' Unlike gold and grain, which one can store, Ricci explained, time passed away with the regularity of the sun and seasons, never to return. How could one speak of having an age, when the past no longer belonged to oneself?

Wasting fifty years, Ricci professed, he had achieved nothing in serving his country, in strengthening his lineage, or progressing in personal virtue. Li Dai exclaimed: 'No, no! Don't be so modest and say you have wasted your time and achieved nothing or not enjoying longevity. There are bad people in the world who insult heaven, hurt people, and shame themselves since youth. Merciful heaven grants them longevity, hoping they would repent, but they use this time to increase their faults. When they are about to die, their age and evil deeds are equally long. How horrible! Do you think they enjoy longevity or not?' Ricci replied: 'Better they were never born.' Impressed by Ricci's words, Li Dai admonished the younger members of his household: use time well in virtue. Continuing his discourse on the transitory nature of time, Ricci again admonished the cognizance of virtue and of God, every moment of one's life.[10]

On life and virtue they concurred. But Li Dai disagreed strongly with Ricci's attack on Buddhism. 'It is wrong for them [the Jesuits] to speak ill of Buddha. If the Lord of Heaven is great in heaven, then Buddha is great on earth,' retorted Minister Li.[11] Two years later, when Li Dai lost his post during the 'Evil Book Incident' (see Chapter 10), Ricci remarked on Li's misfortune, not without malice, 'It looks like God is great in heaven and on earth, and his idols cannot free him and keep him in office.'[12]

Old friends opened doors to new friends. Wang Ruxun, who had learned western mathematics from Ricci in Nanjing, was promoted Vice-Minister (shilang) of the Ministry of Justice. After his arrival in the capital, Wang, a native of Shandong province, introduced Ricci to two other high-ranking mandarins from his home province: Wang's own superior, Minister Xiao Daheng, and Feng Qi, who succeeded Yu Jideng as Minister of Rites, after Yu's death in August 1611.

Scarcely one year in Beijing, Ricci had already cultivated relations with three of the six ministers of state—Li Dai, Xiao Daheng, and Feng Qi—not to mention a grand secretary, Shen Yiguan. Of these powerful men, Feng Qi exerted the most effective patronage: he was the highest official in charge of foreigners in China. Furthermore, Feng Qi showed the keenest interest in the teachings of Christianity, as reflected in a conversation between himself and Ricci about life as a temporary station.

Deeply pessimistic about corruption in his own times, Feng shared with Ricci his reflections on human nature:

I observe that Man is the noblest among the tens of thousands of living beings in the world, incomparable to the birds and beasts, and thus we say that Man is a part of heaven and earth. Yet, when I observe the birds and beasts, they seem more at ease than human beings. Why? They can move right after birth; they know how to look for food and avoid harm; they are born with feathers, hair, skin, and claws, requiring no clothing, agriculture, grain storage, or tools. They eat and breed; they rest and play; and they enjoy leisure. Do they cultivate any distinctions between self and other, rich and poor, high and low, license and prohibition, first and last, or worry about success? Whether resting or running, they spend their days as they wish.

When human beings are born, their mothers suffer great pain; they come naked to the world and start crying, as if they know the difficulty of birth. They are weak after birth and cannot walk. Only after three years do they leave their mothers' embrace. When they are grown, they have their own labor: the farmer plowing earth every season, the traveler spending the year at sea and in the mountains, the artisan laboring unceasingly with his hands, and the scholar exhausting his mind day and night, in short, the gentlemen laboring with their mind, and the commoner with their body. Five decades of life mean five decades of pain. And speaking of illness! I have read in a medical book that there are more than 300 afflictions of the eye alone. How many are there for the entire body! And almost all medicine is bitter ... Human beings hurt one another: they make weapons to chop off limbs; most violent deaths are caused by humans. Today we complain that old weapons are not sharp enough and try to devise new ones. There is more and more killing, littering plains and cities with corpses, slaughter without end. Even in years of peace, is there a single family that lacks nothing? The wealthy have no progeny; those with progeny have no talent; those with talent enjoy no leisure; those who enjoy leisure have no power; and everyone complains of inadequacies. Often, great happiness is eclipsed by a small misfortune. You worry your whole life until it concludes in the great anxiety of death, when your body is buried underground, an inescapable fate.

Therefore, an ancient sage admonished his sons: 'Do not deceive yourself and close your mind: everyone is racing only to their graves. We are not living, rather exist in a state of constant death. When we are born, we begin to die; death represents only the end. A day passes, I lose one day, and step closer to my grave. What we fear we cannot avoid, is there a time of contentment?'

Yet this is only outer pain. Who can bear the inner pain? The labor of the world is real, its happiness false; its worries are normal, its joys limited. If the misfortunes of one day cannot be recounted in ten years, how can we describe the worries of a lifetime in our own lifetime? Our hearts are attacked by love, hatred, anger, and fear, just like a tree on a high mountain blasted by winds from the four directions.

Can there ever be a moment of rest? Be it wine, sex, career, or wealth, we are all led by our desires. Is there anyone who is content with his lot and seeks nothing? Even if one is given the four seas and billons of people, one is still not satisfied. How foolish!

Human beings are ignorant of the true way of being, how can he know other ways? He follows Confucius, then Laozi, and then Buddha; how can all minds in the world be bent under these three teachings? Restless people establish their own schools to propagate novelties; soon, the differences between the three teachings will become more than 3,000 teachings. Everyone says: 'The right way, the right way,' but the way of the world is becoming ever more deviant and chaotic: cruel superiors, insulting inferiors, tyrannical fathers, rebellious sons, rulers and officials in mutual suspicion, brothers in fraternal strife, couples in separation, friends in mutual deception, and the whole world is full of deception, calumny, and madness. Where is the true heart? People in the world are in a shipwreck, bobbing up and down in waves whipped up by gale winds, all trying to save themselves without regard for anyone else. Some hold on to broken planks; some ride on rafts; others grab broken cages, holding on for dear life. Alas, they will all die. Why does the Lord of Heaven create Man to live in this place of suffering? Why does he love human beings less than animals?

Ricci heartily agreed. And yet, human beings clung to this world with all its afflictions. 'Human life is only a temporary abode,' Ricci expounded. 'I think that the Lord of Heaven has placed Man on earth to test his heart in order to rank his virtue. . . . Our true home is not in this world, but in the world after; it is not among men, but in heaven. Our life is the life of animals, therefore birds and beasts look upon the earth. We are subjects of heaven and raise our heads toward the sky.' 'When the Lord of Heaven first created the world,' Ricci continued, 'he made all things and animals for our use, and our kind originally suffered no afflictions. But after our first ancestors had offended the lord, an infringement that their descendants repeated, the things of the world began to turn against us. This was the origins of all suffering; it was not the will of the Lord of Heaven, but our own fault.'

When Ricci was finished, Feng Qi sighed: 'If this view is propagated in China, all doubts will be resolved, and there will be no more talk of blaming heaven, for what fault is there? The saints and sages from antiquity and the past labored their entire lives to save the world. If the Creator were to condemn these moral beings after death to wilt away like trees and grass, without a place of happiness for their eternal enjoyment, and if he had no rewards for their bitter labor, then the world would be filled with doubt.

Your brilliant opinion would lead people to real virtue, rescue them from vacuity, confirm their will to bear sufferings, overcome their embarrassment with poverty, strengthen their determination to follow their own roles and not hanker after shamefulness: it is indeed the truth.'[13]

His interest in Christianity awakened, Feng Qi pressed Ricci to translate the Ten Commandments and other books of Christian doctrine. The Minister of Rites represented a group of intellectuals in the late Ming who despaired over the corruption of their own society. Finding no solution from the traditional teachings in Confucianism, Daoism, and Buddhism, be it for the reform of social mores or for their own spiritual consolation, they found Christianity, in the way it was expounded by Ricci, an attractive and powerful teaching. Convinced that Feng Qi had embarked on the road to conversion, Ricci lamented Feng's untimely death, when an illness carried away the 44-year-old Minister after only eighteen months in office.[14]

Ricci would eventually find converts among the high-ranking mandarins. More typical, however, were those like Ricci's first supporter in Beijing, Censor Cao Yubian, traditional scholars attracted by the convergence between the social ethics of Christianity and Confucianism, but who stopped short of conversion. A conversation between Ricci and Cao is a case in point. The topic at hand was speech, quite appropriate given Cao's official charge to exercise moral vigilance over the actions and words of the ruling elites, including those of the emperor. Collected as the fifth chapter of his *Ten Discourses of the Man of Paradox*, Ricci recalled Cao's question: 'The saints spoke little and wished to remain silent. Why?' Censor Cao told the Jesuit that 'As a boy I read in Confucius [*the Analects*] that a virtuous man is wooden and of few words, whereas the eloquent ones are the self-seekers. I have always wanted to curb my speech and would like to hear the true discourse of your esteemed country.'

Drawing from his immense textual knowledge, Ricci first cited a proverb from the Old Testament (Proverbs 17: 28): 'The fool also if he holds his peace shall be reputed wise, and if he closes his lips, a man of understanding.' After commenting on the proverb, Ricci invoked 'a great sage from western antiquity', Socrates, who taught silence to his disciples, graduating only those who managed to keep silent for seven years. The third example was a great rhetorician from the West, a silent man otherwise; when he was questioned as to his qualifications to teach eloquence, he replied that silence is like a grinding stone that could sharpen knives. Ricci commented that the larger, the more solid the vessel, the less sound it made, thereby implying those without learning would discourse loudly, whereas a true scholar and gentleman would be silent in his solid erudition. A virtuous act spoke louder than mere words. Using an imaginative and vivid metaphor, Ricci explained that the Creator gave Man two hands and two ears, but only one tongue, indicating he should listen more and speak less. Moreover, God has placed the tongue deep inside the mouth, shielding it with a wall of teeth, a moat of lips, and forts of beard, in order to admonish us to be circumspect in speech.

After giving more examples from western texts, Ricci told Cao the story of Xanthus the philosopher and Aesop his slave.[15] Preparing for a banquet, Xanthus orders Aesop to cook the finest dish for his guest. The wise slave purchases pigs' tongues, boiling some, roasting others, and spicing more. To the guests, Aesop serves plate after plate of tongue in different recipes, until Xanthus shouts at his slave. Defending himself, Aesop explains there is nothing finer or greater than the tongue, for all philosophy depends on the tongue, without which nothing gets done by way of buying, selling, or legislating. Since all life is ordered by the tongue, there is nothing greater. The next day, Xanthus gives the opposite command: buy and prepare the worst thing to eat. This time, Aesop prepares the tongues with vinegar and spicy sauce. To his enraged master and grumbling guests, Aesop answers that every bad thing comes from the tongue, for it gives rise to enmity, plots, battles, rivalry, strife, and wars, and is the most abominable thing in the world.

Greek fables and biblical stories provided novel rhetorical commonplaces to enhance the appeal of Ricci's message: the Creator of the world, the Lord of Heaven, was manifest in his work, the Book of Nature, and was known to the ancient Chinese sages; subsequently, knowledge of the true God was displaced by Buddhist and other heterodox doctrines; Ricci merely complemented the teachings of the ancient sages by demonstrating the concordance between Christian and Confucian teachings, and by showing divine providence in the laws of nature and in the beneficial social consequences of a Christian society. The twin arguments of Christian social ethics and western science won two strong supporters for Ricci, who called them his two closest friends in Beijing.

The Director of the Bureau of Water Works for the Capital (*Du shui qing li si shi lang*), one of the four bureaus in the Ministry of Works, Li Zhizao (1565–1630), was a brilliant man. In his youth, Li had produced a map of the fifteen provinces of China. When he saw Ricci's *World Map*, he realized the vast extent of geographic and astronomical knowledge still unknown to the Ming world. Therefore, after Ricci's arrival in Beijing, Li rushed to invite

Ricci. At the banquet, which fell on a feast day, Li noticed Ricci was refraining from all dishes except for vegetables. He asked Ricci the reason for his vegetarian fast, given that the westerner had clearly distanced himself from Buddhism. At this, Ricci took out a sheaf of pages from his sleeve, on which were written a short treatise explaining the principles of Christian fasting (for the repentance of sins, to restrain bodily desires, to discipline the mind in the pursuit of non-sensual moral perfection).[16] Impressed, Li Zhizao asked to have the essay copied. Ricci had come prepared with a sleight of hand to make an intellectual impression.

Impress he did. The older missionary and the younger Chinese scientist quickly became friends. Ricci appreciated Li's quickness of mind, and rated Li one of his two best students in mathematics. Over the next nine years, Ricci and Li collaborated in the translation of several scientific works into Chinese; in fact, Li Zhizao would become the most important transmitter of western scientific knowledge in early seventeenth-century China. Li Zhizao helped Ricci in another important way, by writing prefaces to new editions and reprints of works by the Jesuit missionary. In the Ming literary world, the reputation and circulation of books increased in proportion to the reputation of the scholars who penned prefaces and postscripts. For the first time in his 'apostolate by the book', Ricci would benefit from his close networking with the world of Beijing mandarins.

The first work by Ricci that Li Zhizao sponsored was a reprint of the *World Map*. In his preface, Li mentioned the hypothesis of a spherical heaven in ancient Chinese astronomy and its subsequent achievements. But even during the Yuan dynasty, when astronomy reached its zenith, the measurement of the North Polar Star was still inaccurate. Hence, the great contribution of Ricci's *World Map*, which depicts the world in great detail as well as showing the movements of the sun and moon, and the correct positions of the stars. 'Literati of the past used the north as the median of the heavens . . . using the North Polar Star as the median . . . If you view this *World Map*, you will notice the convergence. How can you not believe that in the Eastern and Western oceans [i.e. China and Europe], there is but one mind and one reason.'[17]

Acknowledging the one truth in the ordering of the universe implied the possible belief in an omnipotent God. Ricci was certainly hoping that Li's intense interest in western science and mathematics would lead to embracing the Christian faith. But Li was resistant, held back in part by his reluctance to accept monogamy and renounce his concubines. The path to conversion would be a long one for Li Zhizao.

Ricci's second intimate friendship was with the imprisoned mandarin Feng Yinjing (1555–1606), a celebrity in the capital. A native of Fengyang, the native place of the founder of the Ming dynasty, Feng Yinjing gained fame as Censor in Wuchang, in the province of Huguang. Upright, honest, and principled, Feng embodied the very image of an ideal Confucian mandarin: in upholding justice, he embraced the cause of the poor and the weak; and he was the only mandarin in the entire province who dared to oppose the Eunuch-Tax Intendant Chen Feng, every bit as rapacious as the notorious Eunuch Ma Tang. Feng's repeated memorials denouncing Eunuch Chen, and the latter's counter-accusations, caused the recall of the upright official, to the general consternation and sadness of the common people. Arriving in Beijing in February 1601 as a hero, Feng was promptly imprisoned by the Wanli emperor; and it was in jail that Ricci first visited the fearless official.

A long-time admirer of Ricci, Feng Yinjing had written a book in his youth defending Confucian orthodoxy against Buddhism. While still in office in Wuchang, Feng sent a disciple named Liu to study mathematics with Ricci. Unable to find the Jesuit in Nanjing, Liu followed his master to Beijing, where he visited Ricci and told the westerner of his master, an ardent admirer and incarcerated mandarin. Ricci went to visit Feng. The two men, similar in age and temperament, developed an immediate rapport, 'and in one hour of conversation', Ricci wrote, 'they formed such a close friendship that all of China was surprised, thinking they have been conversing for many years'.[18] So impressed was Feng by Ricci, 'someone who devoted his life to the cultivation of friendship',[19] that the upright mandarin wrote a preface in praise of friendship and its virtues and paid for a reprint of Ricci's work.

Over the next three years, Ricci regularly visited the imprisoned mandarin and sent Feng copies of his own writings. In prison, Feng was persuaded by the teachings of Ricci and declared his readiness to convert. After three years, the emperor bowed to public pressure and numerous memorials in favor of Feng Yinjing and pardoned his recalcitrant and upright official. Allowed only a few days in the capital after his release, Feng returned to his hometown. Among the crush of mandarin well-wishers, Ricci did not have time to confirm Feng's decision and administer baptism. Later, Ricci instructed the Jesuits in Nanjing to travel to Fengyang to baptize an ailing

Feng, but the mandarin died before receiving the sacrament. When Ricci heard the news, he uttered a prayer in deep regret: 'For the good that he had done for us and the great desire he had shown in helping and following the holy faith, may God count him among the baptized and give eternal salvation to his soul.'[20]

Among the good that Feng had done for the Catholic cause was the preface he wrote for *Tianzhu shiyi*, *True Meaning of the Lord of Heaven*, Ricci's most important work, the content and impact of which will be described in the next chapter. Here, we will read Feng Yinjing's preface, which succinctly and brilliantly sums up the Riccian method of evangelization and reflects the deep attraction Ricci exerted for many intellectuals of late Ming China. Feng writes:

Tianzhu shiyi is the dialogue between Ricci of the Great West and us Chinese. Who is the Lord of Heaven, *Tianzhu*? He is *Shangdi*, the God on high, a real and not an empty being. The four great sages, our six Confucian classics, and assorted sages all say: 'fear God on high', 'help God on high,' 'serve God on high', and 'investigate God on high'; Who can say there is anything empty about this?

The discourse of emptiness came from India during the reign of Emperor Ming of the Han dynasty. The saint mentioned by Confucius was this Buddha, so the troublemakers claimed; and they so inflated their talk as if Buddha was higher than our *Six Classics*. They were ignorant that India lies to the west of China, and to the west of India is the Great West. The Buddhists plagiarized some ethical proverbs of Pythagoras and called it reincarnation; they stole the idea of an amoral universe from Laozi and called it *samsara* . . . In antiquity heaven was called the highest, and now it is Buddha. In antiquity, people made offerings to heaven, earth, the temple of the state, mountains, rivers, and ancestors, and now to Buddha. In antiquity, scholars knew and obeyed heaven, now they recite Buddhist prayers and sponsor Buddhist rituals. In antiquity, officials diffused reverentially the work of heaven to bring benefits to the people of heaven, not daring to indulge in their own leisure, now great hermits reside at the imperial court, escaping the world in Chan meditation.

Who is Buddha but the national teacher of India? Our country has its own national teachers: the three rulers, the five emperors, the three kings, the Duke of Zhou, Confucius, and our own Taizu emperor. Their national teacher insults heaven and puts himself above it; our teachers succeed heaven and stand underneath it. If their country follows him, I have nothing to say. But why should we abandon what we have learned and follow? . . . This book cites many passages from our *Six Classics* to support the real substance of its arguments, and profoundly criticizes the error of the discourse of emptiness, thus using the west to correct the west, using Chinese culture to reform Chinese culture. Its argument is clear: abandoning human relations (*ren lun*) and things of the world, and claiming ridiculous purity from pollution is the heterodoxy of reincarnation. It argues clearly for the cultivation of the self, the expansion of civilization, the respect for filial piety, and the respect for the common ultimate father. It states that human nature is greatly different from that of animals; it advocates that all learning should begin with curbing desire and end in cultivating humanity. It contains things unbeknownst to our country or not yet put into practice. Sir Li [Ricci] has traveled for eighty thousand miles and investigated the nine heavens and nine rivers most accurately. The natural phenomena that we have not profoundly investigated, he has demonstrated with proof, and therefore we ought to accept his reasoning on divinity.[21]

This was a resounding endorsement indeed.

IO

The True Meaning of the Lord of Heaven

R icci's most famous book was a long time in the making. His correspondence suggests a first version of this work had already been completed in Nanchang in 1595. His mind sharpened by the many conversations with the Confucian scholar Zhang Huang and his disciples, Ricci was inspired to find parallels between the sayings of the ancient Confucian classics and the fundamental principles of a pared-down Christianity, stripped clean of the doctrines of original sin, the Crucifixion, and the Resurrection. Ricci advanced a simple, radical two-step argument: the Chinese sages knew and worshipped the true God in antiquity, but that knowledge and practice had been subverted by literati of subsequent ages and especially by the introduction of Buddhism to China. Ricci aimed at demonstrating, using natural reason and invoking Confucian textual authority, the existence of an omnipotent God, creator of heaven and earth, called the Lord of Heaven, *Tianzhu*, in the discourse of the Jesuits, but named God on High, *Shangdi*, or simply heaven, *Tian*, in the ancient classics. By the time he had settled in Nanjing in 1599, Ricci had already developed the first part of his idea—the Confucian–Christian synthesis. The second, anti-Buddhist part slowly came together after Ricci's debates with Abbot Hong en in Nanjing, as we have seen, and with Huang Hui, an academician at the Hanlin Academy.

In many ways Huang Hui resembled Jiao Hong, the eminent scholar and Buddhist layman in Nanjing whom Ricci met: both triumphed in the same *jinshi* examination; both were appointed to the Hanlin Academy; both enjoyed stellar literary reputations; both officials served as tutors to the Eldest Prince, whose cause they pleaded before the emperor; and both men believed fervently in Buddhism and were especially devoted to the practice of Chan meditation.

Unwilling to meet the anti–Buddhist westerner, Huang Hui obtained a manuscript copy of Ricci's work, presumably a version of the *True Meaning of the Lord of Heaven*, through his friend, Mandarin Cai of the Ministry of Rites. With the descriptions of the Christian God, Huang Hui took no issue, but he was livid with Ricci's criticism of Buddhism. A short time later, Ricci received this copy back from Huang Hui, filled with marginal rebuttals and notes. Reluctant to confront and offend such a prominent man, Ricci incorporated his replies in the final version of the *True Meaning of the Lord of Heaven*, which he was busy revising with the help of Feng Yinjing in the autumn and winter of 1602. 'He is scrupulous in altering a single word without first consulting me,' as Ricci wrote in a letter of 2 September.[1] The book appeared in print in 1603.

Divided into eight chapters, *True Meaning of the Lord of Heaven* is written in the form of a dialogue between a westerner and a Chinese scholar.[2] A favorite genre in both Renaissance Europe and Ming China, the dialogue reflected in part the learned conversations at colloquies and scholarly gatherings. In Ricci's case, the dialogical text represented an ordered synopsis of the numerous conversations between himself and the Chinese literati. His intended readership was the Confucian scholar, manifest in Ricci's appeal to Confucian principles in the introduction to the book: 'All doctrines of peaceful and just rule depend on the principle of oneness; therefore the sages admonish officials to be loyal. What is loyalty but devotion to the one [lord]. Among the Five Human Relationships, the most important concerns the ruler, and the relationship between the ruler and his official represents the first of the Three Bonds. A just man understands and acts on this.' More explicitly, Ricci continues: 'Every country has a lord; can it be that only heaven and earth do not have a lord? A country is unified under one lord, how can heaven and earth have two lords? A gentleman cannot but know and reflect on the origins of the universe and the source of creation.' Yet, there are usurpers who rebelled against the Heavenly Emperor (*Tiandi*), who punishes human beings with disasters and sufferings. From his youth, Ricci exclaims, he has wanted to lead the deluded back to the true lord, for which reason he has traveled to China and learned its language and customs.

After this introduction, Ricci uses natural reason to demonstrate the existence of an omnipotent Creator. In chapter 1, 'The Lord of Heaven creates all things and nourishes it', Ricci states that the true doctrine is not limited to one country, but universal to all men. Endowed with reason, a mark that distinguishes us from the animals, man cannot but seek truth. 'Anyone who gazes upon the wonders of heaven must sigh in amazement: "Who then is the lord of all this?" This is the Lord of Heaven, whom we call *Deus* in the West.' Ricci proceeds to demonstrate the existence of God: First, in every country of the world, people worship a supreme being, looking to him for succor and fearing his retribution for sins. Second, natural phenomena, not endowed with souls, cannot move on their own; yet the movements of wind, water, and the stars must come from an external force, which regulates the enormous complexities of movements in the physical world. Third, how can animals, living beings without souls, instinctively seek life and nurture their young without the design of a supreme lord?

Continuing to demonstrate that all things are created, Ricci argues: First, that things cannot create themselves: just as buildings are fabricated by artisans, so too the sun, the moon, the stars, the mountains, the oceans, and all living things cannot create themselves and are created. Second, all created things manifest the order of creation: just as the layout of a house and the style of an essay reflect the designs behind them, so the celestial spheres, earth, air, and water nourish all living beings; and just as men are endowed with organs and senses, and animals with feathers, hide, scales, beaks, horns, or sharp teeth, 'everything in this world is regulated and ordered', thanks to an original sentient creator.

At this point, the Chinese scholar expresses his doubt: 'If everything has an origin in what you Sir call the Lord of Heaven, may I ask who gave birth to this Lord of Heaven?' In reply, Ricci resorts to Aristotelian logic, arguing for the distinction between essence and accident, an omnipotent, essential God and the accidents of his creation. He explains further the oneness of God by appealing both to the idea of a natural perfection in the universe and to Confucian political ethics: 'In a household there is only one elder, in a country there is only one ruler; if there are two, there will be disorder. A person has only one body, and a body has only one head; if they are two, it will be monstrosity. Therefore I know that while there are many spirits in the universe, there is only one Lord of Heaven, creator of all things, who governs and regulates all things. Why do you doubt it?'

Persuaded by logic, the Chinese scholar inquires further into the nature of God. Ricci answers with a parable. Wanting to write a definitive book about the nature of God, St Augustine wanders on the beach one day lost in thought. He sees a boy digging a hole in the sand, filling it with water from an empty seashell. 'What are you doing?' the saint asks. 'I want to empty the sea into this hole with this shell,' answers the boy. St Augustine laughs at the foolishness. The boy retorts: 'If you know this small shell and this small hole cannot contain the vastness of the sea, why do you strain your mind with your puny human capacity to exhaust the great mystery of God and squeeze it into your little book?' With these words echoing in his ears, the boy disappears before St Augustine's eyes; and the saint knows it was a sign from God. Delighted with the story, the Chinese scholar told Ricci that he 'has explained the inexplicable, investigated that which cannot be investigated'. Having heard this discourse, he begins to see the 'Great Doctrine' and the 'Great Origins', and asks for permission to return for further elucidation.

In chapter 2, Ricci refutes the three Chinese views of divinity. First, he dismisses out of hand the ideas of 'Nothingness' and 'Emptiness', the Daoist and Buddhist explanations for the origins of the universe. While affirming the sincere and realistic approach of Confucian scholars, Ricci judges this to be an inadequate knowledge of the true God. At this, the Confucian scholar nods in vigorous agreement: 'The gentlemen of our country also deeply despise the two [Daoist and Buddhist].' Nevertheless, the Chinese interlocutor resists Ricci's critique of neo-Confucianism: 'Are the scholars of my country correct in their statements about the Supreme Ultimate, *taiji*?' The western scholar [Ricci] replies: 'Although I entered China when I was a mature man, I have never neglected studying the ancient classics. I have only heard of ancient men of virtue worshipping the Emperor on High of heaven and earth and never worshipping the Supreme Ultimate. If the Supreme Ultimate were the ancestor of the Emperor on High and of all things, why would the ancient sages suppress this doctrine?'

The Chinese scholar says: 'In antiquity the name [*taiji*] did not exist, but it existed in principle (*li*); only that the diagrams and interpretations have not been transmitted to us.' Ricci disagrees: 'The gentleman must not oppose any discourse that is reasonable. I am afraid the explanation about *taiji* is unreasonable. When I look at the diagrams of *wuji* and *taiji*, I see only random and exotic patterns. Where does the real phenomenon exist? From this you can know the fact that heaven and earth did not originate from *taiji*. As for the principle of the Lord of Heaven, it has been passed on in perfection from antiquity to the present. When I wish to set it down in writing and transmit it to other countries, I dare not but explain the proofs of its principle; how can this be compared to a fantastic phenomenon that has no real principle?'

The Chinese scholar objected: '*Taiji* is nothing else, only principle. If you say this whole principle is no principle, what principle can we talk about?'

Here, Ricci runs up against the materialistic philosophy of Song dynasty neo-Confucianism, which postulates a self-generating universe, born out of undivided primal matter, the Supreme Ultimate, the forces of yin and yang, and the five elements in successive stages of evolution. All this self-generating matter, human beings included, is united in the First Principle, *li*; hence, whether one affirms *li* in one's mind by investigating nature, or sees the mind's principle reflected in all things, these are merely two roads to the same truth.

Ricci's rebuttal focuses on using the Aristotelian distinction between essence and accident. One must distinguish between independent (essential) and dependent (accidental) phenomena. Whereas God, spirits, and souls belong to the former, all things, including the concepts of *taiji* and *li*, belong to the second. Using a famous truism from the ancient Chinese School of Logic, Ricci argues that the essence of horse precedes that of whiteness; hence, a white horse is a compound that consists of an essence and an accident, and the latter, whiteness, cannot exist without the former, just as *taiji*, the Supreme Ultimate or a materialistic universe, cannot exist without a first cause, an essence, the Creator.

Aristotelian logic aside, Ricci only clinches his argument by invoking the authority of the ancient Confucian classics: 'Our Lord of Heaven is the Emperor on High (*Shangdi*) mentioned in the ancient classics. In the *Doctrine of the Mean*, Confucius is quoted as saying: "The ceremonies of sacrifices to Heaven and Earth are meant for the Emperor on High." Zhu Xi comments that not mentioning Emperor Earth was for the sake of brevity. In my humble opinion Confucius wanted to say that the One [i.e. Emperor on High] cannot be mistaken for a duality. How could it have been for the sake of brevity?' Showing off his erudition, Ricci cites seven more quotes from the other ancient classics—the *Shijing* (*Book of Odes*), the *Yijing* (*Book of Changes*), the *Liji* (*Book of Rites*), and the *Shujing* (*Book of History*)—to impress his Chinese interlocutor.

It was a bold move to criticize the authority of Zhu Xi, the great scholar of neo-Confucianism. But Ricci trumped the commentary of Zhu Xi with the texts of the ancient classics. In spite of all their erudite scholars, Ricci ventures, perhaps there are still some things that the Chinese do not see: they worship heaven instead of the Lord of Heaven the way a foreigner comes to the imperial capital, and on seeing the magnificent palaces kneels down in prostration, mistaking the buildings for the person of the emperor. The Lord of Heaven, Ricci admonishes, is the true father and mother of humankind, to whom we owe obedience and reverence.

In chapter 3, Ricci introduces the doctrine of the immortal soul. It opens with a Chinese scholar lamenting that the fate of human beings is less happy than those of animals. With very minor variations, this is identical word for word with Feng Yinjing's discourse in chapter 2 of *Jiren shipian*, which we have seen in Chapter 9. Here, Ricci launches into a far more extensive reply. In Christian doctrine, the doctrine of an immortal soul buttresses the foundations of heaven and hell: without immortal and sentient souls, what would be the point of eternal bliss and endless pain? 'But if you speak about the afterlife,' objects the skeptical Chinese scholar, 'and about heaven and hell, this is Buddhism. We Confucian scholars do not believe in this.'

This provokes Ricci into a vigorous and long-winded defense, in which he invokes and explains in detail Aristotle's idea of the three souls. In *On the Soul*, the Greek philosopher proposes a hierarchy of souls, which corresponds, from lowest to the highest, to plants, animals, and men. The lowest, the nutritive soul, allows plants to reproduce; the middle, the sensitive soul, is possessed by all animals and determines perception and locomotion; only human beings, however, are endowed with the highest, the rational soul, which is capable of intellectual activity. While the Chinese scholar finds this hierarchy persuasive, he ventures that 'The gentleman leads a life different from that of a commoner; hence, it is fitting that after death there should also be a difference. Since in living and dying, they are the same, the difference must lie in the soul. Therefore, some scholars say that the virtuous gathered their mind by following the true path and their minds do not dissipate after death, whereas the wicked, having corrupted their minds in life, would experience the dissipation of both their bodies and minds. This should entice people to virtue.' Ricci immediately objects, repeating that the souls of all persons, good or evil, are eternal and destined for reward and punishments.

The next chapter, 'On the differences between spirits and soul, and against the doctrine that all things are one', consists of a long and rambling dialogue over metaphysics. It starts with the Chinese scholar discussing the nature of spirits and souls, which Ricci uses to argue for the immortality of the latter. Citing passages from the *Book of Odes* and *Book of History*, Ricci points out that in the Shang and Zhou dynasties in antiquity, the rulers often invoked their ancestors, thus proving the immortality of the soul. The conversation next turns to whether all things—plants, animals, and stones—possess some force of spiritual animation, which was the view of the Daoist, and whether all natural phenomena participate in the same essence or substance, which represented the view of Mahayana Buddhism.

Not the easiest of debates, this metaphysical discussion hinges on fundamental differences of concepts. To aid the reader, Ricci includes an elaborate diagram, adapted from Aristotle's work (*Organon* and *On Physics*), in which the categories of form and matter, self-generating and accidental phenomena, and other abstract Greek philosophical concepts are visually presented. In this debate, Ricci takes a basic line: there is an absolute difference between God and his creation, introducing the figure of Lucifer as a spirit who dared to claim equality with his creator; moreover, how can one equate the maker and his tool, omnipotent God and his creatures, and suggest they all share the same body and essence? Let us follow the debate.

The Chinese scholar says: 'Our ancient scholars understood that the nature of all things in the universe is good and possesses reason; it remains unalterable. Although things can be big or small, they share in the same essence, that is to say the Lord of Heaven or the Emperor on High dwells within each thing and is one with it. Therefore, they admonish people to virtue so as not to blemish the original goodness. . . . But I am afraid this is not the same as your discourse about the Lord of Heaven.' Ricci exclaims: 'This is more absurd than what you have said before! How can I agree?' Later on, the Chinese scholar suggests: 'Buddha does not yield in dignity to the Lord of Heaven. He respects and values human life and morality, there is much to be said. God on High may possess great virtue, but we human beings also possess supreme virtue.' He goes on to praise the work of the legendary kings of ancient China, who created civilization and established moral laws. 'Hence, even the Emperor on High may not exceed the virtue and achievements of men; how can you say that only the Lord of Heaven can create heaven and earth!' To this, Ricci can only answer: 'The foundation of virtue is the cultivation of the self and is perfected in serving the Emperor on High. The virtue of Zhou [King Wen of Zhou and the Duke of Zhou] is defined by serving the Emperor on High. Now you say we are equal to the one, whom we ought to worship, how rebellious!'

There is no doubt that Ricci used his heated debates with devotees of Buddhism as material for parts of this chapter. One can imagine that in real life, the Jesuit missionary and his Chinese hosts ended their inconclusive debates before the flames of passionate opposition should scorch the links of courteous friendships. Here in the text, in a bit of wishful thinking, Ricci emerges the winner, with his opponent conceding the truth of the Jesuit discourse.

In chapter 5, Ricci turns to attacking the Buddhist teachings of reincarnation, vegetarianism, and the rule against the killing of animals. The reincarnation of souls, Ricci argues, was a doctrine first invented by Pythagoras as a moral injunction for ignorant commoners. Somehow this doctrine spread to India, where the Buddhists plagiarized and embellished on it. 'India is an insignificant land without culture and ceremonies,' dismisses Ricci; 'how can it serve as a model for the world!'

At this point, the Chinese scholar mentions that there are many examples of people recalling their past lives: is this not proof of reincarnation? Ricci retorts that all these memories of past lives are fabricated by Buddhists, who are in fact listening to the whispers of the Devil. Continuing to criticize reincarnation, Ricci denigrates it as an absurd doctrine that suggests that human souls can be reincarnated in the bodies of animals or plants. Repeating the Aristotelian distinction between vegetative, animal, and the human soul, Ricci argues for the exact correspondence between physical appearances and the nature of the soul: the idea of human souls in animal bodies is simply impossible and absurd. Continuing his attack, Ricci mocks the admonitory intention of reincarnation: evil people cannot wait to cast off their human faces and moral restraints; being reincarnated as ferocious or cunning animals would simply suit their evil natures and is hardly punishment inflicted by God. Not only is the belief in reincarnation ineffective as a moral admonition, it is actually harmful to morality.

Ricci gives examples. The belief in reincarnation leads Buddhists to advocate non-killing, since horses and buffaloes could well be the reincarnations of one's parents. According to this logic, Ricci reasons, one would have to abandon agriculture, since it would be equally offensive to filial piety to ride horses or yoke buffaloes who may turn out to be one's parents! Moreover, this doctrine runs contrary to Confucian ethics. Since there is the danger of incest in marrying a woman who may be the reincarnation one's mother, or the possibility that one lords over servants reincarnated from one's father and brothers, all bonds of human relations would dissolve in this regime.

The Chinese scholar raises more questions. If souls are immortal, would the world not be overcrowded with dead souls? Ricci says this reflects ignorance of the infinity of the universe. His Chinese interlocutor then says: 'Very few of us Confucian scholars believe in reincarnation. However, their rule against killing is like our teaching on *ren*, humanity, why should the Lord of Heaven, who is the source of mercy, forbid it?' To counter this, Ricci launches into a long speech on the nobility of man; all created things are placed at man's service by the Creator. The Chinese scholar doubts that all things are indeed beneficial to man: what about poisonous snakes and predatory beasts? But one has to distinguish between the external and inner man, Ricci reminds him. God has created the world to nourish man's bodies, and has placed physical dangers to admonish man to avoid evil and do good. Still, the Chinese scholar is not quite convinced that the Christian God is not a merciful deity that treasures all life. Using a counter-argument, Ricci retorts that those who keep vegetarian fasts are also killing life. 'Yes, vegetables are living things, but they are without blood or consciousness, therefore Buddha's mercy does not extend to them,' the Chinese scholar argues. Ricci replies: 'Plants have no blood? You say this only because you think blood is red; how do you know that the white and green fluids [of plants] are not blood?' Employing dialectic, Ricci elaborates: what is the difference between using animals for hard labor and killing them for food? The animals suffer in both cases. And if people have no use for animals, they would not raise and feed them, leading to their extinction. In the long run, this is far more harmful than using them for food.

'Well, is there no point to fasting then?' the Chinese scholar asks. Ricci: 'It is misguided to keep a vegetarian feast because of the rule of non-killing, but there are three true reasons for fasting.' The first, Ricci explains, is to expiate sin; the second is to curb bodily desires; and the third is to exercise in virtue. In conclusion, Ricci enumerates the different kinds of fasting in the West and the exemption from fasting for the old, the young, nursing mothers, and those who perform hard labor.

Chapter 6 is a key text. Entitled 'An explanation of why man cannot be free of intentions, and a discussion of the reward of good and evil in heaven and hell after death', this chapter addresses the central Catholic concept of free will and salvation. The discussion begins with the Chinese scholar acknowledging God on High as the great sovereign. But he then poses a difficult moral question: 'But surely talk of heaven and hell has no place in the teachings of the Lord of Heaven. To persuade people to do good or to prohibit them from doing evil because of the gain or loss that will accrue from such conduct is to try to profit from good deeds and to avoid harm by refraining from evil; it is not to delight in goodness or to hate evil, which should be one's true ambition. Our ancient sages taught men not to discuss profit, but only humanity and righteousness. The superior man does good without any ulterior motive, and certainly without any thought of gain or loss.'

This statement goes to the heart of the ethical dilemma: will and utility. Should utility be the motive for virtue? Do actions and intentions carry equal weight in moral judgments? And what is the exact role of the individual will in moral choices?

Ricci attacks this problem head on by equating the Catholic doctrine of free will with the Confucian ideal of sincerity: both serve as foundations of morality. He says: 'Confucianism regards sincerity as the foundation for the rectification of the mind, for self-cultivation, for the regulation of the family, for the ordering of the state, and for bringing peace to the world.' The human will, in short, is the origin of all actions; it is characterized by the ability to choose between good and evil; and it distinguishes man from animals and inanimate objects. Thanks to human will, his intentionality, one can establish moral distinctions and, by extension, rewards and punishments for the effects of his actions.

Acknowledging intentions, however, brings up another dilemma, as the Chinese scholar is quick to point out. A child who steals to feed his parents is fulfilling the duties of filial piety; yet, his actions are punishable by the law: is this a virtuous or an evil act? Having stressed the centrality of human will, Ricci invokes the concept of 'wholeness' as the criterion for moral judgment: goodness consists in both will and action; mere good intentions without a consequential virtuous act do not constitute virtue. The inverse holds true. Ricci gives the counter-example of an evil man who performs many charitable acts in order to gain reputation and cover up for his immorality. Here, good actions performed out of evil intention also cannot constitute an act of virtue. 'Even if only the smallest of evil deeds is required to save everyone in the world, it still may not be done,' concludes Ricci categorically.

Next, Ricci and his Chinese interlocutor discuss the role of utility: should rewards and punishments be inextricably linked to virtue and evil? Resorting to the Confucian Canon, Ricci cites eleven episodes and statements in the *Shu jing*, the *Book of History*, to bolster his position. The two men then debate on *The Spring and Autumn Annals*, a book purportedly compiled by Confucius. Again, the question is utility: should concerns for benefits underlie moral decisions and virtuous actions? Astutely, Ricci pinpoints the central meaning of *The Spring and Autumn Annals*. It was a chronology of ancient history, a mirror for princes and officials, that assigns blame and approbation; in its utilitarian intentionality, it served to promote virtue, and hence, there is no contradiction between utility and virtue, concludes Ricci.

The greatest utility, however, is not concern for historical reputation, but for the afterlife, expands Ricci. His Chinese friend is skeptical: 'Why trouble oneself about the future? The best thing to do is to limit one's concern to the matters of today.' 'What nonsense!' Ricci replies. 'If dogs and pigs could speak, they would say the same!' Without naming the philosopher (he has Epicurus in mind), Ricci denigrates the followers of Epicurean Hedonism in ancient Greece—'there is no happiness after death'—as 'disciples of the pigpen'. 'Could it be that in your noble country there are those who secretly agree with this philosophy?' Ricci's aggressive tone is hard to miss. The two continue to cite ancient Chinese texts in debating the question of foresight and provision, and to what extent they should extend to the afterlife. Their differences are sharp:

Ricci: 'When I die I shall leave two things behind me: (1) an incorruptible spirit, and (2) a corpse which will rapidly decay. I regard my incorruptible soul as that which requires my urgent attention, but you are chiefly concerned with a body that will speedily decay. How can you accuse me of being impractical?' Chinese scholar: 'A superior man is not concerned to do good in order to win benefits in this life and to steer clear of worldly losses. How can the question of gain or loss in the next life be worth discussing?'

To convince his skeptical friend, Ricci turns to an extended metaphor: human life as a theater, full of sights and sounds, with all of us playing the roles of kings, ministers, officials, scholars, slaves, queens, concubines, and wives. But in the end, we, players one and all, will disrobe and leave the world the way we entered: naked and alone. Here, Ricci is adumbrating the great metaphor in European Baroque theater: the vanities of life, merely a stage of empty sights and sounds. The metaphor of theater also struck a deep chord in Chinese sensibilities, for the sixteenth century was the great age of Chinese drama and the development of the Kun opera: for there, in the realm of the Great Ming, the adopted home of the Jesuit missionary, the passions and sorrows of life were likewise played out on the dreamlike stage of human theater.

Next, Ricci analyzes three motives for virtuous acts: out of fear of hell, out of gratitude for God, and in conformity with the divine will. He cites the example of Juniper, a disciple of Francis of Assisi, who led a life of virtue not to gain heaven but for the pure love of God. Yet, most people in this world are so mired in vices that without the fear of hell, they will not reform their lives and turn to virtue.

'What is the difference between this doctrine and the teaching of the Buddhists which uses reincarnation and rebirth in animal forms to induce people to do good?' the Chinese scholar questions. The difference is between the 'empty' doctrine of Buddhism and the 'real' teaching of Christianity, replies Ricci. Still unconvinced, his Chinese interlocutor suggests that if God should reward the virtuous and punish the wicked, these could be imposed on future generations. Opposing this deeply ingrained Chinese idea, which believes in the transmission of merit or harm down the lineage, Ricci postulates the rigorous idea of individual moral responsibility.

Ever so skeptical, the Chinese scholar asks Ricci: 'Sir, have you seen heaven and hell that you can assert their reality so firmly?' Ricci retorts: 'Have you, Sir, seen that there is no heaven and hell that you should so firmly assert their non-existence?' Earthly existence, Ricci continues, is a state of constant longing, for the perfection and happiness that is the eternal life. After further exchanges on the rewards of virtue and punishments for evil on earth, the two men discuss the textual authority of heaven and hell, places which are not mentioned in the writings of Confucius or of any other Chinese sages. As the Chinese scholar puts it: 'Are you saying that the sages were ignorant of this teaching? Why is it concealed and not mentioned?'

Incomplete transmission is Ricci's reply: the ancient Chinese sages did not write down all their teachings; some were transmitted orally; and other texts had been lost. He goes on to cite three passages in the *Book of History* (*Shu qing*) and the *Book of Odes* (*Shi qing*) that place ancient sages and kings in heaven (*tian*). Conceding this point, the Chinese scholar still objects to the lack of textual evidence for the existence of hell. 'If there is a heaven, there must be a hell; the one cannot exist without the other because the reason for the one is the reason for the other,' answers Ricci. Just as the righteous rulers of Chinese antiquity—King Wen, King Yin, and the Duke of Zhou—must be in heaven, its tyrants—King Xia Jie and King Shang Zhou—must necessarily be in hell. Moreover, in western logic, one cannot prove non-existence from the lack of textual evidence, explains Ricci. For example, in the West the Bible mentions Adam and Eve as the progenitors of humanity, but fails to mention the two mythical Chinese emperors Fuxi and Shen Nong; this does not mean, however, that Fuxi and Shen Nong were not, in fact, the ancestors of the Chinese nation. The inverse is also true: the absence of the names of Adam and Eve in the ancient Chinese classics cannot prove their non-existence.

Having half convinced his Chinese interlocutor, Ricci consolidates his gain by arguing that one cannot be a righteous man without believing in heaven. Justice in this world is imperfect, hence the moral necessity of eternal reward and punishment, concludes Ricci. After discoursing further on repentance and on the perfect joys of heaven, the two scholars turn to a different topic.

Acknowledging the existence of the Sovereign on High and the existence of heaven and hell, the Chinese scholar proceeds to ask Ricci to clarify his views on human nature and the correct ways of cultivating virtue. All in all, this chapter strikes a harmonious tone, in contrast to the sharp disagreements in the previous discussions. Ricci asserts the fundamental goodness of human nature, but only after a lengthy dissection of philosophical categories, using the Aristotelian terms of essence and accidents. This is more than Jesuit pedantry. Employing Aristotelian logic, Ricci can demonstrate the composite nature of man and hence deftly avoid at this point the topic of original sin. Human nature is fundamentally good (essence), Ricci affirms, but not all men are good, for God has endowed man with reason (accident), and it is up to the individual to exercise his reason to pursue virtue. Adroitly, Ricci makes room for the existence of evil, which he defines as the absence of good, while shifting its responsibility away from the omnipotent creator to created man.

Ricci makes a second categorical distinction between endowed and acquired virtue to correspond with the Confucian terms *xin* (nature) and *de* (virtue). Being created good does not necessarily imply that man would lead a virtuous life: one has to strive for that. It requires the exercise of reason in knowing God, in loving God, and in extending that love to all men. Using the metaphor of gardening, the first step in the virtuous life is the hard spadework of uprooting evil, followed by the constant care in the cultivating of virtuous plants. In his exposition of the Christian life, Ricci incorporates the Confucian idea of righteousness (*yi*) and humanity (*ren*), rendering a seemingly seamless convergence between virtues West and East. Yet, there is something deficient in Confucian cultivation, Ricci says to the Chinese scholar, who has earlier admitted that the virtuous lives of China's ancient sages do not seem to be followed by contemporary scholars: 'When I observe the learned men of your esteemed country, I find that their common failing is to be found precisely in this point: they speak of the need to cultivate one's illustrious virtue, but are unaware of the fact that the human will tires easily, and that will cannot strive to cultivate virtue by its own strength. They are not aware that they must look up to the Celestial Emperor (*Tiandi*) to plead for the protection and support of the compassionate Father. Therefore, there are so few virtuous men.'

Next, the Chinese scholar asks whether reciting Buddhist prayers is completely useless; perhaps one should not forsake the Buddhas, bodhisattvas, and fairies for they are the officials governing the provinces for the one true and sovereign heavenly emperor. This provokes Ricci into another fierce attack on Buddhism. There can be only one ruler in the realm, one father in the household, hence the inappropriateness of this political metaphor, explains Ricci. He continues to ridicule Buddhism: its absurd astronomical theories, its lack of moral rigor—salvation is promised to those who simply recite the *Lotus Sutra* and the name of Buddha. From this Ricci launches into a denouncement of the Three-in-One cult, created recently by the Ming scholar Lin Zhaoen (1517–98), who devised a syncretistic religion out of Confucianism, Daoism, and Buddhism, a 'monster with three heads', in Ricci's words. In following this cult, one would only triple one's errors. 'There is only one truth, and if the Way harmonizes with the truth, one can gain eternal life.'

The last chapter begins with a query about the customs of the West. In reply, Ricci paints an idealized picture: the highest authority is the pope, which he calls *jiahua huang* in Chinese, the king for culture and moral education, who is elected for his sagacity and virtue. Since the pope does not marry and cannot pass on his dynasty (no word here of papal nepotism!), he can devote himself entirely to the public good. Consequently, all the rulers of Europe respect him as the leading authority. Needless to say, Ricci wasted no word on the Protestant Reformation. This idealized picture of papal authority was far from historical reality, even in the best of times during the High Middle Ages. Be that as it may, Ricci is out to impress his Chinese friend with descriptions of an imaginary perfect Christendom. And in this perfect Christian regime, there are those who join religious societies for the propagation of faith, such as Ricci's own company, the Jesuits.

Here, the Chinese scholar wonders about the necessity for chastity: Is this not too extreme? Would humanity not become extinct? Emphasizing this is merely voluntary and not a commandment, Ricci nonetheless affirms the superiority of celibacy. The most important thing in life is to serve God; marriage and children, though not forbidden by God, represent obstacles to the perfect service of God, for the need to provide livelihood for one's family necessitates the pursuit of wealth. In the service of God, there are two dangers, Ricci admonishes: greed and lust. In practicing celibacy, one can avoid both. Moreover, if one wishes to travel far and wide to spread the knowledge of the true Lord of Heaven, family ties would prove to be indissoluble binds. For this reason, those in China who devote themselves to the cultivation of virtue do not travel abroad because they need to take care of their families. As for human extinction, this is hardly a present danger. In antiquity, virtue flourished with few humans; today, virtue flounders while the world is full of people. Better to attend to the urgent task of salvation than to seek marriage. However, Ricci cautions, not everyone who resists feminine temptation is virtuous. In China, there are those who prefer young boys to women, indulging in an 'unspeakable' vice against nature.

'But there is a saying in China: of the three sins of impiety, not having sons is the gravest,' counters the Chinese scholar. Ricci gives a persuasive answer, showing off his command of the Confucian classics. First, this statement comes from Mencius, a lesser sage, and not from Confucius or any of the ancient Chinese sages. Second, Confucius himself praises three figures in the history of Shang and early Zhou as virtuous sages; yet, Boyi, Shuqi, and Bigan had no heirs. How can you condemn these men for filial impiety according to the criterion of Mencius when Confucius praise them for their righteousness? Filial piety should be redefined in the broader context, Ricci expounds: in the perfect world, one would be filial to the three paternal authorities: the Lord of Heaven, the emperor, and the blood father; in the imperfect world, one may be torn by conflicting commitments; in the eyes of the Lord of Heaven, there is equality of all men. There are many examples of saints in the West who kept celibate.

'It is fitting to refrain from marriage in the pursuit of the Way,' echoes the Chinese scholar. He cites the example of Yu, leader of the people in taming the flood in mythical times (third millennium BC), founder of the Xia dynasty, who journeyed constantly for eight years supervising the work of flood control; even though he passed his home three times, Yu did not visit because of his devotion to public affairs. 'But in this time of peace, what harm is there if the scholar raises a family?' 'Alas! You think we live in peaceful times?' Ricci retorts. The disaster of today is much greater than the flood of antiquity. People have turned away from the worship of the true Lord of Heaven; everywhere, petty officials construct living shrines to themselves; in every nook and cranny, temples are erected in worship of Buddhist and Daoist idols.

Agreeing heartily with this sentiment, the Chinese scholar laments that while it is easy to recognize the Lord of Heaven as the origins of truth, it is far more difficult to devote oneself fully to his cause due to the distractions of the world. 'Why does the [Great Father] not come down to earth and personally lead the lost flocks? It would be magnificent if the sons of all lands can see the one true father!' At this, Ricci bursts out in delight: 'I have waited a long time for you to ask this!' Ricci goes on to expound on the Incarnation, the Immaculate Conception, and the birth of Jesus some 1,603 years ago, the second year of the reign of Yuanshou of Emperor Ai of the Han dynasty. Here, Ricci mentions that Adam and Eve have sinned; that in spite of the fundamental goodness of human nature, humanity needed divine intervention to find the right way again. Christ's coming was predicted by many prophets who preceded him. Jesus lived for thirty-three years on earth, performing many miracles: healing the sick, curing the blind, the deaf, and the lame. Using a bit of historical fabrication, Ricci states that Emperor Ai, having heard the news of Jesus' birth, sent an envoy to the West; but this man arrived erroneously in India and brought back the heretical and erroneous teachings of Buddha instead. What a missed opportunity for China! In Ricci's exuberant summary of the life of Jesus, he pointedly omits to mention the Crucifixion.

With this, the long dialogue comes to an end. Enlightened by Ricci's explanations, his doubts removed by Jesuit logic, the Chinese scholar wants to follow the teachings of the Lord of Heaven. Nothing remains but the sacrament of baptism, a hopeful ending to this work of Christian doctrine.

Celebrated by posterity as Ricci's masterly synthesis of Confucianism and Christianity, at the time of its publication this book had quite a different impact: *True Meaning of the Lord of Heaven* amounted to a declaration of war against Buddhism. Ricci wanted confrontation and succeeded in making powerful enemies. Devout Buddhists the Minister of Personnel Li Dai (see Chapter 9) and academician Huang Hui were particularly angry with the westerner's polemic; they were planning to submit a memorial to the emperor. 'But immediately God has come to aid with his divine providence in punishing His and our enemies,' declared a confident and militant Ricci.[3] The Jesuit missionary was interpreting unrelated incidents in a crisis-ridden Beijing as signs of God's chastisement of the Buddhists.

The first event was the tragic death of Li Zhi. We last met him welcoming Ricci to Shangdong in June 1600 during the Jesuit's long and interrupted voyage to the capital. The two men parted as friends. Li Zhi himself was moving to Tongzhou, half a day's sailing on the Grand Canal east of Beijing. His relentless criticism of his erstwhile patron in Hubei and his disdain for conventional morality had so antagonized the local gentry that they had hired thugs to burn down Li Zhi's monastery. In Tongzhou, a friend and disciple welcomed China's number one non-conformist. Here, the septuagenarian, 'meditation-mad', self-styled Chan Buddhist monk, erstwhile mandarin and official, and the sardonic critic of Confucian orthodoxy and hypocrisy, lived in peace for only one year. Zhang Wenda, an official in the Ministry of Rites, submitted a memorial to the emperor: it accused Li Zhi of spreading heterodox teachings, of writing blasphemies against Confucius and Mencius, of subverting the moral order, and of seducing married women and young girls; his brand of defiant non-conformity had led the youth astray from Confucian orthodoxy to Buddhist madness; his presence in the vicinity of the imperial capital must not be tolerated. The Wanli emperor ordered Li's arrest and the destruction of his writings. Arrested and sent to Beijing, Li Zhi spent his final days in prison. One day in late April 1602 Li Zhi asked his jailer for a shave. Seizing the razor, the old man slit his own throat and died two days later. Ricci reported the tragic end of Li Zhi in a matter-of-fact and distant tone, perhaps the only hint of their former friendship revealed in the description of the suicide as a miserable death.

For Ricci, true friendship only existed in the community of true believers. In his vision, the suicide of Li Zhi merely represented one more defeat in the eventual demise of Buddhism, for his Buddhist mandarin opponents too were being punished by God. The 'Evil Book Incident', which raged in the winter of 1603/4, cost Li Dai his office and the leading Buddhist monk his life.

If these events were divine signs to punish the Buddhists, Ricci was the only one who could interpret them. In fact, the Evil Book Incident had everything to do with politics and nothing to do with religion. At its heart was the crisis of imperial succession, which had been paralyzing court politics since the 1590s; its origins lay in the publication of a harmless little book in 1588, whose twisted and complicated reception culminated fifteen years later in a shocking political scandal.

Back in that year, when Ricci was still mired in Shaozhou, a famous mandarin, Lü Kun (1536–1618), compiled stories of virtuous women from history and published the collection under the title of *Guifan* (*Models for the Inner Chamber*). An official keen on promoting women's education and reforming social morality, Lü Kun asked his friend Jiao Hong (whom we have met in Chapter 8) to write a preface. Boosted by the two men's reputation, the book met immediate success and was reprinted many times. It even captured the attention of Consort Zheng, the emperor's favorite concubine, who commissioned a new edition, with the addition of twelve more historical figures as models of feminine virtue, ending with her. With prefaces by her elder uncle and brother, eminent court noblemen, and the insertion of illustrations, the new edition appeared in 1595 under the title of *Guifan tushuo* (*Models for the Inner Chambers with Illustrations*).

Appearing in the midst of the succession crisis—Wanli refusing repeatedly to declare his eldest surviving son Prince Changlo the heir apparent—*Guifan tushuo* provoked a sharp political reaction. Already widely suspected of wanting to substitute her own son for the legitimate heir, Consort Zheng came under severe criticism for promoting herself as a model of female virtue. A pseudonymous tract was published in 1598. Ostensibly excoriating Lü Kun for unwittingly opening the door for a larger evil, it attacked indirectly the ambitions of Consort Zheng. Two censors also submitted memorials to the same effect, to the chagrin of Consort Zheng. To calm this political storm, Wanli behaved with uncharacteristic restraint. He merely exiled the two censors to faraway Guangdong and refused to enlarge this incident into a political witch-hunt, as some partisans of Consort Zheng had urged. Furthermore, the emperor declared that he himself had given Consort Zheng a copy of *Guifan*, implying that any further criticism would amount to *lèse-majesté*.

The turmoil died down but refused to go away. In November 1603, another tract appeared in Beijing. It struck the capital like thunder. Although Prince Changlo had been declared heir apparent in 1601, the emperor did it against his own wishes, asserted the two writers, who signed off under the names of two actual censors. Consort Zheng was still plotting to overthrow Prince Changlo in order to place her own son, the Prince of Fu, on the throne. Particularly shattering was a purported dialogue between the two officials, who named nine partisans of Consort Zheng, all high civil and military officials, who could be counted on in a palace coup. As for the stance of the Grand Secretary in this intrigue, Shen Yiguan, one of the patrons of Ricci, he was described as 'a devious and evil man, who uses people and is not used by them. Therefore he alone will reap any benefits and will always stay clear of troubles.'[4]

Overnight the imperial capital was shaken to its core. Copies of the pamphlet were left in various corners of Beijing; whispers echoed into a deafening roar of rumors. *Lèse-majesté*, palace coup, political plot: Wanli could hardly ignore his favorite consort Zheng, who came to him weeping and furious for vengeance, having been accused of undermining the foundation of the dynasty. Sensibly absolving the two terrified censors whose names were used for this treatise, the emperor received protestations of innocence from the named parties and launched an immediate investigation. Given an urgent deadline to ferret out the real culprits, the security agents scurried around to hunt down every small lead, arresting people on the slightest suspicion, and using torture to obtain information.

This climate of terror created an opportunity for Shen Yiguan, who lived up to his characterization as 'a devious and evil man'. Jealous of Shen Li, his colleague in the Grand Secretariat, Shen Yiguan concocted an accusation against Guo Zhengyu, a Vice-Minister of the Ministry of Rites and former student of Shen Li. To indict Guo would end Shen Li's political career at the least. To obtain a conviction of the innocent minister, Shen Yiguan's agents arrested several men to elicit forced confessions. One of these was the famous Buddhist monk Zibo Zhenke, whose arrest and death signaled to Ricci God's wrath against the Buddhists.

A native of Wujiang in Suzhou prefecture, the young wandering swordsman Shen Zhenke decided to trade his sword for prayer beads and took the dharma names 'Zibo' and 'Daguan'. After ordination at the age of 20, he wandered to different pilgrimage sites and vowed to revive Chan meditation. Zibo was responsible for the collection, compilation, and publication of the *Jiaxing zang* (the Ming edition of the *Tripitaka*, Buddhist canon)[5] with the help of leading mandarins at court and leading Buddhist laymen, including Qu Ruzi, the elder half-brother of Qu Ruikui. Favored by Empress Dowager Li, the mother of Wanli, Zibo Zhenke was the most prominent Buddhist monk in Beijing, who enjoyed the friendship of many high mandarins.

After Ricci had settled in the capital, Zibo wished to meet the remarkable westerner but did not wish to cede rank by visiting the foreigner. He let the Jesuit know of his wish for a social visit and assured Ricci he would be treated with the courtesies of an equal. His dislike of Abbot Hong an of Nanjing still fresh in mind, Ricci pointedly refused any social intercourse with the Buddhist clergy. For Ricci, these men were ministers of idolatry, servants of the Devil, hence his glee in the demise of Zibo.

Zibo was arrested because he wrote a letter to the physician Shen Linyu, a fellow native of Wujiang and his disciple, in which Zibo criticized the

Wanli emperor for contradicting the pious wishes of his mother, the empress dowager, a devout Buddhist. Some contemporary sources reported that Zibo was horribly tortured in jail to obtain confessions implicating his acquaintance Minister Guo Zhengyu; another stated that the emperor had no wish to execute Zibo, citing the eventual release of the physician Shen Lingyu.[6] In any event, Zibo certainly died in jail due to harsh treatment.[7] Ricci commented: 'Because they hated him, the mandarins of the Ministry of Justice [the Minister was Xiao Daheng] beat him [Zibo] so severely after his incarceration that he soon died. This occasioned much scorn since he had often boasted he did not value his body; but, when he was beaten, he screamed like all the other profane human beings. After his burial, his body was dug up in order to ascertain he had not feigned his own death.'[8] Words echoing Catholic militancy certainly, Ricci's description was perhaps un-worthy of Christian charity.

In his sense of triumph, Ricci even imputed the 1595 disgrace and exile of Hanshan Deqing (1546–1623) to divine vengeance. The erudite monk and Chan master was a close friend of Zibo. A favorite of Empress Dowager Li, Hanshan equaled Zibo in prominence. The dowager's patronage played into the tension between mother and son, the Wanli emperor, who used the excuse of a minor infraction to exile Hanshan to Guangdong. His friend Zibo tried in vain to ameliorate the imperial edict. In the end, Hanshan was the more fortunate. Protected by provincial mandarins, Hanshan was named abbot of Nanhua monastery near Shaozhou, where he set out to institute a series of monastic reforms that would revive the reputation and fortunes of the venerable monastery, where many years ago the western monk Ricci had pointedly refused hospitality. This was one of the ironies in the career of Matteo Ricci.

Back in the search for suspects, the police were desperate to solve the case. Some officials had already lost their posts, due to the emperor's fury at the slow progress. Among them was an officer in the Imperial Body Guard (*jinyi wei*), a nephew of Li Dai, who also lost his own ministerial post, remarked Ricci, not without malice. Eventually, someone denounced a poor elderly scholar, Jiao Shengguang, who had composed slanderous essays to blackmail his victims as purported writers. Grasping at straws, the officials tortured Jiao into confession, although the details in the 'Evil Book' could only have been known to a court official and not to a minor scholar such as Jiao. The condemned man received the maximum sentence and was sliced to death in slow agony. The real composer of the 'Evil Book' was never found.

'And thus the sect of idolaters [Buddhists], of whom we have spoken, became much humiliated. Having heard this news, our Christians and friends, both inside and outside of the court, note that everything has turned in favor of Christianity, which begins to be preached in court, the head of this realm, where formerly that sect [of Buddhism] had flourished.' The ground cleared of his imagined enemies, Ricci and his followers were ready to plant the flag of Christ in the heart of Ming China.

II

Laying the Foundations

'Even the emperor of China has already become a Christian,' boasted the exaggerated report of Ricci's progress, as some would believe in Rome.[1] Even though this was not true, Ricci's superiors had every reason to be pleased. Their pioneer in the China Mission had blazed a trail through the vast domain of the Ming; Ricci and a handful of helpers had planted small communities of converts in Shaozhou, Nanchang, and Nanjing; and in Beijing the Society had gained a foothold in the very heart of the Chinese empire. Valentim Carvalho, the new rector of the Jesuit College in Macao, ordered Manoel Dias the Elder (1559–1639) on an inspection tour of China. Dias traveled with Brother Giacobo Niva (1579–1638), born of a Chinese father and a Japanese mother, who entered the Society and was trained as a painter in Macao. In July 1602, after visiting the three Jesuit residences in the south, they arrived in Beijing, where they stayed for two months. Highly impressed by his tour, Dias left Niva to help Ricci and returned to Macao, where he briefed Valignano on the encouraging developments in China. The Visitor of the Asian Missions arrived there on 10 February 1603 after leaving Japan for good, a country where the new rulers were turning against Christianity. The author of the China Mission, who first summoned Ruggiero in 1578 to this task, Valignano was fired up by the success of his erstwhile protégé at the Roman College. China was the future. Against the strong protests of the fathers in Japan, Valignano created a separate and autonomous Chinese Mission in the Vice-Province of Japan. He also sent a new batch of missionaries, six Portuguese and two Italian: Bartolomeo Tedeschi and Jerónimo Rodrigues went to Shaozhou, to help the energetic but overworked Niccolò Longobardo and Francisco Martins (Wang Ming-sha); Alfonso Vagnoni, Pedro Ribeiro, and Feliciano da Silva reinforced João da Rocha in Nanjing, who was the sole priest in the important residence after the sickly Cattaneo had departed for Macao to recuperate; Manuel Dias and Brother Pascal joined João Soeiro in Nanchang; and Gaspar Ferreira became Ricci's newest companion in Beijing, bringing with him a valuable copy of the 1569 Plantin Bible, published by Christopher Plantin in Antwerp, richly illustrated and with the biblical text in Hebrew, Greek, Chaldaic, Syriac, and in Latin translation. While Ricci remained the overall superior of the China Mission, his busy schedule and the distance of Beijing from the south necessitated the appointment of Dias as superior of the three southern residences, thereby freeing Ricci from the excessive administrative burden that such a far-flung mission entailed.

Ricci had work enough in Beijing. The Jesuits baptized the first converts in the imperial capital. Unlike the Christian churches in Zhaoqing, Shaozhou, and Nanchang, which died out in the course of the mid-seventeenth-century crisis, the Catholic community in Beijing remained continuous from the time of Ricci until today. In the first two years, the missionaries baptized some 70 converts, an impressive figure, compared to the 120–130 conversions during Ricci's twelve years in Guangdong. More important than the number was the quality of the converts. For the first time, elites of Ming society accepted the foreign faith. True, those who belonged to elite families represented younger or minor figures, such as the two sons of the first physician to the imperial court, a brother-in-law of the empress, Ignatius Tung, a relative of Tung Yu, a future Minister of Justice (appointed March 1605–January 1606), and the 18-year-old Michele Xiao, nephew of the current Minister of Justice, Xiao Daheng. Or they might be in retirement, such as the 60-year-old Mandarin Cui, a native of Henan, who took the baptismal name Antonio. Rare was a man in active service. Li Yingshi (1559–1620?), an officer in the Imperial Guards (*jinyi wei*), a veteran of the Korean Wars, converted at the age of 42 on 21 September 1602. Attracted by Ricci's mathematical and astronomical learning, Li Yingshi was not an easy catch. An expert in Daoism and Buddhism, Li was particularly devoted to astrological divination and geomancy. It took many patient conversations before Ricci landed this big catch. But once Li accepted Christianity, he showed his fervor in writing a public declaration of conversion and burning all his books on divination and astrology. He also persuaded and cajoled his entire household—mother, wife, two sons, a tutor, and all his servants (including one reluctant resister)—into embracing the new faith.

No doubt, Ricci's charisma accounted for these conversions. Although Pantoja had mastered enough Chinese by 1603 to converse and receive visitors, 'he could not be compared remotely with [Ricci]', opined Shen Defu (1578–1642), the perspicacious and curious writer, whose collection of vignettes and historical facts of the Wanli reign, the *Wanli yehuo bian* (1619), provided unique and insightful information on the last decades of the Ming dynasty. A neighbor of the Jesuits during his residence in Beijing, Shen Defu described Ricci as 'truly a remarkable man . . . who was by nature generous, capable of calming impatience and anger, whose sincerity and humanity was felt by all, and whom no-one would dare to bully'.[2] Ricci's charisma exudes a force through the ages in the commentaries of his Ming contemporaries: both Shen Defu in Beijing and Gu Qiyuan in Nanjing (see Chapter 8) rated Ricci's 'disciples'—the Spaniard Pantoja and the Portuguese da Rocha—as inferior to their brilliant 'master'.

In the China Mission, as in every mission, the personality of the missionary was paramount. Under da Rocha and Soeiro, the Christian communities in Nanjing and Nanchang stabilized, but had nothing spectacular to report in the years after Ricci's departure. Only in Shaozhou did the Jesuits achieve remarkable success, thanks to the strong personality of Niccolò Longobardo, who had replaced Ricci and Cattaneo. This Sicilian nobleman, who would succeed Ricci as superior and become the longest serving Jesuit missionary in China, struck out in a new direction. Recall that the years in Shaozhou represented the doldrums in Ricci's career: few converts, strong hostility, and the death of two companions. Similarly frustrated at first by the indifference of the city folk to the Christian message, Longobardo turned to the villages around Shaozhou, where he found an enthusiastic welcome. As conversions multiplied, a Christian community emerged in the city and its hinterland; and as his confidence increased, Longobardo assumed a more militant stance. To signify the break with their past, Longobardo urged the neophytes to burn statues of Buddhist, Daoist, and Chinese deities. Several incidents rapidly escalated tensions: zealous Christian youths smashing statues in a Buddhist monastery; Longobardo pointedly refusing to make donations for the neighborhood temple festivals; and his snubbing of Abbot Hanshan Deqing, in exile from Beijing and busy reforming the Nanhua monastery, who had expressed an interest in meeting the western religious. For the time being, the Jesuit Mission was safe from attack, thanks to the protection of the mandarins, but the day of reckoning would come.

Both successful in their respective strategies, there was one major difference in the missionary approaches of Ricci and Longobardo. While Ricci valued elite converts and lured Chinese scholars into the net of Christianity through learned conversations on mathematics, natural philosophy, and the afterlife, Longobardo demonstrated his effectiveness as a religious worker, more in the mode of the popular preachers of repentance in the rural areas of early modern Catholic Europe. Ricci paid great attention to the upper-class converts in his writings, noting their social rank and personal details, even though the majority of his converts belonged to the lower social classes. His was a world of *Christianitas*: a measured world of humanistic learning, moral virtue, a synthesis of Christian doctrines and Confucian ethics, and devotion to the afterlife. In contrast, Longobardo's reports depicted a world different from the scene of the Ming mandarin-literati class: inhabited by spirits, evil and good, this world of intense longing, for health and prosperity in this world and happiness in the next, was full of dreams and visions, prophecies and miracles, in which the divide between Christian and pagan was absolute. This was the world of the Chinese masses—farmers, workers, artisans, and merchants—in Confucian discourse, the 'little people' to be governed by the 'gentlemen' of learning.

There was indeed such a man. Xu Guangqi (1562–1633) came to Ricci already a Christian.[3] In early 1604, the 43-year-old Xu traveled to Beijing to take the *jinshi* examination. Looking up Ricci, Xu reminded the westerner they had already met before. In 1600, Xu Guangqi visited his teacher Jiao Hong in Nanjing. Like so many literati, Xu went to listen to the remarkable westerner. So impressed was Xu by Ricci's discourse, '[he] thought to himself that this was the only gentleman in the world who understands the relationships between all things'.[4] But this was not the first occasion that the native of Shanghai was exposed to western learning. In 1595, Xu earned his living as a teacher in Shaozhou. There, he toured the Catholic church and conversed with Cattaneo on religious and scientific questions, the matter of western learning.

Unlike many mandarin acquaintances of the Jesuits, Xu Guangqi came from a humble family. His grandfather abandoned agriculture for commerce, gained prosperity for his family, and died in his forties. His son, Guangqi's father, had neither talent nor taste for profit. A generous and intelligent man, Xu Sicheng failed to make the classic ascent in the ladder of social success: from wealth to scholarship and examination success. Instead, Sicheng gave gener-ously to the poor and satisfied his curiosity with books on medicine, astronomy, and history. By the time of Xu Guangqi, the family was in decline, and the young Guangqi experienced hunger and the dislocation of pirate raids, as mid-sixteenth-century Shanghai, a burgeoning town in Ming China, still lacked a city wall. All hopes of the family were pinned on the young Guangqi, studious, brilliant, a boy genius. In 1581, Xu Guangqi passed the first degree, the *gongshen*, commonly called the *xiucai*, which entitled him to a small government stipend and qualification for the next level of examination. The years between 1581 and 1597 were a time of immense frustration. Xu Guangqi failed the *juren* examination three times, in 1582, 1588, and 1591. Times were getting tougher for the armies of hopeful scholars. Whereas China's population had more than doubled to 150 million between the late fourteenth and late sixteenth centuries, the government did not alter the quotas for degree-holders established in the initial years of the Ming dynasty. Xu Guangqi was but one of thousands whose hopes were dashed. A few unsuccessful scholars turned their talents to other things: Li Shicheng and Xu Xiake sublimated their disappointments respectively in medicine and travel, becoming China's most famous herbalist and geographer of the Ming. Xu Guangqi, however, refused to abandon hopes of service in the imperial civil bureaucracy. Besides strengthening his resolve, these years in the wilderness took Xu Guangqi literally to remote towns in Guangdong and Guangxi, earning his keep as teacher and household tutor to mandarin families, and provoked him to reflect on life's questions beyond that of success or failure.

In 1597 Xu Guangqi once again sat for the *juren* examination in Beijing. His essay failed the first scrutiny. As was the custom, the examiners leafed through the rejected essays to select one whose brilliance had perchance escaped their first grading. Jiao Hong was Deputy Examiner. As he was reading Xu Guangqi's essay, Jiao Hong slapped his palm on the desk and exclaimed: 'This must have been written by a great scholar!' Xu scored first place in the *juren* examination. His profound gratitude for Jiao Hong deepened even more when the Hanlin academician was demoted the next year, due to a memorial from two resentful colleagues, who criticized Jiao Hong for overlooking unorthodox statements in several successful examinations (see Chapter 8). All life long, Xu Guangqi looked upon Jiao Hong as his teacher and benefactor. When Jiao Hong retired from office to his native Nanjing, Xu went to pay respects; and it was then that he met Ricci.

However much he admired and respected Jiao Hong, Xu Guangqi did not share his teacher's devotion to Buddhism or interest in Daoist philosophy. By and large an orthodox Confucian, Xu Guangqi was concerned foremost with the practical results of learning. What was the purpose of decades of scholarship and years of examinations if not the service of the country? Confucian learning must serve to cultivate morality, in oneself and in society, to reform behavior, to improve the livelihood of the people, and strengthen the defenses of the country. A sharp sense of crisis made Xu impatient with metaphysical speculation: heavy taxes drove farmers off the land; the Manchus menaced the northern frontier; and factional struggles paralyzed the imperial bureaucracy. From his later memorials, we see Xu Guangqi as a man of action, planning experimental farms, training troops, buying Portuguese firearms and cannons, and always admonishing his family to austerity, frugality, and morality. This was a man profoundly shaped by the struggles of his family and his youth, who understood the price for success in scholarship and the burden of office.

Between 1600 and 1603, working as a teacher in Shanghai, Xu Guangqi reflected on Christianity. One night, he dreamed of entering a temple with three chapels. In the first chapel was a fatherly figure, in the second a younger man with a crown, and the third was empty. Xu made signs of reverence in the first and second chapels and ignored the third. His desire to learn more about the western creed brought Xu to Nanjing in January 1603, but Ricci had already left for Beijing. Received by da Rocha, Xu Guangqi showed great eagerness. He showed up twice daily for catechism and devoured readings given to him by the Jesuits, including a manuscript copy of Ricci's *Tianzhu Shiyi*, which had not yet been published. Introduced to the doctrine of the Trinity, Xu applied it to his own dream and thought it was a sign. Xu Guangqi received baptism under the name Paul.

For Xu Guangqi, the attractions of Christianity were multiple. It offered a solution to the afterlife, one that profoundly satisfied Xu's desire for justice: if evil men might lord it over others in this world, they would for certain suffer eternal torment in hell. It demonstrated the unity of religious morality and social ethics: in the stories of Jesuit missionaries, Christian Europe resembled a perfect society, spared the afflictions of war, rebellion, and misrule, where virtuous clerics, the West's counterparts to the Ming literati, guided a godly people. It represented a synthesis of religious and practical learning: for were not the westerners, especially in the person of Ricci, superior in their knowledge of mathematics and astronomy, steeped in the secrets of nature, virtuosi in scientific and military techniques that could strengthen the country? It was a religion about the afterlife that was yet deeply anchored in this world.

In 1604, Xu Guangqi traveled to Beijing to sit for the *jinshi* examination. He passed. Ricci attributed this as divine reward. Assigned to a period of three years at the Hanlin Academy prior to an appointment in the mandarinate, Xu moved into a house adjacent to the Jesuit residence. Through a common passage, he could enter the Jesuit compound without going through the street. A frequent visitor to the Jesuit church, Xu attended every Christian service; and when Ricci preached, he sat at a bench with a flying brush, recording the Jesuit's sermons. Xu conversed almost daily with Ricci, learning logic and geometry. Urging Ricci to publish even more books in Chinese, 'which is the only way to stabilize and expand Christianity in China',[5] Xu became the model Christian in the imperial capital, whose fervor won the emulation of his co-religionists, and whom Ricci valued as a talented intellectual, a good Christian, and a friend.

There was good news of another friend. On 25 March 1605, in Nanjing, Alfonso Vagnoni baptized Qu Rukui and his 12-year-old son Shiqu. Despite their long friendship, Qu Rukui had been unable or reluctant to convert. First, there was the obstacle of bigamy, in the eyes of the Church. After the death of his wife, Rukui was still reluctant to marry his concubine, although she had borne him two sons. Perhaps the thought of mortality prompted Qu Rukui to accept the consolation of Christianity. After embracing the western faith, the 55-year-old Rukui entrusted his son to study with the Jesuits in Nanjing. After eighteen years of friendship, Ricci was much consoled by the conversion of Qu Rukui.

On the subject of death, Ricci recorded several conversations with the fervent academician Doctor Paul, as he was called in missionary sources. Once, when Ricci preached that God, at times, explained his mysteries through dreams, Xu Guangqi recounted his own dream in Shanghai about the temple with three chapels. Xu had been reluctant to relate this dream, he told Ricci, because the fathers disapproved of dream interpretations, common among the Chinese who sought omens and signs of their fortunes. In rare cases, God sent signs in divine dreams to the chosen, Ricci reassured Xu, judging him to be possessed of God's special grace. To his good friend and fellow Jesuit Girolamo Costa, Ricci wrote that 'it seems that God has chosen him [Xu Guangqi] to be the strongest pillar of the Christian faith in these parts and wanted to teach him with special help'.[6] On other occasions, Ricci and Xu discussed death. Ricci recorded two conversations with Xu as chapters 3 and 4 in his *Ten Discourses of the Man of Paradox*. In one, Ricci asked Xu why the Chinese were so reluctant to speak of death and used the occasion to discourse on the necessity to prepare for death. When Xu questioned Ricci in turn about the customs in the West, Ricci enumerated five benefits of thinking about death: it disciplines us and liberates us from the great evil after death; it is the best medicine against sexual lust; it makes us despise wealth and fame, things we cannot take with us at death; it humbles our pride and prevents us from becoming arrogant; it helps us overcome the fear of death and accept it with equanimity. Ricci's arguments might have been commonplaces in Christian doctrine; his rhetoric, however, was ingenious. Peppered with examples from his humanistic and religious readings, Ricci also invented vivid metaphors. He tells the story of a hungry fox passing a henhouse, and squeezing in through a narrow crack. For several months the fox feasts on his prey until he fears being trapped by the farmer. Too fat to exit through the crack, the fox has to starve himself back to his former miserable self in order to save himself. The henhouse, explained Ricci, is the world, and we are the foxes who gorge on its riches and pleasures before death frightens us to swear off its enjoyments.

From Ricci, Xu Guangqi learned not only exempla from western history and literature, but western science. Next to Li Zhizao (see Chapter 9), Xu Guangqi was Ricci's closest collaborator in the transmission of western scientific texts. The method may be described as Jesuit oral translation and Chinese written composition. It had three benefits. First, it allowed Ricci, already terribly overworked, to produce a large body of Chinese scientific texts during the last five years of his life. Second, regular and close contact cemented the bonds between missionary and convert. And finally, this method of collaboration allowed for the greatest accuracy and elegance in translation, maximizing the Jesuit understanding of European texts and the Chinese mastery of stylistic elegance. Together, Ricci and Xu translated the first six books of Euclid's *Elements of Geometry*. Ricci's preface to the translation of Euclid described their labor:

Since my arrival in China, I have seen that there are many scholars and works on geometry, but I have not seen any fundamental theoretical works...I had then entertained the wish to translate this book for the use of the gentlemen of our times, in order to thank them for their trust in a traveler. Nevertheless, I am of little talent. Moreover, the logic and rhetoric of East and West are so supremely different. In searching for synonyms, there are still many missing words. Even if I can explain things orally with an effort, to put it down in writing is extremely difficult. Ever since then, I have met colleagues who assisted me left and right to advance, but whenever there is a difficulty I would stop, advancing and stopping thrice already.[7]

The difficulty was only overcome after the meeting with Xu Guangqi. In discussing Christianity and western science, Xu urged Ricci to complete the translation, 'commanding him to transmit [the text] orally, and receiving [the text] by writing, turning over and over the text, in order to reflect its meaning, resulting in its publication only after three versions.'[8]

In addition to translating Euclid, Xu Guangqi also collaborated with Ricci in writing *Celiang fayi* (*The Meaning of Measurement Methods*, 1608) and wrote a preface to the *Tongwen suanzhi*, a Chinese translation of Clavius' *Summary of Applied Mathematics*, jointly translated by Li Zhizao and Ricci.

In 1607, their collaboration was cut short by the death of Xu Guangqi's father. At the urging of his son, Xu Sicheng had received baptism, together with the extended Xu household. In accordance with the law, Xu resigned his official post for the three-year mourning period, and escorted his father's coffin back to Shanghai. On the advice of Ricci, Xu Guangqi used this occasion of mourning to showcase Catholic funeral ritual, purged of purported Chinese superstitions, such as the burning of paper money and the employment of Daoist and Buddhist ritual specialists. Black cloth signaled mourning at the Xu family home, following western custom, in contrast to the traditional Chinese color of white. Cattaneo, back in Nanjing after his recuperation, traveled to Shanghai to officiate at the requiem mass.

Ricci and Xu personified the Christian–Confucian synthesis that explains the great attraction of Christianity to the last generations of intellectuals in the Ming dynasty. A long career still lay before Xu Guangqi, both in the service of his country and his Church. A checkered path in the imperial bureaucracy ultimately led to the Ministry of Rites and the Grand Secretariat at the end of his life; Xu Guangqi became the highest ranking mandarin who entered the Catholic Church. The western suburb of Shanghai, Xujiahui, the Xu family home, would in time develop into one of the major sites of Catholicism in China and remain so to this day.

In this general mood of enthusiasm during the years 1601–6, there were still anxious signs for the fledgling Christian mission. In early 1604, news reached the imperial capital that between 3 October and 14 November 1603, the Spaniards had massacred some 15,000 to 20,000 Chinese settlers in Luzon, wiping out almost the entire community.[9] After the Spanish colonization of the Philippines, Chinese traders flocked to Manila, supplying the Spaniards with foodstuffs and everyday goods, and importing American silver to China. From a few hundred residents in the early 1570s, their community expanded to 5,000 in 1585, 10,000 in the 1590s, and close to 20,000 on the eve of the massacre. Vastly outnumbering the Spanish colonizers, the Chinese established their own community, Parían, which was situated outside the walls of Manila, and became economically indispensable to the Spanish colony. Growing increasingly alarmed at the size of the Chinese community, the Spaniards failed repeatedly to expel them. While the Dominican friars made a few hundred Catholic converts among these South Fujianese migrants, the majority clung to their own ways. In 1602, a carpenter returning to Fujian from the Philippines told of the existence of an immense silver mine. Starved of bullion, the Ming government was already importing large quantities of silver from Japan, an import that would be replaced by the even larger supply of American silver in the seventeenth century. Recall also that the rapacious Emperor Wanli had appointed eunuch tax-intendants to scourge the countryside for mining revenues. Hearing of the news, the emperor ordered his officials in Fujian to investigate. In May 1603, three mandarins sailed from Haicheng County in southern Fujian. Although the Spanish authorities received them with the proper ceremonies, the Spaniards felt insulted by the arrogance of the Ming officials and feared a Chinese takeover. The Ming officials returned empty-handed; tensions on Luzon mounted throughout the summer and early autumn months. When some Chinese residents armed themselves, the colonial authorities took this to be a signal of rebellion. Spanish troops, aided by Japanese mercenaries and Filippino auxiliaries, butchered the Chinese population. In spite of the huge outcry in China, the imperial court undertook no punitive expeditions. But everywhere, especially in the southern coastal provinces, suspicion and hostility intensified toward all Europeans. In this atmosphere, Ricci feared the association of the Spaniards with the Jesuit Mission. Striving to clear the Christian mission of any Spanish connection, he told Xu Guangqi that the God of the Jesuits, *Deus*, was different from the God worshipped by the Spaniards, whom they called *Dios*. Xu Guangqi repeated this piece of Jesuit sophistry in his mandarin circles, apparently to credulous ears. Ricci had underestimated the negative impact of the Manila massacre on Chinese views of Europeans, which would come back to haunt the Jesuit Mission. For the time being, however, the Christian community in the capital suffered no repercussions, and the number of converts continued to increase.

A lesser threat originated within the imperial bureaucracy. A group of mandarins, displeased with Ricci's sharp attacks on Buddhism, petitioned the emperor in February 1605 to revoke the stipends for the westerners and to repatriate the Jesuits. Reporting this development in his letters to Europe, Ricci sounded a confident note: not only were the Jesuits protected by the goodwill of his friend, Feng Qi, the Minister of Rites, the emperor himself needed the westerners to service his beloved clocks from time to time. Indeed, he was right. Nothing came of the memorials.

We have eight letters written by Ricci in 1605 that testify to his optimistic mood. The number of converts in Beijing had climbed from 70 in 1603 to over 100. The other residences also reported new conversions, with Longobardo reporting the largest number of baptisms in Shaozhou, and with Soeiro boasting of the first Catholic converts among members of the Ming princely houses in Nanchang. Altogether, the baptismal registries counted more than 1,000 souls. Ricci's own Beijing community, while not numerically the largest, led by the social quality and the spiritual fervor of the converts. At Christmas 1604, the Jesuits celebrated three to four masses with clavichord and harp; some Christians even attended an all-night vigil. Some converts impressed Ricci with their diligence in learning the Latin prayers, such as the wife of Li Yingshi, who could recite the *Confiteor*, others moved Ricci by their sincere contrition, expressed in self-flagellation and eagerness in confession and in receiving the eucharist; a few brought their Buddhist and Daoist statues to be burned; an 85-year-old man, baptized Fabio in honor of Fabio de Fabii, Ricci's master in the noviciate in Rome, insisted on being carried to church, not wishing to die without the consolation of communion. All in all, Ricci was quite proud of his little flock, for he wrote to his friend and fellow Jesuit Girolamo Costa: 'Pray for me, my dearest father, that one day God will give me the grace of finishing my work with a holy death, for here our Christian community in China is not inferior to others which are marked not only by sweat, but also by blood.'[10]

The spiritual fervor of the converts was manifest in the firm belief in the miraculous. One story went like this. A Christian, falsely accused of robbery and murder, was convicted by a bribed mandarin. While his co-religionists sought the fathers' counsel, God appeared in a dream and told another mandarin, to whom the case was referred, to help the innocent Christian prisoner. This official, although not a convert, freed the Christian innocent from calumny and punished the false accuser. Another convert, an old man, told Ricci that the Virgin Mary, all clad in white and holding an infant in her arms, appeared to him in his dream. Bedridden with a serious illness, the Christian was told to command his family to make him sweat. Upon waking, it was done; and the old man recovered. A third story concerned a schoolmaster, who converted with seven to eight of his pupils. Another boy of 13 also wanted to convert, but the master judged he was not ready. One day, the boy was struck by lightning and lay unconscious for three days. While comatose, the boy saw God, whose image he had adored at school; and God said to him that this time he would spare his life. When the boy came to, he received baptism. The other converts called him Michael of the Lightning. These dreams and visions deeply impressed Ricci, who recounted them in several of his letters. They represented signs of divine favor to the infant mission, so it seemed to Ricci, who was otherwise level-headed and rational, member of a religious order deeply mistrusting of overzealous mysticism.

One day, tending his little vineyard, Ricci learned the fruits of Christianity were once harvested in China's past, and patches of Christian cultivation still existed in the vast landscape of the Ming realm. A 60-year-old scholar came to the Jesuit church. On seeing the statue of the Virgin Mary and images of the patriarchs, the old Chinese gentleman knelt and made signs of reverence. At first, Ricci thought he was a Christian. Ai Tian, the visitor, a native of the city of Kaifeng in Henan province, was on his way to a minor post as Education Intendant in the Confucian Academy in Yangzhou. Not long into their conversation, Ricci figured out that Ai Tian was a Jew. Although Ai Tian's knowledge of Judaism was fragmentary, he told Ricci of the long tradition of his ancestral religion, with its scriptures, laws, dietary prohibitions, and legends. One of three sons, Ai Tian studied for the imperial civil service examination; his two brothers learned Hebrew, and one was currently serving as rabbi of the small community of seven or eight families back in Kaifeng. There were also Christian families in his hometown, Ai Tian said to Ricci. Returning the next day, Ai Tian brought along a colleague, Mandarin Zhang, a descendant of Christians from Shaanxi. Showing great interest in the Jesuit church and in Ricci's conversation, Zhang regretted he had little time to be acquainted with his ancestral religion. It confirmed for Ricci the claim made by Marco Polo, that in his time, during the rule of the Mongols, there were many Christians in China. At least, the Jew Ai Tian converted. Perhaps then the idea came to Ricci to send a missionary to Kaifeng, which he would act on three years later.

Books bound the tiny Jewish community in Kaifeng to their ancestral faith. Books were likewise central for the nascent Catholic Church. The printing press, indeed, spearheaded the advance of Christianity in China. Long before meeting Ricci in person, many Chinese scholars, Xu Guangqi for example, had already learned of his name through his *World Map*. Thanks to the popularity of printing and inexpensive book production in Ming China, the Jesuits could afford to hire Chinese workmen to carve woodblocks, which were kept in the workshops of the Jesuit residences and repeatedly used for printing their own works. As Ricci said, the only cost of producing new copies was merely the cost of the paper. For the liturgical needs of the growing Christian communities, the Jesuits translated and printed the Gregorian calendar into Chinese for distribution among the converts. They also revised the prayer book in a language more consonant with their developing synthesis in Christian–Confucian theology. The new edition of the *Tianzhu jiaoyao* appeared in March 1605, containing the Our Father, Hail Mary, the Ten Commandments, the Creed, the Sign of the Cross, the works of spiritual and corporal charities, the Eight Beatitudes, the Seven Deadly Sins, the Seven Virtues, the Five Senses of the Body, the Three Potentials of the soul, and the Three Theological Virtues.

Books conveyed the Christian message in two ways. First, the Chinese works by Ricci advanced his reputation and thereby the prestige of the western or heavenly learning. We will come back to this theme when we discuss another of Ricci's works, *Ershiwu yan, The Twenty-Five Sententiae*. Secondly, as material objects, European books, more expensive and more elaborately produced than the cheap and popular Ming editions, made a huge impression on the Chinese. Ming China had a huge appetite for books: the Confucian classics, school texts, history books, poems, plays, novels, almanacs, books on astrology, geomancy, medicine, agriculture, and on a wide spectrum of subjects fed a society that venerated the written word and the social status of literacy and scholarship. Compared to Song editions, however, Ming books were produced cheaply: thin and fragile rice paper, shoddy binding, faded ink, and roughly cut wooden blocks. There was a price for accessibility. Book collectors of the Ming searched for Song editions, books far superior in physical appearance. In this context, the expensively produced western books imported by the Jesuits struck a sharp contrast, as Gu Qiyuan recorded (see Chapter 8).[11]

Ricci was well aware of the physical contrast between Chinese and western books as physical objects. In his bedroom, he displayed these on facing shelves, a representation that never failed to impress the learned Chinese visitor with the material superiority of the West, and by implication the cultural preeminence of *christianitas*. The inability of the Chinese to read the Latin alphabet did not matter. Western books represented prestigious symbols, much like the early Buddhist sutras in Han and Tang China before their systematic translation. In the collection of western books at the Beijing Jesuit library, none was more prestigious than the polyglot Plantin Bible brought to China by Gaspar Fereira.

The barge that carried the Plantin Bible actually sank in the Grand Canal, but Fereira managed to salvage the chest with minimal damage to the precious object. Presented with great solemnity at the Jesuit church, this immense and beautifully crafted book stupefied Chinese viewers and awed the converts with its sealed mysteries. Greatly satisfied with the success of the Plantin Bible as an object of prestige, 'which stupefied all of China with its beauty',[12] to quote Ricci, the Jesuit missionary was a bit hard-pressed to handle the following request. 'The Bible would be perfect,' some Chinese visitors suggested, 'if the eight books in four languages could be rendered into Chinese.'[13] From Ricci, the Chinese scholars understood the Plantin Bible contained the Old and New Testaments in Hebrew, Chaldaic, Syrian, and Greek, hence making it eight books, but they had naturally never heard of the prohibition of vernacular translations of the Bible by the Council of Trent. Put in an awkward position, Ricci did not 'know how to respond because it seems in part the request is just and pious'. He temporized by consenting to the request but pleading he has no time. 'This is the work of a long time and of many persons,' Ricci explained, offering by way of excuse the story of the translation of the Septuagint Bible. On other occasions, he said, 'this needs the permission and order of the pope; or, that he had already translated some substance of all of these books [in the Bible] in the Christian Doctrines, the *Tianzhu jiaoyao*, which has been newly translated, printed, and distributed for use in all of China'.[14]

Fortunately for the Jesuit Mission, pictures were more powerful than words. The presence of another book, another Antwerp imprint, obviated the awkwardness concerning Bible translation. Jerome Nadal (1507–80), a Spaniard from Majorca, was one of the first ten members of the Society of Jesus. Ignatius himself urged Nadal to compile and distribute an illustrated guide for meditation on the Gospels. Nadal selected the biblical scenes to be included, commissioned and directed the layout of the illustrations, and composed notes to accompany each scene. With the cooperation and support of Antwerp publishers Christopher Plantin and Martin Nutius, 153 engravings were eventually produced. In 1593, these illustrations were published in a volume entitled *Evangelicae Historiae Imagines ex ordine evangelicorum quae toto anno in missae sacrificio recitantur in ordinem temporis vitae Christi digestae* (*Illustrations of the Gospel Stories from the Gospels in the order of the Life of Christ which are recited throughout the year in the sacrifice of the Mass*), arranged in chronological order of the life of Jesus. The use of perspective in the engravings incorporated a technique long applied in European paintings; the vivid and three-dimensional representation of the story of Christ transformed the Christian message into historical reality for the Chinese converts. Sent to the Jesuit residence in Nanjing by order of Dias, the *Evangelicae Historiae Imagines* would serve future generations of Jesuit missionaries. In 1637, the Italian Jesuit Giulio Aleni adapted fifty-five pictures into Chinese woodcut illustrations and rendered the Latin text into Chinese under the title *Tianzhu jiangsheng chuxiang jingjie*, an important monument in the visual propagation of Christianity in Chinese art.

Echoing Xu Guangqi's admonition to publish, Ricci repeatedly stated the importance of Chinese Christian books for the propagation of Christianity. From the success of his writings, Ricci concluded 'that in China one can reap a great harvest by way of books and our science. And if I have already made such a stir in the school of this realm, I, who was always here alone and still now I can say that nobody has helped me in this, how much more can someone achieve in this, who is less busy and of better talent than I am. On account of this I recommend to all the fathers who are here the study of Chinese letters, as something on which a good part of the conversion of China depends.'[15] Especially gratifying to Ricci was the request for his books from the Jesuit Mission in Japan, which came from Francesco Pasio, his old companion from the early years of his missionary career.

Ricci's upbeat mood was explained by his surprise at the recent success of his newest work, *Ershiwu yan* (1605). Translated from a Latin version of Epictetus' *Encheiridion*, with additions in a Christian sense by Ricci, the *Ershiwu yan* introduced Stoicism to China. Epictetus was an ancient Greek Stoic philosopher who taught that all external events are determined by fate, and are thus beyond individual control. Individuals can only accept whatever happens calmly and dispassionately. Only in self-reflection can individuals examine and control their own actions through rigorous self-discipline. Suffering arises from trying to control what is uncontrollable, or from neglecting what is within our power.

What accounted for the eager reception of this slim book, more successful than his *True Meaning of the Lord of Heaven*? Ricci explained:

In this [book] I do nothing except to speak of virtue and of living well with much interest as a natural and Christian philosopher, without refuting any sect. For this reason, it is read with pleasure by all, whatever sect they may belong to. The other [Jesuit] residences write to me of the great stir that this one book has made in many places, and thus few visitors who come to visit do not entreat me earnestly to write other books, since with this we have given credit to the things of our religion.[16]

He was quite right in describing the attractions of Stoicism, a natural philosophy, to the Chinese. But Ricci failed to mention another dimension to its reception, which was crucial to the work's success. The printing of *Ershiwu yan* was sponsored by Feng Yinjing, the falsely accused and unjustly imprisoned mandarin, Ricci's close friend (see Chapter 9), who, having read the manuscript in jail, was so moved that he paid for its printing and wrote a preface, to which Xu Guangqi added a postscript.

As in many pictures, where the frame, rather than painting itself, captures the gaze, so it was with the reception of *Ershiwu yan*. The painting, as it were, represented Stoic philosophy—the acceptance of fate, the imperative of self-control—as refracted in the Christian perspective of earthly existence as a journey through a vale of tears. The framing was provided by the fate of Feng Yinjing himself, a righteous official who defended the common people against the rapacious cruelty of the eunuch tax-intendant. His imprisonment raised an outcry, and Feng became the symbol of loyal resistance to tyranny in a country that suffered the fiscal exactions of a capricious and rapacious emperor. For Feng Yinjing and other mandarins, self-sacrifice remained the only option in Confucian orthopraxis: it offered the only exit in the conflict between loyalty and tyranny.

'If you consider the possession and loss of external things as the cause of happiness and sadness, if you consider honor and dishonor as the source of fortune and misfortune, and if you should encounter what you do not wish or fail to encounter what you wish, and thus lament your fate, this is the beginning of the loss of your humanity (*ren*).' A gentleman, a true philosopher, in Ricci's Chinese text, can only control himself; there is no choice but to accept with equanimity the injustice done unto him by those in positions of authority—rulers, fathers, elder brothers.[17] Deeply moved by these words, Feng Yinjing could not but feel the twenty-five passages applied not only to his own fate, but to the fate of the country under misrule and tyranny.

Under the pressure of public opinion, Emperor Wanli finally released Feng Yinjing. Tens of thousands hailed the righteous mandarin at the gate of the prison; Xu Guangqi, a kindred spirit, welcomed Feng in his house before the latter's mandated departure from the capital. A year of major significance, the publication and reception of *Ershiwu yan* in 1605 illuminated the powerful attraction of Christian Stoicism for the elites who faced the crisis of late Ming society.

Was Ricci unaware of the general mood of crisis in the country? No, since he would comment in his memoirs on the power of the eunuchs, exercised with stupidity and cruelty, and sanctioned by the emperor. Did he fail to understand the reasons why the Chinese elites were drawn to Christianity, reasons which were multiple, complicated, and perhaps not even well articulated by the mandarin converts themselves? Quite possibly. What we do know, from Ricci's letters, is that China remained an alien land after so many years of sojourn, after learning so well its language and customs, after transforming himself, brilliantly and successfully, from a western Buddhist monk into a western scholar, equal in learning and superior in technical expertise to his Chinese peers. Even at the height of his success, Ricci lamented his absence from Ludovico Maselli, his old professor at the Roman College, whose recent letter had given him so much consolation because 'this your son is posted among millions of gentiles and has suffered so many troubles'.[18] There is more than rhetoric in the self-pitying words in another letter to Fabio de Fabii, Ricci's master in the novitiate and for whom he cherished a lifelong affection. Thanking Fabii for his letter, for remembering his fellow Jesuits in China in the midst of his many important responsibilities in Europe, Ricci wrote that Fabii's graciousness 'is remembered with particular affection by one of his poor brothers, thrust to the end of the world among infidels'. He described himself as 'a poor one, posted to the proximity of Tartary, so far away from our European and Indian friends, but also from the companions in China'.[19] In this imperial capital, Beijing, which lies so far away from the coast, from Macao and Rome, 'I shall finish my life', Ricci told his father, in a moving letter dated 10 May 1605.[20] To his brother Orazio, an important government official in Macerata, Ricci described the fate of the missionary:

We the religious, are in these countries like in a voluntary exile, not only far away from our dear ones, father, mother, brothers, and relatives, but also from Christians and our nation, and sometimes in places, where in ten or twenty years one does not see a single European, and others, such as those who are in China, never eat bread nor drink wine . . . We are here with our long beards and hair down to our backs at home, that not even our workers have it so sad; many times we have to flee the enemies who come to harm us, as it happened to me one time, when I fell from a window and twisted my foot, which still hurts to this day.

Death stares at the missionary, continued Ricci in his letter.

Some drowned at sea or in rivers, as it happened to me one time; some were crucified by enemies; some were pierced by arrows, some by spears; and those who survive always live with death before their eyes, being among millions of gentiles, all our enemies; and all this for the love of God, and may God pardon our sins and deliver us from hell. At all this we cry and shed many tears every day, not knowing what will be God's judgment. And so, what will those do, who remain safely at home with their family and friends, in the midst of ease and pleasures? . . . Truly, there are not many years left to me and I am already all white, and those Chinese who marvel that I look so old in spite of my age do not know that they are the cause of my gray hair.[21]

Scarcely one year would pass after Ricci wrote these words before he too would have to suffer as a Christian Stoic the slings and arrows of fortune.

The death of Alessandro Valignano on 20 January 1606 was the first blow. A domineering figure in Jesuit Asia, the Visitor was preparing to inspect the Society's work in China when he passed away at the age of 67. Ricci keenly felt this loss: 'In this year, among the other troubles, which are never absent here, we have this great loss of the death of Reverend Valignano, father of this mission, with whose loss we are all like orphans.'[22] Shortly after this, Francisco Martins (Wang Mingsha), who had been assigned to escort Valignano around China, was arrested in Guangzhou.

It was in Macao where Valignano died; it was from Macao that the troubles originated. Ricci had a foreboding. On 26 July 1605, he reported to Claudio Acquaviva in Rome:[23]

Even if Macao is inside the boundaries of China, some consider this city to be foreign and the people there to be sufficiently ill-reputed that they are suspected. Thus, all those [Chinese] who have something to do there are people of the lower sorts and suspected everywhere, to the extent that when they accuse one another, in bad-mouthing their enemies, they call them people who frequent Macao, as I have seen myself. We try, whenever we can, to hide the commerce we have with it [Macao]; and if there is any danger to this our enterprise, the greatest of all stems from Macao, and all our enemies speak of this.

The Chinese considered Macao a violent place and the colony—a settlement of some 600 Portuguese families, with Indians, Timorese, Africans, a few hundred Japanese, and a few thousand ill-reputed Chinese—a hotbed of unrest. The Portuguese were not entirely to be blamed for provoking Chinese anxieties. True, in 1602 the Portuguese began to build a wall around their settlement, which would eventually encircle Macao; the center of this new defense was the fortification of St Paul, erected on the highest point of the land, next to the Jesuit College and the new Jesuit church, the Madre de Deus. What lay beyond Chinese horizons were the troubled waters of Portuguese Asia. At the turn of the century, Portuguese maritime supremacy in the Indian Ocean and South China Sea was challenged by a new rising power: the Dutch Republic. More than a quarter of a century after the initial revolt in the Low Countries, the Spanish crown was still trying to pacify its northern dominions. Having proclaimed their independence, the Dutch brought the war to the sea lanes of the Atlantic and the Indian Ocean in the 1590s; in 1601, they formed the Dutch East India Company, to pry away the lucrative spice trade from the Portuguese, who were, much to the regret of many Lusitanians, subjects of the Spanish king. After 1600, by establishing a string of strong points stretching from Bahia to Batavia, the Dutch contested Portuguese dominions in Brazil, Sri Lanka, Malacca, and the Spice Islands. Not even Japan and China lay beyond the sphere of these intrepid Protestant seafarers. In 1601, the Dutch sailed to the coast of Fujian, where they promised to chase the Portuguese out of Macao and the Spaniards out of Manila, if they were granted the right to trade. Rebuffed by Chinese authorities, the Dutch eventually turned their attention to Formosa and Japan. In the same year, two Dutch ships arrived in Macao. A landing party went ashore. They were taken prisoner. The Portuguese mobilized their ships to chase away the two Dutch vessels, the *Amsterdam* and the *Gouda*. With the exception of some who converted to Catholicism, the Portuguese executed the Dutch prisoners. The Dutch returned in force to attack in 1607. Although the assault on Macao failed, the Dutch succeeded in their intrigues in Japan: in 1610, the new strongman, the Shogun Tokugawa Ieyasu, cut off Nagasaki's trade with Macao and ceded the privilege to the Dutch.

Like a barrel of sulfur, charcoal, and potassium nitrate, the cramped city of Macao, with its diverse ethnic mix, and the juxtaposition of Portuguese and Chinese authorities, exploded as easily as gunpowder. The first blowup occurred on Ilha Verde, a speck of an island offshore from the Portuguese settlement and close to the walled barrier erected by the Chinese. There, the Jesuits erected a chapel. A Japanese Jesuit brother was put in charge of this pilgrimage site, destination of refreshing excursions for the inhabitants of Macao, especially in fine weather. One Christian feast day, while the Portuguese and their entourage gathered for high mass in the city, a low-ranking Chinese officer, a Muslim as it turned out, led a group of his countrymen to Ilha Verde. This was Chinese territory, they shouted. Setting fire to the chapel, the Muslim officer tore up an image of St Anthony. Several Japanese Christians wanted to draw their samurai swords, but were dissuaded by the Jesuit brother. Later, when the Portuguese saw the torn image of their saint, an angry mob took by force the Muslim officer. Wisely, the Portuguese authorities freed the man, already badly roughed up, and sent a messenger to smooth things over with the magistrate of Xiangshan.

The Portuguese barely had time to congratulate themselves on their damage control, when another conflict provoked a much more serious conflict with the Chinese. Here, the Portuguese only had themselves to blame. As was the case with many overseas Portuguese settlements, tiny enclaves on the edges of large alien civilizations, the intense self-absorption of the colonials provoked equally intense internal conflicts. After the death of Bishop Leonardo de Sá in 1597, the Archbishop of Goa appointed as Vicar General and Governor of Macao the Augustinian friar Michele dos Santos, formerly known as Rodrigo Colaço, an ex-Jesuit. In March 1605, the Vicar-General placed the entire city under an interdict, barring all sacraments to the faithful. Such an extreme action resulted from a long chain of conflicts: a secular priest of San Lourenço insulting a Franciscan Observant friar; the grievance of the latter to the Judge Conservator, the representative of papal jurisdiction, the Jesuit Valentim Carvalho; the ruling of the latter against the priest; the appeal of the latter to the Vicar-General; and, finally, the interdict, observed only by dos Santos' own order and the Church of San Lourenço. Clearly, resentment against the Society of Jesus played a role in the actions of the Vicar-General, Augustinian friar, and one-time Jesuit. Unfortunately, the conflict of ecclesiastical authority split the Portuguese community. Before long, rumors multiplied against the Jesuits: they had abrogated all power to themselves, secular and spiritual; they were plotting to overthrow the Ming dynasty and establish the Italian Lazarro Cattaneo as ruler of the new Jesuit kingdom, with the help of convert-traitors and Jesuit mission-aries; they schemed to bring in Japanese and Indian mercenaries for the conquest of China, to be inaugurated by the massacre of all Chinese inhabitants in Macao, copying the 1603 Spanish atrocities in Luzon.

The Chinese panicked. They fled the enclave. Many made their way to Guangzhou, repeating the rumor of Jesuit plots and Portuguese invasion, so many agents of contagion in the spread of Chinese xenophobia. Alarmed, the mandarins overreacted. He Shijin, *zongdu* of Guangdong and Guangxi, ordered defense preparations. In Guangzhou, the *haidao*, who was in charge of coastal defense, razed an entire neighborhood between the city walls and the Pearl River, more than 1,000 dwellings of poor people, in order to have a clear field of fire. Furthermore, he cut off all contact with Macao, and posted proclamations ordering the arrest of western missionaries and their minions. Their food supply cut off, the Portuguese dispatched envoys to plead their case: loyal subjects of the Ming, they harbored no intention of rebellion; the city, deprived of shipping from India (due to Dutch attacks), was languishing economically; the cutoff of victuals would spell doom for the enclave. Meanwhile, other Chinese traveling from Macao recounted the discord between the Portuguese themselves. As the intensity of rumor-mongering and panic subsided, popular anger at the wanton destruction of the *haidao* began to mount.

On 20 February 1606, the Jesuit brother Wang Mingsha, alias Francisco Martins, arrived in Guangzhou, a city boiling over with tension. Having been summoned by Valignano from Shaozhou to Macao as an escort for the planned trip to China, Brother Francisco found a letter informing him of Valignano's death. Not sure whether to proceed or return, the Chinese Jesuit wrote for instructions. Naturally, Wang Mingsha saw the proclamations posted at the city gates. He quickly dispatched a letter of warning to Longobardo in Shaozhou, but ignored urgent advice to leave the provincial capital. There were three reasons for this fatal decision: first, he wanted to wait for a reply from Macao; second, he believed his own innocence was the best defense; and finally, Wang Mingsha, a native of Macao, one of the first Chinese Jesuits, with fifteen years of service in the Society, was counting on the prestige of Ricci, and God's providence, for his own protection.

Suffering from advanced tuberculosis, Wang Mingsha was bedridden for more than a month, still awaiting instructions, when he was arrested the night of 26 March. Hoping for a reward, a convert in the very small Christian community had made a denunciation to the Assistant District Magistrate (*tongzhi*): a foreign spy from Macao was in the city. A friend of the *haidao*, the *tongzhi* thought this arrest would furnish proof of a real conspiracy, hence alleviating public anger at the *haidao*. Aside from the Chinese Jesuit, five other Christians were arrested: Ignatius and Athanasius, two servants who accompanied Wang Mingsha from Shaozhou; two brothers, Peter and Paul, nephews of another Chinese Jesuit; and their uncle, the owner of the house where they were betrayed.

Right away, the Assistant District Magistrate ordered judicial torture: their legs strapped tightly between two wooden boards, all six were beaten on their thighs. In Cantonese, Wang Mingsha urged the others to keep their faith. Protesting their innocence, he told the magistrate he had traveled from Shaozhou with an official permit. Sensing the magistrate's hesitation, the accuser turned to one of the boys and asked, in Cantonese, whether the Jesuit had purchased medicine, to which the boy answered in the affirmative. In both Mandarin and Cantonese, the single character *yao* or *joek* is ambivalent: alone, it signifies medicine; with the compound *qiang/coeng* (arquebus) or *huo/fo* (fire), it means gunpowder. His doubt aroused, the magistrate asked the boy to repeat his answer. The frightened boy stuttered it was indeed medicine. At this, the magistrate ordered his men to apply another judicial torture: crushing the fingers of both hands between strips of bamboo, tied loosely together to allow them to be wrapped between fingers and be pulled increasingly tighter at both ends. Screaming, the boy confessed. The presence of books and letters in western languages in Wang's baggage furnished further material evidence for his conviction.

The next day, the prisoners were handed over to the *haidao* who, after ordering a beating of the adults, declared Brother Francisco, his servant Ignatius, and the uncle guilty: spies from Macao, they had come to Guangzhou to buy gunpowder in preparation for a rebellion. The case was handed back to the Assistant District Magistrate for sentencing. Once again, this mandarin commanded a beating for Wang Mingsha. The sick man, deprived of water and food, and repeatedly tortured, expired under the first blows. Fearful of a judicial reprimand from his superiors, the magistrate ordered a hasty burial for Wang Mingsha. The 33-year-old Jesuit brother died on 31 March.

Back in Shaozhou, soldiers surrounded the Jesuit residence. The *haidao* had asked his Shaozhou colleagues to search for gunpowder and weapons. Although nothing came up, everyone feared association with the Jesuits, as news of Wang Mingsha's arrest and death reached town. No Christian dared go to church. While protesting by letters his innocence to the *zongdu* and to other officials in Guangzhou, Longobardo also had to defend himself against an accusation of adultery. A hostile neighbor, having blackmailed some money from a Buddhist monk, tried out this trick with the westerner. But no one else denounced the foreigner, least of all the woman accused, who screamed out her innocence on the streets of Shaozhou. The magistrate dropped the case.

This messy affair came to an end only with the return of a friendly high-level official. The Vice-Commissioner of Provincial Surveillance (*anchaishi fuzhi*), Zhang Deming, a friend of Longobardo, was away in Beijing representing Guangdong province for the imperial birthday. Returning with gifts from the remarkable westerner Matteo Ricci, Zhang Deming promised help. He ordered the District Magistrate to open a formal inquiry into the Jesuits. Aware of their friendship with his superior, this mandarin promptly declared their conduct lawful and above suspicion. Zhang Deming also sent a captain to Macao. Warmly received by Cattaneo, and impressed by a guided tour of the Portuguese enclave, the captain returned with the highest praise for the alleged Jesuit-conspirator. With a few well-aimed pricks, the boil of malicious rumors started to drain; the Christian community passed from danger.

In Beijing, Zhang Deming had also been appointed to the concurrent post of *haidao*. In this capacity, he transferred the Guangzhou case from the Assistant District Magistrate, the *tongzhi* or second judge, to the fourth magistrate, who had criticized his superior for judicial misconduct. Begging for his life, the accuser confessed to giving false testimony. Zhang Deming sent the man to the *zongdu* in Zhaoqing for sentencing, where he bribed his way out of jail and fled. The five arrested Christians were liberated. Exhumed from the common grave, his wrists and ankles still cuffed, the body of Brother Francisco Martins was transported to Shaozhou, and later buried in his native Macao in a solemn ceremony as the first Chinese Christian martyr. The next year, during the triennial review in the capital, both the former *haidao* and the *tongzhi* were declared ineligible for future office due to judicial misconduct. God's vengeance, Ricci thought, for the tragic death of his erstwhile companion.

Although the immediate danger was averted, opposition to the Jesuit Mission did not vanish. In 1607, a petition organized by some scholars in Shaozhou gathered 400 signatures: expel Longobardo and the foreigners; they disturb the peace of the community. Zhang Deming refused to accept the petition. The same year, the gravely ill João Soeiro left Nanchang to recuperate in Macao. He died in August at the age of 41, worn down by work. The setbacks in Shaozhou and Nanchang only highlighted the indispensable role played by Ricci in the imperial capital, who acted as a patron saint and protector for the Jesuit Mission.

12

The Man of Paradox

The patron of the Jesuit Mission was not quite a saint: wily in the ways of power, Ricci acted more like a minister. Like the emperor a minister would serve, Ricci received the mandarins and future officials of the realm without ever setting foot outside the imperial capital. Every three years, between 5,000 and 6,000 mandarins reported for the triennial evaluation in Beijing; every three years, hundreds of scholars sweated ink and blood in their tiny examination cells for the final *jingshi* degree held in the imperial capital. To distract themselves from anxieties—for their future career in the imperial bureaucracy—these mandarins and scholars visited famous sites in the capital, of which the Catholic church had become a regular stopover. During these hectic periods, the Jesuits received visitors from morning to night, day after day. 'Never in my whole life do I have so little time,' wrote Ricci, 'so that at times I pray to beg God for time, when I have the most need for it.'[1] Every time, Ricci had to act as a guide, explaining the sacred objects and images in the church; every visit, Ricci engaged in polite and learned conversations, showcasing western learning, Christian teaching, and European books; every day, the Jesuit residence opened as a museum of curiosities, with maps, books, astrolabes, quadrants, globes, and other marvels to capture the gaze of the Ming ruling elites. Friendships had to be cultivated, new acquaintances acquired: for on the careful maintenance and expansion of their network, *guanxi*, depended the protection of the Christian mission. It saved the day, in March/April 1606, when Zhang Deming, fresh from the capital and meeting Ricci, returned to clear Longobardo and Cattaneo of all charges of rebellion, and to rehabilitate the good name of the martyr Wang Mingsha. On a less dramatic note, Ricci's conversations and writings were carried by mandarins and scholars returning to their posts and native places, ever expanding the message of

Heavenly Learning. In 1607, a year of triennial scrutiny, Ricci gathered ten conversations he had had over the years in China; putting these on paper, the revised dialogues formed his new work, the *Jiren shipian, Ten Discourses of the Man of Paradox*.

This work received an even greater reception than the *True Meaning of the Lord of Heaven*. The Chinese characters *Jiren*, meaning remarkable person, can also signify a man of paradox in the sense that the uncommon qualities of the person arouse disbelief, puzzlement, as well as admiration. Indeed, many Chinese puzzled over a western sage who abandoned home and country even while they praised him for his erudition and virtue. If the biblical prophet receives no honor at home and must proclaim his message among strangers, the Chinese sage was firmly rooted in his soil, because for the Chinese foreign travel represented at best an adventure, more commonly a misery. To them came a western sage discoursing on ethics and virtue, yet he was unmarried, like Buddhist monks. But this celibate sage excoriated the teachings of Buddhism, many of which seemed in Chinese eyes no different from those of the western religion. The learned man from the Great West was indeed a paradox within a paradox. Some mandarins from Zhejiang province made copies of *Jiren shipian* before the book went to print, and brought these back from the capital to the cities of their posting. As this work circulated, a retired mandarin in Hangzhou wrote an open letter to the 'Man of Paradox' from the West. This was Yu Chunxi.

Even in childhood, Yu Chunxi, a native of Hangzhou, enjoyed a reputation as a devout Buddhist. His entry in the *Biographies of Devout Lay-Buddhists (jushi zhuan)* recounts the story of a 3-year-old boy chanting the name of Buddha at night refusing to sleep. Yu learned meditation from his grandmother and was well devoted to Chan Buddhism before learning a more disciplined and prayer-oriented pious practice from Zhuhong, the great Buddhist abbot of Hangzhou and the key figure in the late Ming Buddhist revival. A firm believer in reincarnation, Yu once told Shen Defu, the chronicler of the Wanli reign, a vivid episode from his previous life, when he was so captivated by the glory of a high minister passing through that he was punished to be reborn in the stormy sea of officialdom.[2]

And the waves of that stormy sea tossed Yu Chunxi up and down. His first appointment was in Beijing, after obtaining the *jinshi* degree in 1584. Soon, the death of his father obligated Yu to return to Hangzhou for three years of mourning, during which Yu became the disciple of the great Buddhist abbot Zhuhong, feeding wild animals, practicing meditation, and reciting Buddhist prayers. In the early 1590s, Yu served as a middle-ranking mandarin in the Ministry of Personnel in Beijing, with the title of Vice-Director of the Bureau for Meritorious Examinations (*ji xun yuan wai lang*). During the 1593 review of all mandarins in the imperial capital, Yu was one of the officials criticized by the censors. His superior, the Minister of Personnel Sun Long (the elder half-brother of Sun Kuang, who enabled Ricci to leave Guangdong for Nanchang; see Chapter 6), tried to shield Yu to no avail. Frustrated with Beijing politics, Sun Long retired from office; and Yu Chunxi lost his post a second time. Rising with the next bureaucratic wave, Yu was appointed the Vice-Director of the Bureau of Guest Affairs (*zhu ke si juan wai lang*), one of the four bureaus in the Ministry of Rites in charge of receiving foreign tributary missions. He was serving in this position when Ricci first arrived in Beijing, although there is no evidence that they had ever met. By now in his fifties or perhaps early sixties, Yu retired to his native Hangzhou, where he read the new work by the western scholar.[3]

In 1608, Yu Chunxi wrote an open letter to Ricci.[4] The occasion was the publication of *Ten Discourses of the Man of Paradox*. Yu began his letter by calling himself an 'ineloquent person who does not flatter, *bu ning*', and expressing his admiration for Ricci, whose erudition had been praised by his fellow literati from Zhejiang: 'Although Mr. Li Xitai [Xitai was Ricci's literati name] is not a Chinese, he is a virtuous man, who is also an expert in astronomy and mathematics.' Nevertheless, Yu was provoked into answering the Jesuit's relentless attack on Buddhism. Continuing in his letter, the Buddhist layman wrote:

When I was three, I learned about the teachings of the three saints [Buddha, Laozi, and Confucius] which I have followed my whole life until the present; I cannot do otherwise. I have heard recently that you, sir, who hail from the West, look down on Siddhartha: is this not similar to the people of ancient Lu dismissing Confucius out of familiar contempt? When I read your comparisons of heaven and hell, it seems you have not flipped through the books [of Buddha] and do not understand their meanings. Have you not heard that in the sutra there is a saying, 'Entering the hell without end, not leaving at the end of time, only the longevity of heaven determines his passing, and in one day and night it is already one thousand and six hundred human years'? From this, one can reason that there is something you have missed seeing. If you do not understand its mysteries and rush to attack, how can you penetrate its strong defenses? I dare invite you to peruse the entire Buddhist Canon issued by the emperor, to classify all the points of similarity and difference, to criticize the shortcomings, and then to publish a book and hang it high above the gate of the palace, so that the Buddhist monks with their bare-left chests can shoot arrows at will. If no feather should stick to the target, and the archers have emptied their quivers for nothing, wouldn't that be a great historic achievement! But I see you do not do this, saying instead slanderous remarks that make other people laugh behind your back. Have you no better plan? If you are occupied everyday with your studies and have no time to peruse all the books [of Buddhism], please start with reading these books: *Zong jing lu* (*Selection of the Mirrors of Eminent Monks*), *Jie fa yin* (*Exposition on Buddhist Rules*), *Xi yu ji* (*History of the Western Region*), *Gao zeng zhuan* (*Biographies of Eminent Monks*), *Fa yuan zhu lin* (*Trees from the Park of Dharma*). Find out the subtleties and arguments, if only to begin to offer an apology. Otherwise, if you only say: 'My country has always found this person [i.e. Buddha] despicable; and I know everything about his place of birth.' How do we know this is not a different western heaven, another Siddhartha. . . . How can one individual's skepticism cast doubt on the faith of thousands?

Traveling with white horses to the east and fragrant elephants to the west, preachers and interpreters never ceased their journeys. You can fool one man, but not ten thousand. How can you say that in more than two thousand years, the numerous saints and sages of our noble China have all been fooled by the doctrines of Buddhism? Let us not denigrate any individual but simply discuss the merits of his books. [The Confucian philosophers] Lu Xiangshan and Wang Yangming have transmitted Buddhist learnings, and yet their statues are honored in Confucian temples; thus we know that Buddhist scriptures are similar to the teachings of neo-Confucianism (*li*). Moreover, the Emperors Taizu and Wenhuang [the first two emperors of the Ming] honored statues of the Buddha; wise ministers and famous officials defend Buddhism with their might: is it that easy to burn down its dwelling? Let us wish it is not the case that when a westerner attacks another westerner, and if he fails, his school will collapse. If the Lord of Heaven (*Tianzhu*) can manifest his spirit, how can he bear to arm you with armor and weapon to result in the destruction of his holy city and the loss of his blessed territory?

I, the ineloquent, know that you Sir honor the commandments of the Lord of Heaven as firmly as metal and stone, and will in no way betray your teacher or friends. While the Confucian classics and the history books are indeed worthy of citation, there are also many places in the Buddhist sutras that are harmonious with your teachings. Yet, without a casual reading, you attack them, whereas those who have read your *Ten Discourses of the Man of Paradox* say: 'This is no different from Buddhist teachings!' These are the wild pigs and celeries that you Sir refuse.

Indeed! All of us living beings exist within the seed of a fruit, ignorant of its peel or its shell, not to mention the things outside of the fruit! Whether this is all the same teaching is for you Sir to decide.

Opening my mouth while lying on my pillow, I feel deeply ashamed; may I beg the indulgence of your grand magnanimity for having attacked a foreigner. Your humble servant, your humble servant!

Ricci replied:[5]

I am a lowly person from the West, who having abandoned his family to learn the doctrines of the way, and having sailed for eighty thousand miles to visit your esteemed country, have lived here for many years. There have been more than one or two eminent gentlemen, who have deigned to offer me their advice. What mathematics I know, I have picked up in my youth. The tributary gifts are token offerings and consist of instruments and things that I had brought with me. Those who praise me for my technical skills do not know me well. If it is only about this, then these instruments, fabricated by artisans, are merely the most minor things in your national treasury, and how would I know from eighty thousand miles away that your esteemed country might not have these? Why would I have risked a thousand deaths, sailing for three years just to do this? I do this because I follow the most righteous path of the Lord of Heaven, and I wish to explicate this in order that all men may become his filial sons, that the Great Parent may receive the love of filial piety, for this I had left home and risked my life.

Having received the favor of a stipend from his sacred majesty for eight years, I wish also to publish my views. I, being incapable and unintelligent, composed *Ten Discourses of the Man of Paradox*, in which I cite a few doctrines from my answers to queries. After penning the volume, I asked for criticisms from eminent scholars of the capital, but the book introduces merely a tiny fraction of the doctrines of my religion, not even one hair on the hide of nine buffaloes. I, the unworthy, have cited the brilliant works [of the Confucian classics], and whatever praises my writings might have garnered, I certainly do not deserve them. I feel only that the statement, penned by later [scholars] 'that *Shangdi*, the God on High is born from the *Taiji*, the Supreme Extremity' does not agree with the views of the ancient sages; I feel rather that Confucius' statement, 'the Supreme Extremity gives rise to the two poles', is more appropriate. The doctrine on the genesis of the universe is a great learning in my obscure country, and there are many books on the subject. Allow me to present a few ideas in the future for your criticism. You know how profound this great doctrine must be that it has caused me to abandon everything else.

Your letter, only a thousand words, admonishes me without arrogance to argue with reason in order to explain the ultimate way. There is a proverb in my obscure country: 'harmonious words enhance the debate'; truly you have taught me this! Drums and bells only sound when they are struck, this is exactly what I had wished for. When I read your admonitions, you say that I 'honor the commandments of the Lord of Heaven as firmly as metal and stone.' You do not know my unworthiness; how can I deserve this praise? Yet this one sentence has alerted me that while anxiously worrying about sincerity, I have not sinned, which is most fortunate.

The reason is that of the Ten Commandments I obey, one of them forbids slander. If I attacked Buddhism without knowing its rights and wrongs, would I not be slandering? Ever since I arrived in China what little learning I have acquired has been from the ancient sages and Confucius and not from Buddha. I have persisted in this until now. A mere foreigner, what debt do I owe Confucius and what wrong had Buddha done me? None! If you say I praise Confucius in order to flatter the scholars and expand my teachings, in China there are many more believers in Buddha than in Confucius, why shouldn't I praise Buddha in order to flatter every scholar and expand my teachings? The reason is that I hold firmly to the commandments with all my heart, and judge everything according to them. I affirm the ancient sages for they taught moral cultivation of the self and the worship of the God on High, *Shangdi*; I negate Buddha, for he disobeyed *Shangdi* and wished to put himself in his stead. How could I have dared to do otherwise?

There is only one God on High, *Shangdi*, is it not slander to say there are many heavens? Is it not rebellion for insignificant men to put themselves above the emperor of heaven? There is no greater error than this! There is no need to peruse all 5,000 volumes of sutra to know this. People say that there are many divergent opinions in the sutras of the *Buddhist Canon*. Listening to your masterful teachings—a brilliant scholar who has devoted his attention to the sutras—if you find teachings that agree with the worship of *Shangdi* and the cultivation of virtue, would I dare not rush to follow you? But this is not the case, and it is difficult for me to turn my mind to this. Since you have mentioned this point, even though I have not read them all, I also know that the sutras are full of obscure, contrived, and arcane meanings. This is like some faraway and marginal country that has usurped orthodox institutions and laws and yet remains unorthodox. How can officials [of orthodox rule] praise their culture and civilization? The Buddhist temple might be strong, but perhaps it enjoys only an empty reputation. Nevertheless, I agree heartily with your admonition 'to peruse the sutras and find out the subtleties and arguments.' Since it has been such a short time I have not been able to do it. Admiring your masterful erudition in this doctrine, if we could exchange letters to express and discuss our principles, hoping to find some harmony with the passage of time, it would be a most convenient and delightful task. This is really an excellent proposition. We should attempt to do this into the small hours of the morning. Who knows what fruit might come of this?

As to the teachings on heaven and hell in my modest work, my intention was only to repudiate the error of reincarnation, in order that those who seek virtue would not change their minds, and those who commit evil cannot hope to be spared. Mencius says we should not prize eloquence above style, style above meaning. If people should understand the error of reincarnation because of my words, then how can we debate the statement which has proof that hell is timeless and in heaven a thousand years pass as one day? If you say I denigrate this man [Buddha] because I know his place of birth, this is merely a coincidence. There are thousands of countries in the world: I have briefly investigated what religion existed in which region; in the twenty to thirty thousand miles between India and China, only India acknowledges Buddha. Wherever people congregate, there will be faith, let us reason based on the results and not on the land. This is not the essence of difference. For all religions that seek to spread their teachings far and wide, they all depend on reason and intelligent scholars. Once the religion has been introduced and many writings are produced, people would begin to believe. What is important is to know the origins and end in order to determine what is correct and incorrect. The difference between Buddhists and people like me is this: they are empty, I am practical; they are selfish, I am public spirited; they split into many paths, I stay true to the one origin. These are the small differences. They disobey [God], I serve [God]. This is the big difference. That is all.

Moreover, it has been two thousand years since Buddhism was introduced to China. There are temples everywhere; monks and nuns fill the roads. Yet, the morality of your esteemed country is no better than the three dynasties of antiquity. Scholars actually say that the present is not as good as the past. As to my humble country, we have turned to our religion some one thousand six hundred years ago. I dare not describe our mores in detail for fear you think I am exaggerating but I will just state the obvious: within ten thousand square miles, there are more than thirty countries sharing borders; there have been no rebellions, wars, or recriminations for one thousand six hundred years. Since the time of Yao and Xun, your esteemed country has enjoyed thousands of years of civilization, and if those who believe and worship Buddha turn to the Lord of Heaven, why would this period not last as long as Buddhism? Since it is difficult to convince you of something yet to be seen, we should now investigate and decide on the right doctrines. Once the truth is determined, the rites of sacrifice should be established; why should this be compared to bearing arms and besieging a city?

There is only one thing that raises difficulty. Even though there are many Buddhist sutras, many people study them. As to the texts from my humble country—those explaining the doctrines and those that describe natural phenomena—they are at least double in scope to the Buddhist Canon, but are not translated. I cannot undertake this myself, nor do I have disciples. In view of this, your admonition that 'the doubts of one individual would collapse against the faith of thousands' amounts to coercion, not persuasion. My humble opinion is that, for now let us not consider who is the winner or loser. If the gentlemen of your esteemed country would translate some [Christian] texts, and not even the same number as the Buddhist Canon but merely one or two percent of the entire corpus, we can use this for debate. And if I lose the argument, I would be willing to admit defeat. If this is not the case, then your admonition that 'without perusing all the Buddhist sutras, one cannot attack the citadel of Buddhism' will be countered by me, saying: 'without perusing all the texts of the Lord of Heaven, how can you destroy my holy city and take my blessed territory'? It is my intention to study the sutras in order to investigate the differences and similarities [to Christianity]; may it be the desire of all gentlemen to study Christianity in order to find the ultimate truth! This will have the great merit of turning the future generations from the deviant path to the one true way. I hope you would not ignore my humble advice.

Blown by the winds and confined by our sensual experiences, even sages are not exempt. Your mastership said: 'in our great China, with all her sages, there is no belief except for this [Buddhism]'. Were there then no sages in China before the

Han dynasty? Your mastership argues from the evidence of sages since the Han; what I affirm, however, are the sages of antiquity. If you say that the emperors Yao and Xun, the Duke of Zhou, and Confucius would have believed in Buddha if they had heard of him, then I would say that if the sages since the Han dynasty had heard of the religion of the Lord of Heaven, they would also have believed in it. How can you say who is right? None of this can serve as proof.

Your admonition also describes my humble work as 'not different from Buddhism'. This is not a fault. Why? If I had stolen some remarks from Buddha in order to criticize him, this would amount to a domestic rebellion. But your mastership already knows that I have not perused all the sutras, and why shouldn't there be similarities? I regret only that Buddha does not agree completely with me. If there is complete agreement, we are speaking of twins, how fortunate! Reflect on this, your mastership: having traveled for eighty thousand miles to make friends, I desire only that people agree with me, and why would I want to seek disagreements? Someone who is trying to get out of an uninhabited wild valley would rejoice when he hears footsteps. The animals in the wild may be all different, but I wish ardently they are the same, and would rejoice the day that this comes about.

I have hidden nothing with my pen and have deeply offended you. I beg for your magnificent forgiveness while I remain, in fear and trembling, fear and trembling.

Scholars published Yu Chunxi's letter and Ricci's response. The elegant poses of the opponents belied the violence of the fight, as Buddhist polemicists and Christian apologists would cross swords of words in the years to come.

All that lay ahead. For Ricci, his time was slowly coming to a close. On 27 August 1605, Ricci moved into a new house, where he would spend the final years of his life. Thanks to the foresight of Valignano, the Jesuit Mission was financially well provided for. Enclosed by a high wall, the new residence, to the east of Xuanwumen, the western gate on the south wall of the Inner City (today, on Xi Changan jie), represented a typical dwelling of the Chinese elites: its wealth invisible to outsiders, its novelties shielded from curious eyes, open only to those who crossed its threshold, to gaze, to converse, and to absorb the marvels of the West. The architectural centerpiece of this compound was the Jesuit church. Accustomed to scenes at Buddhist temples, overflowing crowds, burning incense, kneeling, praying, gazing at statues of Buddhist deities, and asking for their fortunes, the Chinese visitor found the Christian church a quiet oasis. Its silence suggested solemnity, dignity; its unusual pictures directed one's gaze to an unfamiliar world. While there are no descriptions of the residence during the time of Ricci, Chinese visitors in the closing years of the Ming dynasty recorded their impressions of a church that remained little changed from Ricci's days, on the same site as today's Nantang, the southern Catholic church.

Liu Tong and Yu Yizheng (1594–1636) described 129 sights and monuments of the imperial capital in their book *Di jing jing wu lue*. The Catholic church near Xuanwu Gate was one:[6]

The church is narrow and long; its roof resembles a sail, and exotic paintings decorate the sides. There is a painting of Jesus, a man of thirty or so, which looks like a sculpture. He holds a celestial globe in his left hand, and points with his right index finger as if explaining something. A raised eyebrow expresses anger, a relaxed one happiness; the roundness of the ears, the stare of his gaze, the voice coming from his mouth: none of this can be matched by Chinese paintings. . . . To the right is the chapel of the Holy Mother, with the portrait of a young woman holding a child, who is Jesus.

The portrait of the Madonna and Child was not an import. The Jesuits in Beijing had their own painter in residence, the brother Giacomo Niva, who fashioned this portrait, modeled after the Madonna of San Luca in Bologna, Italy, purportedly the work of the Evangelist St Luke (see Figure 11).

To the side of the chapel, framing the interior courtyard, lay the secular buildings. Like all Chinese houses, there was a reception hall, behind which were corridors leading to several sets of rooms. One of these was set up for printing and stored the woodcut blocks of Ricci's works; another served as a workshop/display space for western scientific instruments; and the others served as domestic quarters for the residents, including Ricci's room, with the facing shelves of western and Chinese books, including the Plantin Bible.

In 1608, fifteen people lived in the residence;[7] the number remained stable even though some came and went. Ricci was superior, flanked by two other priests: Diego da Pantoja had been at his side for eight years; the Portuguese Gaspar Ferreira (1571–1649) stayed in Beijing between August 1604 and spring 1607 before being reassigned to Nanchang; in his place came the Italian Sabatino de Ursis (1575–1620), trained in astronomy and hydraulics, expertise that Ricci had explicitly demanded for the Beijing mission.[8] We find next the four coadjutors, Jesuit brothers charged with teaching catechism or secular tasks. Three were born in Macao: Antonio Leitão (1581?–1611) or Xu Pideng, Domingos Mendes (1582–1652) or Qiu Liangbin, and Pascoal Mendes (1584–1640) or Qiu Lianghou, the last two obviously brothers; and the fourth, the Sino-Japanese painter Giacomo Niva or Ni Yicheng. Eight servants made up the rest of the household.

Figure 11. The Madonna of San Luca

Ricci treated his household with love and charity, as we would expect, as he himself admonished veteran missionaries to embrace the new arrivals from Europe. He liked Ferreira, 'a person of much virtue and prudence and talented, and has shown me many examples of edification during the two years he has been here', as Ricci reported to General Acquavivia; 'and in spite of his little training in theology (only two to three years), he understands Chinese well and will succeed greatly in Chinese letters.'[9] Did Ricci see in Ferreira a younger version of himself? The superior also liked Ferreira's replacement, de Ursis. With this native of Lecce, Ricci could practice his forgotten Italian and talked about Fabio de Fabii, now superior of the Jesuit Province in Rome, whom the younger man had met on his way overseas, and whose memory warmed the older man's nostalgia for his own days as a young Jesuit novice in Rome.[10] Often lamenting his rusty Italian in his correspondence, Ricci seemed to warm up to all his fellow countrymen in the China Mission. To Acquaviva, Ricci praised both Longobardo and Vagnoni, and recommended both for the Fourth Vow, as *professi*; the former, moreover, demonstrated the qualities to be superior of the mission.[11]

The only person he had harsh words for was Diego da Pantoja, the companion who had spent more years with the master than any other Jesuit, European or Chinese. Back in 1606, Ricci wrote to Acquaviva:[12]

I have another companion, Diego Pantoja, whom two years ago the Father Visitor ordered to be made Professed of the fourth vow, who has not given many examples of edification, neither to the brothers or other people of the house, who consider him lacking in virtue and prudence, or to anyone, and to me in particular, even though I have had him with me for five or six years. Thus I feel it is a shame that he has been professed.

Harsh words indeed. Discreet even in criticism, Ricci did not give any examples of Pantoja's lack of virtue and prudence. We do know, from Chinese sources, that the two personalities were very different. The Chinese scholar Peng Duanwu later described Pantoja in these words: 'In dealing with the Chinese, Pantoja often loses their friendships; he should understand the character of the Chinese, and not bare his heart and chest, saying things that should not be said.'[13] An emotional, frank, and probably choleric man, deficient in discretion and prudence, diplomatic skills crucial in dealing with the Chinese elites, Pantoja personified qualities that Ricci found unattractive. Prudence, moreover, represented more than a personal trait; it determined the success or failure of the mission. Later on in a conversation about neo-Confucianism, Pantoja criticized Chinese scholars for confusing demons with angels, and for losing their right bearing.[14] Such words would endanger the Christian–Confucian synthesis, so carefully developed in Ricci's missionary strategy. In the eloquence of his debates, Ricci never failed 'to address people with politeness', commented Xie Zhaozhe (1567–1624), who expressed his pleasure with Ricci, whose discourse 'was similar to Confucianism'.[15] Recall also the words of Shen Defu, that Ricci was 'capable of calming impatience and anger, whose sincerity and humanity was felt by all'. Ricci wrote these harsh words in the summer of 1606, after the death of Valignano, in the aftermath of Wang Mingsha's martyrdom, and in rumor of Christian sedition. His books showed the Chinese that Christianity dealt with peace and obedience, and not with war and rebellion, explained Ricci;[16] prudence was the singular virtue in these dangerous times. With time, Ricci softened his words. Impetuousness could turn to zeal, indiscretion to warmth: Pantoja distinguished himself, together with Ferreira, in rural missions around the prefectural capital of Baoding, in the environ of the imperial capital; they baptized 142 in four villages in the years 1606–7.[17]

In the last years of his life, Ricci had also settled into a routine established in the first years of his Beijing sojourn: every day, he read a Chinese lesson to the Jesuits in the residence; frequently, he lectured for an hour on mathematics and an hour on dialectics to a Chinese audience; continuously, he received a steady stream of visitors. Every third or fourth day, Ricci paid a return visit. He did this even though all these visits and counter-visits were 'beyond our strength'. On some days, he received more than 20 visitors; on New Year and major feast days, there would be almost 100! Fatigue aside, there was no need to preach, Ricci consoled himself, for the Chinese came continuously to him.[18] He presided over the liturgical and religious life of the mission: in 1606, the Jesuits baptized 36 persons, including some abandoned infants, for in that year the great flood occasioned great misery in Beijing. By 1608, Ricci led a flock of 300 Christians in the capital, out of a total of 2,000 in the country.[19] More time-consuming than the converts was dealing with admirers. Correspondence ate up his time, complained Ricci in a letter to Acquaviva: 'One of the most time-consuming occupations I have here is to respond in Chinese to the continuous stream of letters that come in from different parts of the country, from very important people, some old acquaintances, others never seen before, who all want to contact me because of my fame.'[20] As superior he needed to write: about money, to Acquaviva; and concerning developments of the other residences, a subject of increasing worry.

From Longobardo, Ricci learned of the continuing hostility toward the mission in Shaozhou, which prompted Ricci to reflect on transferring the residence to nearby Nanxiong. Bad news also came from Nanchang. In 1607, a group of Confucian scholars signed a petition denouncing the westerners and their religion. Wang Zuo, the *buzhengshi si*, Commissioner of Provincial Administration, happened to be a friend of Ricci. He defended the good name of the Jesuits. But to appear even-handed and to save face for the scholar-petitioners, Wang Zuo came up with what seemed a perfectly sensible compromise to the Chinese: Jesuits were not spies; they were attracted to China because of the grandeur of its culture and were living blameless lives; they should be allowed to practice their ancestral religion, although the Chinese ought not to follow these rituals. This public proclamation, like so many others in Ming governance, hardly changed the situation: converts continued to visit the Jesuit church for sacraments, although the fathers bade them come in separate, smaller groups, in order not to attract too much attention.

If routine and correspondence shaped the pattern of Ricci's life, unexpected events reminded him of the unexplored contours of his world. First, to follow up on the Jews of Henan: in the winter of 1607, Ricci sent Antonio Leitão to Kaifeng, where he was well received by the Jews. To convert these last members of the once thriving Hebrew nation would not be easy, Ricci cautioned in a letter to Acquaviva: 'When we deal with a people well versed in their books, it is not easy to sell them lead in place of silver.' Prudence and learning, urged Ricci.[21]

Seeking to connect with China's past, the past also came knocking on Ricci's door. On 28 October 1607, the Chinese Jesuit Zhong Mingli (João Fernandes) finally brought the Armenian Isaac to the Jesuit residence in Beijing. His erstwhile companion in Guangdong, Zong Mingli, was dispatched by Ricci in March 1606 to the remote province of Gansu in the northwest. News came to the imperial capital in early 1606 that a Jesuit was trying to reach China from India and was marooned in Gansu. This epic journey, which began in 1602, was meant to retrace the steps of Marco Polo, and link up Portuguese India with Matteo Ricci. The Portuguese brother Bento Goís started his voyage from the court of the Mughal emperor in Agra, in northern India. Accompanied by the Armenian merchant Isaac, fluent in Persian and Turkish languages, Goís traveled to Lahore, Kabul, climbing mountains, crossing rivers, negotiating some of the harshest terrain in the world, before he reached the ancient silk route that led from Central Asia through the narrow corridor of oasis towns, hemmed in between the snow-capped Tianshan to the north and the barren Tarim Desert to the south. When he reached Suzhou within the Great Wall of China, Goís, still 1,000 miles from Beijing, died from sheer exhaustion and a severe illness. The heroic tale of this epic, if foolhardy, journey confirmed Ricci even more in the knowledge that the Cambulec in *The Travels of Marco Polo* was none other than Ming China. The hardy Isaac traveled on to Macao, where he embarked on a ship back to India, to be reunited with his wife and children, who had not seen him for seven years.

For Ricci, there was no going home. He felt old. 'I am already aged fifty-five,' he wrote Acquaviva in 1606, 'and pretty exhausted with this laborious enterprise, in which I have been engaged roughly twenty-five years.'[22] Two years later, he wrote to his friend Girolamo Costa, 'I shall be almost sixty years old, and thus very close to the grave. May it please God that I can finish this final act, which I still need to complete in the service of God, in correcting the faults of my past life.'[23] To his brother Antonio Maria in Macerata, Ricci described himself as 'in an age where I see myself growing feeble, even though in these last years I have been always healthy'.[24] In his last extant letter, dated 17 February 1609, to João Álvares, the Portuguese Assistant to General Acquaviva, Ricci was yet ready to continue his work: 'I am already old and tired, but healthy and strong; praise be to the Lord!'[25]

Travel is for the young. For the last nine years of his life, Ricci never set foot outside Beijing: the rural missions were entrusted to his younger colleagues and the Chinese catechists; and for the last five years of his life, Ricci hardly stepped beyond the threshold of the Jesuit compound, except to pay the obligatory courtesy visits, so 'beyond our strength'. Ricci had no need to travel. The whole world came to him in the form of visitors and letters; and he reached out to the world in his books. Such was the importance of books, Ricci wrote to Girolamo Costa, that it turned animosity to friendship:[26]

A great scholar lived close to our house: he was very haughty, of great fame among them [the Confucian literati], received a continuous stream of auditors in his house, and was promoted from a minor post at court to a higher one due to his virtue. Many times he had been invited to come and visit us on account of the fame of our letters and the novel things and good doctrines we discourse on, but in two years, nobody had succeeded in persuading him to visit. I don't know how he got hold of my *Ten Chapters of a Remarkable Man*, which he liked a lot, so that he suddenly came to see me in great humility, and has already invited me to two or three banquets at his home, and he has brought his friends, many people of importance, to come and visit us. From this, Your Reverence can understand how much you can obtain with the publication of books in China.

Since he lacked western books, Ricci added, he had written all his only from memory. Despite this, the Chinese scholars marveled at his learning. How much more could the younger missionaries achieve, if they were to follow in his footsteps. 'All this is due to the Lord, that such an inept instrument [himself] has served to such good effect, and for this reason I do everything possible that all our fathers study well Chinese books and learn to write books, for verily, while it's not easy to believe, more can be done with books than with the spoken word in China.'[27]

His modesty aside, Ricci was immensely proud of his books. They were his world. Ricci was much consoled that the Jesuits in Japan used his books.[28] When he received copies of Euclid in Chinese, his joint translation with Xu Guangqi, Ricci proudly sent copies to Acquaviva, Costa, and to his old professor, Clavius,[29] whose name was already known to many Chinese.[30] Other scientific works, collaborative translations, were published by his good friend Li Zhizao. To these and other works, important Chinese mandarins added their laudatory prefaces, expanding the fame of Ricci. Even the Muslims in China were reading the *True Meaning of the Lord of Heaven*, Ricci claimed.[31] Surely, the many reprints reflected his success. And none of his works was reprinted more times than the *World Map*. Now, even the emperor demanded a copy. On discovering the woodblocks were worn out, Ricci had fashioned for the imperial palace a new and elaborate representation of the *World Map* on a lacquered screen, the fifth printing and a mobile work, as it were.

If Emperor Wanli remained secluded, inaccessible to Ricci, he was at least open to the Jesuit's world. The imperial reprinting of the *World Map* was as secure a guarantee for the mission as an official edict, which was anyhow impossible to obtain, answered Ricci in a letter to the queries of Francesco Pasio, the new Visitor of the Jesuit Far East.[32] Many Turks traveled to China without official permits; unlike Tokugawa Japan, there was no law in China that stipulated the death penalty for foreigners who entered illegally. Better to just send more missionaries without asking for license, advised Ricci. Summing up a lifetime's experience in China, Ricci thought it better to have a small, high-quality Christian community than a large multitude. Specifically, it was far more important for the Jesuits to know Chinese well than to have another 10,000 new baptisms: 'to know our own [letters] without knowing theirs serves nothing... I myself value it [knowledge of Chinese letters] more than another ten thousand converts, since this is the way for the universal conversion of the realm.'[33] The only danger that existed for the Jesuits came from their continuing connection to the Portuguese in Macao, who remained suspect, as recent memorials by imperial censors demonstrated. On balance, Ricci was optimistic.

As for the Chinese, among whom he had lived so many years, 'the cause of his gray hair', Ricci conceded adjustment at first had not come easily. Not so much eating rice, and going without bread and wine, but in sleeping on hard beds and hard pillows, as the Chinese were wont to do. And while they, the Jesuits, gladly imitated the literati in many things, 'all dressed in honorable Chinese style with long sleeves and square berets, with long beards and long hair, we cannot imitate [the literati] in their fastidious ways with finger nails, which many wear more than a palm and a half in length, and, in order they may not crack, they put long tubes over them, something that seems filthy and deformed to us, but taken very seriously by them, since they are more fragile than glass'.[34] After a lifetime of ambivalence, Ricci had forgiven the unkindness the Chinese had inflicted upon him early on in his career. 'It is superfluous for me to speak of the intelligence of this people,' confided Ricci to Acquaviva on his opinion of the Chinese, 'to whom all the peoples of the Orient yield, and they are very much devoted to letters, and if they do not have great philosophers it is because they have never had true philosophy. But if they are taught this, they will not only be equal to us, I think, but will surpass us in many things. We can say this also about their religion: if they do not believe in their own priests, it is because they perceive that everything is based on falsehood; one can hope that once having been taught the true religion, they will not refuse it.'[35] And leading the way to conversion, Ricci believed, would be the Confucian scholars, 'who had always governed China . . . and [who] never speak of supernatural things, and are almost completely in agreement with us in ethics'. By not disputing the Confucian scholars, but in interpreting their teachings in the manner of Christianity, and in suggesting this was indeed the way of their own ancient sages, 'many of them have become Christians and give manifest signs of being good Christians, going to confession and receiving communion, and showing themselves, to their own strength and will, their love of our holy faith'.[36]

One summer day in 1608, some eunuchs and mandarins invited Ricci for a tour of the city walls. The massive masonry defended the imperial capital against many northern barbarians. Such was the breadth of the wall that ten horses could gallop on top of it or seven or eight carriages could drive side by side. At every stone throw, Ricci came across a sentry post. 'I could not count the numbers, but without doubt, there were many hundreds,' as Ricci recounted his tour of the defensive walls to Fabio de Fabii, continuing: 'Other than this there are many towers and in this part a very broad anti-wall, where one finds two other gates in the square, and that this square anti-wall is located outside of the city gate with towers much higher than the city wall itself. Surely, more than a million soldiers and officers are guarding day and night at the Great Wall itself.' Musing on their fear of invaders, Ricci wrote:

We can hardly believe that a realm so great and with so many soldiers would have a constant fear of other kingdoms that are so small . . . that the Chinese trust no foreign kingdom; and thus they do not let in anyone, except those who do not return, the way we are now. Even if we were to think of returning to our land, they would never consent. In this way, my Father, there is no hope that we will see one another again, except in the other life. Pray, Your Reverence, that God may make me worthy of it, when this comes to an end.[37]

Atop the walls of Beijing, Ricci looked over a brown and dusty plain, extending as far as his eyes could see, the waters of the ocean, and the cities he had lived in—Nanjing, Macao, Goa, Lisbon, and Rome—beyond his gaze if not his imagination. Once he had set foot within the precincts of Beijing, on 24 January 1601, Ricci remained within its massive walls; once he settled in Zhaoqing, on 11 September 1583, there was no returning from the realm of the Great Ming. Ricci had turned his back on the places and people of his youth. And so many memories in China itself, so many companions, now dead, so many acquaintances, so many friends, so many admirers, that the living and the dead, the past and the present, the country of his birth and longing, and the land he had adopted, mingled into a seamless whole.

To that seamless whole, Ricci brought division. Mastering the abundance of memories, Ricci placed each event, every person, all places in his life into specific rooms in his memory, a space so grand as to resemble more the imperial palace in the Forbidden City, rather than his own more modest residence. 'At the end of last year [1608] I don't know how, but it came to my mind that I am the only one left from the first ones who had entered into this realm, and that nobody knows the things that had happened in the beginning. Since it was good to write down everything in the order they happened, I had written down many things that I had experienced myself, but sometimes differently from the way things actually occurred. For this reason, I am beginning to write a report of what I think about these things that will be of great pleasure [to read].'[38]

The year 1610 was another year of triennial scrutiny and metropolitan civil service examination. Once again, thousands of mandarins and aspiring scholars streamed to the capital. 'This flood immensely increased the fatigue of Father Ricci since all the literati either know him personally or are attracted by his books,' wrote de Ursis, Ricci's Italian companion in the Beijing residence, 'and it is incredible how they flood to our residence. These waves of visitors began during Lent, on account of which the Father was constrained to interrupt his meals to receive his guests. And since he had the strictest scruples in observing exactly all ecclesiastical fasts, the fellow Jesuits cannot persuade him to resume his interrupted meals or to eat at another hour or to take some light refreshments.' During this time, Li Zhizao fell gravely ill. Ricci nursed his good friend back to health, all the while admonishing Li to think of the afterlife. Having resisted baptism for eight years, Li relented. He agreed to send away his concubine, the obstacle that had stood in the way of perfect friendship with Ricci, by embracing the faith of his friend and collaborator. For certain, the conversion of Li Zhizao consoled Ricci, whose own strength was further depleted in caring for his sick friend. On 3 May, returning from a visit 'beyond our strength', Ricci retired exhausted to his room. His fellow Jesuits went to their superior, who told them he felt fatigued and that he was mortally ill. Li Zhizao sent his personal physician; the Jesuits hired six of the best doctors in Beijing; they came up with three different prescriptions. When news came out, many converts went to church to join the Jesuits in praying for Ricci's recovery. Lacking medical authority, they placed all three prescriptions in front of the crucifix. Eventually, they chose one to give to the bedridden Ricci, to no effect. On 8 May, after six days in bed, Ricci made a general confession of sins to de Ursis. The next day, Ricci received communion in the morning. At the hour of three or four in the afternoon, the feverish Ricci fell in and out of consciousness. At times, he responded clearly to questions; at times, he spoke a continuous stream of feverish words, of the conversion of China and of the emperor. After twenty-four hours, Ricci regained consciousness. He received extreme unction. Surrounded by his fellow Jesuits and converts, Ricci spoke of the charity they needed to show newly arrived missionaries, of leaving his companions 'at a threshold opened after great effort, but not without many perils and labors', and of his admiration for the French Jesuit Pierre Coton, whom Ricci had never met, confessor to the dauphin of Henry IV, the king who had converted from Calvinism to ascend the throne. Worn out beyond his strength after twenty-seven years of labor, Ricci passed away his last hours in lucid conversations with his companions and converts. In his ultimate moment, Ricci retired to the private chamber of his mind, closing the door behind him, and walked into an infinite flood of images beyond words.

Matteo Ricci died on 11 May 1610 at the age of 58.

Epilogue

U nder the arches formed by dancing branches of cypresses and angled twigs of pines, Ricci lay in a marble tomb with Latin and Chinese inscriptions. The cemetery was located just outside the Fuchengmen, a gate in the mid-point of the western walls of the Inner City, still referred to by its old Yuan name Pingzemen by the Ming residents of Beijing. With their fondness for direct elocution, the people called the cemetery Zhalan, literally the wooden gates, in reference to the fences that marked off the site. In his peaceful loneliness, with only the cypresses and pines to remind him of the Roman countryside, Ricci waited. He was the first, but not the last. Many brothers of his beloved Company, the Society of Jesus, would find their resting places next to him, for Ricci had indeed cleared the hard soil for workers in the missionary vineyard.[1] Some 500 came, between his death and the dissolution of the Old Society in 1773; they hailed from all over Catholic Europe: Portuguese, Spaniards, Italians, French, Belgians, Germans, Austrians, and Poles; a small minority, in the course of time, was recruited among the Chinese converts.

If the dead could gaze at the heavens, Zhalan was a veritable academy of astronomers. Under the starry skies of Beijing other Jesuit astronomers joined Ricci in the cemetery: the German Johann Terrenz Schreck was buried there in 1630, the Italian Giacomo Rho in 1638, another German, Johann Adam Schall von Bell, in 1666, and the Fleming Ferdinand Verbiest in 1688; still others added to the company in the course of the eighteenth century. The first three arrived in China together in 1618, having been recruited by the Belgian Jesuit Nicolas Trigault, who played a crucial role in propagating the Riccian legacy.

Born in Douai in the Spanish Netherlands, Nicolas Trigault (1577–1628) joined the Society of Jesus in 1594. His petition for missionary work in

'the Indies' having been approved, Trigault shipped for Goa in 1607 and
eventually arrived in China in 1610. Serving in Hangzhou, Beijing, and
Nanjing, Trigault was selected as procurer for the Jesuit Mission in China by
his superior Niccolò Longobardo. In February 1613, Trigault traveled back
to Europe, entrusted with the task of raising money and recruiting reinforcements for the budding China Mission; among the papers Trigault carried
with him was the manuscript journal kept by Ricci. During the long maritime
voyage, Trigault translated Ricci's memoirs into Latin, a language accessible to
all educated readers in Europe. After traveling through India, Persia, and
Egypt, Trigault finally arrived in Rome on 11 October 1614.

As spokesman for the Jesuit China Mission, Trigault succeeded brilliantly. With his Chinese silk robe, his scholar's hat, his report of steady
evangelical progress and the prospect of millions of souls to be saved, all
backed up by the master narrative of the master missionary, the late Matteo
Ricci, Trigault scored major successes: he gained papal permission to substitute Chinese for Latin as the language of the Catholic mass, for the
Chinese people, Trigault argued, could not distinguish between many
consonants of the Latin alphabet; he won for the China Mission the support
of the mightiest Catholic monarch, Philip III of Spain; and he persuaded
General Acquaviva to command the creation of an independent Vice-
Province of China within the organization of the Society, one of the last
acts of Acquaviva before his death. Meanwhile, Trigault's edition of the
Riccian memoirs was published in Augsburg in 1615 under the title *Five
Books dedicated to our holy lord Paul V on the Christian Expedition in China
undertaken by the Society of Jesus and Father Matteo Ricci of the same society, in
which are accurately and most faithfully described the customs and laws of that
Chinese realm, and the difficult beginnings of its newly instituted Church.*[2] Trigault
then listed himself as the author. The title page of the book used theatrical
images so well developed by the Jesuits in their sacred drama and forty-hour
devotions during Lent: it depicts Ignatius Loyola (with a halo) and Matteo
Ricci (in the garb of a Ming scholar) standing as column figures framing and
supporting a Jesuit church; a large white curtain containing the title and data
of publication drapes the entrance, complemented by a partial view of
Ricci's World Map (see Figure 12). This mise-en-scène invites the viewer
to imagine the holy drama that would unfold and urges him to enter into the
theater of missionary action by turning the pages. A second Lyons edition
followed in 1616, a third Cologne edition in 1617. *On the Christian Expedition in China* was a great publication and propaganda success. More than a

Figure 12. *De Christiana Expeditione apud Sinas*, frontispiece

translator, Trigault intervened in the presentation of Ricci's memoirs, deleting, adding, and generally presenting the work in a more seamless narrative, thus justifying perhaps his own attribution of 'author'.

In May 1616, Trigault left Rome on his recruitment tour, passing through Lyons, Munich, Cologne, and Antwerp. Everywhere he went, Trigault stayed in local Jesuit colleges, firing up the fervor and imagination of young

Jesuits by his very presence, and by the rhetoric of extraordinary adventure and glorious missions. His passage swelled by new Jesuit missionary recruits, Trigault gained audiences with the leading princes and prelates of Catholic Germany, securing financial contributions from the Duke of Bavaria and the Archbishop of Cologne before passing on to his native Netherlands. There, in the studio of the greatest painter of his age, Peter Paul Rubens (1577–1640), Trigault allowed himself to don the silk robes of the Chinese scholar and posed for a sketch by the great master (see Plate X). This ink and watercolor sketch strikes an interesting contrast to the portrait of Ricci by You Wenhui (see jacket). Both men are attired in the black silk robes and high square hats, the Su Dongbo style of Ming literati dress, but the similarities end here. In You's painting, Ricci's masculine authority is expressed by a lion's mane of white beard, his scholarship exemplified by his long, elegant nose, his diplomacy symbolized by clasped and concealed hands, and his iron will revealed in his steady gaze. In contrast, Trigault seems a delicate, almost fragile figure in Rubens's rendering. He is much thinner, perhaps reflecting the physical strain of two global voyages and numerous journeys within China and Europe in under a decade. His long, thin beard makes him look more Chinese than European. Above all, Trigault's eyes, vivid and intelligent, looking away from the viewer under knotted brows, betray a look of anxiety. Here is a personality altogether more sensitive, nervous, and fragile than the master missionary Ricci. We are perhaps reading too much into Rubens's portrait in view of Trigault's last years, a subject to which we will presently return. Meanwhile, at the height of his glory, strengthened by missionary recruits and his coffers filled, Trigault traveled in triumph, setting sail from Lisbon in mid-April 1618, taking with him a new cohort of young Jesuits, among them Johann Schreck, Giacombo Rho, and Adam Bell, the three missionaries destined to serve as mathematicians for the Chinese emperor and companions in death to Matteo Ricci.

While Trigault galloped about Europe with the wind of success in his back, the Jesuit Mission in China was battered by a storm. In 1616, Shen Que (1565–1624), the Vice-Minister of Rites in Nanjing, petitioned the emperor against the Jesuits in the two Ming capitals. Shen objected to the projected reform of the imperial calendar to be undertaken by Pantoja and de Ursis in Beijing, and he excoriated Alfonso Vagnone (1568–1640) and Álvaro Semedo (1586–1658) in Nanjing for undermining Confucian ethics by prohibiting certain rites of ancestor worship. Despite counter-memorials submitted by Xu Guangqi and Yang Tingyun, another mandarin-convert, an imperial edict of 3 February 1617 exiled the four Jesuits to Macao. There, Ricci's old companions passed away, Pantoja in 1618 and de Ursis two years later, both men, no doubt, crushed by personal disappointments. Other Jesuits prudently went underground, protected by Yang Tingyun in his native Hangzhou. Fierce but short, the 1616–17 persecutions did not damage the foundations of the Jesuit Mission. By 1619, when Trigault and his recruits arrived in Macao, the winds were again blowing in favor of the Jesuit vessel. In 1629, Xu Guangqi petitioned the new emperor Chongzhen (reigned 1628–44) to reform the calendar, after still another failure by the imperial astronomers to predict accurately an eclipse. Worried by the failures of the Ming state and anxious for reform (for were not all heavenly phenomena manifestations of the Mandate of Heaven and had profound messages for statecraft?), the Chongzhen emperor entrusted Xu to establish a new Calendar Office and summon the Jesuit mathematicians to serve in the emendation of the calendar. Schreck, Rho, and Schall were the first Jesuit mandarins, to be followed by Verbiest and a long line of other mathematician-missionaries, astronomical experts in the Directorate of Astronomy, serving their terms even beyond the dissolution of the Old Society of Jesus in 1773.

If the Jesuit side of the Riccian legacy was assured in a line of missionary succession for the next 160 years, its impact on the Chinese Christian community enabled the latter to survive the catastrophic crisis of dynastic change in the mid-seventeenth century. Ricci's friends, at least, were spared that calamity. It may be recalled that Qu Rukui, Ricci's oldest friend in China, only accepted baptism in 1607. His concubinage had represented an obstacle. Only after the death of his first wife and 'marrying' his concubine could Rukui join the Catholic Church. His son Shigu, a boy of 15, followed his father into the new faith. In memory of their friendship, Qu Rukui named the boy Matteo after Ricci, whose prayers, it seemed, had gained for Rukui his precious offspring.[3] Having been forgiven and quietly received back by his clan, Qu Rukui died in 1612 in his native Changshu, two years after the death of his good friend Ricci. A new generation carried on the Jesuit—literati friendship. Qu Shigu became a strong supporter of the mission, welcoming the Italian Jesuit Giulio Aleni in 1623 to his hometown to preach the western faith.

Of Ricci's friends in Beijing, Xu Guangqi not only outlived his western mentor by twenty-three years, but would become the single most important individual in the history of early Chinese Catholicism, whose patronage and protection enabled the Jesuit mission to thrive during the last decades of the Ming dynasty.[4] Between the death of Ricci (1610) and his retirement to Shanghai (1622), Xu Guangqi struggled to maintain his position in the increasingly bitter strife between mandarin factions. Splitting his responsibility between the household of the heir apparent and the urgent task of training troops, Xu Guangqi found time to pursue experiments in agronomy at his private farm near Tianjin. His multiple activities all aimed at one goal: strengthening China. The education of an ethical heir apparent for just rule, the training of effective troops for defense against the Manchus, and the improvement of farming to increase agricultural production all reflected the traditional concerns of an upright mandarin. But for Xu Guangqi, these public concerns merged seamlessly with his private religious devotion. Like other elite converts of the late Ming, Xu Guangqi expected the teachings of Catholicism to result in ethical behavior and social discipline. Christianity, to use a metaphor current in Jesuit literature, represented the best medicine for a sick society, one in profound social, political, and spiritual malaise.

This political malaise, together with Xu's ill health, prompted him to retire from public life in 1622. In imperial politics, the mandarin faction under the patronage of the powerful eunuch Wei Zhongxian emerged triumphant and vengeful. Many mandarins in the opposition faction, the so-called Donglin movement, were executed, imprisoned, or forced to resign. Wisely, Xu Guangqi maintained his neutrality, devoting his years in retirement to promoting the Catholic cause in his native Shanghai. In 1628, Zhu Youjian ascended the throne as the Chongzhen emperor. The young man, ambitious for reforms, swept Wei Zhongxian and the eunuch faction from power. The emperor summoned Xu Guangqi to serve as the Right Vice-Minister of Rites. Inspite of his advanced age at 66, Xu Guangqi readily accepted the nomination. In the last years of his public life, Xu Guangqi labored to reform Ming statecraft and promote Christianity, of which the introduction of Jesuit astronomers into the imperial bureaucracy represented the most tangible and permanent achievement. The highest positions within the imperial bureaucracy distinguished these short years of Xu's career: first promoted to be Minister of Rites, an old and ill Xu Guangqi was named Grand Secretary in August 1633, only three months before his death on 8 November 1633. The Jesuits in China deeply mourned his death and praised him as one of the Three Pillars (together with Li Zhizao and Yang Tingyun) of their nascent Church. The Xu

Figure 13. Statue of Xu Guangqi at Guangqi Park, Shanghai

family compound, to the west of Ming Shanghai and a suburb of today's metropolis, served not only as Xu Guangqi's burial ground but one of the centers of Catholicism in China (see Figure 13).

To the outside, Chinese Catholicism grew by leaps and bounds. The 2,500 converts at the time of Ricci's death matured into a community of 13,000 on the eve of Chongzhen's ascension. During the Chongzhen reign (1628–44), a fantastic 31 per cent average annual growth rate, never sur-passed in the history of Christianity in China, swelled the ranks of the Christian community to 70,000.[5] This robust external growth belied a crisis within the Jesuit Mission. After succeeding Ricci as superior in China, Niccolò Longobardo grew increasingly skeptical of the Riccian method. The Sicilian Jesuit disapproved of Ricci's Confucian–Christian synthesis and doubted the doctrinal understanding of the leading mandarin and literati converts. A charismatic preacher among the common people, Longobardo thought of Confucianism as atheist, and most Ming scholars as materialist philosophers. His misgivings bolstered by criticisms of Ricci's Chinese texts voiced by Jesuits in Japan, Longobardo pushed for a re-evaluation of Ricci's methods and legacy.

Already as a young missionary in Shaozhou, Longobardo began to develop a critical attitude toward Ricci's methods. He wrote:[6]

The Chinese name for [the Christian] God, '*Shangdi*' (Emperor on High) I first saw some twenty-five years ago [1598] and immediately felt uneasy. This was because after I had learned the Confucian classics (a requirement after having arrived in China), I was made aware that the name *Shangdi* has many different connotations which do not at all accord with the natural qualities of divinity. However, when the society's priests first heard the name *Shangdi*, they opened up their troubled hearts to allow for the formulation of a new concept of God; this concept perhaps differed with the scholarly glosses and connotations of the Confucian *Four Books*, but scholars' commentaries can also differ greatly from the meaning of the original canonical texts. I spent thirteen years in Shaozhou without the opportunity for serious reflection on this point. After assuming the position as superior after the death of Father Ricci, I received a letter from the Visitor of the Japanese Province, Father Francesco Pasio. He said that the priests in Japan believed our Chinese writings contained doctrinal errors, causing them to waste their energies in refutation. Thus, he begged me to thoroughly investigate the situation, for he found it difficult to imagine that someone who had written these works in Chinese, an accomplished theologian knowledgeable in the Chinese classics, could fall into such grave doctrinal errors. After reading the letter, my old suspicions were confirmed.

Although Longobardo mentioned no names, he was doubtless referring to Ricci. In the role as superior in the China Mission, Longobardo commanded all Jesuit priests in China to share their opinions of the terms *Shangdi*, *tianshen* (angels), *linghun* (soul), and the Confucian classics (*Four Books* and *Five Classics*). Among the responses, there were some who believed that ancient China did in fact possess a concept of the true God; others understood neo-Confucianism as a materialistic philosophy that acknowledged no divinities.

Convinced that the synthesis of Catholicism and Confucianism had compromised the doctrinal purity of the Church, Longobardo wrote in 1623 the treatise 'Several Views regarding Chinese Religion' in which he expressed his belief that neo-Confucian philosophers propound a materialistic universe, and that the Chinese literati were basically atheists, thereby forcefully opposing Ricci's distinction between a pristine, naturalistic, and quasi-Christian ancient Chinese philosophy and a corrupted neo-Confucianism. In 1627, eleven Jesuit priests in China gathered for a conference in Jiading. Although Longobardo commanded that the use of *tian*, *Shangdi*, and

Tianzhu be prohibited as synonyms for the Christian God, the majority of missionaries under the leadership of the Belgian Nicolas Trigault fervently supported Ricci's missionary strategy, which also enjoyed the complete support of the leading Chinese convert-officials. The result of the conference was that the names *tian* and *Shangdi*, words that are found in the ancient Chinese classics, were abandoned in Catholic discourse, while the neologism *Tianzhu* was retained, thereby drawing a sharper boundary between the Catholic and Confucian worlds.

Regarding the worship of Confucius and ancestors, the conference decided to uphold Ricci's prior policies. Having been ratified by the General of the Society in Rome, Jesuit missionaries in China unanimously supported this modified policy of cultural accommodation. As a result, Longobardo's 'Several Views regarding Chinese Religion' was suppressed after Jiading. In the mid-seventeenth century, however, the French Jesuit Jean Valet, who was sympathetic to Longobardo's position, passed a manuscript copy to the Franciscan friar Antonio Caballero de Santa Maria. The latter, highly critical of the Riccian method of cultural accommodation, in turn passed this on to the Dominican friar Domingo Navarete, who published the tract in a Spanish translation in his own book, *The History of the Chinese Empire, Government, Ethics and Religion*. In time, this would constitute the first barrel of gunpowder in the Chinese Rites Controversy, which would blow apart the foundations of the Catholic mission.[7]

As defender of the Riccian legacy, Nicolas Trigault emerged victorious in the 1627 Jiading Conference, but his nerves were stretched beyond the breaking point. Sensitive, delicate, and anxious, as we have seen from the Rubens portrait, Trigault sank into a prolonged depression and hanged himself on 14 November 1628 in Hangzhou. To save themselves from scandal, the Jesuits hushed up the suicide, referring to it only in secret codes.[8] Yet the saintliness of Ricci remained untarnished by the mortal sin of his chief promoter, just as the Jesuit Mission survived the slaughter of the Manchu conquest of China.

When peasant rebels conquered Beijing in March 1644 and Manchu troops poured in through the Great Wall, the Ming regime started to die an agonizingly slow death that lasted nearly forty years. Jesuit missionaries, Chinese converts, as well as millions of people perished in massacres and natural disasters. For a while, Ricci's words seemed to have come true: 'Even the emperor of China has become a Christian,' as Ricci mused in his 1605 letter about exaggerated reports of his success in Rome. In their desperation, the rulers of the Southern Ming, the resistance regime to the new Manchu Qing conquerors, welcomed the help of the westerners, be it the guns of the Portuguese or the God of the Jesuits.[9] In 1648, the court of Yongli in Guilin, the court of the last Southern Ming emperor, witnessed three key conversions: the empress and two empress dowagers, baptized as Anna, Helena, and Maria. Even Emperor Yongli himself considered conversion, the Jesuits claimed, only to be held back by the unacceptable condition of Christian monogamy. But Yongli reluctantly agreed to the baptism of the baby heir apparent, upon the empress's pressure, when the boy fell into a fever and only recovered after baptism. This Constantine failed to live up to the achievements of his Roman namesake, for he and his father were garroted in 1662 in Yunnan by Wu Sanguei, a Ming general who had surrendered to serve his new Manchu masters.

Others prospered in the new regime. Thanks to his prominence in the Directorate of Astronomy, the German Jesuit Adam Schall shielded the Catholic community in Beijing, first from the rebel troops under Li Zicheng, then under the new Manchu Qing regime. In time, Schall befriended the young Qing emperor Shunzhi, who looked upon the westerner almost as a father figure, bestowing upon Schall the honor of a first rank mandarin. In the mandarin robes of a new dynasty, Schall ensured the survival and prosperity of the Jesuit Mission. In spite of a brief period of persecution after the death of Shunzhi in 1664–5, the Catholic mission flourished under the Emperor Kangxi (reigned 1662–1723). Interrupted by the crisis of the mid-seventeenth century, the line of missionary succession resumed under Kangxi.

One century after Ricci's installation in Beijing, the founder of the Catholic mission would have every reason to smile in his grave. In 1701, there were an estimated 200,000 converts and 153 clerics in China. The latter figure included 9 Chinese priests, all Jesuits, and 82 European Jesuits.[10] Working the vineyards alongside other religious orders, often jealous and hostile, the Jesuits still comprised two-thirds of the clergy and contributed over 80 per cent of all Chinese Catholic writings. Catholic churches were to be found in nearly every province of the Qing empire, and Kangxi himself showed great familiarity with his Jesuit advisers, learning Latin, mathematics, and western science from them, and benefiting from their use of quinine to recover from a relapse of smallpox, a disease he had contracted as a child and one that had killed his father, the Shunzhi emperor. Again, the Jesuits talked excitedly about the prospect of an imperial conversion.

Then everything changed. Only nine years later, on the centenary of Ricci's death, Christianity was forbidden to the Chinese people. The missionaries had only themselves to blame. For half a century, the arguments over Chinese rituals between the Jesuits and the mendicant orders in China increased in intensity and animosity. Had the first Jesuit missionaries accommodated too much to Chinese culture? Had Ricci and his followers diluted the contents of Christianity to such an extent that the Chinese were practicing a cult hardly worth its name? Could students, scholars, and mandarins, if they were Christian converts, show respect to Confucius without compromising themselves in perhaps 'idolatrous' rites? Was it proper to call the ancient Chinese sages saints who might have gained heaven by dint of their virtue instead of confining them to hell fire for living in a state of sin and ignorance of the 'true faith'? Was it filial piety or idolatry to offer food and drink to one's ancestors, inscribing their names on wooden tablets, keeping their pictures in family shrines, and 'honoring them in death as if they were living'? Where did culture end and religion begin? How could Christianity represent itself without its European expression and without compromising its true essence? All these and other questions, cultural and theological, afflicted the expanding and increasingly divided Christian enterprise in China. Delegates to Rome, theological controversies, pronouncements by the Holy Office and the Propaganda Fidei, diplomatic overtures, and even a papal legate to China in 1700 failed to resolve this crisis. Fed up by incessant squabbling among the westerners and angered by foreign pronouncements regarding Chinese cultural practices, Kangxi forbade his subjects in 1705 to practice Christianity. Westerners were allowed the right to worship according to their customs, the edict declared, but they should refrain from proselytizing. All western missionaries who wished to remain in China had to swear by 'the methods of Father Ricci' and promise never to return to the West. The Dominicans, the Augustinians, and the priests of the Paris Missions Étrangères left en masse; the Franciscans were deeply divided over the issue; and among the fathers of the Company, except for a handful of Portuguese, all Jesuits in China swore to uphold 'the methods of Father Ricci'.

Perhaps this was enough of a consolation for Ricci in his grave. The 1705 imperial edict was seldom enforced over the next eighty years. Occasional persecutions owed their origins either to political factors or to the zeal of individual regional and local officials. The Catholic Church continued to grow, albeit at a slower pace, and a larger rank of Chinese priests complemented the work of underground European missionaries. Yet, Ricci was not forgotten. Between 1773 and 1782, Emperor Qianlong commissioned the *Siku Quanshu*, the *Imperial Collection of Four Treasures*, an encyclopedic compendium of over 10,000 books and manuscripts approved by the Qing state. The editors included several scientific works by Ricci, the only Jesuit author to be honored out of the forty who had published in Chinese.

There was little to celebrate at the bicentennial of Ricci's death. Under the grandson and great-grandson of Kangxi, the emperors Qianlong (reigned 1736–96) and Jiaqing (reigned 1796–1820), sporadic persecutions made martyrs of western missionaries and Chinese converts, although they resulted in only a handful of deaths and scores of exiles, almost peaceful in comparison to the bloody martyrdom of thousands killed in the repression of Christianity in Tokugawa Japan. Worse still, the Society of Jesus existed no more. Having made too many powerful enemies, in part due to its pride and success, the Society incurred the wrath of the Portuguese, Spanish, and French monarchies. Dissolved in 1773, Jesuit missionaries were shipped back from the colonial domains of Spain and Portugal, some suffering long years of imprisonment in Portuguese jails. Only in 1814 did Pope Pius VII reverse the bull of suppression.

Like the Catholic Church, the Society of Jesus recovered rapidly in post-Napoleonic Europe. Jesuit missionaries were once again ready to preach the gospel in China, when the Qing empire was defeated, by the British in the First Opium War (1839–42) and by joint Anglo-French attacks in the Second Opium War (1858–60). The treaties forced the Qing regime to open up the empire to foreign diplomats, western goods, and Christian missionaries. Under the diplomatic and military protection of France, Jesuits and other Catholic missionaries came to China with diplomatic status and new powers. To the Chinese, they appeared representatives of western powers and an extension of European aggression. Upon returning, the Jesuits initiated scores of lawsuits, trying to reclaim properties confiscated more than a century earlier. Everywhere, the missionaries protected Christian converts, intervening in civil and property disputes, appealing to local magistrates and to their own consuls. And as their influence increased, so did the Chinese hatred toward all things Christian and western. Forgotten was the synthesis between Confucianism and Christianity, the harmony of East and West. Overwhelmingly, the Confucian elites of the late Qing were staunchly anti-Christian if not outright xenophobic. Rumors and myths multiplied. Some originated in paranoid fantasies: missionaries paid for

conversions, killed babies after baptisms, and gouged out eyes of the living
to make medicine. Others rang true: they furnished intelligence to foreign
governments, they decried Chinese culture as superstitious, and generally
did not hesitate to call upon their diplomats and soldiers for protection and
pressure. In 1870, a mob in Tianjin killed a pistol-waving French consul, and
a dozen missionaries and converts. Under pressure, the Qing government
executed scores of ringleaders to placate France. It was a harbinger of things
to come.

In 1899, local conflicts in Shangdong and Hebei provinces escalated into
a general anti-Christian movement. There were many fuses that led to this
explosion: one was the competition between villages for resources that
assumed an anti-Christian character when the communities in question
involved Christian villages; another was the rise of a regional indigenous
movement, the Boxers, who claimed medical and magical powers in addition to their martial prowess. Soon, the Boxers targeted Christian converts
and foreign missionaries as their chief enemies. 'Expel all westerners, restore
the dynasty', such was the slogan of the Boxers, who allowed themselves to
be maneuvered by the anti-western faction at the imperial court. With the
connivance of the court, the Boxers entered Beijing and laid siege to the
foreign legations, where western missionaries and Chinese converts had
escaped to. An invasion by troops of eight nations lifted the siege and crushed
the Boxers. A humiliating treaty was imposed on the Qing. In addition
to killing hundreds of Christians and scores of westerners, the Boxers
rampaged through Zhalan in June 1900, destroying all eighty-eight graves,
opening the tombs, burning the remains, and scattering the ashes to the four
winds.

In time, the Catholic Church regained Zhalan, reburied any human
remains to be found, and cast new tombstones. It was much harder,
however, for Catholic Europe to absorb the shock of the Boxer violence.
As the tercentennial of Ricci's death approached, the need to remember and
celebrate the pioneer missionary became more urgent, in light of China's
recent xenophobic and nationalistic rejection of western Christianity. The
young Kingdom of Italy expressed its nationalist pride in holding a conference of geographers and Oriental scholars in Macerata, in celebration of its
famous native son, 'geographer and apostle in China'.[11] The Catholic
Church was not left behind. After nearly three centuries, the Jesuits finally
dusted off the manuscript sent by Sabatino de Ursis, one of Ricci's Jesuit
companions in Beijing; this earliest biography of Ricci appeared in print

only on the eve of the tercentenary of his death.[12] Nor was this the only publishing event. Pietro Tacchi-Venturi (1861–1956), official historian of the Society of Jesus, transcribed and published the Italian manuscript of Ricci's memoirs kept in the Roman Archives of the Society. For the first time, Ricci's voice spoke directly to posterity, instead of Trigault's interpreted translations. The first volume of the *Opere storiche del P. Matteo Ricci* appeared in 1911, the year of the republican revolution in China and one year after the inauguration of the Italian colonial empire with the invasion of Libya; the second volume followed two years later. Tacchi-Venturi included letters written by Ricci as well as by other Jesuits in his orbit, although one has to wait until 2001 for a critical modern edition of these letters. In spite of his erudition, Tacchi-Venturi was careless in his use of Jesuit papers not from Ricci's pens: the few folios from Ruggieri's journal included in the documentary appendix were wrongly attributed to Rodolfo Acquaviva. More serious was Tacchi-Venturi's ignorance of Chinese, which meant that the *Opere storiche* remained severely limited in its scholarship and reliability. Well aware of these shortcomings himself, Tacchi-Venturi hardly had the time to deepen his scholarship. During the 1920s and 1930s, the Jesuit historian acted as the chief liaison between popes Pius XI and Pius XII and Mussolini, whom he had befriended in 1922. As the confessor to il Duce, Tacchi-Venturi exerted an enormous informal influence behind the scenes, and played a key role in concluding the Lateran Treaties that established relations between the Vatican and the Italian state. His intimacy with Fascism even provoked an assassination attempt in 1928. In his busy role as 'the man in black', Tacchi-Venturi had not forgotten Ricci. In 1933, he summoned Pasquale D'Elia (1890–1963) to Rome in order to prepare a new critical edition of Ricci's work.

Meanwhile, Jesuit missionaries continued to draw inspiration from Ricci. Trained as a mathematician, the French Jesuit Henri Bernard (1889–1975) identified with the scientific-religious tasks of his sixteenth-century Italian predecessor. Active in China between 1924 and 1947, Bernard briefly taught mathematics in Tianjin, but his interest in Jesuit missionary history soon moved him into full-time research. He is the author of several works on Ricci, notably a shorter work on the scientific contributions of Ricci in Ming China and a two-volume biography on Ricci and Chinese society.[13] A massive tome published in 1937, *Father Matteo Ricci and Chinese Society of his Age 1552–1610*, develops Ricci's career and late Ming society in parallel narratives that often fail to intersect. Relying on Tacchi-Venturi's edition of

Riccian writings, Bernard focuses his story on China, without neglecting Ricci's formative Roman years as well as his short but instructive sojourn in India. In relating Ricci's career, Bernard discourses at length, and sometimes straying far from the main narrative line, on Ming society, culture, and politics. Like Ricci's own *Dell'entrata*, Bernard addresses himself to a western readership, hence the assumption that Europe or Christian civilization need no explanation, and China, the object of curiosity and interest, together with the subject hero of the biography, would constitute the subject matter of the exposition. Without the benefit of a critical edition of Ricci's writings, and without adequate identification of Chinese personae and full consultation of Chinese sources, Bernard's biography remains a monument to the memory of Ricci, rather than a critical work of scholarship. That contribution would come, in the decade after Bernard's book, from a fellow Jesuit and a compatriot of Ricci.

A researcher at the Jesuit center of Zikawei (Xujiahui), the old home of Xu Guangqi in the western suburbs of Shanghai, D'Elia arrived in China as a young Jesuit in Shanghai, where he studied between 1913 and 1917. After further theological training in the United States and England, D'Elia returned to China in 1923 and taught at the Jesuit University Aurore in Shanghai. His training as a Sinologist and his long years of experience in Shanghai made D'Elia the ideal successor to Tacchi-Venturi. The senior Jesuit wanted the Jesuit-Sinologist to produce a new edition of Ricci's work that would incorporate Chinese characters and draw on Chinese sources. Professor of Missiology at the Jesuit Gregorian University and later Professor of Sinology at the State University of Rome as well, D'Elia devoted his life to the three-volume *Fonti Ricciane*, which has become the standard source work for the life and writings of Ricci. His immense erudition ensured that every Chinese person, institution, and event is minutely researched and documented in the *Fonti Ricciane*. In spite of minor mistakes in identification, the *Fonti Ricciane* remains an indispensable work and a monument to the rapprochement of Church and State in Fascist Italy, which projected a benign and civilizing image, both backward to the time of Catholic missions (Italian missionaries being less belligerent and culturally more suave than their Spanish, Portuguese, and French counterparts, so the message implied) and forward to the colonial projects of Fascist expansion. The *Fonti Ricciane* represented a monument to scholarship in dramatic and difficult times. D'Elia undertook and completed the project as Mussolini launched Italians into a reluctant war. The first volume appeared in print in 1942 under the auspices of the State Printing House; the second and third volumes were published only in 1949, long after the death of Mussolini, in the post-war years when the rapport between the papacy and Fascism came under increasing scrutiny.

With the publication of the *Fonti Ricciane*, the heroic and central role of Ricci in the China Mission was established beyond any challenges. Everything and everyone prepared the way for the great missionary. Surrounded by his fellow brothers, Ricci took center stage as the star of the missionary drama. His senior and first companion in China, Michele Ruggieri, is described only as someone who 'prepared the way for Ricci, who introduced him to China, and then faded away in silence from the scene'.[14] It does not help that on the title page of Ruggieri's manuscript, an archivist has written the comment: 'Non e da fidarsene punto, che il faso v'e a tre quarti del vero in molte narration' ('This is not to be trusted for three-quarters of the narration seems to be fabricated').[15] D'Elia, who quoted Ruggieri's barely legible journal much more extensively than Tacchi-Venturi, merely cannibalized it for use in his detailed commentaries on Ricci's text. A Catholic hero, a remarkable individual, seemed just the right antidote to the rising tide of the faceless communist masses. The year when D'Elia closed his work on Ricci was also the year when the Chinese communists slammed the door in the face of western missionaries.

If the Catholics had cast in their lot with Fascist anti-communism in the 1930s, the communists had not forgotten the missionaries. Three centuries after his death, only the spirit of Matteo Ricci remained in Zhalan. That spirit, alternately calm and agitated, hovered over the passing of regimes: the Qing dynasty overthrown in 1911–12, ending 5,000 years of imperial history; and the republic itself, with its precarious balance of Chinese nationalism and openness to the West, succumbing in turn to the Communist Revolution. After 1949, the Catholic Church was co-opted by the Chinese Catholic Patriotic Association, which denounced the history of western religious and colonial invasion; all western missionaries were forced to leave China; and Chinese clerics loyal to Rome spent years in labor camps and behind prison bars. Yet Ricci was not forgotten. In 1954, the Beijing Communist Party Committee built a school for party cadres on the site of Zhalan: most graves were moved, but the premier Zhou Enlai insisted on keeping the tombs of Ricci and other Jesuit missionaries in their original sites as cultural monuments under the protection of the State Council. This move saved the tombstones from the violence of the Red Guards, who descended on Zhalan in August 1966 intending to smash up all things western, bourgeois, and imperialist. School authorities persuaded the young revolutionaries to bury the tombstones instead of smashing them up. When the storm passed, the tombstones once again graced the resting place of Ricci and his companions (see Figure 14).

During the years when China was convulsed by waves of revolutionary fervor, the memory of Ricci seemed restricted to the West. In the United States, with the country's own political, economic, and missionary (albeit mostly Protestant) fantasies of a boundless China, and the subsequent disappointment after 1949, Ricci was remembered in the 1942 publication of his 'journal' in an English translation.[16] Louis Gallagher, however, translated Ricci from Nicolas Trigault's Latin translation; and his failure to adhere to the Latin transliterations of Chinese names conventional to sinology rendered this work a curious read but without scholarly merit. This edition was republished on the occasion of the 400th anniversary of Ricci's birth, an occasion that also inspired the highly readable account by

Figure 14. Entrance to the Jesuit Cemetery, Beijing

Vincent Cronin, the noted British biographer, who benefited from D'Elia's scholarship, and whose imaginative prose painted a wise Jesuit preaching Christianity to a 'fabled Cathay'.[17] A lively book, *The Wise Man from the West* depicts Ricci as he represented himself. Unable to read Chinese (the language of the majority of Ricci's work), Cronin describes the Jesuit's success as almost proceeding in a mysterious or providential fashion. And China, in its communist heyday in the early 1950s, remained in historical memory just a 'fabled Cathay' behind the reality of the bamboo curtain.

When western scholars turned their attention to Ricci, how different were their views! Within a couple of years of the 400th anniversary of the arrival of Ricci in China, two leading western sinologists published studies on Ricci and the Jesuit Mission that reflect profoundly different understandings of the Riccian enterprise. In his 1982 book *China and Christianity, the First Confrontation*, Jacques Gernet analyzes the profound opposition in thought and language between traditional China and the Christian West.[18] Refuting his critics' accusation that he had exaggerated the cultural differences between China and the West, Gernet gave a categorical reply ('Eh bien, non!') to the following questions: are human beings not everywhere the same and does not the most elementary logic impose a belief in the existence of a creator-God? Do similar religious aspirations not exist in all beings? He asserts:

In Europe as in China, religious sentiments and even the most ordinary and basic notions have their histories. What seemed self-evident to the missionaries was in no way the same for the Chinese of that period. Why, one says, could Ricci not have understood better the Chinese among whom he lived in familiarity rather than a historian of the 20th century? It is because Ricci, his companions and their successors were entirely persuaded that the questions which are debated here simply do not arise; and if the Chinese did not embrace with joy the religion that would bring them eternal salvation, it was due to the obstacles posed by their superstitions, the jealousy of Buddhist monks, and the hostility of the literati.[19]

Ricci himself realized the gulf between languages and structures of thought, Gernet argues, hence the Jesuit's heroic effort to learn Chinese and adapt his Christian message to a Confucian audience. Without calling this dissimulation, Gernet does write that Ricci failed to convey Christian doctrines accurately and in their entirety, citing the objection raised by Niccolò Longobardo as well as Buddhist anti-Christian polemics in the mid-seventeenth century. So deep was the abyss in language and thought, Gernet implies, that the vision of a created universe and a personal God incarnated on earth would never have been embraced by more than a tiny minority in Ming China.

Focusing on Ricci rather than on China, Jonathan Spence's book represents a different gaze.[20] Using Ricci's mnemonics as an opening, Spence penetrates Ricci's *Xiguo Jifa* to explore the mental world of the Italian missionary. Eschewing a conventional chronology of Ricci's life, Spence takes seriously the European formation of the Italian missionary. His succinct evocations of Macerata, Rome, and the Europe of the Counter-Reformation are some of the strongest parts of an otherwise idiosyncratic essay, one that focuses on a minor work by Ricci which made little impact in Ming society. Nonetheless, Spence's historical imagination and his ability to weave the different strands of European and Chinese history into a seamless narrative have, no doubt, inspired other accounts of Ricci's story. There is something irresistible in this narrative: by virtue of his intellect, a heroic individual bridges impossible chasms between civilizations, opening up a new world of understanding by the strength of his learning and genius.

It is this *ingegno*—ingenuity, talent, and quickness of mind, the Italian essence—that endears Matteo Ricci to his compatriots, who see in the scientific and religious figure of the Jesuit a model for the cultural and diplomatic relations between contemporary Italy and China. Ingenious in diplomacy and dissimulation, a politician, yet an intellectual: are these not the qualities of Ricci sympathetic to Giulio Andreotti, the Godfather of Christian Democracy and thrice Prime Minister of Italy between 1972 and 1992, who, having successfully defended himself in repeated trials on connections to the Mafia, found time in his retirement and old age to write a biography of Ricci?[21] For others, it is diplomatic and cultural experience in China which has provided the inspiration, as in the beautiful biography written by Michela Fontana.[22] In the tradition of Italian Ricci scholarship, other biographies have come from the pens of Jesuits and sinologists. Gaetano Ricciardolo, Sinologist at the University of Rome, has taken strong exception to the interpretation of Jacques Gernet, pointing out that many Confucian scholars, not converts, valued the cultural contributions of Ricci and his successors.[23] And the latest Jesuit contribution is the short biography written by Francesco Occhetta, editor of the *Civiltà Cattolica*, the official press of the Vatican.[24] Lest we forget local pride, Macerata commemorates its native son with a street and a statue; and in the Ricci Institute, jointly funded by the municipality, province, university, and diocese, one finds a beehive of scholarly production, publishing modern critical editions of Ricci's writings and translating, for the first time and with the help of a team of Chinese researchers, the entire body of Ricci's Chinese works into Italian. The director of that Institute, Filippo Mignini, has also written a biography of Ricci, which evokes imaginary but credible scenes from the childhood of Ricci, bringing to life the pharmacy of his father, the churches, schools, and streets of sixteenth-century Macerata.[25]

Researchers in Macerata are not the only Chinese exports in the Riccian cultural enterprise. The three decades after the Cultural Revolution (1966–76) have witnessed an explosion of interest in early Sino-western encounters, especially after the announcement of economic reform by Deng Xiaoping in 1978. Publications on Matteo Ricci in the Chinese language have matched the rate of economic growth.

One of the first and most important works of scholarship to appear was the 1996 book *Li Madou yu Zhongguo* (*Matteo Ricci and China*) by Lin Jinshui.[26] In spite of its publication date, Lin had finished his first draft in 1981, shortly after Deng's speech on economic liberalization. In those heady years, it seemed China was finally turning its back on xenophobia and toward the West, stepping once more on the long march to modernization, a process interrupted repeatedly over the past 120 years of its history. Matteo Ricci, affirmed Lin Jinshui, had made an important contribution to China, inaugurating the era of sustained encounter with the West. Lamenting that this early cultural encounter failed to bring about Chinese modernization, Lin concluded that the Qing dynasty represented an even more feudalistic regime than the Ming and that the scientific and modernizing techniques of the Jesuits were limited by their primary religious objectives. Then, Lin admonishes:

Nevertheless, we cannot view all missionaries to China as 'cultural invaders' and 'vanguards of colonialism', without consideration of historical periods or actual analysis, simply because there was a relationship between the Jesuits and Iberian colonial-maritime expansion. This is contrary to the spirit of historical materialism.

Religious missions represent one form of cultural exchanges and the main channel of cultural exchanges between traditional China and the West. Through them, western civilization reached China, and China's illustrious civilization spread to all countries . . . Therefore, we should not thoughtlessly criticize cultural exchanges that took place in religious terms; we should analyze concretely concrete historical questions. There is an essential difference between Jesuit missionaries in late Ming and early Qing China and those missionaries who came after the Opium

War. Jesuit missionaries came to China in order to win converts to Christianity in a country that was neither Christian nor Muslim; these were proper missionary activities.[27]

The difference, Lin elaborates, lies in the legal constraints and cultural accommodation that characterized the Ming-Qing Jesuit Mission, as opposed to the western military, economic, and cultural invasion of China after the Opium War of 1842. While these invaders would be exposed and criticized, Lin called for commemorating 'those missionaries, friends of the Chinese people, who had made a contribution to Sino-western cultural exchanges. The renovation of the tomb of Ricci in Beijing is a good example.'[28]

Programmatic statement aside, Lin's book represents an important milestone in scholarship. In addition to analyzing Ricci's mathematical, astronomical, geographical, artistic, musical, and linguistic contributions, Lin provides information on the 141 mandarins and scholars mentioned in the writings of Ricci, with data gleaned from a vast number of Chinese records. This prosopography remains the foundation for all future research into the social history of the early Jesuit mission.

On the intellectual side, Sun Shangyang takes a philosophical view in his 1994 book *Jidujiao yu Mingmo ruxue* (*Christianity and Confucianism in the Late Ming*).[29] In the first part of his book, Sun carefully analyzes the Christian–Confucian synthesis in Ricci's writings; in the second part, he traces thematically the Confucian reactions in the seventeenth century. Only a handful of Chinese scholars, Sun concludes, creatively adopted Christianity, as expounded by Ricci, for their own uses for statecraft, social reforms, or personal salvation. The majority rejected this foreign culture, in order to preserve traditional values and social stability. This stability, however, was bought at the price of cultural exclusion and xenophobia, rendering nineteenth-century China totally unprepared to deal with an altogether less pacific challenge by the West. In missing the peaceful window of cultural exchange at the time of Matteo Ricci, the Chinese elites helped to condemn their country to a century of semi-colonial humiliation.[30]

As we step into the twenty-first century, Chinese scholarship on Catholic missions has long expanded beyond the confines of Chinese Catholic scholarship in the 1930s and 1940s, just as the economic reforms first implemented in the 'Special Economic Zones' have embraced all of China. From art, mathematics, astronomy, religion, philosophy, music, to linguistics, Ricci is a legitimate and popular subject for investigation. A 2001 critical edition of the Chinese writings of Ricci was edited by no less than Zhu Weizheng, professor at Fudan University and one-time campus radical during the Cultural Revolution.[31]

On the 400th anniversary of his death, Matteo Ricci is anything but alone: his tombstone polished up, his writings republished, and his memory celebrated. Three sets of stamps, issued by the Republic of China (Taiwan) in 1983, Italy in 2002, and Macao in 2006, excite the Jesuit-philatelists.[32] Four institutes bearing his name in Taipei, Macerata, San Francisco, and Macao are dedicated to Sino-western cultural exchanges and support scholarship on the Jesuit China Mission. In the busy schedule of conferences, exhibitions, and publications that celebrate his memory, we should remember a time before Nanchang, Nanjing, and Beijing, when visitors beat down the door to converse with the remarkable scholar from the West.

Some years ago, at the beginning of my research, I visited Zhaoqing, the first residence of the Jesuits, where Ricci spent seven unhappy years. Ignorant of Cantonese and modest in his missionary accomplishments, Ricci and his companions stayed in a house adjacent to Chongxi Pagoda by the West River just outside the eastern gate of the city. Touring every historical monument and walking on the city walls, which still surround the old city of Zhaoqing, I looked in vain for signs of Ricci. The largest bookstore, Xinhua, had no books on the history of Zhaoqing, let alone books on the famous Jesuit. This beautiful provincial town in Guangdong seemed to have forgotten the Jesuits the moment Ricci left for Shaozhou. After three days, I left for the ferry terminal to return to Hong Kong. Then, on the spur of the moment, a quick sprint to the Chongxi Pagoda from the river's bank. As I turned the corner around a low wall shielding some undistinguished workshops, with the magnificent silhouette of the pagoda before my eyes, I caught sight of a small plaque to my left. Erected in 1998 by the municipality, it commemorates the site where the Jesuit residence formerly stood and where Ricci once lived.

His head shaven, dressed in Buddhist robes, despised by locals as a barbarian monk ignorant of their tongue, and a world away from home, Ricci would have found comfort in these words that show he would not be forgotten, even in the beautiful provincial backwater of Guangdong.

Appendix:
Magistrate's Verdict in Adultery Accusation against Michele Ruggieri

ARSI Jap-Sin I-198, fos. 183, 187

審得蔡一龍於九月廿五日哄騙番僧寶石到省意圖重價勒贖且因借陸
於充本艮人叉欲寶石私償抵償債隨充往省尋見向論前憤是充執回寶
石送　道驗明發還本僧此一龍解到本府暫收倉監喚僧面賢究懲乃捏羅
洪告詞稱僧明堅與妻通姦即指一龍寫帖張掛 [1]準後慮本府審出真情又
訴匿名詐害今據李主歷回稱羅洪原(187)案住南門與妻先期外躲即
是一龍供報詳看羅洪與明堅素無來往何故將妻自汙告害番僧況南門
去本府頗遠以異言異服之僧私往通姦一路地方鄰佑豈不窺見即使潛
跡亦難逃於近處耳目此中奸棍甚夕脫一瞰知登時捉獲或送官或嚇詐
仍所不遂而始待久出之夫告鳴耶此俚人之所必無可知矣今洪既不出
官對俚即是一龍捏名妄告圖洩私念無(183)疑應將一龍問罪仍追還陸
於充本艮人叉將一龍取問罪犯

The interrogation reveals that on the twenty-fifth day of the ninth month, Cai Yilong tricked the foreign monk into giving him the precious stone and went to the provincial capital, intending to demand a high price for its return. Furthermore, he wanted to use the precious stone to repay Lu Yuchong, who was innocent. Lu went and found Cai in the provincial capital and angrily demanded the return of the precious stone, which, after having been examined by the magistrate, was returned to this monk. Cai Yilong was escorted back to this prefecture and imprisoned, while the monk was summoned for interrogation. To escape punishment [Cai] forged an accusation in the name of Luo Hung to the effect that the monk Mingjian [Ruggieri] and Luo's wife were engaged in adultery. This accusation was posted as a handbill, but since [Cai] worried that this magistrate would find out the truth, he initiated another anonymous denunciation. According to the report of Li Zhuli the accuser Luo Hung and his wife reside at the South Gate, but they have gone away to hide in advance. Examining the information supplied by Cai Yilong, it seems that Luo Hung has never had any dealings with Luo Mingjian [Ruggieri]: why would he denigrate his own wife and accuse the foreign monk? Moreover, the South Gate is far from this magistracy. How can a monk wearing foreign clothes and speaking a foreign tongue go there for liaison without being seen by people along the way? Even if he got there in stealth, he could hardly avoid being heard by neighbors. It is difficult for criminals to escape: he would have been captured and delivered to the magistracy or blackmailed, and would not have to wait to be denounced by a long-absent husband. The vulgar folk naturally would not know this. And since [Luo Hung] does not appear before the magistracy to face the accused, it is clear that Cai Yilong has made the accusation under a pretended name for vengeance, and there is no doubt he is guilty. Therefore, the debt owed the innocent Lu Yuchong should be recovered and Cai Yilong sentenced.

Notes

CHAPTER I

1. *The Ratio Studiorum: The Official Plan for Jesuit Education*, trans. Claude Pavur, SJ (St Louis: Institute of Jesuit Sources, 2005), 137.

2. Figures from Riccardo G. Villoslada, *Storia del Collegio Romano dal suo inizio (1551) alla soppressione della Compagnia di Gesù (1773)* (=*Analecta Gregoriana*, vol. LXVI) (Rome: Gregorian University Press, 1954), 58.

3. Henri Bernard, *Le Père Matthieu Ricci et la société chinoise de son temps 1552–1610*, 2 vols. (Tianjin: Hautes Études, 1937), i. 19.

4. Montaigne, *Travel Journal*, in Michel de Montaigne, *The Complete Works*, trans. Donald M. Frame (New York: Alfred A. Knopf, 2003), 1167.

5. A list of rectors and professors is appended in Villoslada, *Storia del Collegio Romano*, 322–36.

6. James M. Lattis, *Between Copernicus and Galileo: Christopher Clavius and the Collapse of Ptolemaic Cosmology* (Chicago: University of Chicago Press, 1994), 150–1.

7. Gregory Martin, *Roma Sancta (1581)*, ed. George Bruner Parks (Rome: Edizioni di Storia e Letteratura, 1969), 162–3. I have modernized the spelling of Martin's text.

8. Ibid. 164.

9. For these figures see Jean Delumeau, *Vie économique et sociale de Rome dans la seconde moitié du XVIe siècle*, 2 vols. (Paris: de Boccard, 1957), 171.

10. Cited in my 'Mission und Konfessionalisierung in Übersee', in Wolfgang Reinhard and Heinz Schilling (eds.), *Die Katholische Konfessionalisierung* (Münster: Aschendorff, 1995), 158.

11. *Avisi particolari delle Indie di Portugallo ricevuti in questi doi anni del 1551 & 1552 da li reverendi padri della compagnia di Iesu* (Rome, 1552).

12. *Novi avisi di piu lochi de l'India et massime de Brasil . . . doue chiaramente si puo intendere la conuersione di molte persone . . .* (Rome, 1553).

13. *Avisi particolari del avmento che Iddio da alla sua Chiesa Catolica nell'Indie, et spetialmente nelli Regni di Giappon con informatione della China, riceuuti dalle Padri della Compagna di Iesu, questo anno del 1558* (Rome, 1558).

14. *Diversi avisi particolari dall'Indie di Portogallo, riceuuti dallanno 1551 sino al 1558, dalli Reuerendi padri della compagnia di Gesu, dove s'intende delli paesi, delle genti, & costumi loro, & la grande conuersione di molti popoli, che hanno riceuuti il lume della*

santa fede, & religione Christiana. Tradotti nuouamente dalla lingua Spagnuloa nella Italiana (Venice, 1565).

15. See Gian Carlo Roscioni, *Il desiderio delle Indie: Storie, sogni e fughe di giovani gesuiti italiani* (Turin: Einaudi, 2001).

16. For Valignano's career, see Adolfo Tamburello, M. Antoni, J. Üçerler, and Marisa di Russo (eds.), *Alessandro Valignano S.I., uomo del Rinascimento: Ponte tra Oriente e Occidente* (Rome: Jesuit Historical Institute, 2008).

17. For biographies of Jesuits selected for India in 1577, see Joseph Wicki (ed.), *Documenta Indica*, xi: *1577–1580* (=*Monumenta Historica Societatis Iesu*, vol. 103) (Rome: IHSI, 1970), 19*–23*.

18. Gregory Martin, *Roma Sancta*, ed. George Bruner Parks (Rome: Edizioni di Storia e Letteratura, 1969), 167.

CHAPTER 2

1. A. C. de C. M. Saunders, *A Social History of Black Slaves and Freedmen in Portugal 1441–1555* (Cambridge: Cambridge University Press, 1982), has figures for the size and distribution of African slaves in Lisbon.

2. For the general history of the Society in Portugal, the standard work is Dauril Alden, *The Making of an Enterprise: The Society of Jesus in Portugal, its Empire, and Beyond 1540–1750* (Stanford, Calif.: Stanford University Press, 1996).

3. ARSI, Lusitania 39, Catalogii brevii, fos. 7–8.

4. *DI*, xi. 156.

5. For maritime archaeology and research on the Portuguese galleons, see N. Fonseca, T. A. Santos, and F. Castro, 'Study of the Intact Stability of a Portuguese Nau from the Early XVII Century', in Guedes Soares et al. (eds.), *Maritime Transportation and Exploitation of Ocean and Coastal Resources* (London: Taylor & Francis, 2005), 841–9 and the web resources http://nautarch.tamu. edu. On Portuguese seamanship and the history of maritime explorations, see Frédéric Mauro, *Le Portugal et l'Atlantique au XVIIe siècle (1570–1670): Étude économique* (Paris: SEVPEN, 1960).

6. I have used the elegant translation by Landeg White (Oxford: Oxford University Press, 1997).

7. Four Jesuits on the voyage in 1578 recorded their experiences of passage: three of these—by Nicolo Spinola, Francesco Pasio, and Rodolfo Acquaviva—have been published in *DI*, vol. xi, ed. Joseph Wicki, 304–24, 333–79. The fourth, by Ruggieri, is in his manuscript journal, ARSI Jap-Sin 101 I, fos. 8–11, 116^{r-v}. The accounts of Spinola and Pasio are the most detailed. Unfortunately, there does not seem to be an extant record written by Ricci. The account of Ruggieri, who was Ricci's shipmate, is rather brief, reflecting probably the relatively smooth sailing. See also the article by Joseph Wicki, 'As relações de viagens dos Jesuítas na carreira das naus da Índia de 1541 a 1598', in Luís de Albuquerque and Inácio Guerreiro (eds.), *II seminário internacional de história*

Indo-Portugues (Lisbon: IICT-CEHCA, 1985), 3–17. The Jesuit accounts obviously focus on edifying matters, leaving out the vulgar. For a very different description of the Indian passage, from a non-clerical and secular perspective, there is a short but lively record of a journey in 1583 written by the Netherlander Jan Huygen van Linschoten, who was in the service of the Dominican Vincente de Fonseca, assigned to the archbishopric of Goa: *John Huighen van Linschoten: His Discours of voyages into ye Easte & West Indies* (London: John Wolfe, 1598), available online: http//name.umdl.umich.edu/A05569.0001.001.

8. *DI*, xi. 307.

9. ARSI Jap-Sin 101 I, 'M. Ruggiero relaciones 1577–1591'.

10. *DI*, xi. 315.

11. ARSI, Fondo Gesuitico, 723/5.

12. The percentage (15.3%) of deceased among German Jesuits en route for overseas missions comes from Christoph Nebgen, *Missionarsberufungen nach Übersee in drei deutschen Provinzen der Gesellschaft Jesu im 17. und 18. Jahrhundert* (Regensburg: Schnell/Steiner, 2007), 98.

13. *DI*, xi. 307.

14. This anecdote is published in *OS*, ed. Tacchi Venturi, ii. 395. Tacchi Venturi mentions the manuscript from which this extract is transcribed without giving its signature in the ARSI. He wrongly attributed this text to Acquaviva. In fact, this episode is recorded in the memoirs of Ruggieri, ARSI Jap-Sin 101 I, 'M. Ruggiero Relaciones 1577–1591' under the anonymous title 'Relatione del successo dela missione della Cina dal mese di Novembre 1577 sin all'ano 1591 del P. Michel Ruggiero al nostro R. P. Claudio Acquaviva Generale della Comp di Gesu', fo. 11.

15. Information on the Jesuit Province in India is gathered from *DI*, vols. ix–xii, covering the years 1573 to 1583. Ricci's letters are contained in vols. xi and xii, as is correspondence by Pasio, Ruggieri, and Acquaviva.

16. Ines G. Županov, *Missionary Tropics: The Catholic Frontier in India (16th–17th Centuries)* (Ann Arbor: University of Michigan Press, 2005), 76.

17. *DI*, xi. 645–6.

18. Tacchi-Venturi, *OS* ii. 400, Ruggieri's letter to Mercurian, Macao, 12 November 1580.

19. Ibid.

20. *DI*, xii. 435.

21. *Lettere*, 11.

22. *DI*, xi. 638, 699.

23. *Lettere*, 19.

24. Ibid. 24.

25. Ibid. 25.

26. Ibid. 40.

27. On the Inquisition in Portugal and its main victims, the New Christians, see A. J. Saraiva, *Inquisição e cristãos novos* (Porto: Inova, 1969); António Borges Coelho has studied thoroughly the workings of one of the three tribunals in Portugal; see his *Inquisição de Évora 1533–1668* (Lisbon: Caminho, 2002); 231–71 and 598–628 deal specifically with targeting Jewish converts. The former archive of the Inquisition in Goa has not survived; we have a late 17th-century eyewitness account by a French victim: *L'Inquistion de Goa: La Relation de Charles Dellon (1687)*, ed. Charles Amiel and Anne Lima (Paris: Chandeigne, 1997). For cases against *conversos* in India, see Županov, *Missionary Tropics*.

28. For the 1506 pogrom against Jews, see Yosef Hayim Yerushalmi, *The Lisbon Massacre of 1506 and the Royal Image in the Shebet Yehudah* (Cincinnati: Hebrew Union College, 1976).

29. *Lettere*, 31. This quotation and others are from 29–32.

30. On the problem of discrimination in the formation of an indigenous clergy in India, seen from Jesuit sources, see Josef Wicki, SJ, 'Der einheimische Klerus in Indien (16. Jahrhundert)', in Johannes Beckmann (ed.), *Der einheimische Klerus in Geschichte und Gegenwart, Neue Zeitschrift für Missionswissenschaft Supplementa* II (Schöneck-Beckenried: NZM, 1950), 17–72. For a larger discussion of race prejudice in Iberian Catholicism, see Charles Boxer, *The Church Militant and Iberian Expansion 1440–1770* (Baltimore: Johns Hopkins University Press, 1978).

CHAPTER 3

1. See the letter of Leonel de Sousa to the Infante D. Luís, 15 January 1556, in Rui Manuel Loureiro (ed.), *Em busca das origens de Macau (Antologia documental)* (Lisbon: Grupo de Trabalho do Ministéro da Educação para as comemorações dos descobrimentos Portugueses, 1996), 91–9.

2. See Ibid.

3. Lu Xiyan's description of Macao is cited in Fang Hao, *Zhongguo Tianzhujiao Renwu juan*, 3 vols. (Hong Kong: Zhonghua shuchu, 1970), ii. 250–2.

4. On the alliance between the Jesuits and the mercantile elites in early Macao, see Luís Filipe Barreto, *Macau: Poder e saber. Séculos XVI e XVII* (Lisbon: Editorial Presença, 2006), 115 ff.

5. The original verses are more refined: 'He Iapão, onde nace a prata fina, que illustrada será cosa ley divina.'

6. A picul, adapted from the Chinese measure *dan*, equated approximately 133 lbs.

7. Figures from the letter of Francisco Cabral, superior of the Jesuit Mission in Japan, 15 September 1581, fo. 8, in *Cartas que os padres e irmãos da Companhia de Iesus escreuerão dos Reynos de Iapão & China aos da mesma Companhia da India, & Europa, des do anno de 1549 atè o de 1580*, vol. ii (Evora 1598/Maia 1997).

8. Mentioned in Ruggieri's letter of 8 November to General Everard Mercurian, in Tacchi-Venturi, *OS* ii. 398.

9. Ibid. 397.
10. 'Carta do P. André Pinto aos Jesuítas da Índia', in Loureiro (ed.), *Em busca das origens de Macau*, 122.
11. Having first served in Goa and Malacca, the Porto native joined the Company in Goa in 1557. Pinto traveled in the summer of 1563 from Malacca to Macao, where he stayed until 1568. He returned to Goa and later served in Malacca and Japan before joining the Jesuits in Macao in 1581 for a second time and remaining there until his death. See 'Carta do P. André Pinto aos Jesuítas da Índia', 117–29.
12. See documents 46 and 47 in John W. Witek and Joseph S. Sebes (eds.), *Monumenta Sinica*, i: *1546–1562* (Rome: IHIS, 2002) (=MHSI, vol. 153), 232–57, esp. 246–7.
13. An English translation of the report of Gaspar da Cruz is published in C. R. Boxer (ed.), *South China in the Sixteenth Century* (London: The Hakluyt Society, 1953).
14. See letter of João de Escobar, secretary of the embassy, to Manuel Teixeira, superior of the Macao Jesuits, Guangzhou, 22 November 1565, in Loureiro (ed.), *Em busca das origens de Macau*, 179–81.
15. An English translation of the reports of Martin de Rada is published in Boxer (ed.), *South China in the Sixteenth Century*.
16. The reports by the Franciscans are published in Anastasius van den Wyngaert (ed.), *Sinica Franciscana*, ii: *Relationes et Epistolas Fratrum Minorum Saeculi XVI et XVII* (Florence: Collegium S. Bonaventurae, 1933).
17. ARSI Jap-Sin 101 I, fo. 20.
18. ARSI Jap-Sin 101 I, fo. 12^{v}.
19. ARSI Jap-Sin 101 I, fo. 96.
20. Tacchi-Venturi, *OS* ii. 401.
21. For the population figures of Guangzhou and a description of the Ming city, see Wang Zhuo et al., *Jiajing Guangdong tong zhi* and *(Kangxi) Xin xiu Guangzhou Fu zhi, juan* 16.
22. For the diplomatic missions of Alonso Sanchez to China and Macao, see the collected documents and analysis in Francisco Colin, *Labor evangelica: Ministerios apostolicos de los obreros de la Compañia de Iesus, fundacion, y progressos de su provincia en las Islas Filipinas*, ed. Pablo Pastells, 3 vols. (Barcelona: Henrich y Co., 1900/2). For an analysis of Spanish policy toward China, see Manel Ollé, *La invención de China: Percepciones y estrategias filipinas respecto a China durante el siglo XVI* (Wiesbaden: Harrassowitz, 2000). For the trade between Macao and Manila, see Benjamin Videira Pires, *A viagem de comérico Macau-Manila nos séculos XVI a XIX* (Macao: Museu Marítimo de Macau, 1994). For the primary position of southern Fujian in Chinese maritime trade, especially with the Philippines, see Chang Pin-tsun, 'Chinese Maritime Trade: The Case of 16th Century Fu-chien' (Ph.D. dissertation, Princeton, 1983).

23. Agustín de Tordesillas, *Relación de el viaje que hezimos en china nuestro hermano fray Pedro de Alpharo con otros tres frailes de la orden de Nuestro seraphico padre san Francisco de la prouincia de san Joseph etc.* (1578). Archivo de la Real Academia de la Historia, Velázques, tomo LXXV. Available at http://www.upf.es/fhuma/eeao/projectes/che/s16/tordes.htm, 13.

24. For descriptions of the robes and insignia of mandarins, see *Ming shi, juan* 67.

25. ARSI Jap-Sin 101 I, fo. 26^{r-v}.

26. Colin, *Labor evangelica*, i. 281.

27. Ibid. 321–2.

28. Ruggieri's letter is dated 14 December 1582 and Pasio's 15 December. See Tacchi-Venturi, *OS* ii. 407–10.

29. *Lettere*, 45–9, 52.

30. Ibid. 53. The other quotations criticizing the Portuguese Jesuits are also from this letter to Acquaviva, dated 13 February 1583.

31. Ibid. 46.

32. Ricci's words are cited from his letter to de Fornari, 13 February 1583, ibid. 46–9.

33. Ibid. 46–7.

34. Tacchi-Venturi, *OS* ii. 416. Ruggieri's letter of 7 February 1583 to Acquaviva.

35. Letter of Francesco Pasio to Pedro Gomez, 18 February 1583, in Colin, *Labor evangelica*, i. 320.

36. For the relationship between the Wanli emperor and Zhang Juzheng see Fan Shuzhi, *Wanli zhuan* (Beijing: Renmin chubanshe, 1993), chapters 2 and 4; for the memorial attacking Chen Rui and Wanli's rescript dismissing the viceroy, see *Ming Shen zong shi lu, juan* 132, cited in Fan, *Wanli zhuan*, 182.

CHAPTER 4

1. *FR* I, 177.

2. *Zhaoqing Fuzhi*, Chongzhen edn., *juan* 12. In the tenth year of Wanli (1582), the tax register lists 52,901 households and 213,714 heads for the Prefecture (*fu*) of Zhaoqing, and 16,629 households and 47,332 heads for the county (*xian*) of Gaoyeo, which was practically coterminous with the walled city of Zhaoqing.

3. The journals of Ruggieri and Ricci describe their early days in Zhaoqing, which are supplemented by their letters: for Ruggieri's correspondence see Tacchi-Venturi, *OS* ii, nos. 6–7 and 10, 419–24, 434–5; and the long report of Francisco Cabral to Valignano, no. 9, 427–34; for Ricci's correspondence in Zhaoqing, see *Lettere*, 97–124.

4. Tacchi-Venturi, *OS* ii. 422–3.

5. Ibid. 425–6.

6. Archivo General de Indias, Patronato 25, 22, available online at www.upf.es/fhuma/eeao/projectes/che/s16/roman.htm/.

7. For Valignano's scathing critique of Sanchez, see Acosta's two tracts against Sanchez, to be found in José de Acosta, *Obras*, ed. Francisco Mateos (Madrid: Ediciones Atlas, 1954). See also Valignano's letters in *DI*, xiv. 9. 11. 20–1, cited in my 'Valignano e Cina', in *Alessandro Valignano, S.I., uomo del Rinascimento: Ponte tra Oriente e Occidente*, 102–3.

8. Tacchi-Venturi, *OS* ii. 423–4.

9. The Latin synopsis of Ruggieri's Chinese catechism is published in Tacchi-Venturi, *OS* ii, no. 29, 'Vera et Brevis divinarum Rerum Expositio', 498–540.

10. ARSI Jap-Sin 101 I, fos. 28^v–31.

11. *Lettere*, 123.

12. Timothy Brook, *Praying for Power: Buddhism and the Formation of Gentry Society in Late-Ming China* (Cambridge, Mass.: Harvard University Press, 1993), 249–77.

13. Ibid. 268–9.

14. Shi Shengyan, *Ming mo fojiao yanjiu* (Taipei: Dongchu chubanshe, 1987), 239.

15. *Chongzhen Zhaoqing Fuzhi*, juan 20, 777–9; quotation, 779.

16. *Chongzhen Zhaoqing Fuzhi*, juan 46, 296. The 1673 Kangxi edition uses the words 'Guan jie' (官僻) instead of 'Guan lan'(官懶). See *Kangxi Zhaoqing Fushi*, juan 30. The Chinese text reads: 官懶簿書稀, 尋僧入翠微, 白雲依榻靜, 紅葉近人飛, 愛爾能分供, 憐余未拂衣, 禪心共明月, 相對欲忘歸.

17. *Chongzhen Zhaoqing Fuzhi*, juan 46, 270–1. The Chinese verses read: 深尋有丹穴, 乞藥駐朱顔, 興 來招鶴駕, 直欲提飛仙.

18. *Chongzhen Zhaoqing Fuzhi*, juan 49, 493:日射金輪散寶光.

19. Letter of Francisco Cabral to Alessandro Valignano, Macao, 5 December 1584, Tacchi-Venturi, *OS* ii. 429.

20. Ibid. 424.

21. Reprinted in Nicolas Standaert and Adrian Dudink (eds.), *Chinese Christian Texts from the Roman Archives of the Society of Jesus*, 12 vols. (Taipei: Ricci Institute, 2002), i. 1–86.

22. ARSI Jap-Sin 101 I, fos. 33^v–35.

23. *Tianzhu shilu*, 53, 58. (Tianzhu huawei nanzi, 天主化為男子, 'The Lord of Heaven transformed himself into a man').

24. Ibid. 59.

25. Ibid. 77.

26. Letter to Acquaviva, 20 October 1585, Ricci, *Lettere*, 98.

CHAPTER 5

1. *FR* I, 147 n. 2.

2. Compared to the large scholarship on Ricci, only a handful of works have been devoted to Ruggieri. The most important of these is the dissertation written by Joseph Shih, SJ, at the Pontifical Gregoriana University in Rome, only a part of which has been published as *Le Père Ruggieri et le problème de l'évangélisation en*

Chine (Rome: Pontificiae Universitatis Gregorianae, 1964). The thesis of Rossella Turner, 'La figura e l'opera di Michele Ruggieri, S.J., missionario Gesuita in Cina', Tesi di Laurea in storia e civiltà dell'Estremo Oriente (Naples: Istituto universitario Orientale Napoli, 1984), typescript, analyses the *Tianzhu shilu* and letters and does not cite Ruggieri's manuscript journal in the Roman Archives of the Society of Jesus. The publication of Ruggieri's Chinese letters by Albert Chan (see n. 3) is the most significant rediscovery of Ruggieri's importance in the China Jesuit Mission.

3. Albert Chan, SJ, 'Michele Ruggieri, S.J. (1543–1607) and his Chinese Poems', *Monumenta Serica*, 41 (1993), 129–76, here 158–9. The translation is by Chan. The Chinese verses read: 一葉扁舟泛海涯，三年水路到中華，心如秋水常涵月，身若菩提那有花，貴省肯容吾著步，貧僧至此便為家，諸君若問西天事，非是如來佛釋迦.

4. I would translate this verse as: 'The Body is like a bodhi so how can there be flowers?' This would be an allusion to the famous answer by the Sixth Patriarch Weineng to the question of his master on the way to keep pure: 'Bodhi originally has no tree, so how can it be dirty?' Ruggieri's Chinese poem strives for the effect of Chan meditation, which is missed in Father Chan's English translation.

5. Letter by Almeida to Duarte de Sande, 10 February 1586, Shaoxing, ARSI Jap-Sin 101 I, fos. 150^v–151.

6. ARSI Jap-Sin 101 I, fo. 44. This representation of Guanyin seems to have combined the iconographic motifs of the 'Water-Moon Guanyin', and the 'Son-Giving Guanyin', often depicted as riding on a wondrous beast. Ruggieri's explanation to Almeida refers to the legend of Princess Miaoshan, who would become the 'Thousand-Eye and Thousand-Arm Guanyin'. See Chünfang Yü, *Kuan-yin: The Chinese Transformation of Avalokitesvara* (New York: Columbia University Press, 2001), 252, 295–9, 442.

7. For a detailed description of the Sun family, the identification of this personage, and for the relationship between Sun Kuang and the Jesuits, see my article under preparation: 'Who was "Scielou" in Ricci's *Dell'entrata*?'

8. Letter of Antonio d'Almeida to Duarte de Sande, 10 February 1586, Shaoxing, ARSI Jap-Sin 101 I, fo. 152^r.

9. ARSI Jap-Sin 101 I, fos. 48^{r-v}.

10. ARSI Jap-Sin 101 I, fo. 90^v.

11. ARSI Jap-Sin 101 I, fos. 91^r–92^r.

12. ARSI Jap-Sin 101 I, fo. 110^v.

13. For the Chinese text of the judgment, see ARSI Jap-Sin I 198, fos. 183, 187^{r-v}. This text, which is appended to the Chinese–Portuguese dictionary compiled by Ruggieri and Ricci, has not been published in the edition edited by John Witek, *Dicionário Português–Chinês=Pu Han ci dian=Portuguese Chinese Dictionary* (San Francisco: Ricci Institute, 2001). For the Chinese text of the magisterial verdict, see appendix, document.

14. Letter of Ricci to Claudio Acquaviva, 20 October 1585, Zhaoqing, *Lettere*, 103.
15. Letter of Ricci to Giulio Fuligatti, 24 November 1585, ibid. 116.
16. Ricci's letter to Claudio Acquaviva, Zhaoqing, 20 October 1585, ibid. 100.
17. Ibid. 107.
18. Ibid. 115.
19. Ibid. 108–9.
20. Ibid. 112.
21. Ibid. 111.
22. Ibid. 116.
23. Ibid. 123.
24. The idea was first proposed by Ruggieri to General Mercurian in a letter dated 12 November 1581, written in Macao, and repeated in Ruggieri's letter of 8 November 1586 to General Acquaviva. *OS* ii. 403, 449.
25. *FR* I, 250. The syntax of this passage is unclear, although the context obviously refers to the 'I' as Valignano.
26. ARSI Jap-Sin 11, fo. 29^v. Cited in *FR* I, 250 n. 2.
27. ARSI Jap-Sin 9 II, fo. 186^{r-v}. Cited in *FR* I, 222 n. 1.
28. Bibliothèque Nationale de France, Chinois 1320 and 9186; the former is the engraved plaque for printing. A modern Chinese edition of the works of Ricci published in Taipei (Guangqi chubanshe, 1986) has modernized the text and changed all Buddhist terms into contemporary Catholic terms, thus making the text useless for historical analysis.
29. Wang Pan was promoted in the twelfth month of the fifteenth year of Wanli, i.e. January 1588. This item from the *Ming shilu* is compiled in Li Guoxiang and Yang Chang (eds.), Yu Xu et al. (comps.), *Ming shi lu lei zhuan. Guangdong Hainan juan* (Wuhan: Wuhan chubanshe, 1993), 232.
30. Liu was promoted from *xunfu* of Guangxi to *zongdu* of Guangdong and Guangxi, in charge of all military affairs, in the seventh month of the sixteenth year of Wanli (i.e. August 1589). See *Ming shi lu lei zhuan. Guangdong Hainan juan*, 234. His reputation for incorruptibility, 'second only to Hai Rui', is found in a Ming biographical compilation, Guo Tingxun (comp.), *Benchao fensheng renwu kao, juan* 17 (Taipei: Chengwen, 1971; reprint), v. 1448–9.
31. *FR* I, 263.

CHAPTER 6

1. The only source for the history of Nanhua monastery in the Ming dynasty is the *Cao xi tong zi*, ed. Ma Yuan, compiled in the reign of Kangxi in the Qing dynasty. In addition to a sketchy account of its monastic history, there is a detailed description of the physical conditions of the monastery and the environs. Crucial documents of monastic reform in 1600 by Heshan Deqing are also included in this monastic history: Ma Yuan (ed.), *Cai xi tong zi*, published in *Si ku jin hui shu cong kan bu bian*, vol. 27 (Beijing: Beijing chubanshe, 2005).

2. Liu Jiezhai, 'Inscription on Renovating Nanhua si', in Ma Yuan (ed.), *Cao Xi tong zhi, juan* 4, 90–1.
3. Ma Yuan et al. (comp.), *Shaozhou fuzhi,* Kangxi edn., *juan* 4, 1767–8.
4. Zhu Weizheng (ed.), *Li Madou Zhongwen zhuyi ji* (Shanghai: Fudan Daxue chubanshe, 2001), 117.
5. *FR* I, 295–6.
6. The story of Qu Rukui and his family genealogy is reconstructed in Huang Yilong, *Liang toushe: Ming mo Qing chu de di yi tai Tianzhu jiao tu* (Xinzhu: Guoli Qinghua daxue chubanshe, 2005), 33–64; on the adultery, see 49–59. For his biography of his father, see *Ming shi, juan* 216, 28 vols. (Beijing: Zhonghua, 1997), 5696–7.
7. Qu Rukui's poem is published in Ma Yuan et al. (comp.), *Shaozhou fuzhi,* Kangxi edn., *juan* 15, 2004.
8. See entries in *juan* 233 and 235 of *Ming Shenzong shi lu,* published in Liu Chonglai et al. (eds.), *Ming shi lu lei zuan. She guan ren mian juan* (Wuhan: Wuhan chubanshe, 1995), 234.
9. See Guo Tingxun (comp.), *Benchao fensheng renwu kao,* 115 *juan, juan* 17 (reprint, Taipei: Chengwen, 1971), v. 1448–9; *FR* I, 312–13.
10. This conversation forms chapter 9 in *Jiren Shipian.*
11. Ricci to Claudio Acquaviva, 15 November 1592, Shaozhou, *Lettere,* 169–80.
12. Ricci to Fabio de Fabii, 12 November 1592, Shaozhou, ibid. 157–63.
13. Ricci to Giovanni Battista Ricci, Shaozhou, 12 November 1592, ibid. 165–8.
14. Cited in *FR* I, 323 n. 7.
15. Ricci to Claudio Acquaviva, 10 December 1593, Shaozhou, *Lettere,* 183–5.
16. *FR* I, 336.
17. Ricci to Claudio Acquaviva, 15 November 1592, Shaozhou, *Lettere,* 171–2.
18. Ricci to Fabio de Fabii, 15 November 1594, Shaozhou, ibid. 191.
19. Ricci to Girolamo Costa, 12 October 1594, Shaozhou, ibid. 189.
20. Ibid. 187.
21. *FR* I, 337.
22. Ibid. 337 and n. 1.
23. For the identification of this personality, see Chapter 5 n. 7.

CHAPTER 7

1. *Lettere,* 216.
2. Ibid. 218.
3. Ibid. 223–4.
4. Unlike the ministries in Beijing, staffed with one minister (*shangshu*) and two vice-ministers (Left and Right *shilang*), the simplified parallel ministries in Nanjing had only one minister and one vice-minister (Right *shilang*). See *Ming shi, juan* 75, 1833.
5. Letter to Duarte de Sande, Nanchang, 29 August 1595, *Lettere,* 240.

6. *FR* I, 355.

7. Guo Tingxun (comp.), *Benchao fensheng renwu kao*, 115 *juan, juan* 38 (Taipei, 1971; reprint), x. 3084–6.

8. The narration of the dream in Ricci's letter to Girolamo Costa is essentially the same as in his journal, except for the variation in the ending. See *Lettere*, 290.

9. *Didaci Lainez Adhortationes*, 1559, in *Fontes Narrativi de S. Ignatio de Loyola et de Societatis Iesu initiis*, ii: *Monumenta Historica Societatis Iesu* (Rome: IHSI, 1951), 133–4. 'Vendeno noi a Roma per la via di Siena, nostro Padre, come quello che aveva molti sentimenti spirituali, et specialmente nella sanctissima Eucharistia, che egli ogni giorno pigliava, sendoli amministrata o da maestro Pietro Fabro, o da me, che ogni giorno dicevamo messa, et egli no; mi disse che gli pareva che Dio Padre gl'imprimesse nel cuore queste parole: "Ego ero vobis Romae propitious." Et non sapendo nostro padre quell che volesseno significare, diceva: "Io non so che cosa sarà di noi, forse che saremo crocifissi in Roma." Poi un'altra volta disse che gli pareva di vedere Christo con la croce in spalla, et il Padre Eterno appresso che gli diceva: "Io voglio che Tu pigli questo per servitore tuo." Et cosi Gesù lo pigliava, et diceva: "Io voglio che tu ci serva." Et per questo, pigliando gran devotione a questo santissimo nome, voles nominare la congregatione: la Compagnia di Gesù.'

10. See my 'Dreams and Conversions: A Comparative Analysis of Catholic and Buddhist Dreams in Ming and Qing China: Part I', *Journal of Religious History*, 29/3 (October 2006), 223–40.

11. Fan Lai (comp.), *Wanli xin xiu Nanchang fu zhi* (1588), *juan* 7, 122. *Lettere*, 282.

12. *Lettere*, 283.

13. Ibid. 242.

14. *FR* I, 357. *Lettere*, 220.

15. Letter of Ricci to Claudio Acquaviva, Nanchang, 4 November 1595, *Lettere*, 311.

16. Ibid. 245.

17. *Ming shi*, vol. 19, *juan* 107, 5777.

18. Jiangxi led in the number of private academies in the Ming dynasty, followed by Guangdong (234), Zhejiang and Fujian (174 each), Anhui (141), and Jiangsu (117). See Tai-loi Ma, 'Private Academies in Ming China (1368–1644): Historical Development, Organization and Social Impact' (Ph.D. dissertation, University of Chicago, 1987), 153. For figures on *jinshi*, see He Bingdi, *The Ladder of Success in Imperial China: Aspects of Social Mobility 1368–1911* (New York: Columbia University Press, 1962). Among the studies on the place of Jiangxi in Ming intellectual life, see: Kandice J. Hauf, 'The Jiangyou Group: Culture and Society in Sixteenth Century China' (Ph.D. dissertation, Yale, 1987); John Meskill, *Academies in Ming China: A Historical Essay* (Tucson, Ariz.: University of Arizona Press, 1982); Anne Gerritsen, *Ji'an Literati and the Local in Song-Yuan-Ming China* (Leiden: Brill, 2007).

19. *Lettere*, 246.

20. Lettre, 247.
21. Zhu Weizheng, *Li Madou Zhongwen zhu yi ji*, 146–7.
22. This is reported by Ricci himself in a letter to Claudio Acquaviva, Nanchang, 13 October 1596, *Lettere*, 336.
23. *Ming shi, juan* 100, 2503; see Chen Baoliang, *Ming dai shehui shenghuo shi* (Beijing: Zhong guo she hui ke xue chubanshe, 2004), 68–70.
24. Li Qionying and Zhang Yingchao (eds.), *Ming shi lu lei zuan: zong fan gui qi juan* (Wuhan: Wuhan chubanshe, 1995), 1488, 1497.
25. For Zhu Duogang, see *Ming shi, juan* 102, 2732; for the bestowal of the Confucian classics, see Li Qionying and Zhang Yingchao (eds.), *Ming shi lu lei zuan: zong fan gui qi zhuan*, 1238.
26. There is a recent English translation by Timothy Billings, *On Friendship: One Hundred Maxims for a Chinese Prince* (New York: Columbia University Press, 2009).
27. *Lettere*, 262.
28. Zhu Weizheng, *Li Madou Zhongwen zhu yi ji,*. 108–15.
29. Ibid. 117.
30. I am indebted to Professor Chu Hung-lam of the Hong Kong Polytechnic University for elucidating the nuances of this term.
31. *FR* I, 372.
32. 'Quei che più mi contentano sono gli accademici...' *Lettere*, 317.
33. Ibid. 255.
34. Ibid. 282.
35. Ibid. 316.
36. Ibid. 257.
37. For a detailed analysis, see my 'Li Madou yu Zhang Huang', in *Wei le wenhua yu lishi: Yu Yingshi jiaoshou ba she shou qing lunwen ji* (Taipei: Liangjing chubanshe, 2009), 727–49.
38. 'Zhang dou jin xian sheng xing zhuang', in Zhang Huang, *Tushu bian, juan* 127, collected in *Wen yuan ge si ku quan shu*, vol. 972, 850–62 (Taipei: Taiwan shangwu yinshu guan, 1983).
39. Huang Yilong, *Liang Tou She: Ming mo Qing chu de di yi tai Tianzhu jiaotu*, 34–5.
40. Li Yingsheng (ed.), *Bai lu shu yuan zhi* (1622), published in *Bai lu dong shu yuan gu zhi wu zhong* (Beijing: Zhong Hua shu chu, 1995). Zhang Huang's Eight Point speech is on 845–8.
41. Letter to Giuglio Fuligatti, Nanchang, 12 October 1596, *Lettere*, 325.
42. Letter to Claudio Acquaviva, Nanchang, 13 October 1596, ibid. 336.
43. Letter to Antonio Maria Ricci, Nanchang, 13 October 1596, ibid. 329–31.
44. Ibid. 347–8.
45. For an exhaustive study on the subject, see Benjamin A. Elman, *A Cultural History of Civil Examinations in Late Imperial China* (Berkeley and Los Angeles: University of California Press, 2000).

46. The Ming bureaucracy was divided into nine ranks, the first being the highest. Each rank is further divided into full and associate. Mandarins ranked fourth and above wore crimson robes, those beneath blue robes.
47. Letter to Girolamo Costa, Nanchang, 15 October 1596, *Lettere*, 343.
48. Letter to Christopher Clavius, Nanchang, 25 December 1597, ibid. 353.
49. Ibid. 264–5.

CHAPTER 8

1. *FR* II, 30.
2. Fan Shuzhi, *Wanli zhuan*, 169–78.
3. See Leng Dong, *Ye Xianggao yu Ming mo Zheng tan* (Shantou: Shantou Daixue chubanshe, 1996), 220–9 and Adrian Dudink, 'Giulio Aleni and Li Jiubiao', and Erik Zürcher, 'Giulio Aleni's Chinese Biography', in Tiziana Lippiello and Roman Malek (eds.), *'Scholar from the West': Giulio Aleni S.J. (1582–1649) and the Dialogue between Christianity and China* (Nettetal: Steyler, 1997), 85–127, 129–200.
4. *FR* II, 72.
5. Gu Qiyuan, *Ke zuo zhui yu* (Nanjing: Fenghuang chubanshe, 2005), 22.
6. For astronomy in China, the authoritative work of Joseph Needham is indispensable. See his *Chinese Astronomy and the Jesuit Mission: An Encounter of Cultures* (London: The China Society, 1958), and for greater depth, *The Shorter Science and Civilisation in China*, vol. i (Cambridge: Cambridge University Press, 1978), and Joseph Needham and Wang Ling, *Heavenly Clockwork: The Great Astronomical Clocks of Medieval China* (Cambridge: Cambridge University Press, 1960).
7. Zhu Weizheng (ed.), *Li Madou Zhongwen zhuyi ji*, 525.
8. Ibid. 529.
9. Ibid. 530.
10. Ibid. 532.
11. Gu Qiyuan, *Ke zuo zhui yu*, 128–9.
12. Ibid. 267.
13. Ibid. 266.
14. Ibid. 240.
15. *FR* II, 50 n. 1.
16. Ibid. 54.
17. For an English study see Edward T. Ch'ien, *Chiao Hung and the Restructuring of Neo-Confucianism in the Late Ming* (New York: Columbia University Press, 1986). For a succinct biography, see Shen Xinlin (ed.), *Ming dai Nanjing xue shu ren wu zhuan* (Nanjing: Nanjing Daxue chubanshe, 2004), 323–41. The best approach, however, is to read Jiao Hong's work itself, especially his *Jiao shi bi sheng* (Shanghai: Shanghai gu ji chubanshe, 1986), which contains his miscellaneous notes, which reveal an eclectic and original mind.

18. He Xiaorong, *Ming dai Nanjing si yuan yan jiu* (Beijing: Zhongguo she hui ke xue chubanshe, 2000), 142–5.

19. His writings on Buddhism are scattered in his collected works: encomia for Matreiya Buddha, Guanyin, and Buddha statues (*juan* 8), 'Preface to the Engraving of the Huayan Sutra' (*juan* 16), 'Record of the 500 Arhats of Qixia Monastery' (*juan* 21), 'Postscript to the Heart Sutra in Four Calligraphic Styles', 'Postscript to the Diamand Sutra' (*juan* 22), collected in *Jiao shi Danyuan ji*, 4 vols. (Taipei: Weiwen, 1977).

20. Jiao Hong, *Jiao shi bi sheng, juan* 16.

21. For a succinct biography, see Shen Xinlin (ed.), *Ming dai Nanjing xue shu ren wu zhuan* (Nanjing: Nanjing Daxue chubanshe, 2004), 300–15.

22. In *Fen shu, juan* 3, *Li Zhi wen ji: Fen shu, Xu fen shu*, 162.

23. *Fen shu, juan* 4, 192.

24. *Xu fen shu, juan* 1, 370.

25. Ibid., *juan* 2, 426.

26. Li Zhi in *Xu fen shu* (*Book to be Burned: Sequel*), *juan* 1, in *Li Zhi wen ji: Fen shu, Xu fen shu* (Beijing: Yanshan chubanshe, 1998), 378.

27. *Fen shu, juan* 6, 301–2.

28. There is an entry on the Buddhist abbot Xuelang Hong'en in Yu Mei an (comp.), *Xin xu gao seng zhuan si ji* [65 *juan*], 4 vols. (Taipei: liu li qing fang, 1967), *juan* 7, i. 305–8. For studies on the Hua yan School of Buddhism, of which Hong'en was an expert, see Francis H. Cook, *Hua-yen Buddhism: The Jewel Net of Indra* (University Park, Pa.: Penn State University Press, 1977); Guo Peng, *Zhongguo fujiao sixiangshi*, vol. ii (Fuzhou: Fujian renmin chubanshe, 1994), 334–81; Wei Daoru, *Zhongguo Huayanzhong tongshi* (Nanjing: Jiangsu guji chubanshe, 2001), *passim*; there is an entry on Xue lang Hong'en on 283. For a study of Buddhist monasteries in Nanjing, including the milieu of Hong'en, see He Xiarong, *Ming dai Nanjing si yuan yan jiu* (Beijing: Zhongguo shehui kexue chubanshe, 2000).

29. Gu Qiyuan, *Ke zuo zhui yu*, 257–8; *Xin xu gao seng zhuan si ji, juan* 5, 306–7.

30. *FR* II, 75.

31. Ibid. 77.

32. Gu Qiyuan, *Ke zuo zhui yu*, 284–5.

33. Ibid. 23.

34. *Lettere*, 363. In his letter to Girolamo Costa, written from Nanjing on 14 August 1599, Ricci writes that a multitude of visitors 'come to see me, like madmen' ('Vengonon a verdermi, come pazzi').

35. Ibid. 364.

36. Ibid. 361.

37. Ibid. 362.

38. Gu Qiyuan, *Ke zuo zhui yu*, 217–18.

39. These converts were not identified in *FR*. They are first identified by Huang Yilong, *Liang Tou She*, 74–5.

CHAPTER 9

1. The only biography on Diego de Pantoja is *Zhang Kai, Pang di wo [Pantoja] yu Zhongguo* (Beijing: Beijing tushuguan chubanshe, 1997). In addition to Pantoja's Chinese works, which were published after 1610, he also wrote a long letter describing his entry into China and the initial experiences in Beijing: *Relacion de la entrada de algunos padres de la Compañia de Iesus en la China, y particulares sucesos que tuvieron, y de cosas muy notables que vieron en el mismo reyno* (Valencia: Juan Chrysostomo Garriz, 1606).

2. Ibid.

3. The Korean emissaries were allowed free movement until the early sixteenth century, when a Mandarin Director of the *Xiyi guan* restricted their freedom of action. This was lifted later in the century upon petition. See the seventeenth-century work on the palaces and offices of Beijng, Sun Chengze, *Chun Ming meng yu lu* (Hong Kong: Longmen, 1965), *juan* 40, 606–7.

4. Sun Chengze, *Chun Ming meng yu lu, juan* 7, 73.

5. The memorial is cited in full in Shen Defu, *Wanli Yehuo bian, juan* 30, 3 vols. (Beijing: Zhonghua, 2004), iii. 784.

6. In 1566, Pope Pius V issued strict laws banning all prostitutes from Rome. Although the measure failed to suppress Roman prostitution in the long run, it confined them to specific quarters of the city. Ricci was present in Rome when these disciplinary laws were carried out. See Tessa Storey, *Carnal Commerce in Counter-Reformation Rome* (Cambridge: Cambridge University Press, 2008).

7. The extremely low salary of Ming mandarins was acknowledged in the *Ming Shi, juan* 82 (*shi huo, juan* 6), 2003, and gave a strong impetus for corruption.

8. This is a summary and partial translation of the Chinese text, *Shi ke wenda*, 37 unfoliated leaves, Bibliothèque de France, Manuscrits chinois 7024.

9. Ibid.

10. This conversation forms chapter 1 in *Jiren Shipian*, in Zhu Weijing (ed.), *Li Madou Zhong wen ju xi ji*, 443–5.

11. *FR* II, 182.

12. Ibid., 190–1.

13. This conversation forms chapter 2 in *Jiren Shipian*, in Zhu Weijing (ed.), *Li Madou Zhong wen ju xi ji*, 445–8.

14. Feng Qi succeeded Yu Jideng as Minister of Rites in the tenth month of the twenty-ninth year of Wanli (November 1601) and died in the third month of the thirty-first year (April 1603). *Ming shi, juan* 112 (*biao, juan* 13), 3482–3.

15. This story is in 'The Life: The Book of Xanthus the Philosopher and Aesop his Slave', in Lloyd W. Daly (trans.), *Aesop without Morals* (New York: Thomas Yoseloff, 1961), 58–9.

16. The banquet and Ricci's essay on Christian fasts were later published as chapter 6 of *Jiren shipian*, in Zhu Weijing (ed.), *Li Madou Zhong wen ju xi ji*, 470–3.

17. Li Zhizao, 'Preface' to *Kunyu wanguo quantu*, in Zhu Weijing (ed.), *Li Madou Zhong wen ju xi ji*, 180.
18. *FR* II, 165.
19. See Feng Yinjing's preface to the Beijing reprint of *On Friendship*, in Zhu Weijing (ed.), *Li Madou Zhong wen ju xi ji*, 116.
20. *FR* II, 168.
21. Zhu Weijing (ed.), *Li Madou Zhong wen ju xi ji*, 97–8.

CHAPTER 10

1. Ricci to Niccolò Longobardo, Beijing, 2 September 1602, *Lettere*, 369.
2. There is a bilingual English–Chinese text of the *Tianzhu Shiyi: The True Meaning of the Lord of Heaven*, trans. Douglas Lancashire and Peter Hu Guozhen (St Louis: Institute of Jesuit Sources, 1985). The translations in this text are mine and based on the Chinese text in Zhu Weijing (ed.), *Li Madou Zhong wen ju xi ji*, 6–102.
3. *FR* II, 182.
4. Cited in Fan Shuzhi, *Wanli zhuan*, 322.
5. On the *Jiaxing zang*, see Lan Jifu, *Fojiao shiliao xue* (Taipei: Dong da tushu gongsi, 1997), 29–31.
6. On the different accounts of Zibo's treatment in prison, see Fan Shuzhi, *Wanli zhuan*, 326 and Shen Difu, *Wanli Yeyuo bian, juan 27*, 3 vols. (Beijing: Zhonghua shuchu, 2004), iii. 692.
7. Guo Peng, *Ming Qing fojiao*, 190–5.
8. *FR* II, 190.

CHAPTER 11

1. Ricci to Ludovico Maselli, [May] 1605, *Lettere*, 371.
2. Shen Defu, *Wanli yehuo bian, juan 30*, entries under 'Da Xiyang' (Europa) and 'Li Xitai' (Matteo Ricci). I have used the Zhonghua edition, 3 vols. (Beijing, 2004), here iii. 783–5.
3. On Xu Guangqi, there has been a spate of recent scholarship; see Chen Weiping and Li Chunyong, *Xu Guangqi pin zhuan* (Nanjing: Nanjing Daxue chubanshe, 2006) and Catherine Jami, Peter Engelfriet, and Gregory Blue (eds.), *Statecraft and Intellectual Renewal in Late Ming China: The Cross-Cultural Synthesis of Xu Guangqi (1562–1633)* (Leiden: Brill, 2001); Chu Xiaobo, *Cong Hua yi dao wan guo de xian sheng: Xu Guangqi dui wai guan nian yan jiu* (Beijing: Beijing Daxue chubanshe, 2008).
4. These words appear in Xu Guangqi's postscript to *Ershiwu yan*, Ricci's translation of a Latin version of Epictetus' *Encheiridion*, published in 1604, in Zhu Weizheng, *Li Madou Zhongwen zhu yi ji*, 135.
5. *Lettere*, 398.
6. Ibid.

7. Cited in Xu Zongze, *Mingqingjian yesuhuishi yizhu tiyao* (Shanghai, 1949; reprint, Beijing, 1989), 261–2.
8. Ibid. 262.
9. On the 1603 massacre in Manila, see José Eugenio Borao, 'The Massacre of 1603', *Itinerario*, 22/1 (1998), 22–40; Zhang Bincun, 'Meizhou bai yin yu fu nu zeng jie: 1603 nien ma li la dai tu sha di qian yin yu hou guo', in Zhu Delan (ed.), *Zhongguo hai yang fa zhan shi lun wen ji*, vol. viii (Taipei: Academia Sinica, Zhongshan ren wen shehui kexue yanjiu zuo, 2002), 295–326.
10. Ricci to Girolamo Costa, 10 May 1605, *Lettere*, 400.
11. Gu Qiyuan, *Ke zuo zhui yu*, 217–18.
12. Ricci to João Álvares, 12 May 1605, *Lettere*, 405.
13. Ibid. 406.
14. Ibid.
15. Ricci to Ludovico Maselli [May] 1605, ibid. 377.
16. Ibid.
17. Zhu Weizheng, *Li Madou Zhongwen zhu yi ji*, 131.
18. *Lettere*, 371.
19. Ibid. 381.
20. Ibid. 389.
21. Ibid. 401.
22. Ricci to Claudio Acquaviva, 15 August 1606, ibid. 423.
23. Ibid. 409.

CHAPTER 12

1. Ricci to Fabio de Fabii, 9 May 1605, *Lettere*, 381–2.
2. Shen Defu, *Wanli Yeyuo bian, juan* 27, iii. 703.
3. For Yu Chunxi's biography, see *Ming Shi, lie zhuan* (biography), *juan* 112, under Sun Long, xix. 5894–5; Peng Jiqing, *Jushi zhuan* (biographies of Buddhist laymen), 1776, in *Xinbian wanzi xu zang jing* (Newly Compiled Continuation of the Buddhist Canon), 150 vols. (Taipei, 1994, reprint), vol. cxlix, *juan* 42, 946–7.
4. Zhu Weijing (ed.), *Li Madou Zhong wen ju xi ji*, 657–8.
5. Ricci's letter is published ibid. 659–62.
6. Liu Tong and Yu Yizheng, *Di jing jing wu lue* (Shanghai: Yuan dong chubanshe, 1997), 229.
7. The number is mentioned in Ricci's letter to Claudio Acquaviva, 22 August 1608, *Lettere*, 487.
8. See Ricci's letter to João Álvares, 12 May 1605, ibid. 407.
9. Ibid. 427.
10. Ricci to Fabio de Fabii, 23 August 1608, ibid. 498.
11. Ibid. 426.
12. Ibid. 427.

13. Cited in Zhang Kai, *Pang Diwo yu Zhong Guo* (Beijing: Beijing tushuquan chubanshe, 1997), 183.
14. Ibid. 184.
15. Xie Zhaozhe, *Wu zazu*, cited Ibid. 185.
16. Ricci to Acquaviva, *Lettere*, 428.
17. Ricci to Acquaviva, 18 October 1607, ibid. 446–7.
18. Ricci to Masselli, [May] 1605, ibid. 377; Ricci to Acquaviva, 22 August 1608, ibid. 495–6.
19. Ibid. 486.
20. Ibid. 473.
21. Ibid. 471.
22. Ibid. 429.
23. Ibid. 463.
24. Ibid. 507.
25. Ibid. 523.
26. Ibid.
27. Ricci to Acquaviva, 8 March 1608, ibid. 470.
28. Ibid. 469.
29. Ricci to Acquaviva, 22 August 1608, ibid. 487.
30. Ricci to Álvares, 12 May 1605, ibid. 407.
31. Ricci to Acquaviva, 22 August 1608, ibid. 489.
32. Ricci to Pasio, 15 February 1609, ibid. 509.
33. ibid. 519.
34. Ricci to Giulio and Girolamo Alaleoni, 26 July 1605, ibid. 420.
35. Ibid. 496–7.
36. Ricci to Pasio, 15 February 1609, ibid. 520.
37. Ricci to Fabio de Fabii, 23 August 1608, ibid. 504.
38. Ricci to Álvares, 17 February 1609, ibid. 524.

EPILOGUE

1. Edward Malatesta and Guo Zhiyu (eds.), *Departed, yet Present: Zhalan, the Oldest Christian Cemetery in Beijing* (Macao: Instituto Cultural de Macau/ Ricci Institute, 1995).
2. *De Christiana Expeditione apud Sinas: Suscepta ab Societate Jesu ex P. Matthaei Riccii eiusdem societatis commentariis libri V ad S.D.N. Paulum V in quibus Sinensis Regni mores, leges, atque instituta, & novae illius Ecclesiae difficillima primordia accurate & summa fide describuntur* (Augsburg, 1615).
3. This story is related in Giulio Aleni's biography of Ricci, *Daxi Xitai li xiansheng xingji* (1630).
4. For an annotated chronology of Xu Guangqi's career, see Ad Dudink's contribution in Jami, Engelfriet, and Blue (eds.), *Statecraft and Intellectual Renewal in Late Ming China*, 399–409.

5. For figures of Chinese converts, see the various estimates compiled in *HCC*, i. 382–3.

6. Cited in English translation in my 'Christian Conversion in Late Ming China: Niccolo Longobardo in Shangdong', *Medieval History Journal*, 12/2 (2009), 275–301; and in Chinese translation in my 'Tianzhu jiao yu Mingmo shehui', *Lishi yanjiu*, 2 (2009), 51–67.

7. Longobardo's treatise is published in Spanish translation in Domingo Fernandez Navarete, *Tratados historicos, politicos, ethicos y religiosos de la monarchia de China* (Madrid: Imprensa Real, 1676), chapter 5. For a succinct summary of the origins of the Rites Controversy, and for the conflict between the Jesuits and the mendicant orders in China, see J. S. Cummins (ed.), *The Travels and Controversies of Friar Domingo Navarete 1618–1686*, 2 vols. (Cambridge: Cambridge University Press, 1962), i. xliii–xlv.

8. See Liam M. Brockey, *Journey to the East: The Jesuit Mission to China, 1579–1724* (Cambridge, Mass.: Harvard University Press, 2007), 87–9.

9. See my 'Fürstenkonversionen in China', in Dieter Bauer, Wolfgang Behringer, and Eric-Oliver Mader (eds.), *Konversionen zum Katholizismus in der Frühen Neuzeit*, forthcoming.

10. *HCC*, i. 307, 383.

11. This conference resulted in the volume *Atti e memorie del convegno di geografi-orientalisti tenuto in Macerato il 25–27 settembre 1910* (Macerata, 1911).

12. *P. Matheus Ricci S.J.: Relação escripta pelo seu companheiro P. Sabatino de Ursis S.J.: Publicação commemorative do terceiro centenario da sua morte* (Rome: Enrico Voghera, 1910).

13. *L'Apport scientifique du P. M. Ricci à la Chine* (Tianjin: Mission de Tianjin, 1935) and *Le Père Matthieu Ricci et la société chinoise de son temps 1552–1610*, 2 vols. (Tianjin: Hautes Études, 1937).

14. *FR* I, 147 n. 2.

15. ARSI Jap-Sin 101 I, fo. 2. It turns out in fact that Ruggieri was amazingly accurate in his journal jottings. The disorganized and unedited style of the journal is the major reason for its neglect.

16. Louis J. Gallagher, *The China that Was: China as Discovered by the Jesuits at the Close of the 16th Century* (Milwaukee: Bruce, 1942). There is a 1953 reprint of the same book under another title: *China in the Sixteenth Century: The Journals of Matthew Ricci: 1583–1610* (New York: Random House, 1953).

17. Vincent Cronin, *The Wise Man from the West: The True Story of the Man who First Brought Christianity to Fabled Cathay* (New York: Image Books, 1955).

18. *Chine et christianisme: La Première Confrontation* (Paris: Gallimard, 1982). Gernet published a 1990 revised edition with corrections and a new preface in answer to the critics of his book and it is this edition which I have used. An English translation appeared under the title *China and the Christian Impact: A Conflict of Cultures* (Cambridge: Cambridge University Press, 1985).

19. Gernet, *Chine et christianisme*, i–iii.

20. *The Memory Palace of Matteo Ricci* (New York: Penguin, 1984).

21. Giulio Andreotti, *Un gesuita in Cina (1552–1610): Matteo Ricci dall'Italia a Pechino* (Milan: Rizzoli, 2001).

22. Michela Fontana, *Matteo Ricci: Un gesuita alla corte dei Ming* (Milan: Mondadori, 2005).

23. Gaetano Ricciardolo, *Oriente e Occidente negli scritti di Matteo Ricci* (Naples: Chirico, 2003).

24. Francesco Occhetta, *Matteo Ricci: Il gesuita amato dalla Cina* (Cascino Vica-Rivoli: Elledici, 2009).

25. Filippo Mignini, *Matteo Ricci: Il chiosco delle fenici* (Ancona: Il lavoro editoriale, 2004).

26. Lin Jinshui, *Li Madou yu Zhongguo* (Beijing: Zhongguo shehui kexue chubanshe, 1996).

27. Ibid. 284.

28. Ibid.

29. Sun Shangyang, *Jidujiao yu Mingmo Ruxue* (Beijing: Dongfan chubanshe, 1994).

30. Ibid. 257–60.

31. Zhu Weizheng, *Li Madou Zhongwen zhuyi ji* (Shanghai: Fudan Daxue chubanshe, 2001).

32. See illustrations of the sets in http://www.manresa-sj.org/stamps/home.htm. I am indebted to Ms Ellen Peachey of the American Philatelic Society for help in locating these stamps.

APPENDIX

1. This represents the erroneous copying of a Chinese character in the original text.

Chinese Glossary

Ai Tian 艾田

anchasi fushi 按察司副使

Bao en si 報恩寺

Biluodong 碧落洞

buzheng si shi 布政司使

Cai 蔡

Cai Mengshuo 蔡夢说

Cai Yilong 蔡一龍

Cao Yubian 曹于汴

Celiang fayi 測量法義

Changshu 長熟

Chaozhou 潮州

chayuan 察員

Chen Feng 陳奉

Cheng en si 承恩寺

Cheng Hua 成化

Cheng Qiyuan 成啓元

Chen Mo 陳謨

Chen Rui 陳瑞

Chongxita 崇禧塔

chu jia 出家

Chujian lu 吹劍錄

Ci Sheng 慈聖

Cixi tang 此洗堂

Cui Zijun 崔自均

Da Ming hui dian 大明會典

danjia 蛋家

Danyang 丹陽

dao ren 道人

Daxiyang 大西洋

Da xi yu shanren 大西域山人

de 德

Deng Siqi 鄧思啓

Di jing jing wu lue 帝京景物略

Dingan 定安

Dongguan 东莞

Dong Yu 董裕

du shui qing li si 都水清吏司

dutang daren 都堂大人

Er shi wu yan 二十五言

Fang Yingshi 方應時

Fa yuan zhu lin 法苑珠林

Feng Bao 馮保

Feng cheng 豐城

Feng Qi 馮琦

Feng Shengyu 馮生虞

Feng Yinjing 馮應京

Fugu shuyuan 復古書院

Fuxi 伏羲

Gao ling 高嶺

Gao seng zhuan 高僧傳

Gao Yao 高要

gong 公

gongsheng 貢生

Guan Gu 管穀

Guanxiao si 光孝寺

Guan ya 关闸

Gui fan 閨範

Gui fan tushuo 閨范圖說

Guo Yingpin 郭應聘

Guo Zhengyu 郭正域

guozi jian 國子監

Gu Qiyuan 顧起元

haidao 海道

Hai Rui 海瑞

Hanshan Deqing 憨山德请

Han Yu 韓愈

Hao jing ao 濠鏡澳

heshang 和尚

He Shijin 何士晉

He Xinyin 何心隱

hou ru 後儒

Huang Hui 黃輝

Huang Jilou 黃繼樓

Huang Men 黃門

Huang Mingsha 黃明沙

Huang Shiyu 黃時雨

Huang Zongxi 黃宗羲

Huayan 華嚴

Huihui 回回

Huiji 會稽

Huineng 惠能

ji 機

Jiajing 嘉靖

Ji'an 吉安

Jian an 建安

Jiang Bin 江彬

Jiao Hong 焦竑

Jiao Shengguang 皦生光

Jiaxing zang 嘉興藏

Jie fa yin 戒發隱

Jiming shan 雞鳴山

Jingjiang 靖江

jingzuo 静坐

jinshi 進士

jinyi wei 錦衣衛

Jiren shipian 畸人十篇

ji xun yuan wai lang 稽勳員外郎

Jubao 聚寶

junzi 君子

juren 舉人

Jurong 居容

Jushi Zhuan 居士傳

Kai yang 開陽

Ke zuo zhui yu 客座贅語

Kunyu wanguo quantu 坤輿萬國全圖

laoye 老爺

Le an 樂安

li 理

liangzhi 良知

Li Chunhe 李春和

Li Dai 李戴

Li Huan 李環

lijia 里甲

li ke gei shi zhong 禮科給事中

Lin Daoqian 林道乾

linglongyi 玲瓏儀

Linqing 臨清

Linxidao 嶺西道

Lin Zhao'en 林兆恩

Li Ruzhen 李汝禎

Li Shizhen 李時珍

Liu Cheng 劉成

Liu Dong 劉侗

Liu Dongxing 劉東星

Liu Guannan 劉冠南

Liu Jiezhai 劉節齋

Liu Wenfang 劉文芳

Liu Yaohui 刘堯誨

Liuzu 六祖

Li Xinzhai 李心齋

Li Xitai 利西泰

Li Yngshi 李應試

Li Zhi 李贄

Li Zhizao 李之藻

Li Zicheng 李自成

Lü Kun 呂坤

Lü Liangzuo 呂良佐

Luo Fushan 羅浮山

Luo Hong 羅洪

Luo Hongxian 羅洪先

Luo Mingjian 羅明堅

Lu Wangai 陸萬垓

Lu Xiang shan 陸象山

Lu Xiyan 陸希言

Lu Yuchong 陸于充

ma chuan 馬船

Ma tang 馬堂

Mei an 梅庵

Meiling 梅嶺

Mingru xue an 明儒學案

Mozi 墨子

Nanhua 南華

Nanxiong 南雄

Nie Bao 聶豹

Ningxian 寧獻

Ni Yicheng 倪一誠

Ouyang De 歐陽德

Peng Duanwu 彭端吾

Peng Jiqing 彭際请

qiang 槍

Qiankun tiyi 乾坤體義

Qinhuai 秦淮

Qiu Liangbin 邱良稟

Qiu Lianghou 邱良厚

quan 權

Quanzhou 泉州

Qujiang 曲江

Qu Jingchun 瞿景淳

Qu Rukui 瞿汝夔

Qu Rushuo 瞿汝説

Qu Shigu 瞿式穀

ran gui 染鬼

ren 仁

ren lun 人倫

Ru fa jie pian 入法界篇

Ruichang 瑞昌

seng 僧

Shangchuan 上川

Shang di 上帝

Shang Zhou 商紂

Shanyin 山陰

Shaoxing 紹興

Shaozhou 韶州

Shen Defu 沈德符

sheng ci 生祠

Shen Li 沈鯉

Shen Lingyu 沈令譽

Shen Nong 神農

Shen Yiguan 沈一貫

Shi ke wen da 釋客問答

shilang 侍郎

Shi Shen 石申

Shi zi men 十字門

shou chang zhai 守長齋

si 私

siyi guan 四夷館

Siyuan xing lun 四元行論

Su Daiyong 蘇大用

Su Dongpo 蘇東坡

Sun Kuang 孫鑛

Sun Long 孫鑨

Sun Sui 孫燧

Su Shi 蘇軾

taiji 太極

Taisu 太素

Taizhou 泰州

Tiandi 天帝

Tianfei 天妃

Tianmu 天母

Tianning si 天寧寺

Tianshen 天神

Tian shu 天樞

Tianzhu 天主

Tianchu guo jiaohua huang zhi daming huangdi shu 天竺國教化皇致大明皇帝書

Tianchu guo seng 天竺國僧

Tianzhu huawei nanzi 天主化為男子

Tianzhu shilu 天主實錄

Tianzhu shiyi 天主實義

Tianzhugong 天柱宮

tidu xuedao 提都學道

Tongwen suanzhi 同文算指

tongzheng si 通政司

tongzhi 同知

Tongzhou 通州

Tushu bian 圖書編

Wang Bo 汪柏

Wang Kentang 王肯堂

Wang Pan 王泮

Wang Qi 王奇

Wang Ruxun 王汝訓

Wang Shanglie　萬尚烈
Wang Yangming　王陽明
Wang Yinglin 王應麟
Wang Zhongming 王忠銘
Wang Zuo　王佐
Wanli 萬歷
Wanli yehuo pian　萬歷野獲篇
Wei Zhongxian 魏忠賢
wuji　無極
Wu Sanguei 吳三桂
Wu Shan 吳善
Wu Wenhua 吳文華
Xia Jie　夏桀
Xia Yu 夏禹
Xiang shan 香山
Xiao Daheng　蕭大亨
Xiao Lianggan　蕭良幹
Xie Taiqing 謝臺卿
Xijiang 西江
xing xue　性學
xing　性
Xinjian xian　新建縣
xiru 西儒
xi seng 西僧
xishi 西士
xiucai 秀才
Xi yang　西洋
Xi yu ji　西域記
xuan 璇
Xuancheng 宣城
Xuanwu 玄武
Xu Bideng　徐必登
Xu Da 徐達
Xu Daren　徐大任

Xuelang Hong'en 雪浪洪恩
Xu Guangqi 徐光啓
Xu Hongji 徐弘基
xunfu 巡撫
Xu Shi 徐栻
xunshi haidao fushi 巡視海道副使
Xu Sicheng 徐思誠
Xu Xiake 徐霞客
Xu Zhenjun 許真君
yamen 衙門
Yang Daobin 楊道賓
Yang Tingyun 楊廷筠
Yang Zhu 楊朱
yao 藥
Yao guang 搖光
Ye xiang gao 葉向高
yi 義
Yingde 英德
yiren 異人
Yiyang 弋陽
You Wenhui 游文輝
yuan wai lang 員外郎
Yu Chunxi 虞淳熙
Yu Dayou 俞大猷
Yuegang 月港
Yuheng 玉衡
Yuhuatai 雨花臺
Yu Jideng 余繼登
yusha 玉沙
yushi 御使
Yu Wenbao 俞文豹
Yuyao 余姚
Yu Yizheng 于奕正
Zeng yiben 曾一本

Zhang Deming 張德明

Zhang Heng 張衡

Zhang Huang 章潢

Zhang Juzheng 張居正

Zhang Wenda 張問達

Zhang Yangmo 張養默

Zhang Ying 張鷹

Zhangzhou 漳州

Zhao Kehuai 趙可懷

Zhaoqing 肇慶

Zheng 鄭

Zheng de 正德

Zheng yang 正陽

Zheng Yilin 鄭一麟

Zhenjiang 鎮江

zhixian 知縣

Zhonghu men 中華門

zhong ji linglong 中極玲瓏

Zhong Mingli 鐘鳴禮

Zhong Mingren 鐘鳴仁

Zhongshan 中山

Zhong Wanlu 鐘萬祿

Zhou Gongxiang 周公相

Zhou Qixiang 周啟祥

zhuangyuan 狀元

Zhuangzi 莊子

Zhu Changluo 朱常洛

Zhu Changxun 朱常洵

Zhu Chenhao 朱宸濠

zhudong 主洞

Zhu Duogeng 朱多㷿

Zhu Duojie 朱多節

Zhuge Liang 諸葛亮

Zhu Guozuo 朱國祚

zhu ke si yuan wai lang 主客司员外郎

Zhu Shilu 祝世祿

Zhu Xi 朱熹

Zhu Yuanzhang 朱元璋

Zhu Zhifan 朱之蕃

Zibo Zhenke 紫柏真可

Zi Gong 子貢

Zijinshan 紫金山

zongbing 總兵

Zong jing lu 宗鏡録

Zou Shouyi 鄒守益

Bibliography

PRIMARY SOURCES

Manuscripts

Archivo General de Indias, Patronato 25, 22. http://www.upf.es/fhuma/eeao/projectes/che/s16/roman.htm.

Archivum Romanum Societatis Iesu.

   Fondo Gesuitico, 723/5.

   Jap-Sin 101 I.

   Jap-Sin I 198.

   Lusitania 39.

Bibliothèque Nationale de France, Chinois 1320, 7024, 9186.

Printed Sources

Acosta, José de. *Obras*, ed. Francisco Mateos. Madrid: Ediciones Atlas, 1954.

Aleni, Giulio. *Daxi Xitaili xiansheng xingji* 大西西泰利先生行蹟. Taipei: Taibei Li shi xue she, 2002.

Avisi particolari del avmento che Iddio da alla sua Chiesa Catolica nell'Indie, et spetialmente nelli Regni di Giappon con informatione della China, riceuuti dalle Padri della Compagna di Iesu, questo anno del 1558. Rome, 1558.

Avisi particolari delle Indie di Portugallo ricevuti in questi doi anni del 1551 & 1552 da li reverendi padri della compagnia di Iesu. Rome, 1552.

Billings, Timothy. *On Friendship: One Hundred Maxims for A Chinese Prince*. New York: Columbia University Press, 2009.

Boxer, C. R., ed. *South China in the Sixteenth Century*. London: The Hakluyt Society, 1953.

Cao Xi tong zhi 曹溪通志, ed. Ma Yuan 马元. *Si ku jin hui shu cong kan bu bian* 四库禁毁书丛刊补编. Beijing: Beijing chubanshe, 2005.

Cartas que os padres e irmãos da Companhia de Iesus escreuerão dos Reynos de Iapão & China aos da mesma Companhia da India, & Europa, des do anno de 1549 atè o de 1580, vol. ii. Evora 1598/Maia 1997.

Chan, Albert, SJ. 'Michele Ruggieri, S.J. (1543–1607) and his Chinese Poems', *Monumenta Serica*, 41 (1993), 129–76.

Colin, Francisco. *Labor evangelica: Ministerios apostolicos de los obreros de la Compañia de Iesus, fundacion, y progressos de su provincia en las Islas Filipinas*, ed. Pablo Pastells. 3 vols. Barcelona: Henrich y Co., 1900/2.

Cummins, J. S., ed. *The Travels and Controversies of Friar Domingo Navarrete 1618–1686*. 2 vols. Cambridge: Cambridge University Press, 1962.

De Christiana Expeditione apud Sinas. Suscepta ab Societate Jesu ex P. Matthaei Riccii eiusdem societatis commentariis libri V ad S.D.N. Paulum V in quibus Sinensis Regni mores, leges, atque instituta, & novae illius Ecclesiae difficillima primordia accurate & summa fide describuntur. Augsburg, 1615.

de Ursis, Sabatino. *P. Matheus Ricci S.J.: Relação escripta pelo seu companheiro P. Sabatino de Ursis S.J.; publicação commemorative do terceiro centenario da sua morte*. Rome: Enrico Voghera, 1910.

Didaci Lainez Adhortationes, 1559. In *Fontes Narrativi de S. Ignatio de Loyola et de Societatis Iesu initiis*, vol. ii, *Monumenta Historica Societatis Iesu*. Rome: IHSI, 1951.

Di jing jing wu lue 帝京景物略, ed. Liu Tong 劉侗 and Yu Yizheng 于奕正. Shanghai: yuan dong chubanshe, 1997.

Diversi avisi particolari dall'Indie di Portogallo, riceuuti dallanno 1551 sino al 1558, dalli Reuerendi padri della compagnia di Gesu, dove s'intende delli paesi, delle genti, & costumi loro, & la grande conuersione di molti popoli, che hanno riccuuto il lume della santa fede, & religione Christiana. Tradotti nuouamente dalla lingua Spagnuloa nella Italian. Venice, 1565.

Documenta Indica, 1540–1597, ed. Joseph Wicki. 18 vols. Rome: MHSI, 1948–88.

Fonti Ricciane: Matteo Ricci: Storia dell'introduzione del Cristianesimo in Cina, ed. Pasquale D'Elia. 3 vols. Rome: La Libreria dello Stato, 1942–9.

Gallagher, Louis J. *The China that Was: China as Discovered by the Jesuits at the Close of the 16th Century*. Milwaukee: Bruce, 1942.

Gu, Qiyuan 顾起元. *Ke zuo zhui yu* 客坐赘语. Nanjing: Fenghuang chubanshe, 2005.

Guangdong tongzhi 廣東通志, ed. Chen Changqi 陳昌齊. Taipei: Huawen shuju, 1968.

Guo, Tingxun 过庭训, comp. *Benchao fensheng renwu kao* 本朝分省人物考, 115 juan. Reprint, Taipei: Chengwen, 1971.

Jiao, Hong 焦竑. *Jiao shi bi sheng* 焦氏笔乘. Shanghai: Shanghai gu ji chubanshe, 1986.

—— *Jiao shi Danyuan ji* 焦氏澹園集. 4 vols. Taipei: Weiwen, 1977.

Li, Zhi 李贽. *Li Zhi wen ji: Fen shu, Xu fen shu* 李贽文集：焚书，续焚书. Beijing: Yanshan chubanshe, 1998.

Li Madou Zhong wen zhu yi ji 利玛窦中文著译集, ed. Zhu Weizheng 朱维铮. Shanghai: Fudan daxue chubanshe, 2001.

Linschoten, Johann Huighen van. *John Huighen van Linschoten. His Discours of voyages into ye Easte & West Indies*. London: John Wolfe, 1598.

Li Yingsheng 李應昇 ed. *Bai lu shu yuan zhi* 白鹿書院志. 1622. In *Bai lu dong shu yuan gu zhi wu zhong* 白鹿洞書院古志五種. Beijing: Zhong Hua shu ju, 1995.

Loureiro, Rui Manuel, ed. *Em busca das origens de Macau (Antologia documental)*. Lisbon: Grupo de Trabalho do Ministéro da Educação para as Comemorações dos Descobrimentos Portugueses, 1996.

Martin, Gregory. *Roma Sancta*, ed. George Bruner Parks. Rome: Edizioni di Storia e Letteratura, 1969.

Matteo Ricci Lettere (1580–1609), ed. Francesco D'Arelli. Macerata: Quodlibet, 2001.

Ming shi lu lei zhuan 明实录类纂. *Guangdong Hainan juan* 广东海南卷, ed. Li Guoxiang 李国祥 and Yang Chang 杨昶. Wuhan: Wuhan chubanshe, 1993.

Ming shi lu lei zuan 明实录类纂. *Zhi guan ren mian juan* 职官任免卷, ed. Liu Chonglai 刘重來. Wuhan: Wuhan chubanshe, 1995.

Ming shi lu lei zuan 明实录类纂: *Zong fan gui qi juan* 宗藩贵戚卷, ed. Li Qiongying 李琼英 and Zhang Yingchao 张颖超. Wuhan: Wuhan chubanshe, 1995.

Montaigne, Michel de. *The Complete Works*, trans. Donald M. Frame. New York: Alfred A. Knopf, 2003.

Monumenta Sinica, i: *(1546–1562)*, ed. John W. Witek and Joseph S. Sebes. Rome: IHIS, 2002.

Navarrete, Domingo Fernandez. *Tratados historicos, politicos, ethicos y religiosos de la monarchia de China*. Madrid: Imprensa Real, 1676.

Novi avisi di piu lochi de l'India et massime de Brasil . . . doue chiaramente si puo intendere la conuersione di molte persone . . . Rome, 1553.

Opere Storiche del P. Matteo Ricci S.I., ed. Pietro Tacchi-Venturi. 2 vols. Macerata: F. Giorgetti, 1913.

Pantoja, Diego de. *Relacion de la entrada de algunos padres de la Compañia de Iesus en la China, y particulares sucessos que tuvieron, y de cosas muy notables que vieron en el mismos reyno*. Valencia: Juan Chrysostomo Garriz, 1606.

Pavur, Claude, SJ, trans. *The Ratio Studiorum: The Official Plan for Jesuit Education*. St. Louis: Institute of Jesuit Sources, 2005.

Peng, Jiqing 彭際清. *Jushi zhuan* 居士傳. 1776. In *Xinbian wanzi xu zang jing* 新編卍字續藏經 (Newly Compiled Continuation of the Buddhist Canon), 150 vols. Taipei, 1994, reprint.

Ricci, Matteo. *Tianzhu Shiyi: The True meaning of the Lord of Heaven*, trans. Douglas Lancashire and Peter Hu Guozhen. St. Louis: Institute of Jesuit Sources, 1985.

—— and Trigault, Nicolas. *China in the Sixteenth Century. The Journals of Matthew Ricci: 1583–1610*. New York: Random House, 1953.

Shaozhou Fu zhi (Kangxi) (康熙)韶州府志, comp. Ma Yuan 马元, Compilor. Beijing: Shu mu wen xian chubanshe 书目文献出版社, [1988].

Shaozhou Fu zhi (Tongzhi) (同治)韶州府志, eds. Dan Xingshi 單興詩. 1874. In Zhongguo di fang zhi ji cheng. Guangdong fu xian zhi ji. 2003.

Shen, Defu 沉德符. *Wanli Yehuo bian* 万历野获编. Beijing: Zhonghua, 2004.

Sinica Franciscana, ii: Relationes et epistolas Fratrum Minorum saeculi XVI et XVII, ed. Anastasius van den Wyngaert. Florence: Collegiae S. Bonaventurae, 1933.

Standaert, Nicolas, and Dudink, Adrian, eds. *Chinese Christian Texts from the Roman Archives of the Society of Jesus*, 12 vols. Taipei: Ricci Institute, 2002.

Sun, Chengze 孫承澤. *Chung Ming meng yu lu* 春明夢餘錄. Hong Kong: Longmen, 1965.

Tordesillas, Agustín de. *Relación de el viaje que hezimos en china nuestro hermano fray Pedro de Alpharo con otros tres frailes de la orden de Nuestro seraphico padre san Francisco de la prouincia de san Joseph etc.* 1578. Archivo de la Real Academia de la Historia, Velázques, tomo LXXV. Available at http://www.upf.es/fhuma/eeao/projectes/che/s16/tordes.htm, 13.

Witek, John. *Dicionário Português-Chinês=Pu Han ci dian=Portuguese Chinese Dictionary*. San Francisco: Ricci Institute, 2001.

Xin xiu Guangzhou Fu zhi 新修广州府志 (Kangxi 康熙), ed. Wang, Yongrui 王永瑞. In Beijing Tushuguan gu cong kan. Vols. xxxix–xl. Beijing: shumu wenxian chubanshe, 1998.

Xinxiu Nanchang Fu zhi 新修南昌府志 (Wanli曹屠), 1588, ed. Zhang Huang 章潢,. In Riben cang Zhongguo han jian di fang jie cong kan 日本藏中国罕见地方志丛刊. Beijing: shumu wenxian chubanshe, 1990.

Xu, Zongze 徐宗泽. *Mingqingjian yesuhuishi yizhu tiyao* 明清间耶酥会士译著提要. Shanghai, 1949; reprint, Beijing, 1989.

Yu Meian 喻昧菴, comp. *Xin xu gao seng zhuan si ji* 新續高僧傳四集 [65 *juan*]. 4 vols. Taipei: liu li qing fang, 1967.

Zhaoqing Fuzhi 肇庆府志 (Chongzhen 崇禎), ed. Yin Mengxia 殷夢霞. Vol. xii. In Riben cang Zhongguo han jian di fang she cong kan xu bian 日本藏中國罕見地方志叢刊續編, vol. 12. Beijing: Beijing tushu guan chubanshe, 2003.

Zhang, Huang 章潢. *Tushu bian* 圖書編. In *Wen yuan ge si ku quan shu* 文淵閣四庫全書, cmlxxii. 850–62. Taipei: Taiwan shangwu yinshu guan, 1983.

Zhang, Tingyu 张廷玉. *Ming shi* 明史, 28 vols. Beijing: Zhonghua shuju, 1997.

SECONDARY SOURCES

Alden, Dauril. *The Making of an Enterprise; The Society of Jesus in Portugal, its Empire, and beyond 1540–1750*. Stanford: Stanford University Press, 1996.

Andreotti, Giulio. *Un gesuita in Cina (1552–1610): Matteo Ricci dall'Italia a Pechino*. Milan: Rizzoli, 2001.

Atti e memorie del convegno di geografi-orientalisti tenuto in Macerato il 25–27 settembre 1910. Macerata, 1911.

Barreto, Luís Filipe. *Macau: Poder e Saber. Séculos XVI e XVII*. Lisbon: Editorial Presença, 2006.

Bernard, Henri. *L'apport scientifique du P. M. Ricci à la Chine*. Tianjin: Mission de Tianjin, 1935.

—— *Le Père Matthieu Ricci et la société chinoise de son temps 1552–1610*, 2 vols. Tianjin: Hautes Études, 1937.

Borao, José Eugenio. 'The Massacre of 1603', *Itinerario* 22/1 (1998), 22–40.

Boxer, Charles. *The Church Militant and Iberian Expansion 1440–1770*. Baltimore: Johns Hopkins University Press, 1978.

Brockey, Liam M. *Journey to the East: The Jesuit Mission to China, 1579–1724*. Cambridge, Mass.: Harvard University Press, 2007.

Brook, Timothy. *Praying for Power: Buddhism and the Formation of Gentry Society in Late-Ming China*. Cambridge, Mass.: Harvard University Press, 1993.

Chang, Pin-tsun (Zhang Bincun). 'Chinese Maritime Trade: The Case of 16th Century Fu-chien.' Ph.D. dissertation, Princeton, 1983.

—— (Zhang Bincun) 張彬村. 'Meizhou bai yin yu fu nu zhen jie: 1603 nian ma ni la da tu sha de qian yin yu hou guo' 美洲白銀與婦女貞潔:1603 年馬尼拉大屠殺的前因與後果. In Zhu Delan 朱德蘭, (ed.), *Zhongguo hai yang fa zhan shi lun wen ji* 中國海洋發展史論文集, vol. viii. Taipei: Academia Sinica, Zhongshan ren wen shehui kexue yanjiu zuo, 2002, 295–326.

Chen, Baoliang 陈宝良. *Ming dai shehui shenghuo shi* 明代社会生活史. Beijing: Zhong guo she hui ke xue chubanshe, 2004.

Chen, Weiping 陈卫平 and Li Chunyong 李春勇. *Xu Guangqi pin zhuan* 徐光启评传. Nanjing: Nanjing Daxue chubanshe, 2006.

Ch'ien, Edward T. *Chiao Hung and the Restructuring of Neo-Confucianism in the Late Ming*. New York: Columbia University Press, 1986.

Chu, Xiaobo 初晓波. *Cong Hua yi dao wan guo de xian sheng: Xu Guangqi dui wai guan nian yan jiu* 从华夷到万国的先声: 徐光启对外观念研究. Beijing: Beijing Daxue chubanshe, 2008.

Coelho, António Borges *Inquisição de Évora 1533–1668*. Lisbon: Caminho, 2002.

Cook, Francis H. *Hua-yen Buddhism: The Jewel Net of Indra*. University Park, Pa.: Penn State University Press, 1977.

Cronin, Vincent. *The Wise Man from the West: The True Story of the Man who First Brought Christianity to Fabled Cathay*. New York: Image Books, 1955.

Daly, Lloyd W., trans. *Aesop without Morals*. New York: Thomas Yoseloff, 1961.

Delumeau, Jean. *Vie économique et sociale de Rome dans la seconde moitié du XVIe siècle*. 2 vols. Paris: de Boccard, 1957.

Dudink, Adrian. 'Giulio Aleni and Li Jiubiao', in Tiziana Lippiello and Roman Malek, eds. *'Scholar from the West': Giulio Aleni S.J. (1582–1649) and the Dialogue between Christianity and China*. Nettetal: Steyler, 1997, 129–200.

Elman, Benjamin A. *A Cultural History of Civil Examinations in Late Imperial China*. Berkeley and Los Angeles: University of California Press, 2000.

Fan, Shuzhi 樊树志. *Wanli zhuan* 万历传. Beijing: Renmin chubanshe人民出版社, 1993.

Fang Hao 方豪. *Zhongguo Tianzhujiao Renwu juan* 中國天主教史人物傳. 3 vols. Hong Kong: Zhonghua shuchu, 1970.

Fonseca N., Santos, T. A., and Castro, F. 'Study of the Intact Stability of a Portuguese Nau from the Early XVII Century', in Guedes Soares et al., eds. *Martime Transportation and Exploitation of Ocean and Coastal Resources*. London: Taylor & Francis, 2005, 841–49.

Fontana, Michela. *Matteo Ricci: Un gesuita alla corte dei Ming*. Milan: Mondadori, 2005.

Gernet, Jacques. *China and the Christian Impact: A Conflict of Cultures*. Cambridge: Cambridge University Press, 1985.

—— *Chine et christianisme: La première confrontation*. Paris: Gallimard, 1982.

Gerritsen, Anne. *Ji'an Literati and the Local in Song-Yuan-Ming China*. Leiden: Brill, 2007.

Guo, Peng 郭朋. *Ming Qing fojiao* 明清佛教. Fuzhou: Fujian ren min chu ban she 福建人民出版社, 1982.

—— *Zhongguo fujiao sixiangshi* 中国佛教思想史, vol. ii. Fuzhou: Fujian renmin chubanshe, 1994.

Hauf, Kandice J. 'The Jiangyou Group: Culture and Society in Sixteenth Century China.' Ph.D. dissertation, Yale 1987.

He, Bingdi. *The Ladder of Success in Imperial China: Aspects of Social Mobility 1368–1911*. New York: Columbia University Press, 1962.

He, Xiaorong 何孝荣. *Ming dai Nanjing si yuan yan jiu* 明代南京寺院研究. Beijing: Zhongguo she hui ke xue chubanshe, 2000.

Hsia, R. Po-chia. 'Christian Conversion in Late Ming China: Niccolo Longobardo in Shangdong', *Medieval History Journal*, 12/2 (2009), 275–301.

—— 'Dreams and Conversions: A Comparative Analysis of Catholic and Buddhist Dreams in Ming and Qing China: Part I', *Journal of Religious History*, 29/3 (October 2006), 223–40.

—— 'Li Madou yu Zhang Huang 利玛窦与章潢', in *Wei le wenhua yu lishi: Yu Yingshi jiaoshou ba zhi shou qing lunwen ji* 为了文化与历史: 余英时教授八秩寿庆论文集. Taipei: Liangjing chubanshe, 2009, 727–49.

—— 'Mission und Konfessionalisierung in Übersee', in Wolfgang Reinhard and Heinz Schilling, eds. *Die Katholische Konfessionalisierung*. Münster: Aschendorff, 1995, 158.

—— 'Tianzhu jiao yu Mingmo shehui: Chongzhen chao Long Huamin Shandong chuanjiao de ji ge wenti' 天主教与明末社会：崇祯朝龙华民山东传教的几个问题, *Lishi yanjiu* 历史研究, 2 (2009), 51–67.

—— 'Valignano e Cina', in Adolfo Tamburello, M. Antoni J. Üçerler, and Marisa Di Russo, eds. *Alessandro Valignano. S.I. Uomo del Rinascimento: Ponte tra Oriente e Occidente*. Rome: Jesuit Historical Institute, 2008, 102–3.

—— 'Fürstenkonversionen in China', in Dieter Bauer, Wolfgang Behringer, and Eric-Oliver Mader, eds. *Konversionen zum Katholizismus in der Frühen Neuzeit*, forthcoming.

Huang, Yilong 黃一龍, *Liang Tou She: Ming mo Qing chu de di yi tai Tianzhu jiaotu* 兩頭蛇:明末清初的第一代天主教徒. Xinzhu: Guo li Qinghua daxue chubanshe 國立清華大學出版社, 2005.

Jami, Catherine, Engelfriet, Peter, and Blue, Gregory, eds. *Statecraft and Intellectual Renewal in Late Ming China: The Cross-Cultural Synthesis of Xu Guangqi (1562–1633)*. Leiden: Brill, 2001.

Lan, Jifu 藍吉富. *Fojiao shiliao xue* 佛教史料學. Taipei: Dong da tushu gongsi, 1997.

Lattis, James M. *Between Copernicus and Galileo: Christopher Clavius and the Collapse of Ptolemaic Cosmology*. Chicago: University of Chicago Press, 1994.

Leng, Dong 冷东. *Ye Xianggao yu Ming mo Zheng tan* 叶高与明末政坛. Shantou: Shantou Daixue chubanshe, 1996.

Lin, Jinshui 林金水. *Li Madou yu Zhongguo* 利玛窦与中国. Beijing: Zhongguo shehui kexue chubanshe 中国社会科学出版社, 1996.

Lippiello, Tiziana and Malek, Roman, eds. *'Scholar from the West': Giulio Aleni S.J. (1582–1649) and the Dialogue between Christianity and China*. Nettetal: Steyler, 1997.

Ma, Tai-loi. 'Private Academies in Ming China (1368–1644). Historical Development, Organization and Social Impact.' Ph.D. dissertation, University of Chicago, 1987.

Malatesta, Edward, and Guo Zhiyu, eds. *Departed, yet present: Zhalan, the Oldest Christian Cemetery in Beijing*. Macau and San Francisco: Instituto Cultural de Macau and Ricci Institute, 1995.

Mauro, Frédéric. *Le Portugal et l'Atlantique au XVIIe siècle (1570–1670): Étude économique*. Paris: SEVPEN, 1960.

Meskill, John, *Academies in Ming China: A Historical Essay*. Tucson, Ariz.: University of Arizona Press, 1982.

Mignini, Filippo. *Matteo Ricci: Il chiosco delle fenici*. Ancona: Il lavoro editoriale, 2004.

Nebgen, Christoph. *Missionarsberufungen nach Übersee in drei Deutschen Provinzen der Gesellschaft Jesu im 17. und 18. Jahrhundert*. Regensburg: Schnell/Steiner, 2007.

Needham, Joseph. *Chinese Astronomy and the Jesuit Mission: An Encounter of Cultures*. London: The China Society, 1958.

—— *The Shorter Science and Civilisation in China*, vol. i. Cambridge: Cambridge University Press, 1978.

—— and Wang Ling. *Heavenly Clockwork: The Great Astronomical Clocks of Medieval China*. Cambridge: Cambridge University Press, 1960.

Ollé, Manel. *La invencíon de China: Percepciones y estrategias filipinas respecto a China durante el siglo XVI*. Wiesbaden: Harrassowitz, 2000.

Pires, Benjamin Videira. *A viagem de coméríco Macau–Manila nos séculos XVI a XIX*. Macau: Museu Marítimo de Macau, 1994.

Ricciardolo, Gaetano. *Oriente e Occidente negli scritti di Matteo Ricci*. Naples: Chirico, 2003.

Roscioni, Gian Carlo. *Il desiderio delle Indie: Storie, sogni e fughe di giovani gesuiti italiani*. Turin: Einaudi, 2001.

Saraiva, A. J. *Inquisição e cristãos novos*. Porto: Inova, 1969.

Saunders, A. C. de C. M. *A Social History of Black Slaves and Freedmen in Portugal 1441–1555*. Cambridge: Cambridge University Press, 1982.

Shen, Xinlin 沈新林, ed. *Ming dai Nanjing xue shu ren wu zhuan* 明代南京学术人物传. Nanjing: Nanjing Daxue chubanshe, 2004.

Shi, Shengyan 釋聖嚴. *Ming mo fojiao yanjiu* 明末佛教研究. Taipei: Dongchu chubanshe, 1987.

Shih, Joseph, SJ. *Le Père Ruggieri et le problèm de l'évangélisation en China.* Rome: Pontificiae Universitatis Gregorianae, 1964.

Spence, Jonathan D. *The Memory Palace of Matteo Ricci.* New York: Viking Penguin, 1984.

Storey, Tessa, *Carnal Commerce in Counter-Reformation Rome.* Cambridge: Cambridge University Press, 2008.

Sun, Shangyang 孙尚扬, *Jidujiao yu Mingmo Ruxue* 基督教与明末儒学. Beijing: Dongfan chubanshe 东方出版社, 1994.

Standaert, Nicolas, ed. *Handbook of Christianity in China, i: 635–1800.* Leiden: Brill, 2001.

Turner, Rossella. 'La figura e l'opera di Michele Ruggieri, S.J., missionario gesuita in Cina.' Tesi di Laurea in storia e civiltà dell'Estremo Oriente. Naples: Istituto universitario Orientale Napoli, 1984.

Villoslada, Riccardo G. *Storia del Collegio Romano dal suo inizio (1551) alla soppressione della Compagnia di Gesù (1773) (=Analecta Gregoriana,* vol. LXVI). Rome: Gregorian University Press, 1954.

Wei, Daoru 魏道儒. *Zhongguo Huayanzhong tongshi* 中国华严宗通史. Nanjing: Jiangsu guji chubanshe, 2001.

Wicki, Josef. 'As relações de viagens dos Jesuítas na carreira das naus da Índia de 1541 a 1598', in Luís de Albuquerque and Inácio Guerreiro, eds. *II Seminário internacional de história indo-portugues.* Lisbon: IICT-CEHCA, 1985, 3–17.

—— 'Der einheimische Klerus in Indien (16. Jahrhundert)', in Johannes Beckmann, ed. *Der einheimische Klerus in Geschichte und Gegenwart (=Neue Zeitschrift für Missionswissenschaft* Supplementa II). Schöneck-Beckenried: NZM, 1950, 17–72.

Yerushalmi, Yosef Hayim. *The Lisbon Massacre of 1506 and the Royal Image in the Shebet Yehudah.* Cincinnati: Hebrew Union College, 1976.

Yü, Chün-fang. *Kuan-yin: The Chinese Transformation of Avalokitesvara.* New York: Columbia University Press, 2001.

Zhang, Kai 张铠. *Pang Diwo yu Zhong Guo* 庞迪我与中国. Beijing: Beijing tushuguan chubanshe, 1997.

Županov, Ines G. *Missionary Tropics: The Catholic Frontier in India (16th-17th Centuries).* Ann Arbor: University of Michigan Press, 2005.

Zürcher, Erik. 'Giulio Aleni's Chinese Biography', in Tiziana Lippiello and Roman Malek, eds. *'Scholar from the West': Giulio Aleni S.J. (1582–1649) and the Dialogue between Christianity and China.* Nettetal: Steyler, 1997, 85–127.

Index